LIVES OF INDIAN IMAGES

LIVES OF INDIAN IMAGES

Richard H. Davis

PRINCETON UNIVERSITY PRESS · PRINCETON, NEW JERSEY

Published by Princeton University Press, 41 William Street,
Princeton, New Jersey 08540
In the United Kingdom: Princeton University Press, Chichester, West Sussex

Third printing, and first paperback printing, 1999
Paperback ISBN 0-691-00520-6

The Library of Congress has cataloged the cloth edition of this book as follows
Davis, Richard H.
Lives of Indian images / Richard H. Davis.
p. cm.
Includes bibliographical references and index.
ISBN 0-691-02622-X (cloth : alk. paper)
1. Gods, Hindu, in art. 2. Sculpture, Hindu.
3. Art and anthropology—India. I. Title.
NB1912.H55D38 1997
730'.954—dc20 96-22196 CIP
Publication of this book has been aided by a grant from the
Frederick W. Hilles Publications Fund of Yale University

This book has been composed in Dante typefaces

The paper used in this publication meets the minimum requirements of
ANSI/NISO Z39.48-1992 (1997) (*Permanence of Paper*)

http://pup.princeton.edu

Printed in the United States of America

3 4 5 6 7 8 9 10

To MATTHEW

Contents

Illustrations

Acknowledgments

THIS BOOK traces the lives of Indian objects as they have been relocated and revalorized over time by various communities of response. As I reflect on writing it, I realize the book too has taken shape within its own community of response. It has developed gradually, through many conversations, correspondences, public presentations, and written drafts that I have circulated. I recognize just how much I have depended on the comments, suggestions, questions, assistance, and encouragement of others at every step of the way. In many cases I acknowledge specific pointers or special help in footnotes within the text, but I would like to assemble the entire community here, like an imaginary group photograph.

For conversations, comments, and readings of chapters at various stages of coherency, I am grateful to Muzaffar Alam, Catherine Asher, Pravin Bhatt, Susan P. Borden, Kate Brittlebank, John Brockopp, David Carpenter, Francis Clooney, Andrew Cohen, Bernard Cohn, John Cort, Vishakha Desai, Richard Eaton, Jerry Ellmore, Carl Ernst, J. R. Freeman, Phyllis Granoff, Sumit Guha, Charles Hallisey, Ron Inden, Gene Irschick, Ginni Ishimatsu, Igor Kopytoff, Rita McCleary, Jaya Mehta, Michael Meister, Barbara Metcalf, George Michell, Vasudha Narayanan, Rob Nelson, Leslie Orr, Shantanu Phukan, Michael Rabe, Gary Schwindler, Don Stadtner, Cynthia Talbot, Phil Wagoner, Verity Wilson, Irene Winter, and Theodore Wright. Norvin Hein was the first person to read the entire manuscript, and I thank him for his encouragement at every stage of this project.

In England, I am especially grateful to Richard Blurton at the British Museum and John Guy at the Victoria and Albert Museum for helping me out backstage. While working in London, I was able to discuss colonial collecting with James Harle, Robert Skelton, Andrew Topsfield, Thorn Wilkinson, and Wladamir Zwolf. For assistance in sorting out the Pathur Nataraja case, I thank Anna Bennett, Dennis Cooper, Bhasker Ghorpade, Col. G. A. Jackson, Robert Knox, Sunita Mainee, Alexis Sanderson, Nigel Seeley, and John Stephens in England.

During three trips to India while working on this project, I was aided by S. S. Janaki at the Kuppuswami Sastri Research Institute, Madras, and Françoise l'Hernault at the French Institute of Indology in Pondicherry. I also thank P. R. Mehendiratta at the American Institute of Indian Studies, who miraculously intervened to enable one research trip to proceed. While in India, Prema Nanadakumar, S. Sampath Kumaran, and S. R. Sampath Thathachariar helped me out at Sri Rangam. Shantilal N. Bhatt, Shambhu P. Desai, Amritlal Trivedi, and Chandulal P. Trivedi helped answer some of my questions about the rebuilding of Somanatha. U. C. Chandramouleeswaran, R. Nagaswamy, and K. K. Rajasekharan Nair discussed issues pertaining to the theft of religious icons in south India. For helping me along in my Indian travels, I also thank Vimal Shukla and Adam Zeff.

University seminars and conference panels are the arenas in which many of the ideas presented in this book made their first public appearances. I am grateful to the Universities of Chicago, Columbia, Pennsylvania, Texas, Wisconsin, and Yale, and to the professional organizations of the American Academy of Religion, the American Committee on South Asian Art, the Asia Society, the Association for Asian Studies, the Association of Art Historians (U.K.), and the College Art Association for giving me opportunities to try out new notions in front of colleagues.

Finally, I thank the three anonymous readers for Princeton University Press, my editor Ann H. Wald, editorial assistant Helen Hsu, Margaret H. Case who graciously copyedited the manuscript, and others at the Press who helped turn the manuscript into a book. I also thank John Jones for checking over the page proofs.

To all members of this community of response, I am grateful in more different ways than I can say here, and I only hope that each will find something of value in this book to continue the conversations we have begun.

I have been fortunate to receive institutional and financial support for this project as well. The Department of Religious Studies at Yale University has provided me with an atmosphere conducive to research for almost nine years now. I spent one year as a fellow of the Whitney Humanities Center at Yale. I started the project with the help of a Morse Fellowship in the Humanities in 1990–1991, and I also traveled to India that year through the grace of an American Institute of Indian Studies Short-term Research Grant. A Fellowship for University Teachers from the National Endowment for the Humanities in 1994 allowed me to complete my work, and enabled me to conduct further research in London and India. At a time when governmental agencies like the N.E.H. are under extreme duress, I wish to acknowledge my gratitude. Finally, the Frederick Hilles Fund at Yale has helped me in acquiring illustrations for the book.

I feel privileged to have participated in the most extensive interpretive community of all: that found in a library. One often takes for granted the miraculous incarnations by which we encounter the thoughts and words of authors distant in time and place. I am particularly indebted to the library at

Yale University, and to the wonderful superlibrary brought into being through Inter-Library Loan.

This book is dedicated to Matthew Davis, who wonders why his father has been working on just one book during the entire five years Matthew has been alive (and then some), while he often turns out two or three in a single day at kindergarten.

Translation and Transliteration

THIS BOOK draws upon works composed in a number of Asian languages: Sanskrit, Tamil, Pali, Arabic, Persian, and Old Rajasthani. All translations from Sanskrit, Tamil, and Pali are mine, except where otherwise noted. (Most of the exceptions are translations of Tamil bhakti poetry.) I list the editions I have used, and also published translations where available, in the bibliography. Indic texts are listed alphabetically by title.

For works in Arabic, Persian, and Rajasthani, I have relied on the translations of other scholars. Works in Arabic and Persian are listed alphabetically by translator in the bibliography, and they are listed chronologically in a bibliographic appendix.

I follow the usual scholarly conventions in transliterating terms and names from Indic languages. For guidance in the pronunciation of Sanskrit terms, the reader may consult Robert Goldman, ed., *The Rāmāyaṇa of Vālmīki* vol. 1 (Princeton: Princeton University Press, 1984), pp. xix–xx. For pronunciation of Tamil, consult Indira V. Peterson, *Poems to Śiva* (Princeton: Princeton University Press, 1989), pp. xv–xvi. Where a term or name is used in both Sanskrit and Tamil, I have preferred the Sanskrit as more commonly recognizable (e.g., Cola, not Cōḻa; Sundaramūrti, not Cuntaramūrti).

In rendering Arabic and Persian terms and names I have generally followed the conventions of *The Encyclopedia of Islam*, new edition (Leiden, 1960–1993), with some accomodations to common English usage (e.g., Shāh Jahān, not Shāh D̲jahān).

I have tried to avoid intimidating the non-Indianist reader with too many diacritic marks. Modern place names and modern personal names are given in their usual Indian English rendering (e.g. Tiruvengadu, not Tiruveṅkāṭu). In some cases I use common Anglicized terms in preference to more technical Sanskritic renderings (e.g. brahmin, not *brāhmaṇa*). Out of respect, however, deities and temples always receive their proper diacritics. Śiva (not Shiva), Viṣṇu (not Vishnu), and their divine cohorts are the protagonists of these iconic lives.

Abbreviations

ARE	*Annual Reports of South Indian Epigraphy*
BhG	*Bhagavadgītā*
BhP	*Bhāgavatapurāṇa*
BrSBh	*Brahmasūtrabhāṣya*
BS	*Bṛhatsaṃhitā*
CV	*Cūlavaṃsa*
KĀ	*Kāmikāgama*
KO	*Koyil Oluku*
MĀ	*Mṛgendrāgama*
MBh	*Mahābhārata*
MS	*Manusmṛti*
MSBh	*Manubhāṣya*
MV	*Madhurāvijaya*
PA	*Prapannāmṛta*
PS	*Paramasaṃhitā*
RT	*Rājataraṅginī*
SBh	*Śrīvacanabhūṣana*
SP	*Somaśambhupaddhati*
T.	Transcript of *India v. Bumper*
VĀK	*Vimanārcanākalpa*
VS	*Viṣṇusmṛti*

LIVES OF INDIAN IMAGES

Introduction

IN OCTOBER 1917, a young man named Maulavi Qazi Sayyid Muhammad Azimul spied a large square block of stone along the edge of the Ganges River at the hamlet of Didarganj Kadam Basul, in the eastern part of Patna, capital of the colonial province of Bihar and Orissa. Erosion along the riverbank had brought this long-buried piece of sandstone to the surface. Maulavi hoped to appropriate his find for household use as a grinding stone, but as he began to scrape and dig away the dirt, he discovered that the block was in fact the pedestal for a large polished stone statue. When unearthed and set upright, the impressive image stood on its pedestal six feet nine inches tall. It was a voluptuous female figure with wide hips and full breasts, leaning forward slightly toward the viewer. One of her arms was missing; the other held a long fly whisk draped over her shoulder. Though the tip of her nose was chipped off, she maintained a serene and slightly enigmatic smile. Her sandstone body was burnished to a lustrous finish (Figure 1). Maulavi's river find would go on to an illustrious career as one of the most celebrated and well-traveled of all Indian works of sculpture, the Didarganj yakṣī. This was not, however, its most immediate destiny.

Art historians still debate just when the Didarganj yakṣī was fabricated, but judging from its sculptural style and unusual polish, it seems most likely that a sculptor carved her during the Mauryan period of the third century B.C.E., when Pāṭaliputra (modern Patna) was the metropolis of an empire extending over most of the subcontinent. At the time, many inhabitants of northern India regarded male yakṣas and female yakṣīs as powerful divine figures particularly associated with wealth, abundance, and the fecundity of natural processes. From an early period, votaries made anthropomorphic images of these deities, placed them in shrines under trees, and presented offerings of flowers, incense, food, and drink before them.[1] Later, worshipers of other religious persuasions incorporated yakṣa and yakṣī icons into their own cultic centers. At the early Buddhist stupas of the first century B.C.E. and the first century C.E., for instance, yakṣas and yakṣīs appear as subordinate figures, bringing their powers and auspicious presence to guard and attend the preeminent symbol at the core of the stupa complex, the mound containing

FIG. 1. The Didarganj Yakṣī in the Patna Museum. Polished sandstone image, probably of third century B.C.E., unearthed in Didarganj, Bihar, now in the Patna Museum.

sacred relics of the Buddha. As for the Didarganj yakṣī, we cannot know the precise liturgical setting she originally occupied, nor do we know when or how she was dislodged from that spot. Somehow, though, she ended up spending many centuries buried in the sands of the Ganges.

After Maulavi disinterred the statue, some "unauthorized persons" carted it a few hundred yards upriver and built a makeshift shrine for it. As D. B. Spooner, then curator of the Patna Museum, relates, "Here it was again set up, this time under a canopy improvised on four bamboos, which was so speedily invested with the character of an incipient shrine, that tentative worship had been instituted (under the mistaken notion that the figure was a Hindu deity) before the fact of the discovery was brought to the notice of any but the Police, who, however, reported it in due course in the proper quarter" (Spooner 1919: 107). Unfortunately Spooner did not ask the local worshipers with just which Hindu deity they identified the yakṣī, nor does he say anything about the "tentative worship" they instituted. We can assume, however, that the villagers would not have worried unduly about the original historical identity of the awesome new icon. They would have been much more concerned to integrate the image into their current world of belief, and they would have assigned identity and worshiped it accordingly.[2]

Evidently a student at Patna College mentioned the advent of this new deity to Jogindra Nath Sammadar, professor of history and an "enthusiastic antiquarian." Sammadar reported it to the British official E. H. C. Walsh, a member of the provincial Board of Revenue and president of the Patna Museum's Managing Committee. Walsh in turn brought it to the attention of curator Spooner. Walsh and Spooner went out to Didarganj to investigate. "By good fortune," reported Spooner, "it was easy to show that the figure was merely an attendant, bearing a chowry, and thus clearly no member of the Hindu pantheon, nor entitled to worship of any kind by any community" (108). More likely it was the authoritative presence of two British officials backed up by a coterie of policemen that proved persuasive to the residents of Didarganj, rather than the iconographic niceties of fly whisks.[3] With "characteristically energetic steps," Walsh had the Didarganj yakṣī taken away from Didarganj and brought "in safety and triumph" into the Patna Museum.

In this brief confrontation by the banks of the Ganges, two worlds collided, and with them two visions of what the newly uncovered image was and should be also came into conflict. The Didarganj villagers took the appearance of the icon as (we must speculate here, thanks to Spooner's lack of ethnographic curiosity) yet another manifestation of a primordial Mother Goddess, who recurrently makes herself visible in ever new forms to her human devotees, and they immediately took steps to treat the goddess in suitable fashion. Walsh and Spooner, on the other hand, understood the object to be a specimen of ancient Indian statuary. As such, they arranged to have the statue displayed without any accoutrements in a museum for the inspection of interested students of Indian art, they assessed it in terms of the skill and success of its anonymous sculptor in realizing "correct and convincing modelling" (by which aesthetic standard Spooner judged it "primitive"), and they sought to locate it within a historical sequence of Indian sculptures through comparison with other similar objects. These two conceptions of the yakṣī exemplify two polar ways of valuing works of art. In Walter Benjamin's well-known distinction, the Indian villagers accent the "cult value" of the icon, while the British officials esteem the statue for its "exhibition value" (Benjamin 1985: 224).

The resolution of the 1917 dispute over the Didarganj yakṣī was a political one. It was their power and authority, the latent ability to impose their will by force if necessary, that enabled Walsh and Spooner to dislodge the yakṣī from her incipient temple and relocate her in their own recently founded institution, the Patna Museum, which itself represented through its neat classifications and displays British rule over the material remains of India's past. Even Spooner's instruction of the villagers in what was and was not a deity reflected British attempts to master knowledge of native religions and to display that mastery as part of their program of colonial control. Walsh and Spooner, not the inhabitants of Didarganj, were in a position to create the yakṣī's new identity. Only Spooner's brief narration of the Didarganj yakṣī's find in his 1919 article for the *Journal of the Bihar and Orissa Research Society* remains as a residue of that other brief life, her moment of ritual presence in east Patna.

My aim in this book is to explore the different worlds of belief that Indian religious images have come to inhabit over time, and the conflicts over their identities that have often surrounded them. I wish especially to exhume and examine past lives of objects like the Didarganj yakṣī that we have become accustomed to viewing unproblematically, in the modern museums of South Asia and the West, as objects of Indian art.

Biographies of Indian Images

For many centuries, most Hindus have taken it for granted that the religious images they place in temples and home shrines for purposes of worship are alive. They believe these physical objects, visually or symbolically representing particular deities, come to be infused with the presence or life or power of those deities. Hindu priests are able to bring images to life through a complex ritual "establishment" that invokes the god or goddess into its material support. Priests and devotees then maintain the enlivened image as a divine person through ongoing liturgical activity; they must awaken it in the morning, bathe it, dress it, feed it, entertain it, praise it, and eventually put it to bed at night. They may also petition it, as a divine being, to grant them worldly benefits and liberation from all suffering.

Life does not end there for many of these images. In medieval Indian literature we read of images that move their limbs, speak, and perform miraculous feats. Images may act to adjudicate disputes among their human devotees, and they may engage in contests of miracles with one another to resolve their own disputes over status and authority. According to Indian legal literature, central images are the lords and owners of the temples they inhabit. As proprietors they carry out a host of administrative activities through functionaries, who are themselves sometimes images. In some cases, particularly eminent images even rule kingdoms, with human sovereigns acting as subordinate ministers under their command. For medieval Indians, the power and efficacy of the religious images they created and worshiped was indeed great, and today for many modern Hindus these iconic deities retain much of their power.

In this book I take the Hindu theological postulate of religious images as animate beings as the organizing trope for a series of biographies that narrate the lives of Indian religious images. Hindu priests and worshipers are not the only ones to enliven images. Bringing with them differing religious assumptions, political agendas, and economic motivations, others may animate the very same objects as icons of sovereignty, as polytheistic "idols," as "devils," as potentially lucrative commodities, as objects of sculptural art, or as symbols for a whole range of new meanings never foreseen by the images' makers or original worshipers. These new views may well have profound effects on the images themselves. As we will see, humans may steal the images, destroy or disfigure them, transport them, buy and sell them, label them, display them in new settings for new audiences, and even sometimes research their history. In the process, Indian religious objects are sometimes drawn into conflicts that have repercussions far beyond themselves. I consider all such shifts in mode of life as parts of their biographies.

In adopting this approach, I follow Igor Kopytoff's proposal for a "cultural biographical" method for the study of objects in society. "A culturally informed economic biography of an object," as Kopytoff envisions it, "would look at it as a culturally constructed entity, endowed with culturally specific meanings, and classified and reclassified into culturally constituted categories" (1986: 68). Kopytoff goes on to show how a processual approach can elucidate the fluctuations in status, the negotiations of social value, and the transactions that attend and transform an object over time. A similar premise and similar agenda underlie the biographical narrative of Indian religious objects in this book.[4] In recounting diverse adventures of Indian images I portray them as fundamentally social beings whose identities are not fixed once and for all at the moment of fabrication, but are repeatedly made and remade through interactions with humans. Responses to such objects, I will argue, are primarily grounded not in universal aesthetic principles of sculptural form or in a common human psychology of perception, but more significantly in varied (and often conflicting) cultural notions of divinity, representation, and authority.[5]

Images and Their Communities

In attempting to reconstruct lives of Indian objects and their interactions with human audiences, I have found it valuable to combine Kopytoff's biographical method with a notion of "interpretive communities," drawn from reader-response literary theory, particularly as formulated by Stanley Fish in two volumes of essays (1980, 1989). Together, these two approaches provide a theoretical skin light and flexible enough to accommodate the plurality of identities and modes of livelihood in the lives of Indian images I wish to narrate here. Before beginning to look at these lives, though, it will be helpful to say something about reader-response theory and my adaptation of interpretive communities.

Reader-response critics initially set themselves against formalist approaches to literature, which view meaning as embedded within a work of literary art. From a formalist perspective the task of literary interpretation is to analyze and describe the formal properties of texts as the source of their meaning. Against this approach, Fish and other reader-response critics insist that meaning develops within the dynamic relationship between reader and text established during the act of reading. The reader gains joint responsibility in the production of meaning, and meaning itself becomes an event rather than an entity (Fish 1980: 3).

The reader-response orientation that Fish and others advocate validates the subjective responses of readers, but it faces the objection of subjectivism. Are there not as many experiences of a text as there are readers of it? If so, how may we say anything of general interest about common texts? What is the basis for common reading experience or for shared meaning? To counter this objection Fish introduces his conception of "interpretive communities," groups of readers who approach texts in the same way. Communities who share cultural assumptions may also share "interpretive strategies" through which they "write texts"—that is, constitute the properties of texts and assign intentions—in a like manner (1980: 171).

Fish insists that no single way of reading is correct and universal. Different interpretive communities reading the same physical text but working with differing interpretive strategies may engender very different readings. Further, as Fish argues, interpretive strategies are not natural, but learned within particular social settings. Therefore they can and do change. The notion of interpretive communities thus takes reader-response theory back into the social world and gives it a historical dimension. The biography of a literary work may be seen as a history of its interactions with different interpretive communities over time.

Viewing a stone or bronze sculpted icon is not exactly like reading an arrangement of words on pages of a book, but the idea of interpretive communities—or, as I will prefer, "communities of response"—is just as valuable for considering the plurality of ways viewers approach and encounter a visual object. Here too, "meaning" emerges through the relationship of image with viewer, who brings his or her community's own interpretive strategies to bear within the encounter. Here too, these ways of approaching the object are learned, shared, and susceptible to change. Interpretive strategies for encountering objects, like those for texts, have their own social locations and historical genealogies. This book aims to explore and describe some of the significant ways different communities have seen, interpreted, and constructed Indian religious images as meaningful objects. To reinvoke the central metaphor of the book, different ways of seeing animate the objects seen in new ways.

One significant difference between reading a book and looking at an object lies in the relative importance of setting and presentation. Admittedly there are better and worse places to read, but generally location does not enter profoundly into the dynamic relationship established between the reader and the text during the moment of reading. The location of an object, by contrast, plays a constitutive role in the act of looking. The physical display, adornment (or lack of adornment), pedestal, lighting, label, surrounding objects, and even the type of building—what I will call the "frame" of the object—all help guide the attention and responses of the viewer in looking at, and in some cases acting toward, a visual object. The Didarganj yakṣī, for instance, exhibited herself in a very different light in her improvised bamboo sanctuary near the river than she did when later placed on display in the exhibition hall of the Patna Museum. In the first chapter I discuss a similar instance by contrasting the disjoint appearances of the same bronze image of Śiva in a south Indian Hindu temple and in an American museum. Appropriation, relocation, and redisplay of an object can dramatically alter its significance for new audiences.

True to the reader-response spirit of reciprocal encounter, we may well speak of a second kind of frame. Just as the image or object appears in its own physical setting, viewers also bring their own frames of assumptions, understandings, needs, expectations, and hopes to what they see. The viewer's frame is not just a set of interpretive strategies, but something more global and more diffuse: an outlook on the cosmos, on divinity, on human life and its possibilities, and on the role of images in a world so constituted. I occasionally use the theological term "dispensation" as a shorthand way of designating historically grounded and socially shared understandings of the systems, often but not necessarily believed to be divinely instituted, by which things are ordered and administered.[6] For individual viewers, particular dispensations set the epistemic frame within which the world comes to be known and acted upon. Thus, the very different ways in which the inhabitants of Didarganj and the British officials understood the large carved stone "yakṣī" reflected the juxtaposition of two contrasting dispensations. In the broadest sense, communities of response grow out of particular dispensations.

Stanley Fish usefully observes that an interpretive community may be homogeneous with respect to its general purpose and at the same time heterogeneous with regard to the variety of practices it can accommodate (1989: 149). Likewise it would be a mistake to attribute too great a hegemony to any particular dispensation. The dispensation of early medieval temple Hinduism, for example, entailed certain shared premises concerning the divine order and human goals within it, but within that broad consensus lay great room for disagreement and debate over such issues as the character of divinity in relation to the world, the ontological status of the image, and the relative efficacy of different methods of worship. These concerns might have a bearing upon the specific ways in which groups of Hindu worshipers would animate their images, but it would not affect the broader shared view of temple images as ritually consecrated material supports for divinity and as sites for human interaction with the divine. When this dispensation comes to be juxtaposed with an Islamic one, as it was historically in India from the eleventh century on, or with the post-Enlightenment dispensation of the modern West, the areas of agreement among Hindus become more salient than their philosophical disagreements.

Plan of the Book

This book is organized as a linked series of case studies or biographies. Each chapter focuses on one particular religious object or site and traces it over time. I intend these cases to be exemplary. Within each particular biography, I aim to explore significant moments or dramatic shifts in response that have affected many other Indian objects as well.

The first chapter opens with an account of a medieval south Indian bronze image of Śiva that appeared at the National Gallery in Washington, D.C., during the 1985 Festival of India. Like many of the objects that accompanied it from India, the bronze Śiva was originally fabricated for liturgical usage and spent its early life in a Hindu temple. I juxtapose the way the object presented itself to the gaze of American museum goers with the way it would have appeared in its original temple setting to the audience of devotees for which it was initially intended. Using this object as a point of departure, I describe early medieval south Indian theological notions of divine presence and the ritual means by which this presence was instantiated in physical icons. I go on to outline briefly the devotional frame of values within which south Indian communities of this dispensation approached and viewed their enlivened images, a mode of response I call the "devotional eye."

This effort to recover an original intent behind the bronze Śiva might suggest that I am privileging the moment of its creation as the essential meaning of the object, as religious historians and art historians often do. The argument of this book moves in the other direction. I hold that subsequent "reinterpretations" of these objects in new settings are equally worthy of disciplined inquiry. If a religious image is really a living being, we would not confine its biography to an account of its birth. All chapters after the first deal primarily with the ways in which Indian religious images come to be animated with new significances by persons holding different conceptions in altered historical situations. The lives of Indian images may be just as filled with change, disjuncture, and readjustment to new circumstances as those of humans.

Further, I take the goal of recovering an earlier or original meaning as itself a historical phenomenon. In two later chapters I consider moments or situations in which recovery of an image's original identity or meaning has become an important value to late medieval Hindus and to twentieth-century Western historians of Indian art. As a twentieth-century Western historian myself, I share an interest in the historicist project of comprehending Indian art objects by imaginatively relocating them in their original context. However, I argue that a fuller historical study of this category of objects ought to consider all the responses they have evoked during their long lives and all the significances that audiences have given them over time.

The second chapter investigates the appropriation of select religious images by Indian rulers during the medieval period. In medieval India, Hindu kings regularly seized valuable objects from one another in situations of dynastic conflict and war. They relocated and redisplayed them and thereby shifted their significance. I argue that such wartime looting was a common and well-understood signifying practice, part of a larger political rhetoric by which rulers made and displayed claims of victory and defeat, dominance and subordination, and imperial overlordship. In this chapter I focus primarily on a Cālukya door-guardian statue captured by the Cola sovereign Rājādhirāja, and cite other examples to illustrate the range of rhetorical possibilities available to early medieval rulers.

Chapters Three and Four deal with medieval Islamic iconoclasm in India from two sides of the conflict. From the late tenth century onward, Turkic and Central Asian warrior groups adhering more or less to an Islamic religious ideology began to enter the Indian subcontinent. They established new polities that eventually dominated much of India. In certain circumstances the new elites acted upon traditional Islamic directives for warriors to destroy idols and idol houses, the embodiments of polytheism, as an act of conquest and incorporation. Hindu warriors seeking to establish new polities independent of Islamic political control reciprocally reestablished images and temples as a means of publicly proclaiming their autonomy.

The historiography of these contentious medieval events has recently become particularly contentious itself, as a result of recent claims and political mobilizations of Hindu nationalist groups on India. In this book I focus not on the events themselves, but rather on the ways in which Indo-Muslim and Hindu texts of the period narrated acts of image destruction and reconstruction. Chapter Three discusses Indo-Muslim anecdotes of Maḥmūd, the Ghaznavid ruler who destroyed the Hindu temple of Somanātha in Gujarat in 1026. Conservative Indo-Muslim chroniclers of the late medieval period came to portray Maḥmūd's act of iconoclasm as a model for an Islamic conqueror confronting the idols of India. Chapter Four looks at the Hindu literature of recovery, especially that centering around the south Indian Viṣṇu temple at Sri Rangam. Here, Vaiṣṇava devotees act heroically and deceptively to salvage the divine icons, and gods may intervene as well to preserve their images. Not only do these tales of images destroyed and saved illustrate two very different ways of interpreting and responding to Indian religious icons. I wish also to show how the "primary sources" upon which modern historians have necessarily based their reconstructions renarrate these events in accord with their own theological and political purposes.

The following chapter looks at a new historical mode of appropriation: the early acquisition of Indian objects by the British during the colonial period. My discussion centers on "Tipu's Tiger," an effigy that British forces took as wartime prize after their successful the siege of Sri Rangapattana in 1799. British officials transported the tiger back to England and exhibited it in the India Museum, where it became a famous and much discussed display. Comments of early nineteenth-century observers about the tiger indicate how British viewers of the time characterized the tiger as a trophy and symbolic justification of British colonial rule. By following the tiger and other appropriated Indian objects into the twentieth century, we will see how changing conceptions of Indian "art" and the altered political relationship of India and the United Kingdom have transformed the frame within which modern Western museum goers now encounter these icons of colonialism.

We return to Somanātha in Chapter Six. Here I trace the subsequent history of the site where Maḥmūd destroyed the Śiva temple. More importantly I also retrace the history of its rememberings. Over the centuries many groups with differing agendas have laid claim to the image and the site, and they have each retold its story to suit their own ends. I look at the efforts of medieval Muslims, Rajputs, and Jains, nineteenth-century British, early twentieth-century Indian nationalists, and late twentieth-century Hindu nationalists to mobilize Śiva Somanātha and his ever-lengthening biography of loss and reappearance for themselves.

Finally, Chapter Seven examines the current market in the West for ancient Indian art objects by following a twelfth-century bronze image of Śiva Naṭarāja as it enters and eventually leaves the art market. The Pathur Naṭarāja was taken out of its temple in a small village in Tamilnad and buried long ago, accidentally dug up in 1976, sold and resold several times in India, smuggled abroad, sold again, and then seized by London police as a stolen object. It became the center of a legal dispute between the Government of India, which sought to repatriate the image to its village shrine, and the chief executive of a Canadian oil corporation, which sought to retain it for museum display. When the bronze image finally returned to Tamilnad in 1991, the chief minister and other dignitaries hailed it as a new symbol for the successful protection of India's cultural heritage. By following the Pathur Naṭarāja's repeated shifts in location and status, I aim to illuminate a clandestine practice whose workings often remain hidden, and to bring into juxtaposition the conflicting claims and views Indian worshipers and Western collectors may hold toward their objects of devotion.

There are hundreds of thousands of religious images in the Indian cultural sphere. All have their own lives, and many have long and varied biographies. I have selected objects for the interest of their stories, but many other Indian images have equally intricate pasts and would equally repay biographical attention. I have chosen case studies that will illustrate significant historical interpretive shifts and practices that have affected many objects, but I would be the first to admit there are other such moments.

One need not believe Hindu theological premises concerning divinities entering and enlivening icons to accept that Indian religious images are, in some important sense, alive. If I convince the reader that these objects may be animated as much by their own histories and by their varied interactions with different human communities of response as by the deities they represent and support, I will have achieved my purpose.

(*left*) FIG. 2. Śiva Vṛṣabhavāhana of Tiruvengadu. Bronze image, dated 1011 C.E., sponsored by Kolakkavan for Śvetāraṇyeśvara temple, Tiruvengadu. Now in Rajaraja Museum, Thanjavur.

(*right*) FIG. 3. Pārvatī, Consort of Vṛṣabhavāhana. Bronze image, dated 1012 C.E., sponsored by Rajaraja Jananatha Terinca Parivara for Śvetāraṇyeśvara temple, Tiruvengadu. Now in Rajaraja Museum, Thanjavur.

1.

Living Images

IN 1985 a medieval south Indian bronze sculpture of the Hindu god Śiva traveled from southern India to the United States, accompanied by another bronze sculpture of his wife Pārvatī, to appear in a major show of "The Sculpture of India, 3000 B.C.–1300 A.D." at the National Gallery of Art in Washington, D.C. (Figures 2, 3). The eleventh-century image depicts Śiva in his aspect as Vṛṣabhavāhana, "the Lord whose mount is the bull Nandi." Śiva stands in a position of grace and ease, weight on his left foot while his right leg crosses over. His right arm extends to rest on the back of Nandi, who no longer accompanies his master. Śiva wears a short lower garment tied with an elaborate belt ornamented with lion and crocodile forms. His plaited hair has been coiled into a turban, with loose strands dangling onto his back. From a show of many outstanding examples of Indian plastic art, the curators chose this image to grace the front and back covers of the show catalog.[1]

We know something of the earlier life of this icon. The Śvetāraṇyeśvara temple in the village of Tiruvengadu (Thanjavur District, Tamilnad) was reconstructed sometime in the first half of the tenth century, and appears to have enjoyed considerable patronage from the Cola royal family, ruling from Thanjavur about fifty miles away (Figure 4). An inscription etched on the outer wall of the temple records that in 1011 C.E. one Kolakkāvan, a local worthy of Tiruvengadu, presented money and jewels to the image of Śiva Vṛṣabhavāhana that he had installed in the temple. The following year members of a group calling itself the "Rājarāja Jananātha Teriñca Parivāra," apparently royal attendants of the Cola court, had an image of the goddess Pārvatī fabricated and presented it to the temple, to serve as Śiva's consort.[2] Priests performed a ritual consecration for each new icon, and the images joined the retinue of processional icons in the Śvetāraṇyeśvara temple. Priests and worshipers maintained them through a regular round of liturgical activities, and on festival days the images came forth from the temple on palanquins and paraded through the streets of the village.

Sometime over the succeeding centuries, during some period of disruption, Śiva Vṛṣabhavāhana and his consort went into hiding. Temple officials

FIG. 4. Entry Gate to Śvetāraṇyeśvara Temple, Tiruvengadu.

buried the valuable bronze images of the Śvetāraṇyeśvara temple to protect them from marauders and looters. Evidently the information of their whereabouts was lost, for they stayed buried for centuries. Not until the twentieth century were any of the buried Tiruvengadu bronzes unearthed. Altogether there have been four major treasure-trove finds in Tiruvengadu, yielding richest collection of Cola bronze sculpture from any single site.

Village residents returned the first batch of disinterred images, found in 1925, to the temple. They reconsecrated the bronzes for worship and the current residents of Tiruvengadu continue to worship them. In 1951 a farmer came upon a second group of bronzes, including Vṛṣabhavāhana, Pārvatī, and several other works, while plowing a field. The district collector, T. K. Palaniappan, obtained these for the Thanjavur Art Gallery, which he had just established in the district headquarters. Villagers chanced upon another batch of bronzes in 1960, and then again in 1972.[3]

On display in the Thanjavur museum, the images from Tiruvengadu repeatedly caught the eye of visiting museum experts. In 1982 Śiva Vṛṣabhavāhana and Pārvatī traveled to London to participate in the first international

Festival of India, in the exhibition entitled "In the Image of Man" (Michell et al. 1982), and in 1983 they appeared in Delhi at the National Museum, in a show of "Masterpieces of Early South Indian Bronzes" (Nagaswamy 1983). Completing their tour of national capitals, the couple moved on two years later to Washington to take part in the 1985 Festival of India in the United States. Two other bronzes from Tiruvengadu, depicting the legendary Śaiva devotees Brahmādhirāyan and Kaṇṇappar, joined them at the National Gallery. There, American art-lovers and tourists could view these estimable bronze sculptures, nearly a thousand years old, together with even older works of art like the Didarganj yakṣī, representing the ancient civilization of India.

Two Ways of Animating Images

An Indian religious image, however, does not appear to us in a museum the same as it does to Indian worshipers in a temple. The way it is displayed, the frame of surrounding objects, and the expectations the two audiences bring to their encounters with the object differ dramatically.

Those who visited Vṛṣabhavāhana and Pārvatī at the "Sculpture of India" show at the National Gallery of Art saw the couple standing on pedestals by themselves, unadorned, carefully spotlighted by track lights, against a subdued background (Figure 5). Following normal installation practice, the National Gallery displayed this religious icon from another culture as a self-contained aesthetic object, meant to be appreciated for the beauty of its essential sculptural form. The atmosphere was hushed; no extraneous noise (except the unavoidable rustlings and whispers of other visitors) was allowed to detract from the visual experience of the museum goer. Nearby was a label that provided some minimal identifying information: the place and date of the fabrication, its physical dimensions, and the iconographic form of the Hindu deity it represented.

Śiva stood in a large hall with many other such objects, all similarly displayed. These individual "masterpieces" had been assembled from thirty-nine museums in India as well as from museums abroad, private collections, and two temple collections, and brought to the United States as a collective representation of "India's artistic heritage." The purpose of the show, wrote curator Pramod Chandra (1985: 7, 18–20), was "to give the viewer an impression of Indian sculpture as a whole, in all the rich diversity of idioms that flourished in the ancient regions of the country," and "to convey a sense of the contribution of Indian sculpture to the common artistic heritage of mankind." Chandra hoped thereby to counter long-standing attitudes in the West that denigrated Indian art. The arrangement of objects pointedly avoided any divisions into religious groupings. Images of the Buddha, Viṣṇu, Śiva, the

FIG. 5. Vṛṣabhavāhana and Pārvatī at the National Gallery. Special exhibition of "The Sculpture of India, 3000 B.C.–1300 A.D.," May-November 1985. Photograph courtesy of National Gallery of Art, Washington, D.C.

Goddess, other deities, and saints all congregated together with secular and nonliturgical sculptures as equal representatives of "India's artistic heritage." The exhibition presented "Indian sculpture" as a historically produced human artistic achievement unified as a national expression, with regional and temporal variations.

South Indians of the eleventh century who visited Vṛṣabhavāhana in his original setting would have seen the bronze image very differently. In the Śvetāraṇyeśvara temple, he and Pārvatī would have presented themselves to viewers elevated on a pedestal (along with the now-missing image of Śiva's bull Nandi), much as in the National Gallery. However, priests and worshipers would have devoted their primary attention to another object, a smooth cylindrical shaft made of heavy stone emerging from an hourglass-shaped stone pedestal, the Śiva liṅga. Deemed uninteresting as a sculptural form, the liṅga is seldom seen in Western art museums.[4] For Śaiva worshipers, by contrast, it stood at the physical and conceptual center of the temple. Medieval Śaiva texts refer to it as the very "root manifestation" (*mūlamūrti*) of divinity and the emanating source of all other anthropomorphic images in the temple.

Of course, those who attended the Śiva liṅga in a south Indian temple did not approach it as a visual object only to be savored aesthetically. Interactions between priests and their object of worship were much more physical than that. In rites of worship (*pūjā*), they would repeatedly smear it with unguents, shower it with flowers, and bathe it with liquids of many kinds. "Using bowls of various colors," recommends one priestly guidebook, "the priests bathe Śiva with diamonds and other jewels, with the five products of the cow, with nicely prepared powders, with black mustard seed and salt, with tepid water, sandal water, and herb water, with milk, curd, ghee, honey, and jaggery. . . . If money permits, he should also bathe Śiva with coconut milk or the juice of other succulent fruits, with flowers and the like, with gold water, with jewel water, and with sandal water" (*KĀ pūrva* 4.405–9). They would dress it with fine garments and adorn it with all kinds of ornaments: gold diadems, medallions, moons and flowers of gold, pearl necklaces, belts, and much more. They would wave lamps before it, treat it to a sumptuous meal, and serenade it with mantras, devotional hymns, and instrumental music.

Many other images were stationed around the Śvetāraṇyeśvara temple. Some represented Śiva in the whole host of his multiple aspects: as a dancer, a beggar, a conqueror of demons, a teacher, a husband seated peacefully with wife and child, an ascetic, and so on. Śiva leaning gracefully on his bull mount Nandi, accompanied by his consort Pārvatī, was one such aspect of Śiva. Other deities appeared as well. Temple visitors encountered not only Śiva and his own family, but also the deities worshiped by other religious communities, such as Viṣṇu, Durgā, and Brahman. However, in the hierarchy of temple space, all others were rendered subservient to Śiva. In this way, the icons and images of the Śvetāraṇyeśvara temple also formed a collective representation, but one based on theological principles rather than humanistic ones. Emanating outward from the liṅga that embodied Śiva in his highest form, the grouping and arrangement of divine objects offered a hierophanic portrait of Śiva's divine world, hierarchical and eternal. In this world details of human fabrication were deliberately deemphasized, but humans could regularly participate in it through their offerings of worship and devotion.[5]

Like most of the south Indian bronze images we see in Western museums, the Tiruvengadu Vṛṣabhavāhana was fabricated primarily to serve as a processional icon. In medieval south Indian society not all persons were qualified to approach the Śiva liṅga in its inner sanctum. However, Śiva in his grace desires to extend his beneficent presence to all, so he regularly journeys out beyond the confines of the temple for the benefit of all those unable to enter. The heavy stone liṅga embedded in an even heavier stone pedestal is

FIG. 6. Śiva Sundareśvara in Procession, Madurai. Chittrai Festival, May 1982.

immobile, but Śiva's metal icons, though they are sometimes very heavy, are still portable. So daily during the "regular festival" (*nityotsava*) and more ostentatiously during the occasional calendrical "great festivals" (*mahotsava*), Śiva transfers his presence to mobile bronze images and goes on procession.

A processional image presents itself to its audience seated high upon a palanquin carried on the shoulders of temple servants or riding in a large wooden vehicle pulled by ropes (Figure 6). It appears dressed in silk clothing and elaborately decorated with necklaces, bracelets, belts, rings, and a crown of gold and jewels. Heaps of fresh flowers might surround it, virtually hiding the body of the image (Waghorne 1992). Incense burns, and plates piled with coconut, banana, rice, and betel leaf sit before the image. Temple officials walk alongside waving fly whisks and shading the icon with a parasol. Musicians add their raucous accompaniment on reed horns and drums. In procession, Vṛṣabhavāhana and Pārvatī images of Tiruvengadu would have appeared to their viewers not as simple metal icons, but as living beings covered over in the material and social adornments of their livelihood.

This visual contrast between museum bronze and liturgical icon reappears in the souvenirs audiences might carry away from their visits. A visitor to the "Sculpture of India" show in Washington could buy the catalogue, in which photographs rendered each object in its austere exhibition mode. Explanatory text described each image and gave details about what was known of its historical origins and iconographical significance. Through the wonders of mechanical reproduction, modern-day pilgrims to major south Indian shrines like the Śiva Naṭarāja temple in Cidambaram may also take home, for a modest charge of two or four rupees, a lithographic representation of their visit. (This was not possible for eleventh-century Śaiva devotees, of course, and is still not possible at lesser-known shrines like the Śvetāraṇyeśvara temple in Tiruvengadu.) In these "God pictures" (Tamil *cāmipaṭam*), Śiva again appears—properly dressed and decorated, framed within a golden archway, surrounded by family and devotees and all the accoutrements of worship—not as a historically situated material object, but as a living being in his proper situation of worship (Figure 7). A devotee might even place the framed souvenir in his or her home shrine, properly consecrated as an object of worship in itself, for it too partakes of the divine presence that enlivens the temple image.[6]

Differences in visual presentation and placement of the Tiruvengadu Vṛṣabhavāhana in his two abodes correspond to very different ontological and moral premises that his two audiences held about what that bronze image in essence was and how one ought best to act toward it. In each case the encounter between the image and his community of response occurred within a complex framing set of cultural assumptions and ideas, what I call a dispensation, that guided that encounter.

For south Indian Śaivas of the eleventh century, as for traditional Hindus today, religious icons like the stone liṅga and the bronze image of Śiva Vṛṣabhavāhana at Tiruvengadu were most fundamentally living divine beings. The center of an icon's identity and value lay not in its physical materials nor its form, but in the divine presence that was invoked into it through ritual procedures and came to animate it. In medieval Śaiva theology, the animated icon or image was a localized, particularized "manifestation" or "incarnation" of the all-pervading, transcendent God Śiva, who at his highest level of being was considered to be beyond all form, but who simultaneously would inhabit a variety of immanent, physical "embodiments."

Śiva could inhabit all sorts of things. Not only would Śiva enter into beautiful bronze images and stolid stone liṅgas, but also (according to the *Kāmikāgama*) into circular diagrams, cloth paintings, fires, water in consecrated pots, special books on their stands, and various other "supports." These supports need not be made by humans; Śiva also chose to manifest himself in "self-arising" liṅgas (*svayambhūliṅga*) and in the liṅga-shaped stones one might find in the beds of holy rivers (*KĀ pūrva* 4.270–72). Śiva's promiscuity when it came to embodying himself did not mean that Śiva, or his eleventh-century audience of devotees, was insensitive to physical beauty. Iconographic texts urged image makers to make their images as beautiful as they could, and devotional poets of the time repeatedly proclaimed the glorious beauty of their embodied gods. Aesthetic concerns were, however, second-

FIG. 7. Sri Naṭarāja at Cidambaram. Calendar print ("God-picture") of Śiva Naṭarāja by C. Kondiah Raju and T. S. Subbiah, Sri New Karpaga Vilas, Cidambaram.

ary to other criteria: iconographic correctness, completeness, ritual animation, and divine presence.

As a result of Śiva's theophany in physical icons, human worshipers considered it incumbent upon them to treat his physical embodiment as a divine person. The primary liturgical practices of medieval Śaiva temples, accordingly, involved the same kinds of respectful services a diligent host might offer an honored human guest or an attendant at court might offer his mortal lord, but presented in this case directly to God, personalized within an icon. So worshipers before Śiva received the deity graciously, offered him water to sip and rinse his feet, bathed and dressed him, adorned him with ornaments, fed him, gave him after-dinner condiments, entertained him with music and dance, bowed humbly before him, and petitioned him to grant them his all-powerful grace.

At the same time, the physical specificity of the god's presence in an icon or image might lead the devotee to glimpse beyond it Śiva's more all-encompassing nature. The icon was in this sense translucent. While it had a substantive presence in itself, it also allowed a viewer in the proper spirit of devotion and knowledge to glimpse with a devotional eye through it—imperfectly, since all human encounters with transcendence will be limited—to the transcendent reality of the deity as well.

To convey the notion of translucency visually, one modern south Indian God-picture uses two pictorial registers (Figure 8). In the lower portion of the picture, a brahmin priest leads a householder couple in rites of worship addressed to a modest Śiva liṅga. The priest holds his liturgical guidebook, and before the icon stand the offering plate and lighted lamps of pūjā. The liṅga glows with divine presence. Behind this domestic scenc looms a much more awesome depiction of Śiva and Pārvatī in their Himalayan home, gazing directly at the viewer. This, suggests the lithographic artist, is what the devotional eye sees through the Śiva liṅga.

Few of those who attended the Festival of India show at the National Gallery regarded Śiva as the transcendental Lord of the Cosmos, nor did they expect the images of Śiva they saw there to be alive with his presence. Culturally heirs of the Israelite prophets who had disdained the religious idols of neighboring tribes (and of their own past) as false, and Cartesian in their ontological outlook, Western museum goers understood these old images from the past of another culture as fundamentally inanimate objects. The Judaic or Christian God most of them recognize (if they do) certainly does not enter into matter in such a direct way.

However, those attending the National Gallery exhibition also understood the examples of great Indian sculpture assembled there to be, in the modern Western scheme of things, "art objects," and so they recognized that the images deserved careful treatment and were worthy of some special, quasi-religious regard. This attitude is what Svetlana Alpers (1991) has termed the

FIG. 8. Worship of the Śiva Liṅga. Calendar print by C. Murulakshmi.

"museum effect." As a culturally constructed setting in the modern West, the museum encourages its visitors to regard Indian works of religious imagery, as all other objects gathered there, with a close visual attention to their physical forms as both elegant and symbolically meaningful, and to attempt to understand these icons as the refined products of a sophisticated culture of the past. In the hushed atmosphere of the National Gallery, museum goers were implicitly urged to animate the images of Śiva and Pārvatī from Tiruvengadu and their fellow icons not through rituals of installation and feeding, but through visual and interpretive attentiveness.[7]

One reviewer told how the Tiruvengadu bronze had first arrested his attention during its previous 1982 visit to London. "Though my primary interest then was in studying the paintings," wrote Kenneth Robbins (1985: 104), "fully one-third of my time was spent gazing at each feature of this almost perfectly executed bronze." Robbins goes on to praise the impeccable taste of the show's curator for bringing this and several of its compatriots from Tiruvengadu to the United States. In the new exhibition "both novice and experienced viewers" will be able "to luxuriantly bask in the supple, sensuous, sinuous beauty of these idealised forms." The aesthetic lexicon and the promise of a rarefied experience Robbins evokes here reflect something of the hopes and expectations modern museum goers might bring with them to a display of ancient Indian art.[8]

If the Indian sculptures appeared to viewers in the National Gallery at all translucent—if they led viewers beyond their physical selves to some other dimension of reality—it was to a human and historical reality, not a theological one. A viewer with the proper spirit of knowledge and empathy might use the Indian sculptures to envision the concerns, values, and religious beliefs of historical Indians that had led them to produce these human artifacts. The images stood collectively as metonymy for the human society and religious culture of ancient and medieval India. (The metonymic relation of collection and modern nation state was drawn even more closely in the other major show of Indian art in the 1985 Festival of India, focusing on objects from 1300 C.E. to the present, which was titled simply "India!") And in the historicist and cultural pluralism that late twentieth-century museum goers take for granted, viewers understood well that, merely by walking into another section of the National Gallery, they might explore the visual products of another human and historical world, that perhaps of colonial North Americans or medieval European Christians.

Medieval Śaiva temple and modern museum, then, can both be taken as consecrated spaces. Both set aside areas for highly valued cultural activities, where esteemed objects hold court (or in the Indian idiom, give *darśana*) for human viewers, and both engender certain ways of looking and responding on the part of their audiences. Both allow for certain types of experiences that transcend the parochial, though that transcendence leads in quite different directions.

In both temple and museum the principles that organized the institutions and the attitudes that visitors brought to them were themselves the products of historical developments. In the remainder of this chapter, I will consider the dispensation of medieval south Indian worshipers of Śiva and Viṣṇu, the cultural milieu within which the bronze image of Śiva Vṛṣabhavāhana was made and initially seen. In a later chapter I will return to the history of the modern Western dispensation that has come to classify Indian icons as art objects, and in the final chapter I will look also at the conflict of interests between these two ways of regarding Indian images, as seen in a legal dispute over the repatriation of another medieval south Indian bronze image.

The Theory of Divine Embodiment

The Tiruvengadu image of Śiva Vṛṣabhavāhana first came to life within a religious environment dominated by temples and the elaborate worship of images. During the early medieval period, from roughly 700 to 1200 C.E., religious communities devoted to the gods Viṣṇu and Śiva had largely supplanted those loyal to older religious formations, such as that of the Vedas and the heterodox Buddhists and Jains, in elite support and institutional resources. For those Vaiṣṇavas and Śaivas, the worship of images enshrined in temples was a primary way for humans to interact with the gods they considered preeminent lords of the cosmos. Temple Hinduism had some significant opponents, as we will see, but it effectively dominated the sphere of public religious practice in early medieval India.

It is not possible to say for certain just when in India's past the worship of religious images began. Physical images apparently meant for ritual usage have been found among the remains of the Indus Valley civilization (which dates them from 2500 to 1700 B.C.E.), and both stone and terracotta figures from the Mauryan period of the fourth century B.C.E. are abundant. Buddhists and Jains began to fabricate anthropomorphic figures of their founding figures and other divine beings at least by the first century C.E., and the earliest recognizable images of the gods we now classify as Hindu, such as Viṣṇu and Śiva, date from a century or so later. However, there is little verbal record of the practices associated with these religious icons. The earliest texts setting forth practical instructions for the fabrication, consecration, and worship of Hindu images only appear around the fifth century C.E., often as "appendices" to the Vedic corpus of texts.[9]

Starting in the seventh and eighth centuries, new bodies of religious literature began to appear in the subcontinent. The Vaiṣṇava saṃhitās and Śaiva āgamas did not aspire to be parts of the Vedic corpus, but rather claimed to contain the direct revealed teachings of the gods themselves. Within their new liturgical texts, the divine preceptors Viṣṇu and Śiva outlined metaphysical visions of the structure of the cosmos and promulgated the worship of images in temples as the central program through which most humans could best accomplish both their spiritual and worldly aims. The Vaiṣṇava and Śaiva canons are huge and varied, providing various descriptive formulations of the cosmos and many alternatives for liturgical action. Nevertheless, collectively they set forth the dispensation of temple Hinduism that held sway during the early medieval period in India, and would certainly have provided the ritual program for the priests and devotees at the south Indian temple of Tiruvengadu in the early eleventh century.

Transcendence and Immanence

The gods Viṣṇu and Śiva who revealed these texts about themselves, and who contended with one another for religious supremacy during this period, both had two primary modes of being. Texts distinguish the two modes in various ways: undifferentiated and differentiated, formless and corporeal, unmanifest and manifest, without attributes and with attributes, supreme and accessible, and so on. I will use "transcendent" and "immanent" as umbrella terms for the divisions within the nature of the Supreme.

Previous Indian formulations of a theological Absolute, which developed in late Vedic and classical literature, often sought to place the Highest One outside all worldly limitations. The Absolute, they asserted, is beyond all name and form. All worldly things are limited by time, but the Absolute is beginningless and undying, imperishable and unchanging. All worldly things are bounded within space, but the Absolute is pervasive and omnipresent. The world consists in a multiplicity of discrete entities, while the Absolute is one and indivisible. We may approximate this Absolute through such negative verbal formulations, but in the end we must also recognize that the Absolute is unknowable, beyond the purview of our human categories and conceptions. The genre of late Vedic texts known as the Upaniṣads often referred to this attributeless, limitless Absolute as the *brahman*.

As the followers of Viṣṇu and Śiva began to advance claims that their gods were the Highest One, they each appropriated the theological vocabulary of transcendence for their own chosen deity. Yet at the same time they insisted on the physicality and worldliness of their supreme deities. To take one early example, at the beginning of the *Viṣṇusmṛti*, Viṣṇu assumes the form of a giant boar to raise up the Earth from the cosmic ocean at the dawn of creation and establishes all the primary categories of existence. Then he retires to a hidden place.[10] Bereft of her fundamental supporter, the Earth anxiously wonders, "What will support me now?" A Vedic sage advises her to search for Viṣṇu resting upon the milk ocean. When she finally finds him lying there on his snake couch, she bows down and begins to praise him:

> I bow to you, my lord, lord of the gods, destroyer of the strength of the gods' enemies. You are Nārāyaṇa, Protector of the World, who holds the conch, discus, and mace. You are Lotus-navel, Hṛṣikeśa, the very powerful Parākrama. My lord, you surpass all the senses. You surpass all knowledge. You hold the Śārṅga bow. You are the Great Boar, Bhīma, Govinda, the ancient one, the highest of beings. (*VS* 1.49–51)

The Earth goes on in her abundant praises to describe Viṣṇu as undying, imperishable, unalterable, immovable, ethereal, incomprehensible, and the best of all beings. Historians of Indian religions have often dismissed the rhetorical force of panegyric statements like this by speaking of Indian "henotheism," whereby Hindu worshipers supposedly treat whatever god they are worshiping at the moment as the greatest one of all. In the *Viṣṇusmṛti*, to the contrary, the Earth's eulogy of Viṣṇu amounts to an assertion of Viṣṇu's new preeminence. According to the Vaiṣṇava redactors of this text, the Earth herself has come to recognize that Viṣṇu encompasses all the characteristics of the Absolute.

Yet Earth's praise of Viṣṇu also attributes to him a number of features we might not expect in a transcendental Absolute. What is the Absolute doing with a conch, a discus, and a mace? If Viṣṇu is ethereal, how does he have a lotus navel? If he is unalterable, how is it that he appears as the Great Boar, as Bhīma, as Govinda, and in several other guises? Unlike previous formulations of an Absolute *brahman*, the new High God Viṣṇu involves himself personally and vigorously in the world process. He assumes human or seemingly human bodies, as well as a variety of other zoomorphic forms, to advance the interests of his followers and those of the cosmic order as a whole. In honoring Viṣṇu, the Earth interweaves praises both of his transcendent status and of the multiple immanent forms through which he intervenes in the world, since she recognizes that he is simultaneously both.

Viṣṇu's proclivity for worldly engagement is spelled out most clearly in the notion of his "incarnations" (*avatāra*, literally a "crossing down" into worldly form), articulated in the later recensions of the epics *Mahābhārata* and *Rāmāyaṇa* and in early purāṇas like the *Viṣṇupurāṇa*. In the *Bhagavadgītā*, one of his incarnations, Kṛṣṇa, explains the new concept in an often-quoted passage:

> I am indeed unborn. My self is imperishable. I am the Lord of all beings. Even so, I do enter into the material world, which is mine, and take birth through my own powers of appearance. Any time the world order (*dharma*) becomes exhausted and disorder gains the upper hand, then I emanate myself. Time after time I take birth in order to reestablish the world order, so that good people may be protected and evil-doers destroyed. (*BhG* 4.6–8)

The Vaiṣṇavas see no contradiction between transcendence and immanence, at least when it comes to Viṣṇu. He may incarnate himself as a giant boar to dive down into the cosmic waters and rescue the Earth on his tusks. He may equally take birth in the human body of Kṛṣṇa in order to destroy a demonic usurper of the throne of Mathurā, and in another human body as Rāma to put an end to demonic rule in Lanka. Yet since Viṣṇu is truly without limit, his adoption of temporary bounded forms does not in any way subtract from the totality of his being. Equally important, his assumption of these manifest forms allows humans a way to visualize and approach a divinity who might otherwise remain incomprehensible and inaccessible.

Worshipers of Śiva developed a similar notion in speaking of Śiva's "manifestations" (*mūrtis*). Here too, Śiva appears as a transcendent Absolute: "unfathomable, indescribable, incomparable, without defect, subtle, pervasive, eternal, firm, imperishable, and lordly," according to one Śaiva āgama.[11] And he also appears in a whole variety of visible aspects or manifestations, by which he carries out his often-inscrutable purposes among humans and throughout the universe.

The theological result combines transcendence and immanence within a single divine Person, as the condition of His supremacy. Worshipers of Viṣṇu and Śiva were able to combine an assertion of absolute status for their respective deities with a theism centered around personal, engaged divinities who physically appeared and acted in the world. God could be characterized as simultaneously supreme (*paratva*) and accessible (*saulabhya*), as the Śrīvaiṣṇava theologian Rāmānuja put it. This allowed the new religious communities of Vaiṣṇavas and Śaivas to claim successfully that their deities were superior to the older personal gods of the Vedas, and to provide a less austere means of access to the divine than was offered by those who adhered to an impersonal, attributeless Absolute.

The notion of a God who is simultaneously transcendent and immanent also provided the theological foundation for the early medieval theory of images and image-worship.

An Aesthetics of Presence

The worship of images became the dominant form of public religious practice in early medieval India, within the theological dispensation of gods who involved themselves actively and repeatedly in the world process while yet remaining transcendentally aloof. For humans who aspired to gain contact with those gods as the best means of attaining happiness and salvation, the material icon—fabricated by humans and inhabited by God—was taken as a primary site of ongoing interaction and exchange between humans and God. It was this interaction, involving initiatives by both parties and bringing them into a relationship that was unequal but fulfilling for both, that animated Hindu images as living, personal deities.

Vaiṣṇava and Śaiva ritual treatises often frame their discussions of image worship within the question of God's accessibility.[12] If God is by definition unconstrained by form, these texts ask, how may humans praise him, meditate upon him, and offer him worship? In the Vaiṣṇava Pāñcarātra *Paramasaṃhitā*, the creator god Brahman is perplexed by just this problem and raises it with Viṣṇu himself. "You have told me that the Highest God Viṣṇu is the ultimate cause of creation," Brahman observes. "Then how should humans worship him and meditate on him? For He is not ever limited by any conditions, and his form cannot be ascertained through direction, place, time, or shape. So how should one who hopes to be successful worship Him?" (*PS* 3.1–2)

Viṣṇu answers him firmly: "He can be worshiped in embodied form only. There is no worship of one without manifest form." For humans and even for other gods, the only way to approach Viṣṇu is through his immanent bodily forms. This is not a problem for Earth, who may search and find Viṣṇu asleep on the milk ocean, and it was not a problem for the cowherds of Vṛndāvana during Kṛṣṇa's life among them, nor for the citizens of Ayodhya when Viṣṇu was incarnate there as Rāma. However, most humans are not so lucky. For those others, Viṣṇu goes on, there are images. "Thanks to my benevolence toward all beings, there are manifest forms of Viṣṇu, intended for the purpose of ritual action. Therefore humans should construct the Imperishable One in human form and worship him with utmost devotion, in order to gain success. Worship or praise or meditation offered to the god in an image, according to the injunctions set out in the sacred treatises, is offered directly to God" (*PS* 3.6–8). For most humans, images offer the most direct available route to Viṣṇu.

The icons Viṣṇu recommends are, in one sense, physical objects. They are material forms that can be seen and touched, and so allow the sensible contact with god that Viṣṇu says humans crave and require. Śaiva texts say much the same thing about icons of Śiva. Vaiṣṇavas and Śaivas part company, however, on the most suitable kind of form to construct for their gods. According to Vaiṣṇava texts, the best form is an anthropomorphic one. (Perhaps we should call it an enhanced anthropomorphic form, since the icon usually has four or eight arms.) The Śaivas by contrast argue that a liṅga—a nonanthropomorphic, nonpartitive, round-topped cylinder—is the most appropriate physical form for worshiping Śiva, precisely because it parallels in its wholeness and abstractness the highest level of Śiva's being, the Supreme Śiva "without parts" (*niṣkala*). Śaivas consider anthropomorphic images of Śiva such as Vṛṣabhavāhana less complete approximations of the totality of Śiva's being. These images seldom serve as central icons in medieval Śaiva temples, but rather supplement the Śiva liṅga as secondary and processional images.

Icons form an important point of entry of God into the world. Śrīvaiṣṇavas take the image (*arcā*) as an actual and real incarnation (*avatāra*) of Viṣṇu, just as real as his human embodiments of the past like Kṛṣṇa and Rāma. Śaiva siddhāntins speak of Śiva entering and infusing an icon with his presence, much as a soul enters and enlivens a newly formed human body. The various theistic schools of early medieval India employ different metaphors and different philosophical formulations for describing the ontological status of God in the icon, but all agree that these physical objects become imbued with the special presence of God. They become identical with God, and so, as Viṣṇu informs Brahman, worship offered to god embodied in an image is in fact offered directly to God.

As God's entryway, icons reciprocally become the point of access (and ultimately of transcendence) for human devotees. The Vaiṣṇava and Śaiva texts often point out that images thereby reveal a divinity who is difficult or impossible to attain otherwise. The Śrīvaiṣṇava writer Kurattalvan, for example, says of a Viṣṇu image at Hasti Hill, "That great being [Viṣṇu], who is distant to even the minds of the yogis who have conquered their senses, who is not known even in the Vedānta, stands manifest on the Hasti Hill" (tr. Narayanan 1985: 62). Viṣṇu manifests himself in a variety of ways. According to the Śrīvaiṣṇava formulation, Viṣṇu incarnates himself in five different modes: as a transcendent being (*para*) reclining on the milk ocean (as Earth found him in the *Viṣṇusmṛti*), in glorious human personalities (*vibhava*) such as Kṛṣṇa and Rāma, in a series of "emanations" (*vyūha*), as an "inner controller" (*antaryāmin*) deep within the heart of every being, and in images. Of all these, Viṣṇu's incarnation in the image is the most convenient, as the thirteenth-century Śrīvaiṣṇava theologian Pillai Lokācārya suggests.

> Viṣṇu's incarnation as an Inner Controller resembles water hidden deep in the ground. His incarnation as Transcendent Deity resembles the distant water of the oceans surrounding the earth. His incarnation in the form of emanations are like the inaccessible milk ocean. His glorious incarnations in human form resemble rivers that periodically flood, then dry up. But his incarnation in an image is like the full, deep pools in those rivers where water is always available. (*SBh* 24)

Other modes of Viṣṇu's manifestation may be unattainable, irregular, or overwhelming, but Viṣṇu's incarnation in an image is as calm, stable, and easily reached as a pool of water. By rendering God physically present in a particular fixed location, icons enable the whole liturgical system of temple transactions between God and his human worshipers, which the Vaiṣṇava and Śaiva texts prescribe in glorious detail.

According to the Vaiṣṇavas, God takes the initiative in manifesting himself in an image. Sometimes he does this entirely through "self-manifestation" (*svayambhū*), and devotees consider icons that originate in this way to be particularly potent. Yet even icons fabricated and consecrated by humans owe their fundamental holiness to God's favor and compassion. When Brahman asks Viṣṇu how it is that humans, with all their worldly attachments, can install the Highest God on earth, Viṣṇu upbraids him: "God is neither installed nor protected by anyone!" (*PS* 8.12). Viṣṇu goes on to explain how installation of temple images really comes about: "Viṣṇu favors his devotees [with his presence] solely for purposes of worship. The Lord descends into the temples of his various servants and those who have succeeded in discipline through meritorious actions, in response to their various virtues, as an act of sympathy toward his devotees" (*PS* 8.12–14). The seeming paradox of the Highest Lord consenting to confine himself within an inanimate circumscribed piece of stone must be seen in light of Viṣṇu's benevolent disposition.

It is useful at this point to contrast briefly the theory of images here with that of medieval Christianity, articulated by Thomas Aquinas and Bonaventure at about the same time as Pillai Lokācārya composed his Śrīvaiṣṇava works.[13] Heirs to a long Judeo-Christian critique of "idols" and a divine commandment not to make "graven images" that represent or instantiate God, the Christian theologians could not countenance the actual worship of sacred icons. However, this did not preclude all holy images from a place in the Church. According to Aquinas, Christian images could have three primary functions: "first, for the instruction of the unlettered, who might learn from them as if from books; second, so that the mystery of the Incarnation and the examples of the saints might remain more firmly in our memory by being daily represented to our eyes; and third, to excite the emotions, which are more effectively aroused by things seen than by things heard" (Freedberg 1989: 162). Bonaventure retains this tripartite justification, and adds that the need for images results from our human shortcomings: the ignorance of simple people, the sluggishness of our emotions, and the lability of our memory. More than this, they also render the invisible spiritual realm accessible to our senses. Since the divine is not susceptible to ordinary sensory response, we can perceive it only by means of an objectification in the form of visual images. Medieval Christian images, then, are instrumental and representational. Aquinas and Bonaventure locate them within a semiotic aesthetics, where the image is seen as conveying a message separate from the image itself.[14]

Medieval Indian theology also recognizes a transcendental domain that is ultimately unrepresentable, and it also accepts the instrumental functions of the sculpted image. The texts urge sculptors to make their images as beautiful as possible, to engender a taste for God among viewers. Once an image of Viṣṇu has attracted us, notes Pillai Lokācārya, its other attributes begin to act upon its audience. "The *arcā* displays attributes like accessibility (*saulabhya*), which help us to be attached to the Lord; excellence of disposition (*sauśīlya*) which prevents us from fear when we behold the Lord's supremacy; mastership (*svāmitvam*), which builds our confidence in him; and tender motherly love (*vātsalya*), which prevents us from trembling when we behold our shortcomings" (tr. Narayanan 1985: 63). Moral qualities of the Viṣṇu image attract, instruct, remind, and excite viewers, much as Christians intended their images to do. However, Śrīvaiṣṇavas (and other medieval Indian theistic schools) insist that the divine image is both means (*upāya*) and end (*upeya*). It leads the devotee toward God, and it also *is* God, the devotee's object of enjoyment. Rather than simply reminding its audience of the "mystery of the Incarnation," the Vaiṣṇava image serves as the base within which Viṣṇu mysteriously does incarnate himself.

Aquinas recommends images as the "books of the illiterate," but medieval Indians are just as likely to reverse this logocentric view. Śaivas tell the story of the ninth-century poet-saint Māṇikkavācakar, who retired near the end of his life to live near his favored icon, Śiva Naṭarāja at Cidambaram. Devotees at the temple had acquired a written copy of his devotional poems, and they asked Māṇikkavācakar for an explication of their meaning. The old saint took his interlocutors into the Cidambaram sanctum, pointed to the Naṭarāja image, and said, "The Lord himself is the meaning." Then Māṇikkavācakar himself melted into the image.[15] Vaiṣṇava and Śaiva theologians locate their holy icons within an aesthetics of presence. As an instantiation of the godhead, the image is ultimately the message.

Ritual Establishment

The divine presence, as one might expect, has consequences for the substance of the icon. Śrīvaiṣṇavas reserve a special ontological category of fundamentally pure, luminous, immaterial matter (*śuddhasattva*) for the image of Viṣṇu (Narayanan 1985: 61). Śaiva siddhāntins speak of a Śiva liṅga as possessing "Śivaness" (*śivatva*), an attribute that sets it apart from the ordinary stuff of creation, which is inert and inanimate. In an important sense, the object that is infused with or identical with God cannot be composed of ordinary matter; it must undergo a transubstantiation. This requires a combination of divine grace and human ritual labor.

The ritual program by which Indian temple images are brought to life is known as "establishment" (*pratiṣṭhā*). Medieval Indians considered establishment to be an instrumental and efficacious ritual that brought about an actual transformation in the character of the object, rather than simply a symbolical ratification or display of divinity. In a Śaiva temple such as the Śvetāraṇyeśvara in Tiruvengadu, the temple, the central liṅga, and all the primary processional images of the temple would have undergone parallel procedures of establishment, to make them all fit receptacles for Śiva's divine presence. Similarly, when Kolakkavan donated a new bronze image of Śiva in his Vṛṣabhavāhana aspect, he also sponsored a proper ceremony to establish it.

When discussing the animation of images, medieval Vaiṣṇava and Śaiva texts often employ the analogy of a transmigrating soul entering a human body. The fabricated image is a body (*vigraha*) or embodiment (*mūrti*). Divinity in the form of a soul (*ātman*), animating spirit (*jīva*), life breath (*prāṇa*), consciousness (*cetana*), or divine energy (*śakti*) must enter this body to bring it to life, to infuse it with divine presence, just as a soul must enter a human body to instill life into it. This metaphor focuses on God as the divine agency required to animate an icon. The ritual procedures of establishment center more on the material substance of the icon and on the human activities necessary to make it fit for divine entry.

In the view of medieval Indian Dharmaśāstra texts, coming into full human life was not a single event, but rather a process marked and effected by recurrent transformative rituals (*samskāras*) that gradually completed and refined a person's body (Inden and Nicholas 1977:37). So too, ritual establishment does not focus upon a dramatic, abrupt transfiguration from inert matter to living icon. Rather it involves an elaborate sequence of rites that, through repeated imposition of mantras, powers, and substances, progressively constitute the fabricated object as fully imbued with the attribute of divinity. Medieval Śaiva texts like *Kāmikāgama* (*pūrva* 68) list twenty-two constituent rites making up the ritual of establishment, from the initial selecting of materials through the final worship of the fully established temple image.

Another analogy used by the Śaiva ritual texts that better captures this gradualist ritual procedure is that of kindling fire. Because Śiva is by theological definition ubiquitous, they say, he is already present, in a latent sense, even in the raw materials gathered to create the image, just as fire is believed to be latent in the dry wood or in smoldering embers used to build a fire. Śaiva texts refer to this as Śiva's "general" or "common" (*sāmānya*) presence. The aim of establishment is to enhance or manifest that divine ubiety in a particular location, bringing about Śiva's "special" or "marked" (*viśiṣṭa*) presence in the image, much as one stokes up ash-covered embers into a blazing fire by adding grass, sticks, and ladlefuls of ghee.

Accordingly, the rites of establishment commence with the initial selection of materials.[16] When making a wooden image, for example, priest and artisan undertake a field trip to the forest, and take care to choose only specimens that bear an innate resemblance to the intended deity. "Male" trees are destined to serve male divinities, "female" to serve goddesses. The eastern side of the tree is marked as its "face," since the completed image will also face east. At the same time, it is necessary to persuade any other spirits that may reside in the tree to vacate it. "The officiating priest should offer worship at night to any gods, ancestor spirits, ghosts, demons, snakes, antigods, henchmen, obstacles, and the like [in the tree]," recommends the *Bṛhatsaṃhitā*, "and then he should touch the tree and say: 'You have been designated to serve as an icon for such-and-such a deity. We bow to you, tree. Please accept these offerings of worship, in proper manner. May those beings who dwell here receive our tribute, which is given properly, and choose another dwelling. May they forgive us. We bow to them'" (*BS* 59.9–11). After the tree has been properly honored and purified, it is cut and cleaned, transported back to the construction site, and then once again worshiped with mantras and auspicious substances. Even before the first cut of the chisel, the material is treated as a deity in the making.

The second phase of establishment involves the physical fabrication of the image. The priest presents the raw material to the artisan and requests him to make the image. The sculptor must follow iconographic and iconometric guidelines, to insure that the image properly represents the god visually and symbolically. As the artisan sets to work carving, the priest simultaneously performs ritual work: he repeatedly recites the mantra that most fully invokes the deity onto the image as it comes into form. When a sculptor makes a bronze image like the Tiruvengadu Vṛṣabhavāhana following the lost-wax method, the priest swaddles the initial beeswax model in cloth, places it on a bed of grain and sacrificial grass, honors it with a series of oblations, and recites the mantra evoking the deity over it.[17] He returns the wax effigy to the artisan, who encloses it in a clay mold, and the priest once again treats the shell to the same actions of swaddling, honoring, and invoking. Finally, the artisan fires the clay mold, melting the wax, and fills the resulting cavity with molten metal. When the metal has solidified, he breaks open the mold to free the bronze image. The priest immediately subjects this to further mantra recitations identifying the bronze with the deity who is to inhabit it. There is never a time when the image exists as an unconsecrated object; its very coming into being is within ritual.

The third phase of establishment, involving the initial "awakening" of the image, centers around the opening of the eyes (*netronmilana*). After a sacrificial pavilion and a pedestal within it have been carefully constructed, the newly made image is placed atop the pedestal, and the priest uses a golden needle to draw on the outlines of Śiva's three eyes (*KĀ pūrva* 68.35–36). The sculptor then opens the eyes with a diamond needle, and opens the other apertures as well with a chisel. The priest rubs the eyes of the image with unguents and displays before it a series of highly auspicious objects: ghee, a pot of honey, heaps of grain, brahmans reciting praises, virgins in full decoration, and the assembled crowd of devotees (*KĀ pūrva* 68.47–51). The priest immediately washes and purifies the image with clay, ashes, cowdung, and other substances, and then dresses it in clean clothes and adorns it with all suitable ornaments. Temple servants take the image on a palanquin and circumambulate the village. By this point the image has clearly reached an initial stage of livelihood, where it can see objects placed before it and is worthy of going in procession among its community of worshippers, but its ritual metamorphosis is by no means yet complete.

After its circumambulation, the image enjoys a restful interlude, dwelling in water (*jalādhivāsana*) for as many as nine nights. Evidently the purifying effects of the water—which is identified with the most auspicious of all waters, the river Ganges—are needed to remove any lingering defects of earlier ritual processes and to raise the image to a higher level of purity required for the fifth and culminating phase.

Preparations for this phase begin with the elaborate decoration of the pavilion, large-scale feeding of brahmans, and the construction of a couch suitable for a lord. The image is bathed and dressed once more and then brought to the pavilion and raised onto the couch. The priest next performs an "affusion" (*abhiṣeka*). Affusions in Indian ritual idiom are rites that add powers and capacities to a subject by pouring various substances over it. In medieval India affusion rites were performed to install kings, priests, and other persons in positions of authority, and they were employed also to help consecrate divine icons.

The early nonsectarian *Bṛhatsaṃhitā* describes a generic form of affusion for images, in which a wide assortment of substances bathe the image.

> With its head to the east, the image should be bathed with water infused with plaksa-fig, holy fig, ficus, acacia, and banyan trees, with plants deemed auspicious, and with sacrificial grass; with mud from the shores of river confluences, anthills, and mud from lotus ponds; with the five products of the cow and with water from holy bathing spots; and with water containing gold and gems along with fragrant perfumes. The bathing should be accompanied by the sounds of many instruments, shouts of best wishes, and the recitation of Vedic hymns. (*BS* 60.8–10)

The idea behind the repetitive, cumulative procedures of affusion is to concentrate within the body of the subject all the auspicious substances of the world.

The later Śaiva ritual texts that would heave guided south Indian priests at the Śvetāraṇyeśvara temple in Tiruvengadu focus more on the mantras than on the substances used to affuse the image. Only with a "body of mantras," the Śaiva texts explain, does Śiva act in the world, and therefore the most important task in the ritual installation is to impose a mantric body onto the physical body of the fabricated image. To do this, the officiating priest sets up a large number of waterpots, with all proper accoutrements, in a determinate geometrical configuration around the image, and into every one he invokes a deity or divine power by reciting the appropriate mantra for each. Collectively, the pots thereby come to encompass all the most important cosmic forces identified by Śaiva theology. The priest worships each pot, since each is in itself now divine, and then pours the contents of each one over the image. As the water washes over it, the divinities and powers embodied in the pots infuse the image, until it becomes a "divine body" (*divyadeha*) composed of the cumulative mantra-energies of all the pots. The ritual of establishment transfigures the material form of the image not simply as an animate being, but as a divine body of mantra powers, so that Śiva himself will see fit to inhabit and act through it.

After its anointment the image is carried into the temple proper, where it is installed in its own shrine, bathed, dressed, and adorned again. Finally the priest performs full worship (*pūjā*) to the image for the first time, recognizing that it has been fully transformed into a state of "Śiva-ness" (*śivatva*), and that it now serves as the appropriate support for Śiva's special presence in its new setting.

The Devotional Eye

Human responses to rich visual objects such as Indian religious images are sensory, intellectual, and emotional acts that take place in determinate historical settings. In his influential essay on "The Work of Art in the Age of Mechanical Reproduction," Walter Benjamin pointed to the historicity of sense perception itself. "During long periods of history," he wrote, "the mode of human sense perception changes with humanity's entire mode of existence. The manner in which human sense perception is organized, the medium in which it is accomplished, is determined not only by nature but by historical circumstances as well" (1985: 222). In a seminal study of fifteenth-century Italian painting and its original community of response, Michael Baxandall reiterated and specified Benjamin's point. "Some of the mental equipment a man orders his visual experience with is variable, and much of this variable equipment is culturally relative, in the sense of being determined by the society which has influenced his experience. Among these variables are categories with which he classifies his visual stimuli, the knowledge he will use to supplement what his immediate vision gives him, and the attitude he will adopt to the kind of artificial object seen" (1972: 40). Going beyond this general observation, Baxandall was able to demonstrate how certain visual skills and structures of knowledge helped organize the visual activity of the fifteenth-century audience for whom painters like Filippo Lippi and Perugino painted, and how the painters reciprocally sought to meet and challenge their viewers' perceptual expectations. He spoke of this historically grounded, culturally shared way of seeing as the "period eye."

Is it similarly possible to reconstruct the period eye of the tenth- and eleventh-century south Indian worshipers for whom a bronze like the Tiruvengadu Vṛṣabhavāhana was initially fabricated? To make a preliminary foray into this topic, we have, in addition to the theological and ritual literatures I have touched upon, one more key body of source material: the wonderfully rich devotional poetry of the south Indian poet-saints, the Vaiṣṇava āḻvārs and the Śaiva nāyaṉārs.[18] During the seventh through ninth centuries these largely itinerant poets traveled from temple to temple throughout Tamilnad and sang of their gods in each new place. They composed their new hymns in the regional language, Tamil, but they drew upon Sanskritic models as well as an earlier classical Tamil poetic tradition for their literary forms and strategies. Above all, the poets centered their verse around the gods Viṣṇu and Śiva. They approached these deities as divine persons and sought to establish with the personal gods direct, emotional relationships, which they recognized as deeply problematic but also as ultimately satisfying in the highest order.

During the Cola period of the tenth and eleventh centuries, the poetic utterances of these bards were collected and organized into large canonical compilations, the Vaiṣṇava *Nālāyirattivviyapirapantam* ("four thousand divine compositions") and the Śaiva *Tirumurai* ("sacred text"). At the same time the devotional hymns were made an integral part of south Indian temple liturgy. The poet-saints themselves were apotheosized and their images were set up in the temples, facing their chosen deities with hands folded in permanent attitudes of adoration. The poetry of these devotional saints both reflected and modeled a specific, influential way of looking at images and icons of Viṣṇu and Śiva in their medieval south Indian temples, which I will call the "devotional eye."

Connecting through Icons

The devotional poetry of the Tamil saints is most fundamentally a poetry of connections, as A. K. Ramanujan has observed (1981: 166–69). The Indian term most commonly used for it is *bhakti*, usually translated as "devotion," from the verbal root *bhaj*, "to apportion, to share." In religious usage bhakti points to a shared relationship between a devotee and a god, and so in bhakti poetry the crucial connection is that between the poet and God.[19]

The Tamil saints often take the distance between the poet and God as a starting point for thematic exploration. The poets repeatedly address God with their questions: why? how can I understand you? which among all forms is yours? how can I find you? The poets know the theology of God's transcendent nature, and they know the traditions of their gods' incarnations and manifestations on earth, but their quest is for a more direct personal contact. Nammāḻvār asks Viṣṇu:

> O wondrous one who was born!
> O wondrous one who fought the Bhārata war!
> Great one, who became all things,
>   starting with the primal elements:
>   wind, fire, water, sky, and earth.
> Great one, wondrous one,
>   you are in all things
>   as butter lies hidden in fresh milk,
> you stand in all things
>   and yet transcend them.
> Where can I see you?
>
> *(tr. Carman and Narayanan 1989: 89)*

If one takes seriously all the attributes theologians assign to Viṣṇu, as Nammāḻvār does here, it will be hard indeed to "see" Viṣṇu with human eyes. Yet in other poems Nammāḻvār answers his own question affirmatively. One way he can see Viṣṇu is in a temple icon.

> My lord
>   who's both dearth and plenty
>   hell and heaven
>   friendship
>   enmity
>   venom and sweet ambrosia
> my ranging various lord:
>
> I saw him there
>   in Viṇṇakar
>   city named Sky
>   city of rich houses
>
> *(tr. Ramanujan 1981: 14)*

Here Nammāḻvār shifts with the speed of epiphany from the encompassing and abstract characterization of his "ranging various lord" to a specific form of Viṣṇu visible to all in the prosperous city of Viṇṇakar.

The desire to find their gods, to see Viṣṇu and Śiva, leads the devotional poets on constant pilgrimages. They travel around from site to site, visiting temples in each locality. The Vaiṣṇava poets celebrate 108 "divine places," whereas the poetry of the Śaiva saints lauds 274 sacred sites. Much of the Tamil bhakti poetry is insistently local, in one sense, since it purports to render the experience of a particular poet in a specific place. For example, the poetic oeuvre of the Śaiva saint Sundaramūrti consists of one hundred verse compositions, each of ten or eleven stanzas. Each composition centers upon a particular Śaiva temple, and Sundaramūrti incorporates the name of the place into nearly every stanza. The poets describe and praise the landscapes, the villages, and the towns where the temples are located, but their primary concern is the god in the temple.

Poems sometimes record very specific visual experiences, where the devotional saint seems to view and describe a temple image. Tiruppān Āḻvār's only poem in the Vaiṣṇava canon, for instance, offers a detailed description of Viṣṇu Raṅganātha, from feet to head, as he appears recumbent in the central shrine of Sri Rangam (Narayanan 1987: 17). Likewise, the poet Sambandhar observes the processional images of Śiva as they parade on festival days at Naṟaiyūr.

> The Lord of Cittīccaram shrine in Naṟaiyūr,
> who has the river in his hair,
> the poison stain on his throat,
> and the Veda on his tongue,
> goes resplendent in ceremonial dress,
> as his devotees and perfected sages
> sing and dance his widespread fame,
> and the sound of festival drums
> beaten on the streets where the temple-car is pulled
> spreads on every side.
>
> *(tr. Peterson 1989: 183)*

Two stanzas later, Sambandhar observes Śiva in his aspect as Vṛṣabhavāhana:

> A heron feather and the bright datura
> adorn his matted hair.
> His flame-red body
> is covered with white ash.
> Over his girdle and loincloth
> he has bound a tigerskin
> encircled by lovely snakes.
> Thus, with anklets ringing,
> the Lord of Cittīccaram shrine
> comes riding on his bull.
>
> *(tr. Peterson 1989: 104)*

The devotional iconography described by the Tamil saints corresponds rather closely to the sculpted imagery produced in Tamilnad during the Pallava period, though the poets are naturally selective in the details they choose to emphasize. As Indira Peterson puts its, "we encounter a poetic iconography in which selection of detail is governed not by the canons of temple sculpture but by the aesthetic of devotion" (1989: 96).

However, the poets do not imagine that what they are describing are in fact physical objects. When Nammāḻvār speaks of his epiphany at Viṇṇakar, he does not say "I saw an image of Viṣṇu at Viṇṇakar," nor does he say "I saw Viṣṇu present in an image there." He sees Viṣṇu. From our ontological perspective, we might say that the poets conflate image and God. Within the theological dispensation of early medieval temple Hinduism, however, Viṣṇu is actively present at Viṇṇakar and Nammāḻvār sees him there.[20] The way in which Nammāḻvār sees and understands what he is seeing is grounded within the theological premises of a God who is simultaneously transcendent and immanent, ubiquitous and yet forcefully present in certain holy places.

Translucency and Paradox

Devotional literature of early medieval India was fond of epiphany, the momentary glimpse through the window of what appears to be mundane into the totality of things. One of the best-known devotional stories occurs in the *Bhāgavatapurāṇa*, a Vaiṣṇava narrative text in Sanskrit composed in southern India during the same period the āḻvārs were singing their Tamil hymns.[21] When Kṛṣṇa is a child living among the cowherd tribe, some of his young friends teasingly tell his mother Yaśodā that Kṛṣṇa has been eating dirt. Yaśodā grabs her son and asks why he has done that, but Kṛṣṇa denies all charges. "If their words are true," he challenges his mother, "look in my mouth for yourself." Then Lord Viṣṇu, whose lordly majesty, the poet reminds the audience, is not obstructed by his playful appearance as a human child, opens his mouth. When Yaśodā looks there for dirt she sees instead the entire cosmos—the earth with all its mountains and oceans, the sun and moon and stars in the sky, the five material elements, the sense organs and the objects of sensation, the mind, and much more. Her vision of the cosmos, though, is too much for the humble cowherd woman, and she becomes confused and terrified. In his compassion, Kṛṣṇa then spreads over her his "illusion" (*māyā*), which removes Yaśodā's perception of the actual state of things and enables her to see once again within the comforting limitations of every day. Kṛṣṇa's mother retains only her feeling of maternal love for her young son.

The devotional poets of Tamilnad suggest a similar way of seeing. Looking at and into the body of the living God, in the form of a temple image, can open out into the broader vista of the wholeness of God's being. At Tirupparankundram, the Śaiva poet Sambandhar writes:

> Paraṅkuṉṟu is the shrine
> of the Lord who shares his body
> with the girl who plays with a ball,

the god who rose
as a splendid column of light,
whose greatness was beyond the grasp
even of Māl who in a single stride
once spanned this whole earth,
and the ancient god who emerged
from his bright navel,
and gave the sacred Vedas to the world.

(tr. Peterson 1989: 127)

Here the poet offers little physical description of the Śiva liṅga in Tirupparankundram temple, and instead moves quickly on to other ways Śiva manifests himself, in a domestic mode as the lord who has Pārvatī as half his body (Ardhanārī) and in a more awesome manner as the endless liṅga of light that appeared before Viṣṇu and Brahman (Lingodbhava). Once at the beginning of creation, goes the well-known purāṇic story, Viṣṇu and Brahman were arguing over which of them was the greatest, when before them rose an immense pillar glowing like the fire at the end of time. What could it be? Brahman turned himself into a bird and flew up to find the top of the column, while Viṣṇu changed himself into a boar and dove down to find its bottom. But in a hundred years of searching they could find neither beginning nor end. They returned to their starting point and propitiated the God who was the flaming liṅga, Śiva. Pleased by their praises, Śiva became visible to them and gave them a boon. From that time on, concludes the narrator, gods and other creatures have established the Śiva liṅga throughout the world for worship.[22] And so, through the translucency of the stone liṅga that he worships in Tirupparankundram, Sambandhar is able to envision another liṅga, the primordial liṅga, of such overwhelming size and brilliance that even the greatest gods could not grasp its full dimensions.

There is one major difference between Yaśodā's vision and the poetic epiphany Sambandhar relates. In the *Bhāgavatapurāṇa*, Yaśodā does not know of Kṛṣṇa's divinity, and the text portrays her unintended vision as Kṛṣṇa's act of momentary grace. The devotional poets likewise understand God's presence in a temple icon to be ultimately a matter of divine favor. However, Sambandhar does know of Śiva's divinity. He goes to the temple to worship and he brings with him all his knowledge of Śiva's nature. If Śiva in his totality appears in the temple liṅga, then all that one knows of Śiva is true of that liṅga. This carries its own confusion.

When the Śaiva poet Sundaramūrti visits the Śvetāraṇyeśvara temple in Tiruvengadu (later to be home to the Vṛṣabhavāhana image), he sang a composition of ten stanzas. Addressing Śiva directly, Sundaramūrti reminds the god of many of his deeds: how Śiva burned the demon's city of Tripura, how he killed the god of death, how he wanders as a naked beggar, how he defeated the god of love, how he dances, how he swallowed the poison that appeared from the churning of the ocean, how he skinned an elephant demon and wore its skin in a victory dance, how he confounded Viṣṇu and Brahman with his flaming pillar, and more. All this he knows of Śiva. Many of these divine acts correspond to the iconic forms of Śiva that are described in iconographic manuals and realized in stone and bronze sculpture: Tripurāntaka, Kalārimūrti, Bhikṣātana, and so on. Quite possibly these images were present in the Śvetāraṇyeśvara temple when Sundaramūrti visited it in the early ninth century.[23] The full ensemble of Śaiva icons in a temple—the unitary liṅga at the center and the multiple processional and secondary images surrounding it—provides a two-tiered representation of Śiva as both undifferentiated and differentiated.

Sundaramūrti accepts this temple hierophany, but in this poem he is not simply providing Śiva with an inventory of temple imagery. The poet ends each stanza with a short direct question:

> but why, O why,
> lord of Veṇkāṭu, surrounded by sea?

Sundaramūrti enumerates Śiva's versatile activities in order to point to the paradoxical, incomprehensible nature of the single being who can embody himself in so many strange ways. Sundaramūrti does not find an answer to his query within the poem. In its final stanza, instead, he stands back to describe his encounter with a "contrary" Śiva:

> In Veṇkāṭu surrounded by sea,
> home of those skilled in reciting the extensive Veda,
> dwells the contrary lord of the Veda
> questioned avidly by Ārūraṉ [Sundara], devotee and servant,
> from Nāvalūr with its spreading groves.
>
> *(tr. Shulman 1990: 41)*

The temple icon offers a site for vision and even interrogation, but Śiva does not always reply.

The devotional eye takes the icon enshrined in the temple as the living presence of God, sees through its translucency brief glimpses into the fullness of his Being, and then occasionally turns back on itself to observe the paradoxical quality of this transcendence within immanence. Nammāḻvār urges all living creatures:

> Think, and again think
> about the being not contained by any form
> that plunges low, spreads wide, and rises high,
> but after thinking and thinking,
> even in the act of thinking
> the being of the lord is rarely known.
>
> *(tr. Cutler 1987: 135)*

As with the flaming liṅga that stumped Viṣṇu and Brahman, the poets maintain that the top and bottom of their God's nature remain finally beyond their reach.

What is one left with? Yaśodā keeps her human feeling of maternal love, Sundaramūrti retains his question, and all the poets are left with mixed feelings of bafflement, awe, love, and devotion. And they have their poems, verbal icons of God's multiple nature and their own varied responses to him, to present in worship.

> Alone,
> he created me:
> this much I know.
> What have I, then,
> but my song
> to offer at his feet of gold?
>
> *(tr. Shulman 1990: xlviii)*

These offerings have had a much greater afterlife than any of the medieval Tamil poets could have imagined, for later generations collected them and incorporated them into the fabric of south Indian temple worship in the tenth and eleventh centuries. Eleventh-century residents of Tiruvengadu would have heard the songs as part of their temple services, and present-day Hindus of Tamilnad continue to sing them. We should recite the poetry of the Vaiṣṇava saints before the temple image, say the Śrīvaiṣṇavas, because Viṣṇu enjoys hearing it. Moreover, the repeated recitation of the devotional verse instructs and guides worshipers in an exemplary way of looking at and understanding God in the icon. As Norman Cutler puts it, these devotional poems are not simply records of historical events, but rather "the occasion for a ritualized reenactment of the events and emotions portrayed in the poem" (1987: 70). So, just as the gods Viṣṇu and Śiva enter into the world over and over, the responses of the devotional saints to their gods have reincarnated themselves in the experiences of subsequent generations of devotees.

Image Worship and Its Discontents

Judging by both lithic remains and texts of the period, the worship of images in temples had by the eighth century become the central liturgical program for public religion in India. For several centuries, the ritual and theological formulations of icon-worshiping schools such as the Śrīvaiṣṇavas and the Śaiva siddhāntins provided the most authoritative ordering of the cosmos and the human world within it, the dominant dispensation of early medieval India. Ruling elites supported these sacerdotal groups by building monumental temples dedicated to Viṣṇu and Śiva. But the practice of image worship was never without its opponents from within the indigenous traditions of thought and practice we now call Hindu. Many devotional poets, like the twelfth-century Vīraśaiva leader Basavaṇṇa, rejected the worship of material images in favor of a more unmediated encounter with the living deity. Those who were excluded from participating in temple worship anyway, like the north Indian leather worker and devotional poet Ravidās, mocked the cult of images and advocated other forms of devotion.[24] The most sustained intellectual critiques of image worship as a sufficient religious practice, however, came from two brahminic schools of thought, the sacrificial exegetes of the Mīmāṃsā and the philosophical advocates of the Advaita Vedānta path of knowledge.

Exegetical Denial

The staunchest opponents in early medieval India were the authors of the Mīmāṃsā ("interpretation") school, committed to the aniconic ritual program of sacrifice set forth in the Vedas, which were composed between roughly 1200 and 300 B.C.E.[25] The Vedic texts themselves did not take any particular stance toward the worship of images. Based on the assumption that it represented the dominant ritual practice of the Indo-Aryan ruling class, the Vedic corpus simply set forth the system of sacrifice in all its complexity and compelling power. It was left to the later advocates and interpreters of the Vedic system, writing at a time when the sacrifice was being dislodged from its preeminent position and the iconic schools were gaining ground, to do theological battle with the worshipers of images.

The Mīmāṃsā scholars took it as their central task to examine the nature of dharma, as preeminently set forth in the Vedic sacrificial texts. Within this system, they argued, one need not postulate any supreme, divine being. They proclaimed the Vedas themselves to be eternal and authorless. Proper human action follows directly from a correct understanding of the injunctions of the Vedic texts. The rewards that accrue from correct performance of sacrificial duties, according to the Mīmāṃsā interpretation, do not require the intervention of any god, but rather result from the inherent character of the ritual actions themselves.

This denial of divine agency, however, seemed to contradict the contents of the Vedic texts themselves. The hymns of the Vedas repeatedly address a whole pantheon of divine beings—Indra, Agni, Varuṇa, and many others—as if they exist, have bodies, consume the sacrificial offerings, are pleased by them, and reward their votaries. One way of understanding sacrifice was as a reciprocal exchange, in which humans feed the needy gods, who in turn use their vast natural powers to assure the success and prosperity of those who honor them. Mīmāṃsā exegetes asserted that these personifications of the gods are misleading. In his fifth-century commentary on Jaimini's *Mīmāṃsāsūtras*, Śabarasvāmin argued that gods do not have bodies.[26] If they lack bodies, they certainly do not need sacrificial offerings, nor can they act on behalf of their worshipers. To prove his point, Śabarasvāmin subjected a number of Vedic passages that seemed to offer evidence of the gods' corporeal existence to a higher criticism, and showed that these statements were either inconclusive or figurative. A statement in the Ṛgveda that "we have taken hold of Indra's hand," for instance, Śabara interpreted as meaning that "we depend on Indra." In effect, he continued, the passage only reinforces the summons that "we should perform the sacrifice to Indra." The outcome of this skeptical hermeneutics was that, for Mīmāṃsā, gods existed only in the sounds (*śabda*) or mantras addressed to them. The concise Mīmāṃsā formulation was: "divinity is only sound." Indra had no necessary existence apart from the name "Indra" and its semantic functions within Vedic sacrifice. One should offer sacrifice to "Indra" not to nourish or please that divine person, but because the Vedic texts enjoin using that term.

Śabara was arguing explicitly against a way of interpreting Vedic sacrifice, and at the same time he argued implicitly against the theistic schools that advocated the worship of divine icons. As we have seen, the fundamental premises of temple Hinduism held that the gods exist as autonomous beings, and that they willingly assume corporeal forms as suits their purposes. An icon becomes, in this view, a fulcrum of divine presence, a body for the god being worshiped. Śabara's radical denial of divine embodiment subverted the very foundation upon which image worship was grounded.

The theistic schools naturally made their own replies to the Mīmāṃsā position, sometimes satirical. In one early Śaiva siddhānta text, the *Mṛgendrāgama*, the Vedic god Indra himself comes upon a group of Vedic sages who have set up an icon of Śiva in their hermitage and are making pūjā offerings to it (*MĀ vidyā* 1.1–22). To test their faith, Indra disguises himself as an ascetic, enters the grove, and demands to know why they are not following the injunctions of the Vedas. The sages answer by citing Vedic passages that advocate the worship of Rudra (i.e., Śiva). "Your knowledge is wrong, because divinity is only sound" (*MĀ vidya* 1.7), replies Indra, apparently endorsing Sabara's position. The sages stoutly defend their new practice. Words as signifiers must refer to real things, they aver, for "the word 'pot' does not hold water and the word 'moon' does not shine" (1.12). So too, they go on, with a word like Indra: it is the deity and not the word that carries out Indra's divine activities. Delighted by their vigorous defense of image worship (and of his own existence as an autonomous being), Indra reveals his true effulgent body to the sages and consents to teach them what he has learned of Śiva's own teachings. The text goes on to describe a full program for worshiping the Śiva liṅga and related Śaiva practices.

Monist Demotion

A less radical but more effective critique came from the Advaita Vedānta school, especially as set forth in the *Brahmasūtras* of Bādarāyaṇa and the commentary on them by the eighth-century south Indian philosopher Śaṅkara. If Mīmāṃsā refused on principle to accept the embodiment of divinity, Advaita used the more familiar Indian rhetorical strategy of qualified acceptance. Śaṅkara admitted that a worshiper might indeed approach divinity embodied in a physical support, but he consigned this to a distinctly lower level of religious practice than the direct, unmediated realization of oneness with the transcendent *brahman* that Advaitins sought.

Arguing against Sabara's Mīmāṃsā position, Śaṅkara insisted that gods do have bodies (*vigraha*).[27] By virtue of their lordly powers, gods can assume whatever bodies they wish, even normally inanimate forms such as a blaze of light. Gods can even, he asserts, assume multiple forms simultaneously, in order to attend many sacrifices at the same time. Reinterpreting many of the same Vedic passages that Śabara had cited, Śaṅkara argued that statements enjoining us to sacrifice to gods presuppose that these gods have distinct bodily forms. "With Vedic injunctions that compel us to offer oblations to Indra and the other gods, it is necessary that Indra and the others have their own characteristic forms (*svarūpa*), for without such forms it would be impossible for us to produce [or visualize] Indra and the others in our minds, and without producing them in the mind it is not possible to give oblations to the gods" (*BrSBh* 1.3.33). Śaṅkara went on to deny that this inherent form could be merely sound, as the Mīmāṃsakas claimed, because the word and its object, the signifier and the signified, are necessarily distinct from one another.

Up to this point, Śaṅkara's argument paralleled that of the theistic schools. Within the larger context of Advaita metaphysics, however, Śaṅkara demoted image worship as an inferior mode of religious practice. Like the theistic schools, Śaṅkara accepted an Absolute—for which he used the neuter term *brahman*, first employed in the Upaniṣads—that can be both transcendent and immanent. In its highest level, the *brahman* is without qualities (*nirguṇa*): formless, pervasive, and incomprehensible. This *brahman* may also take on, or be given, sensible qualities (*saguṇa*), and thereby it becomes accessible to humans for worship, visualization, and devotion. For Śaṅkara, though, only the first of these two levels had full ontological standing. From a lower, empirical point of view, humans of limited awareness might view *brahman* in saguṇa forms of corporeal divinity or animate image, but this is only a provisional perspective and ultimately it involves a misconception. From the standpoint of transcendent knowledge, *brahman* can only be nirguṇa. The overriding aim of Advaita teaching, as Śaṅkara saw it, was to enable its adherents to leave behind their limited, pluralistic apprehension of things and attain a nondualistic realization of the *brahman* in its unqualified fullness.

On this metaphysical basis, Advaita Vedānta could construct a hierarchized scale of religious forms. Because humans have differing degrees of aptitude for monist insight, Śaṅkara could accept all sorts of practices as useful in a preliminary way. Sacrifice, worship of images, and other exterior ritual observances may provide starting points on a path of knowledge, but they rank here as relatively "gross" stages. A true aspirant to nondualist knowledge should turn progressively inward, toward ever more "subtle" forms of practice, and finally to modes of mental practice that dispense altogether with the dualities of self and other, worshiper and worshiped, knower and known. Those who succeed in this course of progressive realization will regard their former rituals as flawed and even as vaguely sinful.

The sixteenth-century Śaiva Appaya Dīkṣita participated diligently in temple activities and even composed an authoritative manual for the worship of Śiva, the *Śivārcanācandrikā*. Yet as an Advaitin he nevertheless came to look at these activities with regret. "In my meditation I have visualized form for the Lord who avoids all form. By composing hymns in his praise I have contradicted the inexpressible nature of the Supreme. In making pilgrimages to the special holy places I have repudiated the Lord's all-pervasiveness," he reflects. "These are three sins I have committed, in my imperfection. Lord of the World, forgive me" (Venkatarama Iyer 1964: 200). To one who fully recognizes the formlessness, incomprehensibility, and ubiquity of the Absolute *brahman*, the normal devotional practices of temple Hinduism become not merely unnecessary, but also misguiding, because they are based on a misapprehension of the true nature of things.

Without directly attacking the worship of images, Śaṅkara and the Advaita school articulated a new line of critique that would prove resilient indeed. Many advocates of iconic worship and temple liturgy would answer Śaṅkara. The most esteemed was Rāmānuja, the eleventh-century Vaiṣṇava theologian who served as pontiff of the Raṅganātha temple at Sri Rangam in Tamilnad. Commenting on many of the same texts that Śaṅkara employed, Rāmānuja reidentified the impersonal neuter *brahman* as the personal deity Viṣṇu, and argued for the fundamental importance of Viṣṇu's bodily incarnations. By placing the immanence of the Absolute on equal ontological footing with its transcendence, Rāmānuja reaffirmed image worship as a practice of true knowledge, not illusion.[28] But the nondualist principles and criticisms articulated by Śaṅkara and other Advaitins entered into a delicate ongoing dialectic with the physical dualism inherent in image worship as a practice. Many of the philosophical syntheses and ritual reformulations of pūjā in medieval south Indian religious literature may be seen as a series of attempts to accommodate the vision of unitary knowledge advanced by Śaṅkara with the devotional theology underlying the worship of images. And still later, Śaṅkara's demotion of image worship as acceptable for persons of limited understanding but inappropriate for those of higher knowledge would provide a convenient and sophisticated indigenous philosophy by which educated Indian intellectuals of the nineteenth and early twentieth centuries could answer the Western Christian charge that Hinduism was an "idolatrous" religion.

The Temple Effect

The learned Sanskritic debates of Mīmāṃsā, Advaita, and the theistic schools, so important to the development of Hindu philosophy during the medieval period, takes us a good distance away from the world of belief and devotional attitudes toward Śiva that would have informed the responses of residents of eleventh-century Tiruvengadu toward their new images. What would have been most available to devout south Indian villagers were the Tamil hymns of the Nāyaṉārs, sung as part of the temple service, and the visible ritual activities of local Śaiva priests, adhering more or less to the prescriptions of the Śaiva āgamas. In this chapter I have argued that the theological premises embedded in these texts engendered a particular community of response, a "devotional eye" through which Śiva Vṛṣabhavāhana and his iconic cohorts would have been viewed.

To appear later in the national museums of England, India, and the United States, however, the temple images of Tiruvengadu had to be torn from the ritual setting in which they had originally figured. This operation was carried out not by conquerors or art thieves, but by the officials of the Śvetāraṇyeśvara temple itself. In response to some perceived danger they buried their valuable temple icons and then, due to circumstances we can no longer reconstruct, they neglected or were unable to disinter the concealed treasures. The accidental uncovering of Śiva and Pārvatī in 1951 and their subsequent relocations allowed a new type of audience to view the ancient, well-preserved images in an altogether new setting, a museum of art.

As I noted in the Introduction, Walter Benjamin speaks of two "polar types" in the exhibition and reception of works of art: "with one, the accent is on the cult value; with the other, on the exhibition value of the work" (1985: 224). In a long footnote, Benjamin goes on to observe that individual artworks may "oscillate" between these two types of reception. When a religious object is removed from its ritual setting, it is denuded of its context, much as Śiva Vṛṣabhavāhana image lost its sandal paste, garments, and flowers when buried. However, as Svetlana Alpers properly cautions, we should not view its redisplay as a complete disjuncture. "When objects like these are severed from the ritual site" and relocated in museums, she observes of religious objects such as Romanesque capitals and Renaissance altarpieces, "the invitation to look attentively remains and in certain respects may even be enhanced" (1991: 27). On display at the "Sculpture of India" show, and through his photographic reproduction on the catalogue cover, the Śiva Vṛṣabhavāhana from Tiruvengadu undoubtedly received his proper share of close visual attention from a new audience, for his grace of form and "crafted visibility" suited him well for the kind of gaze induced by the "museum effect."

What could be misleading here, though, is the suggestion in Alpers' statement that there is only one kind of attentive looking. Medieval south Indian Śaiva audiences looked at their images attentively, no doubt, but visual experience was not their most highly valued aim. They valued a personal, emotional relationship with the deity mediated through the divine presence in the icon. Through the notion of God's actual embodiment within an object, temple etiquette and ritual practice directed the gaze of worshipers and their actions onto the transvalued icon. In worship it was not only an object of visual interest, but also the recipient of physical services appropriate to the divine, lordly personage inhabiting it. And through the notion of God's simultaneous transcendence and immanence, Hindu theology and devotional poetry directed the worshipers' attention through the translucence of the icon into a broader (and paradoxical) apprehension of God's totality. The temple effect engendered its own way of seeing.

2.

Trophies of War

ONE WHO VISITS the Thanjavur Art Gallery, now renamed the Rajaraja Museum, in the ancient Cola capital, is treated to an exhibition of the most extraordinary collection of Cola-period bronze and stone sculpture anywhere. Exquisite bronze images like the Śiva Vṛṣabhavāhana and his consort from Tiruvengadu line up in the old royal assembly hall, and in the courtyard stand stone sculptures detached from their former temples. Stylistically they form a coherent and compelling group. Looking around, though, one also discovers a few other works of sculpture differing in style from the Cola works. One in particular stands out as an especially impressive intruder in this Cola-dominated museum display: a large black stone door guardian, four-armed, holding trident and snake and leaning on a heavy club. A large lizard climbs his mace, and around the figure other animals appear—a cat attacking a rat, a snake in the process of swallowing another rodent, and a third rat trying to escape by following the lizard (Figure 9). A practiced art-historical eye will quickly recognize this figure as a product of the later Cālukyas, who ruled from Kalyāṇī in Karnataka during the eleventh and twelfth centuries, contemporary with the Colas further south. What, then, is this door guardian doing in Thanjavur, in a museum five hundred miles south of the old Cālukya capital?

There is no historical mystery here. An inscription in Tamil characters of the eleventh century incised on the base conveniently provides the answer. It reads: "This is the door guardian brought by Lord Vijayarājendradeva after burning Kalyāṇapuram" (*ARE* 24 of 1908). We know from other epigraphs that the Cola ruler Rājādhirāja (1018–1054), son of Rājendra I, waged war against the Cālukyas shortly after his father's death in 1044, routed the enemies at the battle of Pūṇṭūr, and marched north to burn their capital. To add ritual insult to injury, he there performed a "heroic consecration" (*vīrābhiṣeka*), and assumed the new royal title of "Vijayarājendra," the victorious Rājendra. Evidently he returned from his successful campaign with the door guardian in tow, brought it to his own capital, and there displayed it as a trophy of war for his subjects. The image later found its way to Darasuram,

FIG. 9. The Cālukya Door Guardian. Stone sculpture from Kalyanapuram, Karnataka, tenth or early eleventh century. Taken by Rājādhirāja to Gangaikondacolapuram, 1045 C.E. Now in Rajaraja Museum, Thanjavur. Photograph courtesy of the American Institute of Indian Studies, Center for Art and Archaeology, Varanasi.

a new Cola capital built by Rājarāja II in the twelfth century, and in the twentieth century it was moved to the nearby Thanjavur Art Gallery for safer keeping.

The case of the Cālukya intruder is not particularly unusual or complex, but in this chapter I will use it as emblematic for reflecting on a practice common in medieval India: the appropriation of religious images and other significant objects by one king or kingdom from another, most often as an act of war.[1] Acts of appropriation, by which objects are taken out of the settings for which they were initially fabricated and placed in new ones, are nothing new in South Asia. We would certainly be wrong to think that Islamic iconoclasm or European commoditization, however profound an impact on the realm of art objects these forces have made, impinged on a previously static Hindu domain where all such objects occupied and remained in their own fixed places, recognized and respected by all. To the contrary, if we judge from inscriptions, chronicles, and the objects themselves, certain objects circulated widely and famously in early medieval India.

The Politics of Images

During the early medieval period, as we have seen, the worship of divinized images in temples was the central public religious cult of the subcontinent. Images were often closely tied to the political order. In the prevailing dispensation of early medieval India, worshipers of Viṣṇu, Śiva, or sometimes the goddess Durgā considered ruling authority to emanate from that highest lord of the cosmos downward to human lords who claimed to rule more limited domains such as empires, kingdoms, territories, or villages. The construction of monumental temples housing images of these divinities, instantiating their cosmic sovereignty within the polity of the sponsor, acted to represent and embody political accomplishments while at the same time locating such attainments within a larger, encompassing divine order.

Early texts portray images as indices of the prosperity and security of their kingdoms. Obversely, unnatural or unusual activities on the part of images portend evil. In his sixth-century *Bṛhatsaṃhitā*, Varāhamihira advises, "If a Śiva liṅga, image, or temple breaks apart, moves, sweats, cries, speaks, or otherwise acts with no apparent cause, this warns of the destruction of the king and his territory" (*BS* 46.8). Similar anomalies befalling a Viṣṇu image indicate danger to the population in general, while those occurring with an image of Brahman foretell a threat to brahmins. In such cases, Varāhamihira advises the chief priest of the kingdom to observe three days of special purification and worship of the image, and the king to declare a seven-day ritual of pacification (*śānti*), in order to prevent the predicted misfortunes from coming to fruition.[2]

Medieval Indians often linked the founding of new kingdoms with the acquisition of significant icons. For example, the tenth-century poet Padmagupta relates in his *Navasāhasāṅkacarita* how Sāhasāṅka, founder of the Paramāra dynasty of Dhārā, acquires a special Śiva liṅga from the king of the Nāgas ruling the underworld. The liṅga has its own pedigree: it had been transferred from Viṣṇu to the sages, to the Nāgas, and then finally to the new Paramāra ruler. When Sāhasāṅka brings it back to his capital and establishes it in the temple of Śiva Mahākāla, he gains with it the authority to rule his kingdom.[3]

Taking this association of kingship and icons one step further, there were also cases where particularly potent images exercised direct earthly sovereignty. Within the medieval Hindu dispensation, with its theological understanding of God's cosmic overlordship and his real manifestation in temple icons, this appears entirely plausible. Just as in the past Viṣṇu ruled terrestrial kingdoms in his incarnations as Rāma and Kṛṣṇa, and just as medieval kings sometimes claimed to be new incarnations of Viṣṇu (as we will see in Chapter Four), so Viṣṇu (or Śiva) might well choose to assume dominion through an iconic incarnation. In such situations human "rulers" became subordinate functionaries of the ruling deity. The best documented example of image sovereignty in India is Viṣṇu Jagannātha's rule of the Gaṅga kingdom centered in Orissa, beginning in the early thirteenth century.[4]

The Appropriation of Images

As divine images were already active, preponderant participants in the medieval system of authoritative relations, it is not surprising that images were often seized publicly by one ruler from another in circumstances of conflict. Alive to the identities and mythic backgrounds of the figures, royal looters dislodged select images from their customary positions and employed them to articulate political claims in a rhetoric of objects whose principal themes were victory and defeat, autonomy and subjugation, dominance and subordination. Such acts were undertaken in deadly earnest, and often had decisive effects for the human actors involved. For the images too, there were notable consequences. When art historians, historians of religion, and others of us who concern ourselves with Indian religious objects regard an image such as the Cālukya door guardian, we focus our attention most often on the aesthetic elegance of its form, on the religious meaning of its iconographic composition, or on the social and political context within which it was fabricated. In these matters, we often think, lies the essential significance of the object, as if meaning were fixed once and for all at the moment of creation. But the later lives of Indian religious images and the ways in which these images come to be relocated and revalorized, I argue, also become intrinsic to their significance. Captured by new proprietors and relocated in new surroundings, their identities shifted significantly from what they had been.

Intrusion and Its Human Agents

I first became interested in the matter of image appropriation through reading a 1984 article by Gary Tartakov and Vidya Dehejia on "Sharing, Intrusion, and Influence." The authors set out to refine the conventional and largely uncritical vocabulary we use to discuss stylistic and iconographic continuities among Indian art objects, and propose a more finely calibrated set of terms for describing what we usually conflate under the vague rubric "influence." They suggest that we replace that single term with three: "sharing" when two works draw upon a common or shared artistic tradition, "influence" in a more restricted sense when one cultural form changes other cultural forms, and "intrusion," indicating cases where something that was not there previously enters into local patterns. Intrusion, they point out, may occur through local invention or through exogenous borrowing.

I found myself most intrigued by their category of "intrusion," since it directs our attention to moments of artistic disjuncture and innovation, to processes that are somehow outside the normal and stationary. One can easily think of many once-extraneous objects that have forced themselves upon new environments. The authors use the example of a recently made Orissan bronze image of Durgā defeating the Buffalo demon that has intruded itself into an Amherst, Massachusetts, home. It stands out unambiguously from the other bric-a-brac above the fireplace mantle as an object that is emphatically not where it was originally fabricated or intended to be.

Tartakov and Dehejia convincingly show that it is not always easy to determine or predict whether an out-of-place object has had or will have an influence on the subsequent development of art in its new home. The Amherst Durgā, I would venture, will not have major repercussions for the local art styles of the Connecticut Valley, but there are many other cases where equally exotic objects have brought about significant restylings in new surroundings. One thinks most readily of the African masks at the Trocadero (now the Musée de l'Homme) in Paris, waiting mutely for an artist with the eye of a Picasso to chance upon them. Lord Elgin even used this possibility to justify transporting the Parthenon friezes to England; he argued that easy access to such classical models would have a positive "influence" (in the restricted sense) on the development of English sculpture.[5] One may argue, too, that the Cālukya door guardian and other objects taken by the Colas from their wartime adversaries were directly related to alterations in twelfth-century Cola sculpture at Darasuram and elsewhere, such as a greater use of close-grained black stone and more emphasis on ornamental detailing.[6]

As a historian, however, I found myself interested less in the tracings of style and more in the human processes through which intruding objects have made their way from one place to another. There is always some human agency involved in the transportation of objects, and there are always social circumstances that are conducive to or allow such intrusions to take place. Such circumstances may be the nineteenth-century colonial expropriation by which, say, the Buddhist sculptures of Amaravati traveled from Andhra Pradesh to the British Museum (Cohn 1992: 312–20; Knox 1992: 17–22). They may include the growth of international tourism and the adaptation of Indian artisans to market production, through which Orissan-style images of Durgā begin turning up in the living rooms of Amherst, Berkeley, and everywhere else tourists in India return to when they go home. Or, as in the case of the Cālukya door guardian, they may result from a war in which one medieval Hindu king seizes an image from his defeated rival and transports it back to his own capital.

Once I had in mind this category of intrusion—or, as I would prefer, appropriation, to stress human agency rather than object's movement—I began to remember and discover a whole series of such appropriations in classical and medieval India, known to us through chronicles, inscriptions, and the objects themselves.[7] Yet the only general treatment I was able to find of the appropriation of art objects in pre-modern South Asia was *Royal Conquests and Cultural Migrations in South India and the Deccan* by the erudite art historian C. Sivaramamurti (1964). In this wide-ranging survey of the relationship between military campaigns and the transmission of artistic themes and motifs in classical and medieval South Asia, Sivaramamurti paints a portrait of essentially benign artistic exchanges among warring kings, motivated by spontaneous aesthetic appreciation. "Sometimes," he writes, "a great victor was struck with admiration and adopted what were essential features of the culture of a dynasty long reduced to dust with all its glory forgotten. Sometimes the politically vanquished sovereign had something glorious to give as a lesson of culture to his victor, who, it must be said to his credit, enthusiastically accepted it, though it was really a cultural conquest of the political victor by the vanquished" (1964: 1). Sivaramamurti repeatedly describes the expropriations of images and other art objects by conquering Indian rulers as if it were the collecting of connoisseurs: "the victor stooped to gather blossoms of culture from the land of the vanquished" (1964: 7).

Undoubtedly many medieval South Asian kings did appreciate the artistry of a finely rendered bronze image or an elegant carved pillar, just as they appreciated well-crafted poetry. As prescriptive texts indicate, a young prince's education might well include a course of instruction in the various branches of art and architecture. Kings often participated directly in the construction of religious edifices as ritual patrons, and several substantial texts on the fabrication of temples and images are attributed to royal authors. However, these same kings did not regard the appropriation of an image primarily as an expression of aesthetic sensitivity, nor did they recognize the strong division of "political" and "cultural" domains implicit in Sivaramamurti's account. Almost all inscriptions and narrative accounts dealing with the matter treat expropriations as predominantly political acts. Such actions were not benign, but highly consequential, not only for the development of art, but for the subsequent course of political events as well.

The Golden Buddha

To gain a preliminary idea of the value attached to appropriations of images, let us consider the case of the pure gold Buddha image of the Jewel Palace in Anurādhapura, seized by the Pāṇḍyans in the ninth century and regained by the Sinhalese king Sena II. The events are narrated by the twelfth-century Buddhist monk and chronicler Dhammakitti in the *Cūlavaṃsa*.

In the early ninth century, the Pāṇḍyan kingdom of southern Tamilnad expanded northward into the Kaveri and Kongu regions, and sometime around 835 the Pāṇḍyan ruler Śrīmāra Śrīvallabha (r. 815–862), filled with imperial ambitions, mounted an invasion of the island of Sri Lanka. The Sinhala king Sena I (r. 831–851) attempted to resist, but the Pāṇḍyan attack proved too formidable. "In an instant," reports Dhammakitti, "the great army of the Pāṇḍyan king swept over the large crowd of Sinhala soldiers and crushed them, moving like Māra's army. And the Sinhala king, hearing that his army had been sundered, took up all his portable wealth and fled the city, heading toward the mountains" (*CV* 50.19–20). With the Sinhalese army dispersed and leaderless, Śrīmāra (like his namesake Māra, deadly to the Buddhists) easily captured the capital and began to plunder it. "He removed all the valuables from the royal treasury, and seized everything that could be seized in the monastery and the city. The statue of the Teacher made entirely of gold in the Jewel Palace, the pair of jewels set as eyes in the Lord of Sages made of stone, likewise the gold plate on the *caitya* in the Thūpārāma, and the golden images in the various monasteries—all these he seized, denuding Lanka island of its wealth and spitting out the once-splendid city as if demons (*yakṣas*) had devoured it" (*CV* 50.33–36).

The solid gold Buddha was not an ancient image. King Mahinda II (r. 772–792) had sponsored its creation about fifty years earlier, at the steep cost of 60,000 copper coins, and had established the image on a pedestal in the Jewel Palace, a pavilion he also constructed in the Abhayagiri monastic complex (*CV* 48.136–37). Mahinda's grandson Aggabodhi VIII (r. 801–812) honored the image with a grand festival as part of his accession to kingship (*CV* 49.44). The sumptuous image was evidently one of considerable importance not only to the Abhayagiri monks who maintained it, but also to the Sinhalese rulers of the period.

Back on the mainland, the Pallavas were organizing a coalition of forces to oppose the upstart Pāṇḍyans, and this undoubtedly made Śrīmāra more eager to come to terms with his defeated opponent. From exile, Sena I was able to negotiate a settlement with the occupying power, giving elephants and all his jewels to Śrīmāra. The Pāṇḍyan king left the island with his booty and tribute. Sena I returned to the capital and took up sovereignty once again, but sovereignty of a decidedly diminished stature.

When Sena I passed away, his nephew Sena II (r. 851–885) became ruler. The new king ruled without incident, Dhammakitti relates, until one day he held a festival for the Tooth-relic.

> Once when the king was celebrating the great festival of the Tooth-relic with all proper offerings, he ascended the excellent Jewel Palace, and there saw the empty pedestal where the golden Buddha had once stood. "Why is this?" he asked.
>
> "Does the king not know?" replied the ministers. "During the time of your uncle, King Sena, O king, the Pāṇḍyan king came here, laid waste to the island, and left, taking all that had become valuable to us."
>
> When the king heard this, he was ashamed as if it were he himself who had been defeated. And that very day he ordered the ministers to assemble his troops. (*CV* 51.22–26)

A disgruntled Pāṇḍyan prince, apparently a passed-over claimant to the throne, had conveniently appeared in Lanka requesting aid, and Sena II saw in him an opportunity to redress his grievance. The Sinhala king sent an expeditionary force to accompany the prince and support his claim to rule in Madurai, the Pāṇḍyan capital. "Go!" he ordered his commander Kuṭṭaka, "Kill the Pāṇḍyan king! Bring back all the jewels he once took from here! Grant sovereignty to this prince, and return quickly!" (*CV* 51.30–31).

Meanwhile, the Pāṇḍyan armies had been engaged with the Pallava-led coalition, fighting three costly battles. When the Sinhalese armies attacked from the other flank and marched on Madurai, the Pāṇḍyans were unable to resist. Śrīmāra died shortly afterward of wounds sustained in battle. "Then the Sinhalese armies fearlessly entered the city and plundered the place completely, like gods sacking the city of the demons," the chronicler reports. "The commander inspected the treasury in the royal palace, and took all the valuables that had been taken from our island, as well as those found in the town and the countryside" (*CV* 51.39–41). A good patriot, Dhammakitti compares pillage when done by others to the work of Māra's army and demons;

when it is done by his own countrymen, however, it is like gods plundering demons.

Kuṭṭaka had the Pāṇḍyan prince crowned as King Varaguṇavarman II, and after a brief tour returned to Lanka, where Sena II received the victorious army with rejoicing and rituals of solidarity. The king held a great feast for them in the capital, celebrated a festival of victory, and distributed gifts to the poor. The repatriated objects he conscientiously restored to their proper places. "Without attachment he placed all the valuables in their original places on the island, and he ritually established the golden images just as they had been before. He filled the empty pedestal of the Teacher in the Jewel Palace, and he secured the land by setting up guardposts" (*CV* 51.48–49). The restoration of images had remarkable effects on the community, for from that time on Lanka became as prosperous as Uttarakuru, the legendary land of plenty beyond the Himālaya.[8]

In this simple moral tale of treasure lost and recaptured, we begin to see more clearly how medieval kings and their advisers regarded the expropriation of images. The stolen image, disclosed to the young king by its empty pedestal, serves as an objectification of defeat not only for his uncle who had suffered the loss, but for the very institution of Sinhala sovereignty. The humiliation the king feels and his immediate resolve to retrieve the golden Buddha indicate how powerfully the empty pedestal provoked him, how clearly he understood its message in this discourse of objects. His orders to Kuṭṭaka, and the commander's careful search in the royal treasury at Madurai, confirm that recovery of the missing images was a central purpose of the invasion, and the jubilation upon their successful return is in the narrator's eyes a celebration of the restoration of the country's wholeness. For Dhammakitti, whose principal concern throughout the *Cūlavaṃsa* is to delineate proper relations between Sinhalese sovereignty and the Buddhist community, loss and recovery of the golden Buddha is a synecdoche for the integrity of the Sinhalese polity itself.

Looting: Morality and Motivation

On the base of the door guardian he brought back, the Cola ruler Rājādhirāja had an inscription engraved explaining that he had seized it from the Cālukya capital. Evidently he did not intend to conceal its origin or his act of appropriation. Rather, he wished to make clear to all that this was a captured trophy.

In their inscriptions, medieval Indian rulers proudly and repeatedly proclaim their expropriation of objects from other kings. Here, for instance, is the epigraphic account of another Cola king's victory over a Cālukya opponent at the battle of Kudalsangamam: "Vīrarājendra halted his hot, impetuous elephant and donned the garland of victory. He plucked out his opponent's wives, the family treasure, his conches, his fringed white parasol, his trumpets, his war drum, his canopy, his white yak-tail fans, the boar banner, the crocodile gateway, 'Blossom' the female elephant, a herd of war elephants, and a troop of prancing horses. Amidst shouts of praise, he put on the victory crown adorned with splendid red jewels" (Hultzsch 1899: 34). Not only does Vīrarājendra (r. 1063–1069) "pluck" his defeated enemy of these properties, he also places them on display in the capital for his subjects to view. A later inscription continues: "Seated on a throne of bright jewels, Vīrarājendra exhibited in orderly rows the great heaps of treasures he had seized in the Vengi territory, while all the kings on earth did homage at his feet and praised him" (Hultzsch 1899: 67). There is nothing furtive about all this. Just as the subordinate rulers bowing at Vīrarājendra's feet visibly signify their acceptance of his overlordship, the orderly exhibition of Cālukyan treasures is meant to represent objectively to all observers Vīrarājendra's battlefield victory. In medieval South Asia, looting was an important element in the rhetoric of kingship.

The forcible expropriation of valued objects from another defined as an enemy in circumstances of military conflict, which we designate by the Anglo-Indian term "looting," is of course a longstanding practice in many cultures.[9] However, this activity may be constructed and construed differently, in different times and places. We in the modern West have come to regard looting as a species of theft, a side effect of war that is predatory, disorganized, and economically gainful in motivation. Indians of the medieval period, by contrast, did not consider such seizure as theft, nor did they leave it a disorderly and surreptitious activity.

As the inscriptions of Vīrarājendra suggest, medieval South Asian rulers and their retinues carried out plunder as a normal and public aspect of war, organized by and around the person of the king, and directed as much toward symbolic objects as toward economic resources. To consider more closely the cultural construction of such wartime appropriations, let us begin with the Dharmaśāstra of Manu (*MS*) and his ninth-century Kashmiri commentator Medhātithi (*MSBh*).[10]

In his discussion of proper royal conduct, Manu is very concerned to circumscribe battlefield behavior within a code of chivalrous conduct. Manu sets down prescriptions concerning whom a warrior may strike, when he may strike him, what weapons he may use, and much more. While urging discipline upon the troops in many respects, Manu indicates no similar compunction about the propriety of plunder. "Chariots, horses, parasols, money, grain, cattle, women, all kinds of goods, and base metals all belong to the one who wins (*jayati*) them" (*MS* 7.96). It is a matter of "victory" (*jaya*), not of theft (*steya*).

Manu elsewhere discusses theft in some detail (*MS* 9. 251–93 and 11.55–71), and it is helpful to consider the implicit distinction he draws between the theft of property in an orderly kingdom and its appropriation on the field of battle. Manu classifies theft as one of the five "great faults" involving serious moral transgression, and stresses that the king is responsible for preventing theft and apprehending thieves. To do this, Manu suggests various methods of surveillance and punishment. The settled order of the king's domain is established and maintained through the king's sovereign activity, and one of his principal duties is to remove those "thorns" that tear the skin of the body politic. In war, by contrast, no settled order exists. Two rulers meet in an antagonistic situation, each seeking to assert dominance over the other. Victory and defeat in battle are the primary means of determining a new hierarchical ordering, and the appropriation of property by the winner in this context appears as an objective correlate to battlefield victory.

The moral question for Manu is not whether one may expropriate objects (and living property as well) from defeated opponents, but how one should properly distribute the booty. Certain valuable commodities, such as gold, silver, and land, are reserved for the king alone, Medhātithi tells us. This includes, as we will see, all regalia and images. It is impermissible, however, for the king as master (*svāmin*) to appropriate all loot himself. Other items, those listed in Manu's verse, belong to the individual warriors who acquire them. But here too, a portion (and, Medhātithi specifies, the best portion) must be presented to the king: "One should give a share to the king. So it is stated in the Veda" (*MS* 7.97). The king occupies the center of all looting transactions; sharing the spoils reiterates substantively the moral relationship between king and troops.

The Vedic precedent to which Manu alludes, his commentator tells us, is none other than the primordial battle between Indra, king of the gods, and the demon Vṛtra. When Indra defeated the demon in combat and so became great, he requested and received the best portion of all the loot obtained (*Aitreyabrāhmaṇa* 3.21). As Indra among the gods, so too the king among his subordinates is entitled to the choice part of every expropriation. By sharing loot hierarchically, suggests Manu, Hindu rulers should attempt to replicate in human society the model set by the Vedic gods.

Medhātithi records an additional provision concerning spoils gained by the king himself and those acquired by the army as a collectivity. Of such loot, he tells us, "the king should distribute it among those he supports according to the principle of 'bestowing acquisitions on a worthy recipient'" (*MSBh* 7.97). This principle, Medhātithi explains elsewhere, means that a king should apportion his acquisitions to such "worthy recipients" as gods, hermitages, intellectuals, and moral exemplars; he may also employ his resources in sponsoring public festivals (*MSBh* 7.56). In inscriptions, by that same principle, we often learn of looted objects being presented to temple deities and to those who have served the king in battle.[11] Booty engenders those substantive transactions that link the king both with the god or gods whose cosmic sovereignty includes and surpasses his own and also with eminent subjects within his own dominion.

Far from avoiding wartime appropriations, then, medieval Hindu rulers placed themselves forthrightly in the center of a redistributive network involving looted objects. Not surprisingly, this was closely linked to the medieval Hindu ideology of royal authority, which viewed the king as the central agency responsible for integrating the dispersed segments of his domain into a unitary polity and bringing about its prosperity. By appropriating objects during military campaigns he embodied the victory he had attained over his rivals, symbolically incorporating their signs, and by reapportioning those objects within his own domain he replenished it and reiterated the ties that bound together the dominion of which he was moral center.

The Rhetoric of Appropriated Images

In Vīrarājendra's list of appropriated objects, as in most loot lists, there are two types of things: "wealth" or economic resources such as gold, elephants, and horses, and specific named objects of symbolic import, like the boar banner, the crocodile gateway, and "Blossom" who appears to have been the royal elephant. (It should be noted that this division between practical and symbolic commodities is our distinction, derived from common Western ontological premises, and is not observed in medieval Indian inscriptions.) Historians George Spencer (1976) and Burton Stein (1980) have stressed the economic significance of plundering in medieval warfare. Spencer goes so far as to argue that the plundering of resources, not acquisition of territory, was the primary purpose of war. Kings too powerless to collect taxes on a regular basis required the "free-flowing resources" that could be gained most effectively by predatory raids on neighboring kingdoms. No doubt such recyclable assets were required by rulers to pay the army through distribution of booty and to make conspicuous displays of devotion to religious institutions. I want to focus here, however, on the significance of the other appropriated objects these historians tend to deemphasize, for I believe these objects were more central to the motivations of medieval warriors.

Over and over, Indian inscriptions refer to a repertoire of symbolic objects as primary targets of royal appropriation: banners, yak-tail fans, umbrellas, crowns, thrones, musical instruments, and gateways. These objects were referred to in general as *aṅgas* ("limbs"), *cihnas* ("physical signs"), or *lakṣaṇas* ("attributes"), suggesting their metonymic participation in the king's sovereignty. This close association of regalia with the king's person was constituted and sustained through the ceremonial activity of kingship. Regalia participated in the royal consecration (*abhiṣeka*), they were displayed on festive occasions, and they were transported, as well, onto the battlefield.[12] In some cases, dynasties traced their sovereignty directly to the acquisition of particular items of regalia.[13] To call them "symbols" representing a king's dominion does not do justice. Rather, they were viewed as physical instantiations of a king's authority, inseparable from his capacity to rule rightfully. Accordingly, appropriating them on the field of battle was equivalent to "plucking out" the opponent's sovereignty and incorporating it into one's own. This is why medieval inscriptions were so careful to list the exact objects taken from defeated kings. They were making specific substantive claims to authority, in a discourse of objects understood by all involved.

With looted images, though, the question of choice is more complicated. It is clear to see why a victorious king would wish to capture the regalia of his opponent, but why should Rājādhirāja have appropriated a door guardian? If he was plundering and burning the enemy capital, presumably he had his pick of a great number of Cālukya images. Why would Rājādhirāja content himself with an image of clearly inferior status within the temple hierarchy?

The Cālukya door guardian was fabricated to stand in the entryway of a temple in Kalyāṇī. Temple doorways were highly charged places both of transition and differentiation, where worshipers passed through into the sacred precincts of the temple and those unqualified to enter needed to be turned away. The task of preventing demons and other unwanted enemies from approaching the interior of the temple was assigned to fierce stone door guardians (*dvarapālas*). Accordingly, they looked fearsome with four arms and terrifying fangs, and they wore snakes as ornaments. They wielded weapons such as maces and axes in their hands, and made hand gestures indicating menace. Yet their function was not only to guard but also to worship. Door guardians enacted their own subservient position within the temple hierarchy by continually paying homage to the supreme lord within.[14] All who saw the Cālukya door guardian in its original setting would have clearly understood its protective intent and its subordinate status.

One could argue that Rājādhirāja's selection of a door guardian was arbitrary, or that this appropriated object alone survives out of a larger set of looted objects, since destroyed. One could postulate, as C. Sivaramamurti has, that Rājādhirāja chose his target on aesthetic grounds, as a particularly fine example of Cālukya sculptural art—which it surely is (1964: 9). However, I will argue that Rājādhirāja chose this particular image for its homological possibilities. Before making this argument, though, I wish to describe some general features of the medieval political rhetoric of objects.

Appropriated Images and Secondary Signs

The appropriation of Indian images recasts their significance without altering what they are and represent in the first place. To clarify this point, it is useful to keep in mind Roland Barthes' well-known model of mythology as a second-order semiological system (1957: 111–17). Myth uses an existing semiological chain, namely language, to construct a new system of significance. In doing so, Barthes argues, myth takes the first-order unity embodied in the linguistic sign and employs that as signifier in the encompassing system of mythical discourse. "Everything happens," he comments, "as if myth shifted the formal system of the first significations sideways."

In the case of appropriated images, the first-order sign system consists not of language but of physical objects: sculpted objects that represent something visually according to known conventions, and that may also serve as the embodiment of that something. The golden Buddha image, as signifier, evokes immediately in its audience the concept of "Buddha as Teacher," the signified. Their associative unity, drawn even more closely when the Buddha is ritually invoked into the image, constitutes the sign. It is this first-order pairing of image and signified concept (or divinity) that we refer to when we "identify" an Indian image iconographically. When seized by the Pāṇḍyan king, however, the signification of the golden Buddha shifts, as Barthes would have it, sideways. The appropriated image in its new situation serves now as the signifier also of the military victory of the Pāṇḍyan ruler over the Sinhalese. It has not lost its previous identity, but a secondary signification augments it.

This enhancement of identity may be asserted explicitly, as in the case of the Cālukyan door guardian, where details of its origin and appropriation are inscribed onto the object itself. The source of the looted image may become a permanent part of its name. The "Vātāpi Gaṇapati" at Tiruccengattangudi, for instance, denotes the image of Gaṇeśa that, according to local tradition, was brought to Tamilnad by the Pallava ruler Narasiṃhavarman I (630–68) and his general Parañjyoti, after sacking the Cālukyan capital of Vātāpi in 642 A.D.[15] Images may even carry with them entire pedigrees of previous proprietors and appropriators. In the Lakṣmaṇa temple of Khajuraho constructed by the Candella ruler Yaśovarman shortly before 950 C.E. to house a solid gold image of Viṣṇu Vaikuṇṭha, the foundation inscription traces the background of the image: "The king of the Tibetans got it from Mount Kailāsa, and then Sahi the king of Kangra received it from him out of friendship. With his troops of elephants and horses, Herambapāla [Pratihāra] thereupon seized it from him. Obtaining it from his son, the [Pratihāra] prince Devapāla, the illustrious [Candella] king Yaśovarman—an ornament among kings and a crusher of enemies—performed the ritual establishment of Vaikuṇṭha"

(Kielhorn 1892: 129). From "Kailāsa" (Kashmir?) to Tibet to Kangra to Kanyakubja to Khajuraho: the epigraph carefully recounts the past journeys of this eminent Viṣṇu image as indicative and constitutive of its identity and value.[16]

The Udayagiri Bālakṛṣṇa

Appropriated images are, nevertheless, still also divine images. The object may be removed from its original and intended situation, but this does not empty it of its previous significance as a fabricated icon that may, under proper ritual conditions, serve as an embodiment for a god or goddess. Looted images should therefore receive respectful treatment from their new proprietors, and for the most part during this period they do. We do not hear of the intentional humiliation of divine images, nor very often of their public mutilation, by those who seize them.

Often looters made a considerable effort to erect new temples to house appropriated images in the manner to which they were accustomed. One of the most notable practitioners of royal appropriation was the Vijayanagara emperor Kṛṣṇadevarāya (r. 1509–1529). Shortly after assuming the throne, the emperor attacked the forces of the Gajapati ruler Pratāparudra at Udayagiri, a hill stronghold in Andhra Pradesh. After a bitter siege lasting some eighteen months, the fortress fell. This paved the way for further victories over the Gajapatis and led finally to Pratāparudra's acceptance of Vijayanagara suzerainty.

Vijayanagara celebrated the victory at Udayagiri as a momentous event. As part of the celebrations Kṛṣṇadevarāya transported back to his capital an image of Bālakṛṣṇa from a small temple at Udayagiri (Krishna Sastri 1912: 164–200). It was a modest figure, just over three feet with its pedestal, carved in the greenish black granite typical of the Udayagiri area, portraying Kṛṣṇa as a chubby boy seated with his right foot on a lotus flower, holding a butterball (Figure 10). To house the looted image, he had specially constructed the Kṛṣṇasvāmi temple, resembling in plan and design the Udayagiri temple from which it had been removed. At its consecration ceremony, the king presented gold and silver vessels to the Udayagiri Bālakṛṣṇa, and endowed it with the royal share from nine villages for maintaining regular daily worship on a suitable scale (Krishna Sastri 1923: 44–50). Vyāsarāya, a favored intellectual of the royal court, composed a series of hymns to honor the advent of this image in Vijayanagara (Nilakanta Sastri and Venkataramanayya 1946: 1.203). Evidently his new dynastic hosts meant to treat Bālakṛṣṇa as a valued and honored guest.

There is good reason to suppose that another Vijayanagara monument of Kṛṣṇadevarāya's time, the Viṭṭhalasvāmi temple, also housed an appropri-

FIG. 10. Udayagiri Bālakṛṣṇa. Stone sculpture of Kṛṣṇa as a child, from Udayagiri, Andhra Pradesh, fifteenth century. Taken by Kṛṣṇadevarāya to Vijayanagara in 1514. Now in Government Museum, Madras. Photograph courtesy of the Institut Français d'Indologie, Pondicherry.

FIG. 11. Viṭṭhala Temple, Vijayanagara. Constructed in early sixteenth century, probably to house icon from Pandharpur. Photograph courtesy of the Institut Français d'Indologie, Pondicherry.

ated image. Viṭṭhala is a form of Viṣṇu-Kṛṣṇa worshiped almost exclusively in Maharashtra, and his cult is centered at Pandharpur. In 1520 and 1521, Kṛṣṇadevarāya led a successful campaign against Ismā'īl 'Ādil Shāh, sultan of Bijapur, bringing him temporary control over the Pandharpur area. Considerable evidence suggests that the Vijayanagara ruler took the image of Viṭṭhala from its cult center and brought it back to the capital to animate his own Viṭṭhala temple, which was then under construction (Khare 1936; Figure 11).

For Kṛṣṇadevarāya, the appropriation of such images does not appear to have been simply a matter of personal religious predilection, nor of offering refuge from the threat of Islamic iconoclasm to gods of other regions (Longhurst 1916–1917: 27; Krishnasvami Aiyangar 1936: 20–21). Rather, I would argue, it was part of a ritually incorporative imperial policy, requiring the conspicuous, ceremonial presence of subordinated polities in the capital.

The principal royal festival of Vijayanagara was Navarātri, the "nine nights" celebration in the autumn. As Burton Stein has argued in his study of this ceremony, all feudatory "chiefs" were obliged at this event to participate in a series of hierarchical transactions with their overlord, enacting and reconstituting annually their subordinate share in Vijayanagara sovereignty (Stein 1983). In addition, divinities of the subject regions likewise made yearly treks to attend the ceremonies, along with retinues of priests and temple dancers, arriving in great "triumphal cars." While the human servants of these divinities made obeisance to the Vijayanagara emperor and danced for him, the images themselves expressed homage to the presiding deity of the festival, an image of the goddess Durgā, slayer of the Buffalo demon.

The more permanent presence of the Udayagiri Bālakṛṣṇa in Vijayanagara conveyed much the same message as the visiting deities of Navarātri. Transported to the capital and housed in its own temple, it spoke with a double message, not only of the glorious child-god Kṛṣṇa who received the homage of Kṛṣṇadevarāya and his retinue, but also of the encompassment of Gajapati polity within the overarching imperial lordship of the Vijayanagara sovereign.[17]

Redistribution: The Emerald Pedestal

Not only does the seizure of objects from opponents in war convey political messages; so too does the subsequent redistribution of those objects. If an image forcibly taken from an unwilling opponent and repositioned in one's own capital can serve as a figurative incorporation of that opponent's polity, then by the same token an image accepted willingly by a subordinate ruler from his overlord may signify a subjugation voluntarily accepted. The operative principle in such cases is Manu's phrase, "bestowing acquisitions on worthy recipients."

Within the system of loot distribution described by Manu and Medhātithi, as we have seen, all important appropriated objects reverted to the king, who then "bestowed" them as warranted. The "worthy recipient" he chose to favor might be, first and foremost, the god he worshiped as his own lord. So when the Kalacuri king Lakṣmaṇarāja II, ruling in the Dahala region of Madhya Pradesh, undertook in the tenth century a western military campaign, he pointedly made a pilgrimage to the Śaiva temple of Somanātha on the Gujarati coast, and there "presented in reverence to Śiva an image of Kāliya [presumably Kāliyavadha Kṛṣṇa] made of jewels and gold," which he had appropriated in an earlier battle with the king of Orissa on the east coast (Mirashi 1955: 213–14).

Alternatively a king might chose human subordinates as worthy recipients for looted images, not as an act of devotion to a superior but as one of favor or grace to an inferior. To consider the political semantics of such a gift, let us take the case of an "emerald pedestal" (*marakatapītām*) employed as a central ritual object in an impressive performance of Navarātri in Ramanathapuram in the year 1892 (Sivasankara Pandiyaji n.d.; Breckenridge 1977).

The pedestal was a looted object. According to local tradition, it had been acquired in the mid-seventeenth century by the setupati Raghunātha Tevar, an ancestor of H.H. Raja Bhaskaraswamy Avargal, the setupati sponsoring the 1892 celebration.

In the seventeenth century, the Madurai nāyakkar ("governor") Tirumalai (1623–1659) ruled over southern Tamiland, and was virtually autonomous from the fading Vijayanagara imperium that had established the nāyakkar rule in Madurai a century earlier. Raghunātha Tevar, the setupati of Ramnad, was his subordinate. During Tirumalai's reign, the southern kingdoms of Madurai and Mysore had fought a series of inconclusive battles, and in 1656, with the aged Tirumalai sick in bed, the Mysore ruler Kaṇṭhīrava Narasa attacked once again. Apparently the Mysore forces penetrated all the way to Madurai, and Tirumalai's only recourse was to call on his loyal subordinate. The Madurai chronicles narrate it this way:

> Now the king Tirumalai nāyakkar wrote and sent a letter to the setupati. On the very day the setupati read the letter, he immediately prepared 60,000 men and brought them. He defeated the Mysore army, drove it into the Ghats, attained victory, and returned to the king.
>
> The king was very happy, and held a feast for him in the palace. He presented him with many elephants and horses, clothing, ornaments, and the like, and he gave him the title "Tirumalai's Setupati." He also gave the setupati his own lion-faced palanquin and other emblems such as a banner and a canopy. Calling him a son of his own lineage, Tirumalai dismissed all revenue assessments, saying that the setupati no longer had to pay tribute. And from that time on, the setupati ruled his territory without paying tribute, and he had the Ramanathapuram fort rebuilt as a stone fortress. (Taylor 1835: 2.26)

The transactions between the Ramnad setupati and the Madurai nāyakkar described here reflect a characteristic medieval south Indian patterning of authoritative relations, by which ruling kings "shared" their sovereignty with lesser kings who thereby became subordinate participants within the overarching system. In his ethnohistory of this political formation, Nicholas Dirks (1987) points to the Vijayanagara ceremony of Navarātri as the dramatic ritual paradigm of the system in action. During the nine-day ceremony, the Vijayanagara emperor at the center of the festival expressed his homage to an image of the goddess Durgā, the presiding deity of the festival, and received from her his authority to rule in the objective form of royal sword and scepter. In her defining mythic action, Durgā had herself received weapons from all the gods to aid her in killing the demon that none of them but she could defeat. The subordinate governors, nāyakkars, who were compelled to be present in the capital would in turn express their devotion to the emperor, and would receive from him portions of his authority in the physical form of emblems. "The sharing of the king's sovereignty through the transactions of the festival," Dirks argues, "had the effect of incorporating the disparate elements of the kingdom into his sovereign being and rendering them all parts—metonyms—of himself, even as the emblems were themselves metonyms of his sovereignty" (Dirks 1987: 42). This personalized and embodied authority was passed down from level to level, from emperor to governor to subordinate chieftain and so on, through similar ceremonial exchanges.

The primary stocks in trade of this hierarchized transactional system, Dirks tells us, were "services" and "honors": the subordinate offering service to his superior, the superior in turn granting honors of various sorts to the subordinate. So the Ramnad setupati unhesitatingly offered his military service and troops to the beleaguered Madurai nāyakkar, saving Tirumalai from defeat and attaining victory over the Mysore invaders on behalf of his overlord. The emerald pedestal was presumably part of the substantive "victory" Raghunātha acquired during the campaign and presented to his lord. Tirumalai in turn recognized Raghunātha's service with a host of honors: gifts, titles, emblems, and rights to the unfettered enjoyment of land. These royal gifts were in fact gifts also of limited, shared sovereignty within Tirumalai's encompassing dominion.

In this light, it is not difficult to see why Tirumalai chose the looted pedestal as a suitable object to bestow upon his worthy recipient. During an earlier campaign on behalf of the Madurai ruler, Raghunātha had helped repel a Muslim invasion led by "Khub Khān," and had been honored with the title "He Who Propped up the Kingdom" (Nelson 1868: 3.138). As a subordinate ruler and warrior, the setupati certainly had acted as a prop to the nāyakkar's rule, and so the identity of the appropriated object once again refers to a political relationship. The emerald pedestal was a homologue not for an involuntarily subjugated source, but for a willingly subordinate recipient.

The Gift of Submission

There is still another variation on this general trope whereby images are made to refer secondarily to rulers. One might give an image as a token of submission, a metonymic acceptance of ritual subordination, in order to forestall an actual invasion and a more forcible incorporation. Our example here concerns the Rāṣṭrakūṭas and Sinhalese.

In the early part of the ninth century, the Rāṣṭrakūṭa king Govinda III (c. 790–815) undertook two southern expeditions, during which he decisively defeated the most potent southern kingdom, the Pallavas of Kanchipuram, and occupied their capital. Other kingdoms of the south came under direct threat from this powerful Indian empire, and the frightened Sri Lankan king Aggabodhi VIII ruling in Anurādhapuram did what he could to fend off a direct attack: he sent two images to Govinda. As a Rāṣṭrakūṭa inscription reports, "Just as if he [Govinda III] had forcibly subdued the self-centered [Lankan] king and his indolent chief minister with his own scepter and brought them deaf and dumb to the City of Delight, while staying in Kanchipuram Govinda received from Lanka two images of their lord (*prabhu*) and then set them up in a Śaiva temple here [in Mānyakheṭa, the Rāṣṭrakūṭa capital], like two pillars of his fame" (Bhandarkar 1925–1926: 246). The epigraphical simile makes it clear that these images were to be regarded as "deaf and dumb" representatives of a Sinhala polity that had, by this very gift, accepted the overlordship of the Rāṣṭrakūṭas. For Govinda III, more concerned with pillars of fame and ritual hegemony than the acquisition of territory, this was sufficient. The diplomatic offering of images did dissuade the Rāṣṭrakūṭas from invading the island, but only at the expense of incorporating Lanka metonymically into the Rāṣṭrakūṭa imperial formation.

What exactly were the images the Sinhalese king sent to Govinda? Various possibilities have been suggested: statues of the demon Rāvaṇa as "the most ancient and traditional ruler" of Lanka, or perhaps likenesses of the king and chief minister themselves (Bhandarkar 1925–1926: 241; Altekar 1934: 69). In light of the general rhetoric we have investigated here, it seems much more likely that Aggabodhi sent two images of the Buddha, as his own personal lord and the highest lord of the Sinhala polity. (Agghabodhi, we recall, celebrated his royal consecration by honoring the solid gold Buddha of the Jewel Pavilion.) It is possible too that the similitude of image and ruler had been drawn even more closely by casting the Buddha image according to the proportions of the king, a Sinhala practice of "reign-images" documented for the tenth century if not earlier (Wickremasinghe 1912: 213–29; Gunawardana 1979: 175). Even without this close visual resemblance, though, none of the agents involved would have mistaken the clear statement of Sinhala subordination in the two Buddha images displayed "like pillars of fame" in a Śaiva temple of the Rāṣṭrakūṭa capital.

Imperial Sovereignty: The Capture of Rivers

The appropriations and relocations of art objects we have looked at so far speak primarily of personalized relations of dominance and subordination among rulers and of the incorporation of particular kingdoms into other polities. However, there are other targets of appropriation that make more far-reaching assertions.[18] Consider the inscriptional claims of Vinayāditya, ruler of the Cālukyas of Vātāpi in the late seventh century.

The Cālukyas at this time were the dominant power of the Deccan, and had battled repeatedly with the Pallavas of Kanchipuram for control of southern India. Taking advantage of a period of dynastic confusion in north India following the death of Harṣa in 647, Vinayāditya and his son the crown prince Vijayāditya undertook a northern campaign in about 690, where they were successful against a series of unnamed foes. They returned to the Deccan with great spoils, including a series of significant symbolic objects: the *pāli* banner, the *ḍaḍhakka* drum, the "great sounds" (*mahāśabda*, probably conches), and the "Gaṅgā and Yamunā." Gaining these, inscriptions tell us, Vinayāditya possessed "all the insignia (*cihna*) of highest overlordship (*paramaiśvarya*), beginning with the powerful pāli banner, which he had acquired by defeating all the lords of the northern regions" (Pathak 1907–1908: 202). They were passed on to Vijayāditya (696–733) when he assumed the Cālukya throne, and he also came to possess "sovereignty illuminated by insignia such as the pāli banner that cause the manifestation of complete overlordship" (Pathak 1909–1910: 16). The Cālukya inscriptions portray this particular bundle of loot not merely as the regalia or second-order signifier of a single enemy ruler, but as the embodiment or representation of "universal sovereignty," imperial lordship of the highest order.

Evidently we are dealing here with some extraordinary imperial objects. The pāli banner (or literally, "flags in rows"), singled out in Cālukya inscriptions as the insignia par excellence, seems to have been a particular arrangement of banners, where a central flagstaff with the Cālukya insignia, Viṣṇu's Boar incarnation, on top was surrounded by rows of flags bearing insignia of all other dynasties in lower and peripheral position (Chidanandamurthy 1973: 85–88). It was thus, as Ronald Inden points out, an indexical sign of the Cālukya's claim to the highest degree of sovereignty, which encompassed and surpassed all other rulers of India (Inden 1990: 250–52).

The most curious and intriguing items in this set of transportable objects, however, are the two rivers Ganges and Yamuna. The Ganges may shift course gradually over the years, but how could the Cālukya king, ruling some eight hundred miles to the south of the river, claim to "take" Gaṅgā? What exactly did he appropriate? Gaṅgā and Yamunā are not just rivers, but also goddesses whose images often adorn the entrances of north Indian temples. Is that perhaps what Vinayāditya seized?

The Cālukyas, it turns out, were not the only southerners to obtain Gaṅgā and Yamunā. Within sixty years of Vinayāditya's northern expedition, the Rāṣṭrakūṭas had supplanted the Cālukyas as the dominant power of the Deccan and had acquired the authoritative pāli banner, replacing the Cālukyan Boar on top with their own insignia, Viṣṇu's mount Garuḍa. Around 800, the Rāṣṭrakūṭa king Govinda III also made an expedition into north India, directed against the Gurjāra and Pāla kings who were then battling for control of the Doab and the imperial city of Kanyakubja. He defeated the Gurjāra king Nāgabhaṭa II, then marched farther north, where the Pāla king Dharmapāla and his Kanyakubja protégé Cakrāyudha also deferred to the royal Rāṣṭrakūṭa progress. During this campaign, say the inscriptions, Govinda "took from his enemies the Gaṅgā and Yamunā, made beautiful by their waves, and acquired at the same moment that supreme lordship of which they are a visible sign" (Fleet 1883: 156–65). Once again epigraphs linked acquisition of the two northern rivers with the attainment of imperial sovereignty.

Two hundred years after that, when the Rāṣṭrakūṭas were no more and the Colas were the dominant power of peninsular India, the Cola emperor Rājendra I sent an army from Tamilnad north to capture the Ganges. Though well aware of the historical precedents for such an expedition, Rājendra instead chose to have himself compared with the mythical ascetic who had also altered the course of the Ganges. "Mocking the great sage Bhagīratha, who had brought the Ganges to earth through the power of his austerities," proclaims his inscription, "this light of the Solar lineage decided to purify his own domain with the Ganges waters, brought there by the strength of his arms" (Krishna Sastri 1920: 400). The Cola army made its way north, engaging and defeating a variety of opponents, until they finally reached the banks of the holy river. From there they had golden pots of Ganges water transported south, according to inscriptional accounts, atop the heads of kings defeated along the way (Krishnan 1984: 74).

A pattern is clear. Three major peninsular dynasties of the early medieval period, each in its time the most powerful kingdom in the subcontinent, mounted military forays into the Gangetic plain, won skirmishes with whatever powers they encountered there, and claimed to have brought back to their own domains Gaṅgā and Yamunā in some sort of visible substantive form.

Moreover, none of them made any attempt in these raids to capture or retain territory in the Gangetic plain. Rāṣṭrakūṭa accounts admit this quite explicitly: "In battles Govinda seized the noble, unshakable fame of the kings Nāgabhaṭa and Candragupta, and then—holding the acquisition of fame as his highest aim—he plucked out the remaining kings, now deprived of support, from their own lands as if he were picking grains of rice, and replanted them again in their very own places" (Bhandarkar 1925–1926: 245). The seemingly nonacquisitive character of the expeditions perplexed earlier dynastic historians, who generally dismissed them as inconsequential, quixotic, and purposeless. The rulers themselves clearly did not regard their campaigns as inconsequential, however, for they repeatedly proclaimed them in inscriptions. First of all, the "plucking and replanting" maneuver incorporated the subjugated opponents into the imperial system, even while leaving them in place. Further, the raids were concerned predominantly with, in Rāṣṭrakūṭa terms, the "acquisition of fame"—and fame that could be objectified in the capture of particular symbolic objects. The peninsular powers regarded these objects as necessary to "manifest" or "make visible" their claims to supreme sovereignty. In one inscription, Govinda III claimed to have seized the insignia of virtually every notable dynasty in the subcontinent:

> The fish from the ruler of the Pāṇḍyan country, the bull from the Pallava king, the tiger from the Colas, the elephant from the Gaṅgas, the bow from the Keralas, the boar from the Andhras, Cālukyas, and Mauryas, the board bearing the doorkeeper from the Gurjāra king, the names of the Kosala and Avanti kings and also the Sinhala, and the famed goddess Tārā from Dharmapāla, king of Bengal—all these and still other insignia the preeminent King Govinda, whose own mark is Garuda, seized from the other rulers of the earth, and hence commanded the entire world.[19]

In medieval India, appropriating these signs of imperial sovereignty was a crucial part of constructing what Ronald Inden calls an "imperial formation."

An imperial formation in medieval India, as Inden describes it, was not a single state under centralized administrative control, nor was it a congeries of petty states warring against one another. Rather, it was a single complex polity ruled by a king of kings who exercised his sovereignty, directly or ritually, over other would-be claimants throughout the subcontinent (Inden 1990: 29–33, 213–17). In the "scale of kingships" (or "circle of kings," as Indian treatises on statecraft call it), other kings would be compelled to recognize the imperial sovereign as preeminent, for instance, by rendering ceremonial homage at his court or through the forced attendance of an iconic stand-in at the imperial capital. They became, willingly or not, subordinate sharers in the transcending sovereignty of the king of kings who managed to create or maintain an imperial formation. Of course, subordinated rulers could always contest the ruling hegemony, by claiming autonomy and seeking to construct their own "circle," but always with the risk that the empire might strike back. Given the considerable strategic problems in holding together such a polity, only a few dynasties succeeded in constituting longstanding imperial formations in early medieval India, and the Rāṣṭrakūṭas of the eighth through tenth centuries and the Colas of the eleventh and twelfth centuries were the most formidable exemplars.

What did the rivers Ganges and Yamuna have to do with all this? Prior to the time of the Cālukya ruler Vinayāditya, every major imperial kingdom of India had been centered on the Ganges-Yamuna river system. The Magadha and Maurya empires had ruled from Pāṭaliputra, and the imperial Kuṣāṇas had maintained a capital at Mathurā. The Guptas originated at Prayāga, the very confluence of Ganges and Yamuna, and ruled from either there or Pāṭaliputra. From the time of Candragupta II, imperial Guptas prominently featured statuary of Gaṅgā and Yamunā in shrines throughout their domain, evoking their own political center even as they invoked the presence of the two goddesses (Goyal 1967; Williams 1982: 45–46).[20] More recently, Harṣa had moved his capital from the relatively peripheral Sthāneśvara, along the upper reaches of the Yamuna, to the more central Kanyakubja when he had attained imperial status.

Faced with this political Gangocentricity, a regional power aspiring to more encompassing imperial sovereignty had a choice of moving to the center, as Harṣa had, or of attempting to relocate the center at one's own capital. The Cālukyas, Rāṣṭrakūṭas, and Colas evidently chose the second option. In their own version of Muḥammad and the mountain, they brought not only the mountain—in the form of the Mount Kailāsa-style temples of Śiva they each constructed—but also the river that issued from that mountain to their own sovereign selves. In the process they sought to remake the imperial topography of the subcontinent (Inden 1990: 256–62).

In what form did they effect this? In the case of the Colas, inscriptions state explicitly that Rājendra had Ganges water transported in pots. With the Cālukyas and Rāṣṭrakūṭas, the evidence is not so clear. Gaṅgā and Yamunā are simply mentioned in lists of insignia, along with other items of regalia such as banners and musical instruments, indicating only that they are material things of some sort. A Rāṣṭrakūṭa inscription does tell us that Gaṅgā and Yamunā are "made beautiful by their waves," which describes the rivers themselves, of course, but would also apply to banners waving in the breeze or to graceful sculpted images. Scholars have offered at least three hypotheses: the Cālukyas and Rāṣṭrakūṭas seized images of the goddesses Gaṅgā and Yamunā, banners with Gaṅgā and Yamunā imprinted, or pots containing water from the two rivers. All are plausible. In light of the recurrent appropriation of images to make political statements during the medieval period, however, I consider it most likely that the Deccan powers looted images of Gaṅgā and Yamunā from existing temples at Prayāga or Kanyakubja.

Even if they were not themselves images, though, the appropriation of Gaṅgā and Yamunā had an important bearing on the art of their new homes. Both Cālukyas and Rāṣṭrakūṭas appear to have commemorated their acquisitions by constructing shrines with Gaṅgā and Yamunā prominently featured. At Lād Khān temple in Aihole, probably built during the reign of the Cālukya king Vijayāditya, images of the two river goddesses stand on the outer columns of the porch, displayed like trophies. Further, Gaṅgā and Yamunā appear as important icons in Cālukyan art only from this time on. It is not a matter of a slowly permeating northern iconographic figure finally reaching the Deccan; rather it appears that the Cālukyas only now felt they had attained the degree of sovereignty such that they could display with confidence (and without fear of retribution) the north Indian river goddesses.[21] As for the Rāṣṭrakūṭas, Govinda III was probably responsible for construction of the shrine of the Three River Goddesses at Ellora, an adjunct to the great Kailāsa rock-cut temple built there by his predecessor Kṛṣṇa I (Goetz 1974: 91–107). Three large panels on the rear wall depict Gaṅgā at the center flanked by Yamunā and Sarasvatī, the subtle river that joins the other two at Prayāga. And after the Rāṣṭrakūṭa exploits in the Doab, they began to include Gaṅgā and Yamunā on their imperial seals, just as the Cālukyas had.

The most dramatic commemoration of Gaṅgā capture, however, was that of Rājendra. When the waters reached the Cola territories, Rājendra had a "liquid pillar of victory" made of Ganges water, designated the "Cola-Gaṅgā," constructed in the new capital he had just built Gangaikondacolapuram, the "city of the Cola king who took Gaṅgā." Presiding over the city was a new Kailāsa-like imperial Śiva temple (Figure 12). Rājendra furnished the city and the temple with objects and images he had appropriated in the course of his conquests: from the Cālukyas a Sun pedestal, several images of Durgā, and a Gaṇeśa image; from the Eastern Cālukyas a resting Nandi, Śiva's bull mount; from the Kaliṅgas of Orissa three large stone images of Bhairava and Bhairavī and an awesome eight-armed Kālī image; from the Pālas of Bengal a bronze image of Śiva dancing on Nandi's back; and undoubtedly many more since removed by later plunderers.[22] At the four entry gates of the fortified city he located images of the powerful goddess Durgā or Kālī to act as guardians of the community within. One of the guardians, at least, was a Cālukyan conscript: a dramatic stone image of eight-armed Durgā defeating the Buffalo demon, her left foot firmly planted on the chest of the demon, who is on his knees and fading fast (Figure 13). Though the pāli banner itself was no longer a target of imperial aspiration, the new capital Rājendra built was a sort of city-scale pāli banner, with the tower of the Śiva temple looming over the rows of loot, insignia of the kings he had subordinated.

The Homology of the Captured Door Guardian

Let us now return to the case of Rājendra's son Rājādhirāja and his appropriation of the Cālukya door guardian. This action should be seen as part of this more general phenomenon of wartime looting in medieval India. For medieval rulers, as far as the historical evidence allows us to see it, such plundering was moral, orderly, and one of the primary objectives of war. Moreover, Hindu rulers of the medieval period appropriated and relocated select religious images, it appears, with attention to their mythical identities, as part of a political discourse. Within this discourse, I would argue, the key to Rājādhirāja's choice of a door guardian as a special trophy from the Cālukyan capital was a past event that was certainly well known to him, the Rāṣṭrakūṭas' famous "golden womb" (*hiraṇyagarbha*) ceremony at Ujjain.

FIG. 12. Rājendra's Great Temple at Gangaikondacolapuram. Constructed by Rājendra I, Cola ruler, in c. 1030 C.E.

Capture and Display

According to Rāṣṭrakūṭa accounts, the first great emperor of that dynasty, Dantidurga, commenced in the mid-eighth century a "conquest of the directions" (*digvijaya*) that vastly extended the Rāṣṭrakūṭa domain and soon brought him into conflict with the Gurjāra-Pratihāra king ruling over the Malwa region. Dantidurga defeated the Gurjāras in battle, occupied their

FIG. 13. Durgā Slaying the Buffalo Demon, Gangaikondacolapuram. Stone sculpture fabricated during Cālukya period, early eleventh century, in Karnataka. Removed to Gangaikondacolapuram to serve as city guardian in eleventh century. Photograph courtesy of the Institut Français d'Indologie, Pondicherry.

capital, and there performed a royal gift-giving ritual, the golden womb ceremony. Rāṣṭrakūṭa inscriptions tell us, "When Dantidurga directed warriors to perform the golden womb ceremony in Ujjain, he made the Gurjāra ruler and other kings serve as his doorkeepers (*pratihāra*)."[23] Clearly the Rāṣṭrakūṭa king was enacting a powerful ritual statement of political subordination here, forcing his defeated opponent Nāgabhaṭa I to act in a lowly capacity in this royal ceremony, and in his own capital to boot.

Dantidurga's digvijaya was the first of a series of acts that established and maintained the Rāṣṭrakūṭas as the preeminent dynasty of India in the ninth and tenth centuries. In the course of his campaigns, Dantidurga also overcame the Cālukyas of Vātāpi, the dominant Deccani power of the time, and thereby attained "supreme overlordship" (*parameśvaratā*) of the subcontinent. Govinda III continued the process in the early ninth century when he defeated a renewed Pratihāra force in north India and claimed to have appropriated the two central rivers of India, the Ganges and Yamuna.

The Cola kings of the eleventh century were acutely aware of the Rāṣṭrakūṭas. For one thing, the Rāṣṭrakūṭas had in the mid-tenth century dealt the Colas a humiliating defeat at the battle of Takkolam, and had occupied Cola territory for several decades thereafter. More important, the Colas aspired to supplant the Rāṣṭrakūṭas as the major imperial power of the subcontinent, and under the kings Rājarāja I (985–1016) and Rājendra I (1012–1044), who both carried out successful digvijayas, they largely accomplished this. Rājarāja extended the Cola dominion into the former Rāṣṭrakūṭa territories, and Rājendra replicated Govinda III's celebrated appropriation of Gaṅga and Yamunā by mounting his own symbolic raid upon the Ganges.

Rājādhirāja looked back to Rāṣṭrakūṭa precedents in his political rhetoric, just as his father had. His appropriation of a door guardian from the later Cālukyas reenacted Dantidurga's treatment of the Gurjāra king during the golden womb ceremony, in a less personal and less compelling but more permanent manner. Mimicking the earlier conqueror of the Cālukyas, Rājādhirāja also performed a royal ritual in the capital of the defeated king, in this case a "heroic consecration." Unable to force his rival to take on the role of ceremonial doorkeeper in person, since Someśvara had successfully fled, Rājādhirāja contented himself by seizing a door-guardian image from the enemy capital and transporting it to the Cola country.[24]

The parallelism of captured door guardian and Cālukya king was clear. Just as the door guardian was unable to prevent the forcible entry and destruction of its temple, Someśvara had been unable to prevent the Cola armies from entering and destroying his capital. Both had failed in their primary responsibility. Waiting in attendance at the Cola court in Gangaikondacolapuram, the looted door guardian could serve as a permanent visible homologue of the subjugated Cālukya ruler.

Appropriation and Vengeance

Royal homologies are not necessarily accepted as political realities by all parties involved, of course. Hyperbole is one of the primary tropes of this rhetoric. While the Cālukya door guardian stood in the Cola capital, a taunting reminder of Someśvara's shameful flight, Someśvara himself acted as if his sovereignty was quite intact, judging from the inscriptions issued during this period in Karnataka.[25] But the political rhetoric of appropriated objects in medieval India did not consist simply of benign figures of speech, either. It was often highly consequential for the subsequent course of political events. The capture of regalia, for instance, could act as a powerful motivating force on the battlefield. In the Sinhalese chronicles, Dhammakitti tells how the Sinhala king Saṅghatissa once, in battle with the rebel Moggallāna, dropped the royal umbrella when his elephant brushed up against a shade tree. Alert rebel troops immediately snatched the insignia and took it to their leader, who raised it high. Saṅghatissa's troops, we are told, thereupon abandoned their king and flocked to Moggallāna, considering that he must now be their lord. All Saṅghatissa could do was to flee to the forest along with his son and one faithful minister (*CV* 44.18–20).

Similarly, looted images could serve as potent reminders of past humiliations and as the basis for renewed struggle, as we have seen in the case of the Golden Buddha. There is no explicit evidence to show that the missing door guardian acted in an equally powerful way on the sensibility of the Cālukya ruler Someśvara. However, his engagement with the Colas did not end with the burning of Kalyāṇī, and Rājādhirāja's appropriation of the door guardian appears as the opening gambit in a new phase of Cola-Cālukya wars. The detailing surrounding the door guardian even offers an ironic and seemingly prescient commentary on the cat-and-mouse dynastic conflicts to follow. As Sivaramamurti describes it, "a snake swallows just a rat and a cat close by pounces on another rat while a huge loathsome lizard appears on the club" (1964: 20). We no longer possess the code to translate fully the artist's zoological allegory, but it certainly evokes the *matsyanyāya* (anarchy, lit. "rule of the fishes") of the eleventh-century Deccan.

Not satisfied with a stand-in for the Cālukya king, Rājādhirāja made a second foray into Karnataka around 1054, pillaging the countryside as he went. Someśvara could not let this offensive go unchallenged. The Cola inscriptions relate, "When the proud and impetuous king Someśvara received word that the Cola king had reached the Raṭṭa domain (that is, the former Rāṣṭrakūṭa core territories) and was pulverizing rivers, counties, and towns, he jumped up, eyes wide open and burning with anger, and exclaimed, 'This is a disgrace to me!' He went to Koppam . . . and began attacking his enemies" (Hultzsch 1899: 58–64). In the ensuing battle, Someśvara managed to avenge his earlier defeat by killing Rājādhirāja. But immediately Rājādhirāja's younger brother Rājendra II stepped to the fore and took command of the Cola forces. Leading a renewed attack, he routed the Cālukya army, "turning it into raw corpses that covered the earth," until Someśvara had once again to retreat. The Cola inscriptions describe the flight mockingly: "Trembling violently, his hair untied, turning his back, looking behind him, Someśvara went running away on foot, and had to plunge into the western ocean."

This time it was Rājendra II who performed the battlefield expropriations. "Then he captured what Someśvara had left on the battlefield: herds of royal-born elephants like Catturupayaṅkaraṉ, Karapattiraṉ, and Mulapattiraṉ, horses, herds of camels, the royal insignias beginning with the all-conquering boar banner, a harem of queens led by the matchless Cattiyavai and Caṅkappai, a throng of other women, and all the rest. As drums sounded on the field of battle, Rājendra performed the 'victorious consecration' (*vijayābhiṣeka*)." In what appears to have been an innovation in royal ceremonial, Rājendra had himself crowned Cola king right on the battlefield, his battle wounds still fresh (Hultzsch 1899: 111–13; Nilakanta Sastri 1955: 257).

Now it was Someśvara who set out for revenge. Marching into the Veṅgi territory, he met the Cola forces—under the command of the third son of Rājendra I, Vīrarājendra—at the confluence of the Tungabhadra and Krishna rivers, Kuṭalsaṅgamam. This is the battle mentioned earlier, at which Vīrarājendra succeeded in driving Someśvara from the field, donned the garland of victory, and appropriated another long list of booty from the defeated Cālukyas.

Humiliated three times by three different sons of the great Cola emperor Rājendra I, Someśvara became ever more ashamed. Reflecting (according to the Cola eulogists) that "It would be better to die than to live with this disgrace," he sent a message from his exile to Vīrarājendra, challenging him to a grudge match on the same field of Kuṭalsaṅgamam. Vīrarājendra, greatly pleased by this invitation, proceeded forthwith to the appointed spot. Someśvara, however, failed to show up. Vīrarājendra dutifully waited on the field for a month, but his opponent never arrived. The details are not clear, but it appears Someśvara around this time was suffering from an inflammatory fever, and finally committed ritual suicide by drowning himself in the Tungabhadra River, the "Ganges of the Deccan" (*Vikramāṅkadevacarita* 4.44–68). Vīrarājendra meanwhile amused himself with some symbolic humiliation of his absent foe. "[The king] had an effigy (*pirattan*) made to represent the Cālukya king, tied the beautiful necklace [*sundarakaṇṭhikā*, a royal insignia of the Cālukyas] onto it, and wrote clearly and fully on a board how Someśvara had escaped the trunk of a haltered elephant and had run away in full knowledge of all people."[26] Then he tied the board onto the effigy, and affixed to it also a closed quiver of arrows, to represent Someśvara's powerlessness to prevent these Cola depredations.

Through all this, the Cālukya door guardian remained captive in Gangaikondacolapuram, icon of the continued subordination of the Cālukyas and the inability of Someśvara to do anything about it. One wonders if it too was subjected to some of the same derisive treatment Vīrarājendra meted out to Someśvara's effigy at Kuṭalsaṅgamam. In any event, when Rājarāja II (1146–1172) constructed a new imperial Cola capital at Darasuram in the mid-twelfth century, he had the Cālukya door guardian transported there.[27] Evidently it still served as a potent trophy for the great victories the Cola princes had won over the Cālukyas of Kalyāṇī in the previous century.

Destruction and Devotion

Of all modes of expropriation, certainly the most radical involves the destruction of images. Here it is not just a matter of change in proprietor, but a radical transformation in form. The image is reduced to its material elements, denying or extinguishing any divine presence that may have inhabited it, and risking in the process the possibility of divine retribution. Instead of continuing to exist as a second-order signifier, the object is at one moment deconstituted in an act that is indeed powerful in rhetorical impact but limited in duration.

There is no question that medieval Hindu armies frequently destroyed religious edifices, as part of more general rampages and the Colas seem to have been particularly fearsome warriors. When the Cola armies led by Rājarāja I campaigned in the area around modern Bijapur in northern Karnataka in 1007, for instance, a contemporary inscription speaks of them "ravaging the whole country, perpetuating murders of women, children, and brahmins, seizing women, and overthrowing the order of caste" (Barnett 1921–1922: 74–75). And when Rājendra I invaded Sri Lanka ten years later, the Cola forces proved equally devastating. The Ceylonese chronicles describe it:

> As soon as it reached shore, the Cola army began to harass the inhabitants as it advanced toward Rohaṇa. During the rainy season of King Mahinda V, the Colas seized the chief queen, the jewels, the crown passed down through succession, all the royal ornaments, the priceless diamond bracelet given by the gods, the unbreakable sword, and the torn cloth relic. Though the king had fled in fear to the forest, they captured him alive as well through the pretense of a treaty meeting. Then they quickly sent the king and all the booty that had come into their hands back to the Cola ruler. Throughout Lanka, among all three assemblies, the Cola army forcibly broke into the relic cham-

> bers and all the monasteries around, and seized many valuable images made of gold and other precious materials, like blood-sucking ogres, seizing the very essence of Lanka. (*CV* 55.15–21)

However, Hindu narratives and inscriptions do not often describe destruction of images as a directed, politically meaningful act. When they do, they most often treat it as an extraordinary action, something morally ambiguous that may be justified only in extreme situations.

The south Indian Vaiṣṇava poet-saint Tirumaṅkai Āḻvār was celebrated for his great devotional zeal toward the god Viṣṇu. According to the *Divyasūricarita*, the thirteenth-century collection of āḻvār hagiographies, Lord Viṣṇu Raṅganātha himself commissioned Tirumaṅkai to rebuild and enlarge his temple at Sri Rangam, and the saint undertook the project with his usual assiduity. He supported the costs of restoration through highway robbery. When his workmen demanded their wages he had them thrown into the Kaveri River and told their distraught relatives that the laborers would be happier at the feet of Raṅganātha than they had been on earth. Finally, needing gold for gilding the shrine, Tirumaṅkai went to the port city of Nagapattinam, stole a large gold image of the Buddha from the stūpa there, and had it melted down for reuse in Viṣṇu's temple. The Buddhists brought him to trial before the Cola king, but Tirumaṅkai's plea of devotional fervor proved effective and the king honored him instead of imprisoning him (Bharati 1968: 69–73).

One of the primary themes in Tirumaṅkai's own poetry was *maṭal*: erotic passion or devotional longing leading a person beyond all conventional moral constraints (F. Hardy 1983: 371–402). Likewise, the later biographical account of Tirumaṅkai explored the extremities of conduct to which bhakti might lead, and used the destruction of a Buddhist image as a dramatic illustration of the devotional antinomianism it endorsed.

Another example of intentional destruction is the muddled raid of the Gauḍa soldiers described by Kalhaṇa in his *Rājataraṅginī*.[28] The great eighth-century Kashmiri ruler Lalitāditya, according to Kalhaṇa's reckoning, was for the most part a high-minded monarch, but he was also capable of duplicity in the service of imperial policy. Once, after making a promise of safe conduct to the king of Gauḍa (Bengal), and offering as surety (*madhyastha*, lit. "intermediary") on his pledge the image of Viṣṇu Parihāsakeśava, Lalitāditya treacherously ordered the ruler assassinated. Such a brazen act clearly departed from all standards of proper royal conduct, and called for revenge. As we might expect by now, the reprisal was directed not at the perpetrator of the deed but at its intermediary. A troop of the murdered king's dedicated attendants snuck into Kashmir, posing as pilgrims, and made their way toward the temple of Parihāsakeśava.

Now, Parihāsakeśava was not just any image. After Lalitāditya's successful conquest of the directions in the mid-eighth century, making him the premier ruler of north India, he returned to Kashmir and established a new capital at the confluence of the Vitasta and Sindhu rivers, Parihāsapura. In and around the new capital, Lalitāditya and his retinue established a number of shrines, but the dominant one was a *sarvatobhadra* ("auspicious in every direction") temple dedicated to Viṣṇu Parihāsakeśava (Inden 1985). A four-doored sarvatobhadra temple was considered the highest form of temple structure, and the immense silver Parihāsakeśava who stood at its center was an image of Viṣṇu Vaikuṇṭha, the cosmic overlord whose four visages facing in the cardinal directions represented Viṣṇu's four primary emanations. This was the principal ruling image of the empire Lalitāditya had established, and to attack it was to threaten the very center of that polity.

Outside the temple the Gauḍa soldiers mustered, preparing to destroy the imperial image. Fortunately for Lalitāditya, however, the priests of Parihāsakeśava were a vigilant lot, and the Gauḍa image raiders were not well acquainted with the fine points of Kashmiri images. "Though the king was abroad," Kalhaṇa relates, "the priests observed that the soldiers wanted to enter, and they closed the gates of the Parihāsakeśava shrine. Aroused with boldness, the soldiers got hold of the silver Rāmasvāmin image, which they mistook for Parihāsakeśava. They carried it out and ground it into dust. And even as Lalitāditya's troops who had come out from the city were killing them at each step, the Gauḍas continued to break it into particles and scatter them in every direction" (*RT* 4.326–28). Lalitāditya had excavated the image of Rāmasvāmin, silver like Parihāsakeśava, some years earlier in a remote part of Kashmir (*RT* 4.265–76). The king had it brought to the capital, and a small stone shrine was built for it near the Parihāsakeśava temple. Though supposed to be an ancient image (Lalitāditya claimed it had been established by Rāma himself), it certainly did not possess the imperial grandeur of Parihāsakeśava. As clearly indicated by the shrine housing it, Rāmasvāmin occupied a position subordinate to the imperial image of Viṣṇu within the hierarchy of Kashmiri divinities.

By this token, then, the raid of the Gauḍa avengers was a botched affair. They failed to destroy Lalitāditya's central ruling image, the image that had stood as deceitful assurance of their own king's security, and they mistakenly crushed a lesser icon. But this is not the moral Kalhaṇa draws from the incident. Rather, he chooses to praise the extraordinary devotion the raiders showed to their former lord. "The showers of their blood illuminated their uncommon devotion (*bhakti*) to their lord, and the earth itself was enriched. . . . What a lengthy path they traveled! And what devotion they showed to their deceased ruler! The Creator himself could not accomplish what the Gauḍa soldiers achieved that day" (*RT* 4.330–32). Utter devotional commitment to a lord (whether divine or human) may in certain circumstances transcend normal moral evaluation. Where the provocation is great, devotion may transmute normally immoral acts into exemplary ones. The Gauḍa raiders, however, were not the only ones to demonstrate loyalty to their superior. "When those Gauḍa demons (*rākṣasas*) brought destruction," Kalhaṇa concludes, "the holy Parihāsakeśava, the king's favored image, was protected through the sacrifice of Rāmasvāmin" (*RT* 4.334). Images too are capable of bhakti toward their lords.

Modern Forms of Appropriation and Defense

The "past" does not exist as such. Rather, it exists only as it is incarnated and reincarnated in memories, texts, objects, and our ongoing collective activity of reconstruction. Nor is the past that is embodied in an object a fixed quality. It comes to be transformed as its audience and the circumstances in which it is encountered are themselves transformed. The historical significance of an object may itself be reconstituted historically.

The location of the Cālukya door guardian as stylistic intruder among Cola images and Rājādhirāja's epigraphical labeling of it have led us to recover a series of events by which the image was removed from its original site and made to serve new ends, to act as a new signifier in a politicized rhetoric. By this medieval act of appropriation, Rājādhirāja turned the statue's previous occupation as temple sentinel against it, pointing ironically to its failure of duty and alluding to Someśvara's parallel failure to protect his own capital. By the same act, Rājādhirāja linked the door guardian through historical allusion to a well-known action of the great Rāṣṭrakūṭa king Dantidurga, and used it to reinforce the Cola claim of supreme overlordship in the subcontinent. We saw this as one case of a more general political rhetoric involving religious images, regalia, and other marked objects practiced by medieval Indian rulers.

However, this supervening value through appropriation no more constitutes the essential significance of the Cālukya door guardian than does that of the sculptor's (or priest's, or patron's) originating intentionality. Rājādhirāja's employment of his captured trophy for rhetorical ends does not finally fix the identity of the image, for the frames of reference in which such identities are formulated are always susceptible to change. If we follow the subsequent fortunes of the Cālukya door guardian, we find that its circumstances shifted dramatically again in the second half of the twentieth century. It resided within a new political formation, the secular Republic of India, and it came to be threatened by a new form of appropriation more far-reaching than any Rājādhirāja could have foreseen: market commoditization and export abroad.

In the twentieth century, objects from non-Western cultures have come increasingly to be incorporated and valued within the Western category of "art." (I will discuss this "taxonomic shift" more fully in Chapter Five.) Medieval Indian temple images and African masks could take their places in museums and homes of the wealthy alongside the more familiar artworks of the West. In this new context Indian images have frequently been appropriated not as tokens of military conquest, but as signs of Western economic dominance. The market for such objects is voracious; one UNESCO report estimated that 50,000 art objects were smuggled out of India over a ten-year period (Greenfield 1989: 239–40).

Modern Indians have not been unaware of this new manner of expropriation, nor have they been passive in the face of it. T. K. Palaniappan, the Collector of Thanjavur District in the early 1950s, spoke eloquently of how "disturbed and neglected" objects themselves entreated him to protect them from nefarious peddlers in art wares:

> Even a civil servant like myself, who is lost in the daily routine of humdrum life and finds very little time for other interests or activities much less for fine art, could not escape being attracted by these disturbed and neglected pieces of art and could not resist their mute entreaties for better treatment and for being given an opportunity to entertain the art lover and to serve the people of Independent India. I was distressed to hear that several pedlars in artware were and still are, by all methods which human ingenuity could devise, acquiring and selling valuable pieces of bronze and even stone for fabulous prices to the rich to adorn their drawing halls. It is sad to reflect that much mischief had already been done and several valuable pieces had been spirited away not only to the bigger cities in this land but also to lands beyond the sea.[29]

Patriotic Indians like Palaniappan have refigured these former religious objects not simply as "art," but further as part of the collective cultural patrimony of the Indian peoples.

Just as the Cola seizure of significant ruling objects had once threatened the integrity of the Cālukya polity, so now the expropriation of this national heritage of art objects posed a new menace. There was a pressing need to save its inherited corpus of images from exportation. As Palaniappan put it, "These will be lost to the nation, if they are not collected and preserved for the benefit of the public and art lovers" (129). To prevent any further "mischief" to vulnerable objects in his district, Palaniappan appropriated and refurbished the disused royal palace of the former Thanjavur rulers (long ago displaced by the British) to serve as a museum. He relocated loose images like the Cālukya door-guardian, then standing unguarded at Darasuram, and treasure-trove finds like the bronzes of Śiva Vṛṣabhavāhana and his cohorts from Tiruvengadu, in this new secular institution where they would be protected from further depredation.

So the impressive Cālukya door guardian stands now in the Rajaraja Museum after its several displacements. Long ago freed from religious responsibilities in its Cālukya temple, and now standing together with an array of Cola bronzes—no longer its dynastic enemies—the image can "entertain the art lover" and "serve the people of Independent India" as a particularly impressive work of medieval Deccani stone sculpture. More than this, it can also act as the starting point for our reflections on the transformations history may bring to its objects. In this new capacity the Cālukya door guardian, though stylistically an intruder in a Cola domain, appears very much at home.

3.

Images Overthrown

At THE ONSET of the eleventh century Maḥmūd, the Turkic ruler of Ghazna in present-day Afghanistan, launched a series of military campaigns into the Indian subcontinent. He conquered and incorporated the fertile Punjab into the Ghaznavid state and made Lahore his provincial capital. Then he mounted raids eastward into the Gangetic plain as far as Kanyakubja, and later southward into Gujarat. Maḥmūd was an observant Sunnī Muslim and the Ghaznavid polity was an Islamic state. Though this was not the first encounter of an Islamic ruler with India, the campaigns of Maḥmūd in many ways set the stage for later Turkic and Central Asian Muslim warriors who would seek to establish new regimes in South Asia.

At that time, the worship of temple images, believed to be animated by powerful immanent divinities, was the central public religious cult of India. Indeed, the Indian landscape that confronted the Ghaznavids was covered with myriad temples, each filled with what must have seemed an astonishing and bewildering host of divine images. For Muslims, who worshiped a god they considered unique, absolute, transcendent, and exclusive, these Hindu practices appeared as "idolatry" and "polytheism" (*shirk*), anathema to the True Faith. Moreover, as Muslim warriors correctly surmised, the Indian temple cult was closely tied to the political order, with kings and ruling groups sponsoring and participating ostentatiously in the building and grand festivities of royal temples and images. So it was important for Muslim conquerors not only to denounce Hindu images for theological reasons, but also to act against them as a statement of conquest. Muslim chronicles of the medieval period repeatedly portray the destruction of politically significant images and temples, coupled with the establishment of mosques, as a conversion, a transformation of the land of the heathens into the land of Islam.

Confronted by these acts of conquest against religious images associated with the existing political order, it was equally important for Indian elites to reassert the longevity and miraculous capacities of images apparently destroyed. As physical instantiations of the Highest God or Goddess, temple images were manifestations of an Absolute that was by theological definition eternal and all-powerful. Any public demonstration by Muslim conquerors of the seeming inability of divinity to resist human attack required a rejoinder, a reassertion of the power of images. Throughout this period, Hindu chieftains and rulers repeatedly reconsecrated important Hindu temples as statements of political autonomy. So it was that certain divine images and the temples housing them took on enhanced political roles in late medieval India. Images often became crucial indices of political control among the contending warrior elites affiliated with Muslim and Hindu forms of religiosity.

Not surprisingly, both cultures developed narratives around the disputes over the status and power of religious icons. In this chapter and the next I examine these stories of Islamic iconoclasm and Hindu recovery. This chapter focuses primarily on the conquest of the Śiva Somanātha temple in Gujarat by the Ghaznavid ruler Maḥmūd in 1026 and on the Indo-Muslim literature that grew up around this event. The next chapter will explore the narratives of Viṣṇu Raṅganātha at Sri Rangam in Tamilnad, particularly the traditions concerning the displacements and restorations of its images during the fourteenth-century invasions of southern India by the Delhi Sultanate.[1]

Medieval Epic and Counter-epic

The new social and political situation of late medieval India brought about by the entry into the subcontinent of new warrior elites affiliated with Islam was reflected in new literary productions. In his ground-breaking 1963 essay, Aziz Ahmad identified two paired genres characteristic of the late medieval period: Islamic "epics of conquest," written mainly in Persian and addressed to a Muslim audience, and Hindu "epics of resistance," composed in Hindi and other Indian vernaculars and speaking primarily to a Hindu audience.

Indo-Muslim epics of conquest, Ahmad observes, grew out of the panegyrics written in the Ghaznavid court during the eleventh century, which celebrated the Indian campaigns of Maḥmūd. The genre later developed in the works of Amīr Khusraw Dihlawī and Fakhr al-Dīn ʿIṣāmī, and continued up through the time of Muḥammad Jan Qudsi, who composed his epic of conquest during the reign of Shāh Jahān in the seventeenth century. These works stress the destiny of Turkish warriors to subjugate India, celebrate their victories over Hindu opponents, and glorify the India that was brought into being through Islamic rule. In his *ʿAshīka*, Amīr Khusraw proclaims, "Happy Hindustan, the splendour of Religion, where the (Muslim holy) Law finds perfect honour and security. . . . The strong men of Hind have been trodden under foot and are ready to pay tribute. Islam is triumphant and idolatry is subdued."[2] Yet as Ahmad indicates, these literary works are not simply martial panegyrics. They often interweave elements of romantic court epic (*bazmiya*) within the fabric of the war epic (*razmiya*). Most common is the theme of romance across religious boundary. The Muslim hero falls in love with a Hindu princess, "asserting the conqueror's right not only to love but to be loved" (471). The Indo-Muslim epic of conquest concerns itself with military victory, but also with social acceptance in the new homeland.

Hindu epics of resistance, says Ahmad, focus on the chivalry and heroism of Rajput warriors in their defiant and most often doomed struggles to resist Turkish dominion. These epics center around historical figures like Pṛthvīrāja, the Cāhamāna ruler of the late twelfth century who fought the Ghorids, and Rājā Hammir Dev, the king of Ranthambor who bravely resisted ʿAlā al-Din Khaljī's attacks in the late thirteenth century. Yet they also embellish the historical deeds of these individual heroes with "an accumulated arena of heroic resistance spreading over several centuries" (473). Like the Indo-Muslim epics, these Hindu counterepics celebrate battlefield heroics, and they also explore the problematics of cultural boundaries in a society composed of competing elites through the metonymn of sexual crossing. Here the Hindu women are often called upon to display their own powers of resistance in rejecting the Other. Rather than give in to the demands of Muslim suitors, Rajput heroines bravely enter the fire of martyrdom to preserve their unalloyed purity.

Ahmad portrays the paired epic types as growing out of "two mutually exclusive religious, cultural and historical attitudes, . . . confronting the other in aggressive hostility." In many respects, though, they are quite similar. Most of the authors of both genres write as court literati addressing ruling patrons; most give retrospective accounts that celebrate the acts of past heroes and urge their own patrons to follow these illustrious predecessors. Both types of epic praise vigorous royal action to uphold conservative, religiously based values and social orders. Although Ahmad characterizes the two epic genres as literary growths that developed largely in ignorance of one another, the framework of conflictual events upon which they center and the language of symbolic action they describe were certainly shared.

Together, these two bodies of literature conduct a vigorous debate over the status and power of Hindu religious images and temples. As the Hindu cult of divine images and the proliferation of temples posed a challenge for Turkish warriors adopting an Islamic frame of values, Muslim epics of conquest portray their destruction as a necessary feature and symbol of conquest. Ahmad quotes Amīr Khusraw's comment on the Khaljī conquest of the Deccan as an example of the "irrepressible bravado of iconoclasm": "There were many capitals of the *devs* (meaning Hindu gods *or* demons) where Satanism had prospered from the earliest times, and where far from the pale of Islam, the Devil in the course of ages had hatched his eggs and made his worship compulsory on the followers of the idols; but now with a sincere motive the Emperor removed these symbols of infidelity . . . to dispel the contamination of false belief from those places through the muezzin's call and the establishment of prayers."[3] Islamic epics depict the destruction of idols and the replacement of temples with mosques as unmistakable signs of purification, as a primary symbolic representation of the conversion of Indian lands into the world of Islam.

Hindu epics of resistance and other literary works of the period not only describe the heroic defense of temples, but also the recovery and reappearance of images. Hindu images are not passive victims in this literature. With foresight of impending invasions, divine images go into exile. They move to less vulnerable temples. They hide in forests or in underground beds and await their chance to return. Sometimes images thought to have been destroyed miraculously reincarnate themselves and are rediscovered by cows or in the dreams of holy men. When danger has passed they ceremoniously emerge from retreat and reenter their temples to be reconsecrated. The return of the image is often coupled with the declaration of autonomy by a new local Hindu ruler. In response to Islamic denunciations, Hindu texts reaffirm the powers of divinities instantiated within images, assert an essential connection between images and their places, and reiterate the value of devotion and worship directed toward temple images.

Because of the retrospective, hyperbolic, and rhetorical character of these epic genres, Ahmad properly cautions his readers not to view them as transparent factual accounts. They make sense "as a historical attitude rather than as history," writes Ahmad. Reading them as history is a serious error in which many colonial and nationalist historians have indulged. Yet even with "historical attitude" we must be cautious. We cannot take the worlds depicted in the epics of conquest and resistance as representatives of medieval "Islamic" or "Hindu" attitudes as if these were monolithic entities. Islamic epics and Hindu counterepics present the views of elite courtiers who defend conservative ideologies within settings of religious plurality and debate, and seek to persuade royal audiences to adopt vigorous military programs of conquest and resistence, respectively.

The Main Characters

Within conventional Indo-Muslim literature, there was a paradigmatic moment in the encounter with Indian religious images: Maḥmūd's successful raid on the Somanātha temple in Gujarat in 1026, where he destroyed the famous Śiva liṅga.[4] There is no question that this event did take place, in one form or another. An archeological excavation led by B. K. Thapar in 1950 revealed the foundations of the tenth-century temple buried

FIG. 14. Defaced Image of Śiva Naṭarāja from Somanātha. Stone sculpture of Solaṅki period, tenth century. Excavated in 1950, and now on display in Prabhas-Patan Museum, Somnath, Gujarat.

beneath two later structures. Thapar found evidence of deliberate breakage on the entrance steps, the pavilion floor, and the foundation stone where the Śiva liṅga had once rested, and also observed charred spots indicating an intense firing of the former shrine. Excavators unearthed a plethora of hacked-up tenth-century Śaiva images (Thapar 1951: 105–33; Dhaky and Shastri 1974: 13; Figure 14).

However, although later historians have often confidently recounted the destruction of Somanātha based on Muslim accounts, the details of the event itself prove to be intractable.[5] Rather than offering another attempt at historiographical reconstruction, I want to look at the ways later Muslim narratives reimagined and retold Maḥmūd's encounter with the liṅga of Somanātha as an archetypal encounter of Islam with Hindu idolatry. These accounts, built upon the famous event, reinforced the status of Maḥmūd as an archetypal Islamic warrior bringing new lands into the Islamic fold. More significantly, they acted as a theological and political rhetoric, constituting and affirming an orthodox Sunnī Muslim community of response toward Hindu images by dramatizing and subverting the miraculous claims made on their behalf by their worshipers.

Somanātha as the World Center of Idolatry

Muslim narratives dramatized the confrontation of Maḥmūd and Somanātha, first of all, by elevating Somanātha to be the cultic center of Hinduism. In the eleventh century, the Somanātha temple was a fairly large temple of a regional power. It stood at an old pilgrimage site on the Saurashtra coast of present-day Gujarat, one of hundreds of such sites in the subcontinent. Originally the place was known as Prabhāsa, and older texts such as the *Mahābhārata* describe it as the place where Soma, the Moon God, periodically recovers from King Dakṣa's curse by bathing each new-moon night. (I will return to this story in Chapter Six.) Later the Śaivas evidently appropriated the site, and subsequent versions of the local myth require the Moon to worship Śiva as his lord in order to recover his brilliance. Hence the place and the form of Śiva worshiped there became Somanātha, Śiva as "Lord of the Moon."

In around 950 C.E. the Solaṅki ruler of Anahilapataka, Mūlarāja, defeated the ruler of Junagadh and brought the Saurashtrian peninsula within Solaṅki dominion. Not long after, most likely between the years 960 and 973, Mūlarāja constructed a large and ornate royal temple to the god Śiva Somanātha at Prabhāsa. Mūlarāja was a devout worshiper of Śiva; at the same time he undoubtedly wished to signal Solaṅki control over the area through his conspicuous act of devotion. Medieval purāṇas and pilgrimage compilations such as Lakṣmīdhara's *Kṛtyakalpataru* (Tīrthakāṇḍa, ch. 19) do not single out Somanātha for special treatment, as they do more important places of pilgrimage. There is no evidence that Indians of the early eleventh century recognized Somanātha as anything more than an important regional holy site, sacred to Śiva and promoted by the new Solaṅki overlords as a sign of their dominion over Saurashtra (Dhaky and Shastri 1974: 16–17).

When confronting the polycentric Indian political and religious order, however, Muslim chroniclers wished and needed to identify a center, the Indian equivalent of Mecca or the caliphal Baghdad. They chose to promote Somanātha to this preeminent position in their own accounts, and turned Maḥmūd's victory over Somanātha into a synecdoche for the conquest of India.[6]

Muslim accounts claimed that Hindus considered Somanātha to be the "lord of all idols," the central site of the Hindu cult of images. According to the belief of the Hindus, reported Ibn al-Athīr, "all the other idols in India held the position of attendants and deputies of Somnāt" (Elliot and Dowson 1867: 2.472), and Abū Saʿīd Gardīzī observed, "the city is to the Hindus as Mecca is to the Muslims" (Parekh 1954: 292). Starting from Maḥmūd's own letter of conquest to the caliph in Baghdad, Muslim observers took delight in relating the size of the temple, its grandeur, and the arrangements necessary to maintain its liturgy: "the *wakfs* settled on it consisted in ten thousand considerable villages of those countries, and its treasury was filled with all kinds of riches. It was served by one thousand bramins; three hundred youths and five hundred females sang and danced at its gate, and each individual of these classes received a fixed sum out of the *wakfs* settled on the idol" (de Slane 1868: 3.332). Al-Bīrūnī, who may have accompanied Maḥmūd on the expedition, added in his *Taʾrīkh al-Hind* that jugs of water were brought daily from the Ganges and baskets of flowers from Kashmir to adorn the idol (Sachau 1964: 2.104).

With equal vigor they reported the various religious beliefs they were told about Somanātha. "According to the Hindoos," reported the letter of victory, "this idol giveth life, inflicteth death, worketh what it willeth, and decideth what it pleaseth. . . . They believe in transmigration, and pretend that the souls, on quitting the bodies, assemble near this idol, and are born again in whatever bodies it pleaseth. They believe also that the ebb and flow of the sea are the signs by which that element adores it" (de Slane 1868: 3.332). Moreover, they claimed, the temple was supported by fifty-six pillars, each of which bore the name of a different king of India as donor. Just as water and flowers arrived daily from throughout the subcontinent to support the deity, so all the rulers of India paid homage to it. In Muslim accounts, Somanātha was not only the preeminent religious image in India, but also its political center.

Some Muslim narratives portrayed India as the original home of all idolatry. Briefly, the Islamic euhemerist tradition, retold in Ibn al-Kalbī's *Kitāb al-Asnām*, held that Adam, after leaving Paradise, descended onto an Indian mountain, and the children of Seth later came to worship his deceased body. One of Cain's sons subsequently carved an idol so that they too would have an object of worship. He was the first human to make a graven image. Later, during the deluge, the idols were washed from the Indian mountain to various parts, and some came ashore on the Arabian coast.[7] This genealogy of idolatry derided the worship of images as deriving from the veneration of a human corpse and the subsequent forgetfulness of its votaries. By taking the battle against idols to its very source in India, Maḥmūd's victory became a symbolic defeat of polytheism itself.

Where did the Somanātha idol come from? Muslim chroniclers dutifully reported some of the strange claims made by Hindus. One account held that there were thirty rings found in the idol's ears, each of which was said to represent one thousand years of worship (de Slane 1868: 3.332). Such estimations reflected the Hindu belief in the eternality of the world, an erroneous postulation from the Muslim perspective. Other observers sought to locate the image more credibly within finite Islamic history. Somanātha (or Somnāt as they called it), they claimed, was in fact Manāt, an idol worshiped near Mecca before Muḥammad's time. Muḥammad had dispatched ʿAlī to destroy Manāt in A.H. 8, but the idol's votaries, according to these accounts, had secretly transported it to the Gujarati coast, where the inhabitants came to worship it as So-manāt.[8] ʿAlī failed in his mission, and the Arab idol took on a new role among a new group of heathens.

This identification of Somanātha with the pre-Islamic idol of Mecca led the fourteenth-century poet ʿIṣāmī to portray Somanātha as the *last* remaining idol in the world. Muḥammad, of course, was the exemplary destroyer of idols, and the paradigmatic moment was the Prophet's destruction of the idols of the Kaʿba in Mecca. As Ibn al-Kalbī describes it, "When, on the day he conquered Mecca, the apostle of God appeared before the Kaʿbah, he found the idols arrayed around it. Thereupon he started to pierce their eyes with the point of his arrow saying, 'Truth is come and falsehood is vanished. Verily, falsehood is a thing that vanisheth.' He then ordered that they be knocked down, after which they were taken out and burned" (Faris 1952: 27). But even after the Prophet Muḥammad had destroyed all the idols of the Arab peninsula, ʿIṣāmī reported, he felt anxious since one escaped idol still existed in Gujarat. "By the power of Faith," he prayed, "I have removed all the idols from the face of the earth. No idol has remained in the world except Manāt [Somanātha], which has become the deity of the territory of Gujarat." How could he destroy it? The divine messenger Gabriel quickly brought Muḥammad a prophecy that a king by the name of Maḥmūd would one day destroy that last vestige of idolatry. The Prophet was reassured, and prayed, "O Lord, give him the key to the world" (Husain 1967: 92–93).

Faced with an exotic Śaiva cult centered on an upright, cylindrical stone, Muslim chroniclers anthropomorphized the object (liṅgas like Somanātha do not have ears with thirty rings in them) and identified it with an idol already familiar from their own past. What might have appeared radically different and incomprehensible turned out to be, in the retelling, something known historically. Not only did this domesticate Somanātha within the Muslim scheme of things, it also linked Maḥmūd's expedition against it with the Prophet himself. As the court poet Hakīm Sanai had put it, "The Kᶜaba and Somnāth both were made clean like the sky by Maḥmūd and Muḥammad. While Muḥammad threw out the idols from the Kᶜaba, Maḥmūd did the same at Somnāth through war" (Husain 1967: 93). By destroying Somanātha, Maḥmūd not only reenacted Muḥammad's destruction of the Kaᶜba idols, but also carried out the Prophet's direct order, left incomplete by ᶜAlī, to destroy Manāt and thereby completed Muḥammad's mission to remove all idols in the world.

Maḥmūd as Exemplary Islamic Warrior

At the same time as it expanded the eminence of Somanātha, Muslim literature was reconstructing the image of Maḥmūd himself.[9]

When Maḥmūd succeeded his father as ruler of the kingdom of Ghazna, the caliph of Baghdad sent him a robe of honor, a valuable jewel, and a new title, "Right Hand of the Empire and Guardian of the Religion." Shortly thereafter Maḥmūd undertook the first of seventeen campaigns into Indian territories. The initial expeditions gradually extended Ghaznavid sovereignty over the Punjab and into the upper Gangetic plain. By 1018 Maḥmūd was able to march on Kanyakubja, which was still the political center of northern India, even though the once-imperial Gurjāra-Pratihāra dynasty ruling there had become weakened over the previous several decades. Maḥmūd took the city in a single day. He launched two more campaigns into the Doab, but both times an army led by the Candellas of Khajuraho evidently prevented the Ghaznavids from further conquests. Frustrated in his eastward advance, Maḥmūd next turned his attention south, toward Gujarat and the temple of Somanātha. He defeated the Solaṅki ruler Bhīmadeva and sacked the temple in 1026. This was the last major campaign Maḥmūd undertook into India.

As the ruler of an expanding empire, Maḥmūd gained great renown in the Islamic world of his own time (Bosworth 1966: 85–88). He regularly dispatched proclamations of his victories to Baghdad, and his claims of Islamic conquest in India—the first major increase in the boundaries of Islam in over two centuries—served as compensation for the losses of Meditterranean territory to the expanding Byzantine empire. After Maḥmūd's victory at Somanātha, the caliph conferred on him the honorary title, "Refuge of the State and of Islam." Maḥmūd surrounded himself with great literary figures, several of whom, like Abu'l-Kāsim Hasan ʿUnṣurī, specialized in royal panegyric. Eminent as he became during his own lifetime, Maḥmūd's reputation as an exemplary orthodox Sunnī ruler became still greater in the centuries after his death.

Already in several eleventh-century Persian "mirrors for princes," which taught statecraft through anecdote and story, Maḥmūd was set forth as a ruler upon whom the princely audiences should model themselves. Kai Kāʾus related several stories involving Maḥmūd in his *Qābūs-nāma*, and Nizām al-Mulk's *Siyāsat-nāma* reported many more (Levy 1951; Darke 1960). Anecdotes originally told of other rulers were now ascribed to Maḥmūd, who was presented as powerful, impartial, just, and pious. For the Seljuqs of this period, threatened by Ismāʿīlism and radical Shīʾism, the Ghaznavid defense of Sunnī orthodoxy made Maḥmūd a particularly appropriate hero.

A more complex picture of Maḥmūd emerged in the work of Farīd al-Dīn ʿAṭṭār, the twelfth-century mystical poet.[10] ʿAṭṭār both condemned and praised Maḥmūd: he criticized Maḥmūd's pride and despotism, while celebrating him as the destroyer of Indian idols. In this latter respect, ʿAṭṭār restated, Maḥmūd was like the Prophet himself. If Maḥmūd was a paradigm for others, it was because he followed the example of the greatest human paradigm. ʿAṭṭār also wrote of Maḥmūd's romantic relationship with his young lover and slave, Ayāz. This love affair between sultan and catamite, which became the focus of an extensive poetic elaboration, added a human and mystical dimension to Maḥmūd's otherwise rigorous literary personality.[11]

In mid-fourteenth-century India, two important Indo-Muslim works by Diyāʾ al-Dīn Baranī and Fakhr al-Dīn ʿIṣāmī advanced Maḥmūd more than ever as "the archetype of the perfect Muslim hero, a model for imitation by succeeding generations of Muslims" (P. Hardy 1960: 107). During this period, as Carl Ernst has argued, Mongol invasions of the central Islamic regions and the destruction of Baghdad led the Turkish Sultanate of Delhi to view India as a bastion of Islam. Within this embattled ideological setting, Indian Muslim elites began to ascribe a religious identity to the subject population of pagan "Hindus" within their own dominion, as a threatening Other (Ernst 1992: 24–25). Maḥmūd was offered as exemplary champion against these threats.

Baranī served as aristocratic courtier to Muḥammad bin Tughluk for twenty-seven years and then found himself imprisoned at age sixty-nine, when Fīrūz Shāh became the new sultan of Delhi in 1351. In poverty and exile, Baranī wrote several bitter works of history and political advice. He called himself a "well-wisher of the sultan's court," and evidently hoped to regain the sultan's favor. In his *Fatāwā-yi Jahāndārī* (1358), Baranī made Maḥmūd the mouthpiece for his own cranky political philosophy, even though (as translator Mohammad Habib comments) the historical Maḥmūd "would probably have repudiated it from A to Z" (iii). Maḥmūd set forth Baranī's view that the Islamic ruler in India must above all else seek to establish "Truth at the center" through vigorous efforts to overthrow infidelity and polytheism. "Sons of Mahmud and kings of Islam!" Baranī advises in the voice of Maḥmūd, "You should with all your royal determination apply yourself to uprooting and disgracing infidels, polytheists, and men of bad dogmas and bad religions. . . . You should consider the enemies of God and His Faith to be your enemies and you should risk your power and authority in overthrowing them, so that you may win the approval of God and the Prophet Mohammad and of all prophets and saints" (Habib and Khan 1961: 47). Baranī considered contemporary Islamic rulers in India far too lenient toward Hindu practitioners, and placed Maḥmūd in the anachronistic position of criticizing future Muslim rulers of India. In Baranī's account, Maḥmūd observed that "the desire for overthrowing infidels and knocking down idolators and polytheists does not fill the hearts of the Muslim kings of India" (48). Such a desire, by contrast, had formerly filled the heart of Maḥmūd, or at least the literary construct of Maḥmūd.

Meanwhile in the Bahmani court of the Deccan, ʿIṣāmī composed the first literary epic of Muslim India, the *Futūhu-Salāṭīn* or *Shāh Nāmah-i Hind*.[12] ʿIṣāmī advanced Maḥmūd as the exemplary hero of his epic and the first conqueror of India.

> Even if any king before him [Maḥmūd] marched on Hindustan he retreated after raiding this beautiful land and made peace. . . . No one set his heart on settling in this meadow; none captured even a fortress, nor won a siege. No one demolished the idol-house of Somnath and none made the blood of enemies flow like the Euphrates. . . . No one uprooted the Hindu power and none demolished the old idol-houses. But his troops overran the country in such a manner that the Hindu power was destroyed completely. (Husain 1967: 66)

For ʿIṣāmī, destruction of "idol-houses" was a significant part of Islamic conquest in India, and Somanātha was preeminent among Hindu temples. ʿIṣāmī also stressed that Maḥmūd should serve as a model for action in the present. (I will return to ʿIṣāmī's agenda within his own political situation in Chapter Six.) As with Baranī, ʿIṣāmī used the example of Maḥmūd to chastise later Indo-Muslim rulers for their failures to carry out his rigorous policies. At the same time, both authors augmented Maḥmūd's retrospective status.

ʿIṣāmī's epic set an important precedent. Two centuries later, the Mughal court official and historian Nizām al-Dīn Ahmad established a new genre, the Indo-Muslim history, by leaving aside the universal history of worldwide

Islam in order to concentrate on the Muslim conquest of India. The teleological frame of the new history was a narrative of gradual, progressive subjugation of India that led up to the Mughal suzerainty. "Now that all the Provinces and Divisions of Hindustan have been conquered by the world-opening sword of His Majesty," began Nizām al-Dīn writing at the height of Akbar's reign, a historical account of how this had come to pass seemed a worthy endeavor (De 1913: iv). Like ʿIṣāmī, Nizām al-Dīn (as well as other Indo-Muslim historians who followed him, such as al-Badauni and Firishta) located the starting point for this conquest with the Ghaznavids and particularly with Maḥmūd, making him progenitor of Muslim rule in the subcontinent.

In his full Indo-Muslim portrait, Maḥmūd appeared as a commander of great determination, leading many campaigns to extend the bounds of Islam and to accumulate great wealth. Occasionally he was reproached for avarice and made an illustration for the vanity of wealth. He was portrayed as a spokesman for conservative and orthodox Islamic values, and in this vein he was proclaimed as the preeminent breaker of idols. It was his iconoclasm that linked him closely with the Prophet, as in Muḥammad's dream about the last idol on earth. The extraordinary demise of various Hindu idols came to be associated with him as well. Minhāj-i Sirāj reported that on the night of Maḥmūd's birth, "the idol temple of Wahand or Bihand . . . on the bank of the river Sind, split asunder" (Ranking 1898: 76). Expansion, avarice, orthodoxy, iconoclasm, prophetic dreams, and birth miracles—all pointed to Maḥmūd's victorious encounter with Somanātha as the culmination and essence of his career.

The Confrontation of Maḥmūd and Somanātha

Why did Maḥmūd march on Somanātha? Modern historians have most often portrayed the campaign as predatory. Lured by reports of the fabulous wealth of the Somanātha temple, Maḥmūd seized the opportunity to make a great economic gain. However, medieval Muslim chronicles ascribed to him a different motive. Ibn al-Athīr reported that Maḥmūd, after his many victorious campaigns into the Gangetic plain, learned that the undaunted Hindu devotees of Somanātha were making a boast. The only reason Maḥmūd had been able to destroy the other idols of north India, the Hindus bragged, was because Somanātha had been displeased with them. Maḥmūd was understandably uncomfortable at being cast as the unwitting instrument of a Hindu god's design and set out on his final great campaign into India to assert Islamic supremacy over even this presumptuous deity. Besides, he reflected, perhaps destruction of *this* idol would help deluded

Hindus turn to Islam. When he reached Somanātha, Ibn al-Athīr goes on, Hindus continued to taunt Maḥmūd: Somanātha had lured him there to destroy the Muslims, to avenge the destruction of the north Indian images (Elliot and Dowson 1867: 2.469–70).

Somanātha's Supposed Powers

Audacious claims made by Hindus on behalf of the Somanātha image constituted the first part of the central peristrophe of Muslim accounts. Such assertions of an idol's power were acknowledged only to be overthrown, when, revealed by Maḥmūd's superior force to be groundless. Indo-Muslim anecdotes thereby turned Hindu claims around on the claimants, by satirically illustrating their foolish attribution of animate powers to inanimate objects.

Several accounts narrated apparent miracles performed by the Somanātha idol. In some accounts Somanātha flew—that is, he floated in the air without visible support. "It [Somanātha] was held," reported the geographer Zakariyya al-Kazwīnī, "in the highest honour among the Hindus, and whoever beheld it floating in the air was struck with amazement, whether he was a Musulman or an infidel."[13] Upon reaching the temple, however, Maḥmūd was skeptical. After investigations, he discovered that an ingenious builder had fabricated the idol of iron and the canopy above it of lodestone. His attendants removed some stones from the canopy and the idol swerved to one side. When more were taken away, the image fell powerlessly to the ground.[14] What first appeared as a marvelous feat by the idol was revealed, through the expanded perspective provided by Maḥmūd's action, to be merely a mechanical contrivance.

The thirteenth-century Sufi poet and traveler Saʿdī related a similar anecdote of Somanātha (though not involving Maḥmūd), in which he observed the image miraculously raising its two hands (Figure 15). Presently he was able to explore behind the scenes, and discovered the truth: "One night, I closed fast the door of the temple and, searching, discovered a screen of jewels and gold that went from the top of the throne to the bottom. Behind this screen the Brahmin high priest was devoutly engaged with the end of a rope in his hand. Then did it become known to me that when the rope was pulled the idol of necessity raised its arm" (Edwards 1911: 109). It was human deception, Saʿdī revealed, that empowered the idol. Hindu priests carried out the fraud.

The Sufi poet, however, was a more subtle narrator than most chroniclers, and concluded his anecdote by turning the marionette image back upon himself. "Whenever I supplicate at the shrine of the Knower of Secrets," Saʿdī reflected, "the Indian puppet comes into my recollection—it throws

FIG. 15. Saʿdī's Visit to an Indian Temple. Painting by Mīr ʿAlī al-Husaynī, Mughal period, 1531–1532, in illustrated manuscript of Saʿdī's *Bustan*. Courtesy of the Arthur M. Sackler Museum, Harvard University Art Museums, Cambridge, Mass.

dust on the pride of mine eyes. I know that I raise my hand, but not by virtue of mine own strength. Men of sanctity stretch not out their hands themselves; the Fates invisibly pull the strings." After revealing the inanimation of the supposedly miraculous Hindu idol, Saʿdī shifted the image into a metaphor for his own powerlessness in the grip of greater forces.

Maḥmūd's own letter of victory to the caliph also sardonically considered the dynamics of Hindu belief in Somanātha's powers. "If it feel inclined," he reported of the idol, "it cureth every malady, and it sometimes happened, to their eternal misery, that sick pilgrims, on visiting it, were cured by the goodness of the air and by exercise; this increaseth their delusion, and crowds come to it on foot and on horseback from distant countries: if they obtain not the healing of their maladies, they attribute it to their sins, and say: 'He that does not serve him faithfully, meriteth not from him an answer'" (de Slane 1868: 3.332). Here Hindu worshipers deceive themselves by assigning supernatural causes to natural effects and by explaining away divine failures as the result of their own moral shortcomings. As with more visible miracles, Maḥmūd's explanation of Somanātha's supposed feats of healing naturalized the Hindu claims within and for a Muslim world of values, where divinity does not enter into objects and stone idols do not effect cures.

In *The Formation of Islamic Art*, Oleg Grabar argues that Muslim "iconophobia" was not an essential feature of Islam, but developed within the specific historical situation of its cultural and religious encounter with an image-saturated eastern Christianity in the late seventh and early eighth centuries. Reacting to the seductive threat posed by the wealth of visual imagery in Christian churches like the Hagia Sophia of Constantinople, Muslims "immediately interpreted this potential magical power of images as a deception, as an evil" (1987: 95). The later Indo-Muslim accounts revealing Somanātha's deceptions reiterated this response in the new and even more icon-filled environment of Hindu India.

Islamic Miracles and Others

It is worth reminding ourselves here that these Muslim observers were not simply pre-modern rationalists, seeking to explain all superstitious beliefs through duplicity, mechanical causality, and psychological credulity. Many were deeply interested in the marvels of creation, and viewed India as possessing an overabundance of the miraculous. As the Persian mariner Buzurg ibn Shahriyār had put it, introducing his tenth-century collection of Indian "marvels": "God—blessed is His name and great His praise—having created marvels in ten parts, attributed nine of them to the eastern quarter and only one to the other three quarters of the earth, the west, north, and south; after which He attributed to China and India eight parts, and only one to the remainder of the east" (Sauvaget 1954: 190). This unequal world distribution of marvels explained why the Arab sailors working the eastern trade routes to China and India brought back so many extraordinary anecdotes. Along with various sorts of zoological and botanical wonders, Buzurg also reported such marvels as the giant bird who carried seven shipwrecked sailors to safety and the women of Kanyakubja who broke areca nuts with their lips. He included as well strange Indian customs like the ritual suicide practiced by the inhabitants of northern Lanka before their Lord, a large black statue (193).

Within Islamic ontology, extraordinary objects and events were manifestations of Allāh's creative omnipotence. Allāh had created the world and set it along its normal course. However, in the predictable routine of every day there was the danger that humans might forget about Allāh's overarching mastery. Precisely by breaking with the ordinary course of things (*ʿāda*), marvels served as signs (*āyāt*) that pointed to their unique Creator (Wensinck 1979: 224–25).

Likewise, Islamic authors generally recognized the possibility of miracles performed by human beings. Anecdotes collected in the hadīth described in detail the marvels practiced by the Prophet Muḥammad. The great Islamic philosopher ʿAbd al-Raḥmān ibn Khaldūn viewed extraordinary human acts as signs by which Allāh singles out those he has chosen for special roles (Rosenthal 1958: 1.188–92). There were two main types. The prophetic miracle (*muʿdjiza*) was a public and rhetorical event. An opponent's challenge initiated it. The man of faith in response produced a marvel, which served to demonstrate the sincerity of the actor as well as the impotence of the opponent to reproduce any such result. Within the framework of a contest of faith, the prophetic miracle was intended to produce conviction in the audience of witnesses. By contrast, the interior miracle or wonder (*karāma*) was not a sign of prophetic mission, but rather a private sign of grace bestowed upon friends of God. Muslim authors ascribed both types to the agency of Allāh, and viewed them as expressions of Allāh's power to transgress the normal order of things in order to realize His own purposes.

Considering the status of Maḥmūd in many texts of eastern Islam, it is no wonder that extraordinary occurrences clustered around him. As Minhāj-i Sirāj put it, "The Almighty has endowed that ruler with great power of performing many miraculous and wondrous acts, such as He has not bestowed since upon any other sovereign" (Raverty 1881: 83). From Muḥammad's own prophetic dream foretelling Maḥmūd's mission and the marvelous events on the night of his birth, Maḥmūd appeared singled out to play an extraordinary role. ʿIṣāmī related that once, while Maḥmūd was participating in Friday prayers, his ablution became invalid. Momentarily perplexed by the dilemma, Maḥmūd was saved when a miraculous stream of water appeared before him and enabled him to repurify himself (Husain 1967: 111–12). On another occasion, according to ʿAṭṭār, Maḥmūd was given a cow by an old woman and made it give unceasing milk, symbolic of bounteous divine power (Bosworth 1966: 90).

Of course, many recognized Maḥmūd's greatest miracle to be his defeat of Somanātha.

> When the potent sovereign made the expedition to Somnāth,
> He made the working of miracles his occupation.
> He staked the Chess of dominion with a thousand kings:
> Each king he check-mated, in a separate game.
>
> *(tr. Raverty 1881: 82)*

So celebrated ʿUnṣurī, a poet of Maḥmūd's court. In contrast with other, more private miracles, this was a public act in a contest of faith. Beginning with the challenge posed by Hindu claims, Maḥmūd's destruction of the idol followed the structure of a prophetic miracle: it illustrated the sincerity of Maḥmūd's actions and the inability of his Hindu opponents, both human and divine, to counteract them.

The world presented in Islamic chronicles and epics, then, was not a demystified one. Marvels might well break through the usual course of things, pointing to Allāh's ever-present creative potency. This world required, however, that one carefully evaluate claims of a miraculous nature. It was necessary to distinguish clearly between true miracles, such as acts of Allāh, and those false wonders that resulted from human acts of sorcery, magic, and deceit. Otherwise, warned Ibn Khaldūn, proof could become doubt, guidance become misguidance, and truth untruth; the world itself could be turned upside down (Rosenthal 1958: 1.190). As for marvelous claims made on behalf of Hindu idols, these needed to be repudiated even more forcefully. Not only might realities become absurdities, but any admission of idol power would encroach on the terrain of special activity exclusive to Allāh.

The Breaking of Somanātha

The most famous anecdote of Maḥmūd at Somanātha involved the priests' attempt to ransom their idol. The twelfth-century mystic poet Farīd al-Dīn ʿAṭṭār first narrated this tale in his *Mantik al-Tayr*. It was repeated in the authoriative account of Firishta, and then in the West by Edward Gibbon, James Mill, and many others up to the present.[15] When Maḥmūd had fought his way into the sanctum and was about to destroy the idol, goes the story, the temple brahmins offered him vast wealth if he would spare their god. Overawed by the offer, Maḥmūd's advisers counseled him to accept. They argued that destroying one idol would not do away with idolatry altogether, while so much money distributed among true believers would be a very meritorious act. Maḥmūd steadfastly refused their advice. He wished posterity to remember him not as a "seller of idols" but as a "breaker of idols." He proceeded to aim a powerful swing of his mace at the belly of the idol, and it burst open. Out came a jackpot of diamonds, rubies, and pearls, even greater in value than what the brahmins had offered.

Apocryphal though it was, this incident earned its historiographical longevity by serving as a dramatic and personalized epitome of the confrontation at Somanātha.[16] Once again, Indian images were not what they pretended to be; what first appeared as an object of great religious value to the brahmins turned out to be merely a hiding place for treasure of a more material character. The episode identified the brahmins as the chief charlatans, just as they usually were in the accounts of counterfeit miracles—a suitable motif for a Muslim orthodoxy that disdained priesthood.

Most important, it provided the theme for the issue of Maḥmūd's motivation, answering a question historians have long since debated. Were his campaigns primarily concerned with plunder and economic gain, or did he attach real importance to the iconoclastic policy prescribed as proper to an Islamic warrior faced with the objects of polytheism?[17] Refusing to view the Somanātha icon as a commodity reducible solely to an economic value, Maḥmūd insisted that it was primarily a Hindu religious object, and his first duty as a Muslim was to destroy it. The story then rewarded his righteousness with wealth, just as Allāh bestowed his mercy on those who acted as his servants.

Ghaznavid Looting

Whatever his actual motivations, Maḥmūd and the Ghaznavid state surely did realize great economic gains through their Indian campaigns. The Sunnī Ghaznavids, much like the Śaiva Colas, considered looting defeated opponents and their capitals as a legitimate and productive part of war. And, like the Colas, they too could cite authoritative precedents in their own cultural tradition for such appropriations. As the Qur'ān put it (in the sūra entitled "Victory"), "God was pleased with the believers . . . and rewarded them with an expeditious victory and the many spoils they were to take" (48.18–19; Ali 1984: 440–41). Allāh revealed this verse to Muḥammad at the battle of Badr in A.D. 624, after which the Prophet received divine legislation on the proper distribution of wartime spoils: "Know that one-fifth of what you acquire as booty [of war] is for God and His Apostle, and for relatives and orphans, the poor and wayfarers, if you truly believe in God and what We revealed to Our Votary on the day of victory over the infidels when the two armies clashed [at Badr]" (8.41; Ali 1984: 157). After one-fifth was reserved for divine and charitable recipients, the remaining four-fifths was left to the warriors.

On this basis, legal scholars in the eighth and ninth centuries developed general principles by which the acquisition of spoils (*ghanīma*) from non-Muslims by force was classified as "original acquisition," taking possession of things in the state of nature, rather than as theft, since the ownership previously exercised by those opponents had been "alienated as a punishment for persistence in disbelief by all those who refused to adopt Islam (or submit to Islamic rule) and resorted to fighting with the Muslims" (Khadduri 1955: 118–19). But other conditions were also necessary. The warriors must have received the initial permission of the imām formalizing their battle as jihād, "striving in the way of Allāh." Second, one must secure the victory before any discussion or consideration of the spoils could be entertained, for alienation of property rights took place only at the moment of victory. As a practical matter, too, premature looting could easily distract warriors from the battle at hand.

As with the dharmaśāstrins, Muslim legalists concerned themselves primarily with the most contentions question, distributing the loot. All of the confiscated property, they assumed, should be collected in a single pot from which shares could then be disbursed. Following the divine edict of Badr, a share of one-fifth clearly belonged to the state, to redistribute for religious and charitable purposes, but various legal schools proposed differing ways of subdividing that portion, based on differing interpretations of the Qur'ānic passage. The remaining four-fifths by general agreement went to those warriors who had directly participated in the battle, in accord with Muḥammad's statement (reported by Caliph ʿUmar) that "the spoil belongs to those who witnessed the battle" (Khadduri 1955: 119). Here too, though, legal authors heatedly disputed the subdivision. What about reinforcements on their way to the front when the battle was won? What about those warriors who could not take part due to illness? What proportion should be given to cavalrymen, and what to foot soldiers? What about those who employed other animals—mules or camels, or elephants in the Indian campaigns—in battle? Such matters preoccupied the learned jurists and those directly affected by their rulings, but they need not detain us here.

The Ghaznavids followed the general procedures of the Hanafī legal school in distributing the loot they acquired during their Indian campaigns. After a victorious expedition, the appropriated property would be transported from India back to the capital, where the head of the Military Department would have it valued and distributed. "The sultan took a fifth from the slaves, animals and general booty, reserving to himself within this fifth all precious metals, arms and elephants; and he had a right of first pick, *safiyya*, from other choice articles," observes the historian C. E. Bosworth. "The remaining four-fifths went to the troops in proportion to their ranks, and with cavalrymen getting two shares to the infantrymen's one" (Bosworth 1963: 126). The sultan would use his portion of the loot to make gifts to his favorites in the court, to decorate his palaces, and to make pious donations to religious institutions. As al-Utbī relates, "When the Sultan returned from Hind in victory and light, with abundant wealth and no scanty amount of gems, and so many slaves that the drinking-places and streets of Ghazna were too narrow for them, and the eatables and victuals of the country sufficed not for them, . . . the Sultan began to feel an earnest desire to expend the plunder of those princes upon some liberal work of piety and lasting benefit" (Reynolds 1858: 462–63). So with the great revenue from his 1018 campaign against Mathura and Kanyakubja, Maḥmūd was able to build in Ghazna a magnificent mosque, the "Bride of Heaven," meant to challenge the great mosque of Damascus. Gilding it was the bullion of melted Hindu icons: "They spared not the purest gold in their painting and gilding, nay they employed lumps of gold; and they crushed the body-like idols and corporeal images, and fastened them into the doors and walls" (Reynolds 1858: 464–65).

The Relocation of Somanātha

Generally, early Islamic chronicles showed little interest in the past identities of Hindu images that the Ghaznavid warriors captured and destroyed. However, the objects clearly did hold interest and value for their constituent elements. Here is a typical accounting, from the contemporary chronicle of al-Utbī.

> And amongst the mass of idols [of Mathura] there were five idols made of pure gold, of the height of five cubits in the air; and of this collection of idols there were especially two, on one of which a jacinth was arranged, such a one that if the Sultan had seen it exposed in the Bazar, he would have considered as underpriced at fifty thousand dinars, and would have bought it with great eagerness. And upon the other idol there was a sapphire [hyacinth] of one solid piece of azure water, of the value of four hundredweights of fine *miskals* each, and from the two feet of an idol they obtained the weight of 400,400 *miskals* of gold. And the idols of silver were a hundred times more, so that it occupied those who estimated their standard weight a long time in weighing them. (Reynolds 1858: 455–56)

The gold, silver, and jewels that often constituted or covered Indian images were valuable materials and could be redeployed, as Maḥmūd did, to decorate his palace and gild the great mosque of Ghazna. Chroniclers carefully recorded the weight and value of the raw materials obtained from Indian shrines. Images of stone, less valuable and less convertable than gold and silver, were most often simply knocked over, defaced, and left behind.

Stanley Fish observes that certain interpretive strategies are designed to make all texts one. He cites as his example Augustine's directives in *On Christian Doctrine* for reading the scriptures and the world itself as all pointing to God's love for us and our responsibility to love our fellow creatures (1980: 170). Islamic chronicles similarly reduced the complex world of Indian images, with their varied iconographic forms and complicated mythological backgrounds, to a single interpretive criterion. All were classified under the general rubric of "idols," and the various identities the Hindus might have assigned them were presented as the results of ignorance and delusion. As idols they were valuable only for their constituent elements, since in Islamic ontology, that was all they in fact were.

Somanātha, however, appears as a partial exception to this homogenizing perspective. This idol received special treatment in accord with his special status as the "lord of all idols." The contemporary observer al-Bīrūnī explained, "He [Maḥmūd] ordered the upper part to be broken and the remainder to be transported to his residence with all its coverings and trappings of gold, jewels, and embroidered garments. Part of it has been thrown in the hippodrome of the town together with the Cakraswamin the idol of bronze that had been brought from Taneshar [Sthāṇvīśvara]. Another part of the idol from Somnath lies before the door of the mosque in Ghazni" (Sachau 1964: 2.103). The other idol Maḥmūd singled out for public humiliation was a large bronze image of Viṣṇu Cakrasvāmin taken to be the palladium of Sthāṇvīśvara city. Maḥmūd had already brought back the Viṣṇu image to Ghazna and unceremoniously thrown it down in the hippodrome, where part of Somanātha later joined it (Sachau 1964: 1.107). Firishta also compared Sthāṇvīśvara city to Mecca, and he recounted how there as in Somanātha the image's devotees unsuccessfully attempted to ransom the idol (Briggs 1966: 29–30).

Later writers such as Badauni stated more explicitly that, placed at the entrance of the Jāmi Masjid, the broken idol of Somanātha was to be "trodden under foot" by the faithful (Ranking 1898: 28). Lying at the gate of the Bride of Heaven mosque, the Śaiva icon from Somanātha in its new situation echoed the Hindu trope by which defeated enemies were subordinated into door guardians, but in a rather more humiliating mode.[18] And in Ghazna as in Gangaikondacolapuram, the new audience was encouraged to interact with the appropriated object. Far from offering worship to the looted deity as a subordinate member of a hierarchized pantheon, however, the faithful of Ghazna could tread on the idol of another religious community with their bare feet as they went to prayer, repudiating the polytheism it represented and reenacting as they did Maḥmūd's own victory at Somanātha.

Another contemporary of Maḥmūd, Abu'l-Hasan Farrukhī Sīstānī, claimed that the sultan uprooted the idol "with the intention of restoring it to Mecca" (Parekh 1954: 294). Putting several earlier versions together into a synthetic account, Minhāj-i Sirāj narrated that Maḥmūd broke the idol and dispatched the pieces to four destinations: "He led an army to Nahrwālah of Gujarāt, and brought away Manāt, the idol, from Somnāth, and had it broken into four parts, one of which was cast before the entrance of the great masjid at G͟haznīn, the second before the gateway of the Sulṭān's palace, and the third and fourth were sent to Makkah and Madīnah respectively" (Raverty 1881: 1.82). This expanded list of final destinations for the remains of Somanātha represented Maḥmūd's subordination of the Hindu deity as simultaneously religious and political, by having it placed at both mosque and palace gateways. At the same time it reaffirmed Maḥmūd's own recognition of the religious center of the Islamic world, Mecca and Medina in the Arabian peninsula.[19]

Some later accounts turned the motif of incorporation in a different and more insidious direction. According to ʿIṣāmī, Maḥmūd had the idol ground into lime, and then served betel leaves spread with the lime paste to the unsuspecting temple brahmins. When the brahmins then asked for the return of their idol, as part of an earlier agreement, Maḥmūd laughed and replied that he had already given it back to them. "You misdirected people! The idol which you are demanding of me and for which you are raising such a clamour has been already consumed by you along with your betel-leaf. Give up the vain hope now, for henceforth your temple is your own stomachs which you should worship instead of the idol" (Husain 1967: 87–88). The deceit enables Maḥmūd to honor his word while avoiding any charge of selling or ransoming idols. Here the precedent for Maḥmūd's action perhaps comes from the Biblical narrative of Moses (Exodus 32.20), who in his fury at the Israelites' idolatry had the golden calf melted and forced its worshipers to eat it. ʿIṣāmī had lived for twenty-five years in the Deccan and knew Hindu liturgical practice. He may have also meant this anecdote as a sarcastic play on the distribution and ingestion of *prasāda*, the leftover food of an Indian image's meal. Besides rewarding enemies of the faith with a rather indigestible meal, such stories reminded their audience of the simple material nature, lime paste, of the Hindu deity.[20]

Reappearances Miraculous and Otherwise

Even reduced to paste, though, Hindu images had a way of reappearing. Hindu religious literature of the medieval period was filled with stories of "buried" or "hidden" or "long-lost" images, whose locations were revealed in the dreams of holy men or by the devoted behavior of cows.

Disinterred, the images were then returned to their temples to be reconsecrated, in a show of divine resurrection and Hindu autonomy.

These miraculous reappearances, too, invited Islamic satire. After Maḥmūd's destruction of the Somanātha idol, ʿIṣāmī related, a brahmin temple priest secretly buried a stone idol just like the destroyed one in the forest. Then, using barley as bait, he trained a calf to go every day to the spot where it was buried. When the calf was reliably habituated, the brahmin announced to the local population that Somanātha had appeared to him in a dream, and advised him that a certain calf would lead the townspeople to the idol's burial place. The calf did as it had been trained. The townspeople uncovered the new Somanātha, proclaimed it as the destroyed idol wondrously risen again, held a great festival, and restored the idol to worship (Husain 1967: 88–90). Playing upon the most common motifs of the Hindu narratives of recovery, the Muslim narrator subverts the apparent miracle worked on a credulous Hindu public once again, by allowing his audience to see at the same time the priestly trickery producing the marvelous effect.

The Somanātha liṅga did reappear, but not precisely in the way ʿIṣāmī described. According to the prevailing theology of Pāśupata Śaivism, Śiva himself was not affected by destruction of one of his iconic "supports," and he would gracefully return to inhabit a new, ritually prepared Somanātha liṅga if it were provided. The temple was rebuilt by the local Solaṅki ruler Bhīma not long after Maḥmūd's withdrawal from Gujarat, and then rebuilt again much more impressively by the Solaṅki emperor Kumārapāla in the mid-twelfth century.

According to the foundation inscription of Kumārapāla's new Somanātha, it was Śiva himself who ordered the reconstruction. Observing that, with the passage of Kali-yuga, his Somanātha temple had been knocked down, Śiva commanded his devoted bull-mount Nandi to incarnate himself as a human in order to carry out the necessary renovations. Nandi took birth in a brahmin family in the holy city of Varanasi. Named Bhāva Bṛhaspati, he soon became famous throughout northern India for his intellect and austerities. He traveled around northern India, visiting and teaching in pilgrimage centers and royal courts. Eventually the Solaṅki emperor Jayasiṃha and his successor Kumārapāla invited Bhāva Bṛhaspati to their court and made him chief priest.

Śiva then reminded the preceptor of his true identity and the reason for his earthly incarnation. Bhāva Bṛhaspati examined the decrepit temple and persuaded Kumārapāla to sponsor the rebuilding of Somanātha temple, under his own supervision. "King Soma, the Moon, built Somanātha's temple in gold," says the epigraph. "Kṛṣṇa, whose bravery equals that of the demon Rāvaṇa, then made it of silver. Lord Bhīmadeva built the 'Jewel Peak' temple with huge beautiful stones. And when in time that had become worn out, the majestic Kumārapāla, best of all kings, built the temple for Bhāva Bṛhaspati's overlord, Śiva, repository for all virtues, and named it 'Meru,' the World Mountain" (P. Peterson 1895: 186–93). The new temple, far more than a simple restoration, was an imperial-scale temple (as the denomination Meru suggests), consonant with the expanded dominion of the Solaṅki regime under Jayasiṃha and Kumārapāla. By the mid-twelfth century, the Solaṅkis had become the predominant power of western India, and Śiva's desire to have his Somanātha temple rebuilt coincided with Kumārapāla's wish to give form to his imperial status.

The Hindu narrative of reconstruction acknowledged the deterioration of the temple, but only in a depersonalized and dehistoricized form, as the consequence of evil times rather than human action. It went on, though, to reassert Śiva's eternality, transcending the deterioration or destruction of any of his earthly habitations, and his continuing interest in the site of Somanātha. As in ʿIṣāmī's satirical view, the restitution of the Somanātha temple resulted from human effort, but in the Hindu inscription the narrator let his audience understand that the human agent Bhāva Bṛhaspati was acting as the incarnation of Śiva's divine bull and as the appointed agent of Śiva himself. We will consider other medieval Hindu narratives of recovery and restoration of images in the next chapter.

Yet Kali-yuga was still in force, and the new Somanātha temple and its icon did not survive uncontested. Due to the exemplary fame of Maḥmūd's victory throughout the world of Islam and the diligence of the Solaṅki rulers in rebuilding the temple, Somanātha subsequently became a primary site of regional contention, a marker of political control over the Gujarat area. Accordingly, Islamic epics of conquest like Amīr Khusraw's poetic celebration of the fourteenth-century campaigns of ʿAla al-Dīn Khilji, the *Khazāʾinul Futūḥ* (Habib 1931), and Hindu epics of resistance such as the *Kānhaḍade Prabandha* of Padmanābha (Bhatnagar 1991), recounting the revolt against ʿAlā al-Dīn's rule led by a Chauhāna chieftain of Jalor, center on new acts of desecration and resurrection of the Somanātha icon. The subsequent history of the Somanātha site and the literary recountings of that history form a complex topic in itself. I will return to these later developments in Chapter Six.

Conclusion: The Implicit Antonym

At the time of Maḥmūd's conquests in northern India, Hindu worshipers of Śiva believed that Śiva, a divinity simultaneously transcendent and immanent, would enter into fabricated objects like Śiva liṅgas and images, and that such animated icons could act powerfully as direct instantiations of Śiva's presence in the human world. In accord with their own theological premises, Muslim invaders set out to reconstitute this world of Hindu icons, at times through physical actions directed against idols and more commonly through discourse about them.

Over time, Islamic authors created a narrative tradition concerning the paradigmatic encounter between a Muslim conqueror and a Hindu idol, a collective "epic of iconoclasm," to adapt Ahmad's term. Not only did these accounts present Maḥmūd as an exemplary Muslim leader of miraculous powers and as the forefather of the Islamic conquest of India, but they also articulated and reinforced an orthodox Islamic response toward Hindu religious images. Focusing on the icon they took to be the preeminent Hindu idol, Somanātha, the epic of iconoclasm portrayed it as anthropomorphic, fabricated, material, temporal, inanimate, powerless, and deceitful. Any Hindu claims that such an idol could act miraculously were subjected to satire and subversion. Like the interpretive strategies Fish identifies as intended to make all texts one, these narratives sought to collapse all Hindu religious images into a single interpretive category, and to define a proper mode of Islamic response toward them.

In such characterizations, there lurked always an implicit antonym. Just as the miracles attributed to Maḥmūd pointed directly to the God acting through him, so the Islamic depictions of the hapless Hindu deity Somanātha were meant to lead their audiences to reflect on the God who was the complete opposite, Allāh. As his very name indicated, Allāh was the unitary and unique One. He was eternal, supremely animate, self-originating, and absolutely true. As sole Creator, He alone was responsible for both the normal order of things and for those miracles that occasionally break with normalcy. He was theologically defined as radically nonanthropomorphic, immaterial, unrepresentable. Surely he would never enter into material objects fabricated by humans. No other deity could be allowed to disturb his all-encompassing divinity.

4.

Viṣṇu's Miraculous Returns

WHEN THE ARMIES of the Delhi Sultanate led by Malik Khān invaded southern India in 1310, they learned of a golden temple in the city of "Barmatpur," the Śiva Naṭarāja temple of Cidambaram.[1] Immediately they marched there, captured the 250 elephants of the royal elephant corps, and then they began to destroy the temple and its idols. The Indo-Persian court poet Amīr Khusraw describes it:

> The stone idols, called "Ling-i-Mahadeo" [Śiva liṅgas], which had been for a long time established at that place—*quibus, mulieres infidelium pudenda sua affiant*,—these, up to this time, the kick of the horse of Islam had not attempted to break. The Mussalmans destroyed all the *lingas*. Deo Narain [Viṣṇu Nārāyaṇa] fell down, and the other gods who had fixed their seats there, raised their feet so high, that at one leap they reached the fort of Lanka; and in that affright the *lingas* themselves would have fled, had they any legs to stand on. (Habib 1931: 103–4)

They dug up the foundations of the temple and pulled down its jeweled walls. "Wherever there was any treasure in that desolated building, the ground was sifted in a sieve and the treasure discovered" (104).

After their sack of Cidambaram, the armies moved on to Madurai, capital city of the Pāṇḍyans, the dominant power of Tamilnad at the time. There they found that the king had fled with his queens and his treasures. They captured the southernmost capital in India and brought Malik Khān's campaign to successful completion.

> Through the favour of the Lord of men and *jins*, and assisted by the sincere motives of the Imam and the Caliph of the age, the orthodox Sunnī victors had now piously compelled all false houses of worship to bow their heads on the prayer-carpet of the ground and had broken all stone idols like the stony hearts of their worshippers. How clean the breasts of those who broke with the greatest severity these contaminated stones, which Satan had raised like a wall before himself! (Habib 1931: 107)

The armies returned to the imperial capital, Delhi, with all their captured elephants and booty.

The audacious campaign of Malik Khān at the behest of his sultan, ʿAlā al-Dīn Khaljī, was the first of several major attempts in the early fourteenth century to bring all of the subcontinent under the sway of Delhi. In 1318 Mubārak Shāh Khaljī commanded his general Khusraw Khān to conquer all the south, and after a dynastic coup in Delhi the Tughluk rulers continued the efforts of the Khaljīs to extend their dominion over southern India. Muḥammad bin Tughluk's forces captured Madurai again in 1327–1328. In 1333 Jalāl al-Dīn Ḥasan Shāh declared himself ruler of the autonomous Madurai Sultanate, a Muslim polity at the southern tip of India. In south India this abrupt encounter with Muslim Turkic armies from Delhi was the most significant political event of the period. "Within a remarkably brief period in the fourteenth century," observes Burton Stein (1989: 18), "all older centres of authority in the peninsula were obliterated by Muslim horsemen, leaving a vacuum that was to be filled by the able fighters who established Vijayanagara on the grave of the Kampili kingdom."

It was a literary as well as a political event. Like Maḥmūd's conquest of Somanātha, the glorious campaigns of ʿAlā al-Dīn Khaljī and his general Malik Khān inspired literary panegyric within Indo-Muslim circles, including the "epic of conquest" by poet laureate Amīr Khusraw, the *Khazāʾinul Futūh* or "Treasures of Victory." The events of the period—both the invasions from Delhi and the establishment of new polities under Vijayanagara and other Hindu-affiliated warrior elites—also formed the basis for Hindu "epics of resistance" or, as was more appropriate to the south Indian case, a literature of recovery.

This chapter examines the ways in which medieval authors in southern India narrated the transformative events of the fourteenth century. The south Indian literature of recovery portrays the Turkic invasions as fundamentally disruptive of existing social norms and relations, and it depicts the new rulers who defeated the invaders as restoring a preexisting Hindu social order grounded upon a shared religious ideology. In the literature of recovery, not surprisingly, images and temples at significant sacred sites like Cidambaram, Madurai, and Sri Rangam play important roles. In the converse reflection of Islamic treatments like that of Amīr Khusraw, where attacks on idols signify the removal of a pollution traced ultimately to Satan, Hindu texts of the period employ dislocation and restoration of key icons as a synecdoche for the disjuncture and recovery of a supposedly ancient Hindu religious and social order.

Yet true recovery is seldom a simple matter. In the literature of recovery, images themselves must often experience considerable travails before returning home, and may return altered by their adventures. Likewise, the new rulers and the new polities they established in the wake of Khaljī and Tughluk invasions differed in origin and in organization from the old dynasties of the south. Covering their originality, the new Hindu elite sought to validate and enhance its ruling authority through the public restoration of the most visible and esteemed icons of former times. In the process, I will argue, particular icons like the Viṣṇu Raṅganātha images at Sri Rangam gained a status still greater than they had enjoyed previously.[2]

The Conquest of Madurai

To gain an idea of the main themes in the south Indian literature of recovery, let us look at one of the finest epics of resistance, the fourteenth-century Sanskrit poem *Madhurāvijaya*, the "Conquest of Madurai," composed by Gaṅgādevī, wife of Prince Kampaṇa, the protagonist of the poem. Sometime in the 1350s the Vijayanagara ruler Bukka I sent his eldest son Kampaṇa southward to extend Vijayanagara dominion into Tamilnad. Kampaṇa first marched on the Sambuvarāya ruler of Tondaimaṇḍala, the old Pallava territory, and set himself up as regional potentate in Kanchipuram. When he had consolidated his forces in that area he attacked and defeated the Madurai Sultanate and made himself king of Madurai, under Vijayanagara overlordship. Gaṅgādevī took Kampaṇa's life and his two successful military campaigns as the subject for her narrative of victory.

Gaṅgādevī's Narrative

Gaṅgādevī classifies her poem as a *carita*, a term often translated as "biography" but more accurately understood as a narrative of actions. As V. S. Pathak has noted in his study of royal caritas, works in this genre never aim to describe the entire lives of their subjects but rather limit themselves to a particular trajectory of events, an ordered sequence of actions culminating in the achievement of royal glory by the king (1966: 27). In some cases, such as the paradigmatic royal carita of King Harṣavardhana composed by Bāṇa Bhaṭṭa in the seventh century, poets personify royal glory as a goddess, Rājyaśrī. The king must overcome great obstacles to win her love. In caritas dealing with "victory" (*vijaya*), such as the *Madhurāvijaya* and Jayānaka's twelfth-century *Pṛthvīrājavijaya*, events culminate not in winning the goddess' love but in "some remarkable victory of the hero over a notable adversary" (101).

Gaṅgādevī's primary theme in *Madhurāvijaya* is the overriding importance of purposeful exertion. All the signs before and at Kampaṇa's birth point to his destiny as warrior and king. While pregnant, his mother has a craving to eat sweet-tasting dirt, "as if she thought to instruct him in the royal duty of bearing the earth" (*MV* 2.3). At birth the infant bears insignia of conch, discus, parasol, and lotus on his feet, and has the curled tuft of hair known as *śrīvatsa* on his chest, clear signs that he is an incarnation of Viṣṇu and will enjoy unbroken prosperity (2.28–29). He grows up handsome, strong, and truthful. Yet Gaṅgādevī also portrays the young prince as something of a voluptuary who enjoys too keenly the many sensual and aesthetic pleasures offered by his privileged courtly life. Kampaṇa requires the directives of others to nudge him out of his indulgences and into action. Gaṅgādevī articulates this instigation primarily through the speeches of Kampaṇa's father Bukka and a mysterious goddess.

When Kampaṇa has grown to maturity and married, his father decides it is time to challenge him. "Darkness spreads over us in youth," Bukka advises his youthful son, and only through paying heed to proper instruction can we free ourselves from that darkness (3.21). He goes on to lament the passions that control us in youth, "for youth is a stage of life where the darkness of intoxication is like the darkest night, whose blackness prevents the moon from shining [or: obstructs the moon of knowledge]. On its flag is the rutting elephant of passion, born in the mind. Those of us with bodies seldom escape it" (3.24). However, continues Bukka, a young prince like Kampaṇa, whose mind has been shaped and purified by good education, should be able to overcome passionate attachments and carry out his proper duties (3.36). Now is the time for Kampaṇa to arise and demonstrate his maturity and prowess.

Bukka then gives Kampaṇa his marching orders. First he must proceed to the region of Tondaimaṇḍala and destroy the armies of the Sambuvarāya king. He should set himself up as ruler in Kanchipuram and prepare for his second and more significant campaign, against the Turkic ruler of Madurai. Bukka suggests an analogy: "That demonic king is perpetuating all sorts of bad deeds in the southern territories, so you should emulate the flawless action of Rāma and remove this disease from the three worlds" (3.43). In former times Viṣṇu's incarnation Rāma had extinguished the demon (*rākṣasa*) Rāvaṇa ruling the southern kingdom of Lanka. Now, it would seem, another "demon" had gained sovereignty over another southern domain.

Kampaṇa sets out the next day and soon accomplishes the first phase of his mission. After several engagements with Sambuvarāya forces, he finally sends the Sambuvarāya king to a place "where all that remains is his story." With this victory he receives a royal charter from his father granting him subordinate sovereignty over Tondaimaṇḍala. Kampaṇa rules Kanchipuram with justice, compassion, and liberality. His subjects consider him an incarnation of Viṣṇu. He surrounds himself with poets, courtesans, and dancers. In spring he becomes so engaged in his lovemaking that the women of the harem begin to mistake the prince for the love god Kāma. As Gaṅgādevī comments, "Thus fearlessly enjoying the special forms of lovemaking that should be practiced during the different seasons of the year with his many clever and beautiful courtesans who longed for him whenever separated, King Kampaṇa fulfilled the third aim of life, Kāma" (5.76). Kampaṇa is satisfied with his life of royal enjoyment, until an unnamed goddess appears to remind him of the second phase of his father's orders.[3]

The goddess begins by describing the situation in the south. A new regime has displaced the old order. In the temples, she says, the howls of jackals have replaced the sound of *mṛdaṅga* drums. The dresses of fine Chinese silk draped on the statues guarding the city gates are covered now with tangles of spider webs. In the brahmin settlements, the odor of raw meat has supplanted the fragrance of sacrificial smoke, and the bellowing of drunken Turks drowns out the chanting of Vedas. Along the highways the jingling sounds of women's jewelled anklets cannot be heard for the screams of brahmins as they are dragged about in leg chains. The new order has even thrown the natural order into disarray. "Its waters no longer restrained," reports the goddess, "the Kaveri River now overflows its ancient banks into all the wrong places, as if it has suddenly decided to imitate the Turks in following wicked pathways" (8.6). In this verse Gaṅgādevī suggests through double entendre that the young women of the area, like the flooding Kaveri, are transgressing the ancient codes of proper conduct and following the Turks into immoral pasttimes. The new rulers pose a sexual threat. Earth no longer produces wealth and Indra does not send rains.

So bad has the deterioration become that Viṣṇu himself is in danger. "The great snake Ananta is distressed! It seems he is trying to wake Viṣṇu up from the deep yogic sleep he has attained at Sri Rangam, while at the same time he protects Viṣṇu under his circle of snake hoods from the bricks that keep falling from the temple tower" (8.2). The image of Raṅganātha at Sri Rangam depicts Viṣṇu asleep upon his snake Ananta in the midst of the milk ocean. Normally this image represents the creative omnipotence of Viṣṇu in its latent state, but in the current political situation, the goddess suggests, yogic sleep seems more like divine negligence. It is time for the deity to awaken before his temple tumbles down all around him.

Concluding her description of the old order gone topsy-turvy, the goddess declares that it is Kali-yuga: "The Vedas have ended. Reason has disappeared. The voice of dharma is silent. Good conduct is gone. Noble birth is set aside. What else is there to say? Kali alone flourishes." (8.16) The cyclical theory of four ages was already an old notion in Indian thought, first articulated in classical works such as Manu's Dharmaśāstra and developed fully in early purāṇas such as the *Viṣṇupurāṇa*.[4] Underlying the theory was a concept of moral deterioration over time. The first age is a golden age (the Kṛta-yuga), when human life is characterized by an effortless virtue. With the arising of passion and greed, virtue begins to require effort and society takes on a hierarchical shape. A gradual deterioration ensues over the next two ages until one reaches the moral nadir, the Kali-yuga.

For a late medieval poet like Gaṅgādevī, the notion of Kali-yuga provided a vocabulary of imagery and a means of naturalizing unprecedented disruptive events within a time-honored conceptualization. However, she altered the concept. In earlier purāṇic treatments, Kali-yuga was brought on through the progressive moral failure of human society as a whole. The *Viṣṇupurāṇa* points to the predatory practices of rulers during Kali-yuga only as a symptom of more general decline, not as its cause. Gaṅgādevī's goddess by contrast suggests that the Kali-yuga of the Madurai Sultanate results directly from the imposition of exogenous rule. The new rulers, she implies, directly overturn the social and religious bulwarks of the traditional order. For Gaṅgādevī, moral transgressions like those of the Kaveri Valley girls are the consequence of foreign rule, not its cause.[5]

In a cyclical model of time all eras must end sometime, and the Kali-yuga fortunately is susceptible to human endeavor. Indian kings often take credit for overturning the Kali-yuga and returning their dominions to the golden age. So in the *Madhurāvijaya* the goddess has chosen Kampaṇa as her special agent for removing Kali. She presents him with a terrible-looking sword, and explains its history.

> King, once Viśvakarman made this sword with particles of all the gods' weapons and presented it to Śiva so he could defeat the demons. That god gave it to the Pāṇḍyan king as a favor for his rigorous austerities, and the king's descendants kept it and ruled the earth without opposition for a long time. But, king, the sage Agastya has ascertained that the Pāṇḍyan lineage has now lost its heroic vigor (*vīrya*) through the passage of time, and so he has passed this round-bladed sword on to a ruler with stronger arms—namely you. (8.23–25)

Kampaṇa is already daring in battle, she tells him, and this sword will make him truly invincible. The goddess then reiterates Bukka's command, selecting a different incarnation of Viṣṇu as the model Kampaṇa should emulate. "You are powerful!" she observes. "Now, by cutting down that cruel Yāvana ruler in southern Madurai, who is as oppressive as Kaṁsa [the demon who ruled northern Mathura], you should prove that you are the incarnation of Viṣṇu [as Kṛṣṇa did]" (8.29). Kampaṇa must restore the proper order of things, the goddess tells him. Only when he rules will the Kaveri River return to its former boundaries (8.36).

The prince goes on to Madurai. His army routs the Turkic forces and he meets the sultan in single combat. With the Pāṇḍyan sword he cuts off the sultan's head. Heaps of flowers fall on Kampaṇa's head, as if the goddess Rājyaśrī had just chosen him as bridegroom at her ceremonial assembly of suitors (*svayamvara*) (9.38). Gaṅgādevī ends her narrative with Kampaṇa crowned and the south regaining its luster. "With the Persians destroyed, the south shone again. It shone like the luster of forests when a forest fire has been put out. It shone like the bowl of the sky when an eclipse has just ended. It shone like the Yamuna River after Kṛṣṇa killed the serpent-demon Kāliya" (9.39). In accord with the conventions of the genre, Kampaṇa has carried out the commands of his preceptors, accomplished his victory, gained the favor of Rājyaśrī—and that is the end of the story.

Vijayanagara Conquest as Hindu Reconquest

Gaṅgādevī's poem of victory illustrates much of the basic thematic repertoire of Hindu literature engaged with the threat of Turkic Muslim rule in India. This literature denotes the invaders as ethnically distinct *turuṣkas* (Turks) or *pārasikas* (Persians), and classifies them in terms of foreign origin, *mleccha* (foreigner) and *yāvana*. The category *yāvana* originally designated Greeks and was subsequently generalized to signify all foreigners from the west of India (including in a later period the French *yāvanas* of Pondicherry). Never do Hindu texts of this period use terms denoting religious affiliation for the Turks, who understood themselves to be members of the Islamic community.[6] However, Gaṅgādevī does identify and criticize some distinct customary practices of the Turks, such as drinking wine and eating meat, that transgress her idea of proper conduct. As Gaṅgādevī's allusions to Rāvaṇa, Kaṁsa, and Kāliya suggest, the invading Turks are often metaphorically figured as demons, homologized with famous antagonists of the gods and disrupters of the social order from the epic literature of the past.

The literature of recovery portrays Turkic rule through imagery of conflagration, through value-laden dichotomies, and through suggestions of sexual threat. An inscriptional account of the Telugu warrior Prolaya Nāyaka, for instance, likens the onset of Turkic rule to pitch darkness enveloping the world after the sun sets, and compares the territory under the Yāvanas to a forest scorched by fire.[7] Gaṅgādevī employs the rhetorical strategy of antithesis, juxtaposing old and new to disparage Turkic dominion and highlight its disastrous consequences. In her punning verse describing the Kaveri River transgressing her former bounds, Gaṅgādevī also touches on the theme of sexual threat. North Indian epics of resistance develop this motif more vigorously. Hindu women are called upon to maintain their purity, often to the point of death, in the face of aristocratic Muslim suppliants. Finally, the literature of recovery frequently comprehends the new situation within the framework of cyclic time, as the Kali-yuga, where greed and passion dominate and dharma totters on one foot.

The defeat of the old orders calls for new heroes. The old Hindu dynasties are not able to reassert themselves, for they have lost their former vitality through the debilitating passage of time. In Gaṅgādevī's narrative, the goddess herself locates her new hero, Kampaṇa, and compels him to take action. To do so she cites exemplary divine heroes like Rāma and Kṛṣṇa, whose legendary victories over their demonic foes should serve as models for Kampaṇa's own conduct. The literature of recovery depicts the victories of new heroes over their Turkic opponents as the restoration of a preexisting order. The new rulers purify the lands from contamination and recover dharma. They overturn Kali-yuga and return society to the former golden age.

Successful heroes often turn out to be incarnations of Viṣṇu. Gaṅgādevī suggests throughout her poem that Kampaṇa is Viṣṇu incarnate. Similarly Jayānaka's *Pṛthvīrājavijaya* argues that the Cāhamāna ruler Pṛthvīrāja is Rāma, returned to earth "to complete the task he had started."[8] Even the low-caste Telugu warrior Prolaya, without any previous connections to royalty, claims in his inscription to be a "partial incarnation" (*aṃśāvatāra*) of Lord Viṣṇu. The poets do not present these as metaphors but as facts of identity. Considering Viṣṇu's multiplicity of manifestations and his continuing interest in maintaining social order, these literary statements would not have appeared as outlandish hubris to Hindu audiences of the time, but as plausible claims to be evaluated carefully.

Often the heroes of restoration are not members of the former ruling elites, but the texts find ways to integrate them into the older dynasties. Gaṅgādevī has her goddess present a sword embodying Pāṇḍyan prowess to Kampaṇa, which makes him proper successor to the deposed rulers of Madurai. By acquiring objects of continuity, such as regalia, new rulers can overcome their humble or exogenous backgrounds and proclaim themselves legitimate lords of their new domains.

Many historians of south India have accepted the literary representations of disruption and restoration such as that of the *Madhurāvijaya* as factual accounts. In his study of *The Tamil Country under Vijayanagar*, A. Krishnaswami speaks of the "pathetic conditions of the Tamil country owing to the tyrannical rule of the Sultans of Madura," and judges Gaṅgādevī's depiction as accurate. "Gaṅgādevī has described the political and social conditions in such a way that it looks like a faithful portrait of the actual state of affairs" (1964: 22). More cautiously, K. A. Nilakanta Sastri comments that "the poem throws much welcome light on the political conditions of the time" (1972: 212). Once again we must remember Aziz Ahmad's admonition to read these texts for "historical attitude" rather than as historical facts.

Texts like *Madhurāvijaya* seek to portray the accomplishments of their heroes as bringing about the reestablishment of a preexisting, stable, harmonious social order that had been temporarily disturbed. Yet historically the Vijayanagara polity that Kampaṇa extended into Tamilnad represented a significant change from the early medieval regimes of the south. Most important, as Burton Stein has argued, was a shift in dominance whereby new dynastic rulers based in the upland dry zones of the Deccan displaced older polities centered in the rich agricultural river valleys. In the plateau areas of sparse rainfall, Stein writes, "hardy peasant groups, prevented by insufficient water from achieving high levels of multi-crop production, were compelled to pursue plundering expeditions with fighting skills honed by turbulent relations with herdsmen and forest peoples" (1989: 21). At the same time, the new and superior military techniques introduced by the fourteenth-century invaders from Delhi intensified an emerging martial ethos in southern India. The new heroes of the age came from precisely those peasant warrior groups of the uplands who were best able to put into practice the military tactics they learned from the Turkic armies. According to some historians, Bukka and his brother Harihara, founders of Vijayanagara, were captured Telugu warriors who temporarily embraced Islam and served in the army of the Delhi Sultanate before renouncing Islam to strike out on their own.[9] After establishing themselves first in a plateau center, they soon extended their dominion over the more prosperous lowland regions through ambitious campaigns like Kampaṇa's forays into Tamilnad.

Parvenu rulers from humble backgrounds legitimated their new sovereignty by emphasizing continuity with the past, whether through claims of reincarnation or through acquisition of regalia. By a dialectical process, this conservative strategy also led them to stress the otherness of the Turkic regimes they were replacing. "By accentuating the threat from Muslims, and their strange alien ways," Cynthia Talbot observes, "these aspiring kings could successfully cast themselves in the role of defenders of the Hindu social order, the most fundamental justification for kingly status. The representations of Muslims as demons may therefore have been instrumental (that is, secondary) to the primary goal of providing Telugu warrior lineages with a secure identity and legitimate authority" (Talbot 1994: 6). Talbot's comments apply particularly well in the case of Kampaṇa, a young warrior from the recently established Vijayanagara kingdom in Karnataka, bringing Tamilnad under Telugu rule. To make himself less of a foreigner in Tamil country, it would help to make the Turks more so. In this context Gaṅgādevī's *Madhurāvijaya* should be seen, just as she suggests, not only as a fine courtly poem designed to "arouse delight," but also to promote Kampaṇa's "fame" and his legitimacy as a proper conqueror and ruler in the classical mold (1.23).

Of course Kampaṇa had other ways of making the same rhetorical point through media more widely accessible than a court epic in high Sanskrit. Hindu temples and their divine images were a key part of the project. Inscriptions throughout Tamilnad record Kampaṇa's many benefactions to temples.[10] He intervened in local temple affairs by abjudicating disputes and replacing old administrators with new ones. More than this, Kampaṇa also reopened key temples that had been converted or closed over the previous decades.[11] At Kannanur, the former regional capital of the Hoysalas in Tamilnad, the Turks had converted the royal temple built by Vīra Someśvara in the mid-thirteenth century into a mosque; Kampaṇa reconverted it into a temple in 1372 (*ARE* 162 of 1936–1937). He reopened the great temple at the center of Madurai. Kampaṇa's officer Gopaṇa restored the image of Viṣṇu Govindarāja to the Śaiva temple at Cidambaram and, as we shall see, Gopaṇa also brought the portable image of Viṣṇu Raṅganātha back from its place of hiding and had it reinstalled in the sanctum of the temple at Sri Rangam, thereby (claims the verse commemorating the event) "reuniting the ground of Sri Rangam with the Golden Age."[12]

During much of the fourteenth century, all of southern India became part of a shifting frontier contested between warrior groups affiliated with Muslim and Hindu ideologies. The literature of recovery, like the dramatic reconsecration of important south Indian holy sites, was primarily the product of this period of crisis and transition. With the establishment of a relatively stable balance of power in peninsular India by the end of the fourteenth century, lasting through the mid-sixteenth century, the dichotomizing rhetoric diminished, as both Cynthia Talbot and Philip Wagoner have recently shown. Texts of the later period envision the peninsula as divided into three major polities, with the Muslim Bahmani Sultanate based in the northwest Deccan (and its various successors) considered as an inescapable and legitimate part of the ruling order of things. "Far from being alien intruders whose very existence was abhorrent to the natural order of the universe," Talbot comments, "Muslims are now conceived as an essential element in the sociopolitical world" (1994: 8).

Flights of Reclining Viṣṇu

Gaṅgādevī's *Madhurāvijaya* viewed Hindu temples and images as an essential part of a larger cultural unity, but as only one element among many. The poet devoted little direct attention to religious objects, but rather focused her narrative upon the warrior-prince Kampaṇa, whose task it was to reestablish and protect all elements of the preexisting Hindu social order. However, in other genres of late medieval south Indian literature, temples and their divine images figure more centrally. In Vaiṣṇava devotional hagiographies and temple chronicles, stories of images recovered signified the restoration of cosmic order.

In the face of actual destruction and alienation of religious objects from their temple settings during the fourteenth century, narratives of recovery reaffirmed the continuing vitality of icons and the gods that inhabited them. They asserted that a special relationship linked the deity's image to its particular site, and that this connection resulted from divine choice rather than human initiative. In implicit rejoinder to Indo-Muslim narratives of iconoclasm, they argued for the capacity of the divine protagonists to act on their own behalf, in concert with humans, in defending their images from danger. They emphasized the community of interest between the deity's image and the devotees, and stressed the power of human devotion toward divinity in overcoming adversity. Finally, they suggested (though only indirectly) that aniconic forms of religiosity such as orthodox Islam did not meet the emotional needs of humans for a loving personal relationship with divinity. Overall the stories offered a dramatic restatement and reification of existing ideas about temple images in light of the challenge posed by iconoclastic Turkic warriors and the Islamic critique of idolatry.

In the remainder of this chapter I will focus on narratives that grew up around the movements of images in the Vaiṣṇava temple at Sri Rangam. The stories come from texts of the sixteenth through eighteenth centuries, though they are based no doubt on earlier written records and oral recountings. At a historical remove from the events they relate, they offer a retrospective view of the iconoclasm of the fourteenth century without the sense of social crisis and the martial ethos that characterizes the *Madhurāvijaya*. Yet these narratives also indicate ways in which the events of that period of crisis became inscribed into the identity of the images for later Hindu audiences, and how those same images assumed new roles in the postinvasion political order.

Raṅganātha of Sri Rangam

The temple of Viṣṇu Raṅganātha at Sri Rangam became the principal center for south Indian Vaiṣṇavism in the early medieval period. Located on an island in the Kaveri River near the city of Tiruccirappali (Anglicized as Trichi), the temple complex occupies a vast area of over 150 acres, arranged in seven rectangular courtyards surrounding the central shrine of Viṣṇu. As with many south Indian temple complexes, the inner core of this sacred center may be very old, whereas the outer sections represent later structures added mostly during the Vijayanagara and Nāyakkar periods. At Sri Rangam, construction continues up to the present. Only in 1987 did workmen finally complete the towering southern gateway, 236 feet tall, that a Vijayanagara-period provincial ruler in Thanjavur had begun in the second half of the sixteenth century (Figure 16).[13]

At the center of the temple complex reclines a large stucco image of Viṣṇu Raṅganātha ("Lord of the stage"), in deep yogic sleep on the great snake Ananta ("endless"). The snake forms for him a couch of coils floating on the milk ocean, and spreads its five hoods over Viṣṇu's head like an umbrella.

FIG. 16. Rājagopuram under Construction, Raṅganātha Temple, 1982. Building started in the sixteenth century, completed in 1987. Sri Rangam, Tamilnad.

Iconographic texts label the form Viṣṇu Anantaśayana, "Viṣṇu sleeping on Ananta." This icon of cosmic relaxation, seemingly so indolent, is in fact an image of creation, for from the navel of this sleeping figure at the dawn of creation emerges all being. In medieval Vaiṣṇava cosmology Viṣṇu recurrently creates and rescues the world, and then retires again to his resting place on the milk ocean, where he awaits yet another call upon his supreme potency.

In front of this reclining Viṣṇu stands a smaller metal image of Viṣṇu, known as Aḻakiyamaṇavāḷa Perumāḷ ("the Lord as handsome bridegroom"), flanked by seated images of his two wives, goddesses Lakṣmī and Earth (Figure 17). This mobile icon is the primary processional deity of the Raṅganātha temple. Another smaller bronze icon of Viṣṇu stands at Raṅganātha's feet. This image is known as Māḷikaiyār ("Lord of the palace"), or more commonly as Yogabherar. Surrounding these primary images is a veritable city of shrines and subsidiary icons.[14]

FIG. 17. Śrī Raṅganātha, Sri Rangam. Viṣṇu Raṅganātha reclines. Viṣṇu Aḻakiya-maṇavāḷa, the main processional icon, stands in foreground center, flanked by two consorts. Viṣṇu Māḷikaiyār is depicted in lower right, at Raṅganātha's feet. Calendar print by C. Kondiah Raju and T. S. Subbiah. Printed by permission of the National Litho Press, Sivakasī.

A Viṣṇu temple certainly existed on Sri Rangam island by the seventh century. Vaiṣṇava poet-saints of the seventh through ninth centuries vigorously praised and promoted Sri Rangam as the special home of Lord Viṣṇu Raṅganātha. The Āḻvārs celebrated many sacred sites throughout Tamilnad—the later conventional enumeration was 108 holy places—but none more so than Sri Rangam. They referred to Sri Rangam simply as *koyil*, the temple par excellence. All but one Āḻvār composed hymns of Sri Rangam, and altogether the poets sang 247 verses of praise devoted to Viṣṇu at Sri Rangam, more than those directed to any other place (Narayanan 1987: 34). Friedhelm Hardy speaks of this as a gradual "apotheosis" of Sri Rangam, by which it gained preeminent position among all Viṣṇu temples in Tamilnad by the ninth century.[15]

The later hagiographical traditions that grew up around the āḻvār poet-saints continued to present Sri Rangam as the preeminent stage for south Indian Vaiṣṇava devotionalism. The ardent saint and prolific poet Tirumaṅkai Āḻvār, as we saw in Chapter Two, accepted Raṅganātha's own command to rehabilitate the temple at Sri Rangam and engaged in some dubious labor and supply methods to carry out the task. The Cera king Kulaśekhara Āḻvār renounced his kingdom in order to live at Sri Rangam near his favored embodiment of Viṣṇu.

The best-known of the devotional biographies concerns the female saint Āṇṭāḷ. According to the Vaiṣṇava hagiographies, Periyāḻvār found her as a baby under a tulsi plant and adopted her. Already as an infant Āṇṭāḷ showed precocious piety. When she babbled it was the names of Viṣṇu. As a young girl she fell in love with Raṅganātha of Sri Rangam, selecting him from "all the Viṣṇus of south India." She adamantly refused any human suitor. Her foster-father became increasingly anxious about her marriage prospects, until Viṣṇu appeared to him in a dream and informed him that Raṅganātha himself would accept Āṇṭāḷ as a bride. Periyāḻvār had Āṇṭāḷ dressed in wedding clothes and together they walked to Sri Rangam. Āṇṭāḷ entered the sanctum, climbed up onto Viṣṇu's snake-couch, clasped the feet of the icon, and disappeared into the image of Raṅganātha. The young bride had merged with her groom. The text explains that Āṇṭāḷ was in fact an incarnation of the goddess Earth, Viṣṇu's second wife.

In addition to the poet-saints, virtually all the theologians and teachers who formulated the Śrīvaiṣṇava school, the primary order of south Indian Vaisnavism, were associated with Sri Rangam. Nāthamuni was a priest in Raṅganātha temple when he collected and organized the compositions of the twelve āḻvār saints into canonical form, set them to music, and arranged to have them recited for Viṣṇu in the temple sanctum (Cutler 1987: 44–45). He became the first preceptor (*ācārya*) in the Śrīvaiṣṇava lineage. His first two successors, Yāmuna and Rāmānuja (d. 1137), were key figures in integrating the Tamil poetic devotionalism of the āḻvārs with the liturgical practices of the Pāñcarātra school and the Sanskritic philosophical teachings known as Vedānta into a coherent new religious formation. Yāmuna taught at Sri Rangam, and Rāmānuja served for many years as manager of the temple.

Along with its continuing centrality to the Śrīvaiṣṇava order, the Raṅganātha temple at Sri Rangam also became a significant site in south Indian politics in the thirteenth century.[16] When the Pāṇḍyan king Jaṭāvarman Sundarapāṇḍya invaded the former Cola territories in the mid-thirteenth century and defeated the Hoysala ruler Someśvara at Kannanur, he visited the two most important religious centers of the area, Cidambaram, and Sri Rangam, during his victory tour. At the Śiva temple in Cidambaram, Sundarapāṇḍya worshiped at the feet of Naṭarāja and put on a victory garland. Then he went on to the Viṣṇu temple at Sri Rangam to perform the ceremonial *tulābhāra*, a royal gift-giving ritual in which a king donates his own weight in gold or other precious substances to some virtuous recipient. According to the inscription commemorating his visit, Sundarapāṇḍya set up a new golden image of the Highest Being, Viṣṇu, covered the central shrine with gold, built several new shrines, and gave numerous gifts of precious gems including an emerald garland he had appropriated from the Gajapati ruler of Orissa on a previous campaign (Hultzsch 1894–1995).[17]

When the armies of the Delhi Sultanate invaded in the early part of the fourteenth century, they directed their iconoclasm selectively against temples that they believed to be particularly wealthy and politically significant. They chose the temples at Cidambaram and Sri Rangam, the most important Śaiva and Vaiṣṇava centers of Tamilnad, as primary targets. Amīr Khusraw's contemporary epic of conquest described the sacking of Cidambaram temple, as we have seen. For the events at Sri Rangam we must turn to later Hindu accounts maintained in temple chronicles and hagiographies. Not surprisingly, these narratives do not dwell on the physical destruction of icons, but on the strategies of concealment, dissimulation, flight, and subsequent return by which devotees preserved the lives of the prominent images of the temple and on the role Viṣṇu himself played in his own self-preservation.

Images in Exile

Under pressure of iconoclasm, concealment and flight became important means of preservation for portable icons. Images might find refuge underground, or they might abandon their wealthy and vulnerable temples for more out-of-the-way sanctuaries. The assumption, or at least hope, behind these evacuations was that, when danger had passed, the images would return to their accustomed homes.

Defensive burial was one common practice. As the *Vimānārcanākalpa*, a medieval priestly handbook of the Vaiṣṇava Vaikhānasa school, advises, "When there is danger on account of thieves or enemy armies, and when there is disorder in the community, one should conceal the metal images used for festivals, bathing rites, processions, and tribute offerings" (*VĀK* p. 435).[18] Judging from the hundreds of bronze icons unearthed by accident in Tamilnad during the twentieth century, temple protectors must have frequently taken recourse to burying their icons, not only in the fourteenth century but also in many subsequent times of political and social uncertainty.[19] The *Vimānārcanākalpa* goes on to outline the ritual procedures one should follow when burying images.

> In a clean and hidden place the temple priest or worshiper should dig a pit, sprinkle sand in it and strew sacrificial grass over the sand. He worships the Earth Goddess in the pit, reciting the mantra "Apohiṣṭhā." Together with the patron and devotees, he enters the sanctum of the god, bows to the deity, and makes a request: "As long as there is danger, O Viṣṇu, please lie down in a bed

> with the goddess Earth." He transfers the divine energy (*śakti*) located in the image into the fixed image, or in lieu of a fixed image he may transfer the energy into his own heart. (*VĀK* 435–36)

Accompanying each action with the appropriate mantra, the priest picks up the image, lays it down carefully in the pit, and fills the hole firmly with dirt. He then returns to the temple and prepares a *kūrca*, a bundle of fifty stalks of sacrificial grass. He invokes the animating spirit of the buried image into the bundle, and henceforward worshipers are to honor the bundle much as they would the image itself. The *kūrca* serves as the temporary support for the divine presence, and one not likely to excite the wrath of iconoclasts or the avarice of thieves.

Clearly the medieval ritualists devised these procedures to preserve both the physical icon and its animating spirit, even though they must be temporarily separated from one another. As soon as danger is passed, the *Vimānārcanākalpa* goes on, the priest should disinter the image, clean it with tamarind, perform a rather lengthy reconsecration, return it to the temple, and finally transfer the divine presence back into the resurrected icon.

Another common strategy involved retreat to some hidden or inaccessible place. Amīr Khusraw recognizes this tactic in his description of the sack of Cidambaram, where he refers with sarcastic personification to gods leaping away to Sri Lanka. Only the fixed liṅgas, he observes, cannot escape since they have no legs to stand on, and the recumbent Viṣṇu Nārāyaṇa (Anantaśayana) falls down in his effort to escape. Some of the most eminent icons of late medieval India did flee their homes to escape destruction. During the struggles for control of Orissa during the Mughal period, for instance, the Viṣṇu Jagannātha image of Puri left for the hinterlands of southern Orissa or for islands in Chilka Lake more than a dozen times.[20]

Independent rulers might offer refuge to prestigious threatened images, to enhance their own prestige and ruling authority. In the 1660s, the increasingly antagonistic policies toward major Hindu temples of the Mughal emperor Aurangzeb led to a veritable exodus of Vaiṣṇava images from the Braj area around Mathura, the original homeland of Kṛṣṇa. Most famous of these was Śrī Nāthji, a four-foot black stone image of Kṛṣṇa raising his left arm. The icon depicts a famous moment in Kṛṣṇa's life on earth, in which he held up Mount Govardhana to protect his cowherd community from a deluge sent by the Vedic god Indra. After its miraculous appearance from the ground on Mount Govardhana, the image remained at Gokul until 1669, when its custodians decided the threat was too great. First Śrī Nāthji journeyed to Agra, then to the state of Kota, whose ruler offered protection. Next the icon travelled to Kishangarh, then to Chaupasani near Jodhpur. Finally the Mewar ruler Rana Rāj Singh requested that Śrī Nāthji come to stay in Udaipur, and the priests set out with the image once again. But gods do not always comply with the aims of terrestrial kings. Twenty-four miles shy of Udaipur, Śrī Nāthji's cart got stuck in the mud. His entourage took this as a sign that Śrī Nāthji wished to remain there, rather than continue into Rāj Singh's capital, and so they built a shrine for the image there. This became the site of Nāthadvāra, the "Lord's door," the primary center of the Puṣṭimārga sect and one of the major Vaiṣṇava pilgrimage centers of India.[21]

The status that exiled images lent to peripheral rulers granting them temporary asylum might naturally leave the chieftains reluctant to give them up later. In 1688 the officials of three main temples in Kanchipuram, those of Viṣṇu Varadarājasvāmin, Śiva Ekāmreśvara, and the goddess Kāmākṣī, received reports that Mughal armies were about to invade the south. They disguised their temple images as corpses and transported them secretly out of town. Viṣṇu Varadarāja and his consort took refuge with a local ruler in the hinterlands of Udayarpalayam. By 1710 danger had passed and the temples tried to get their images back. The little king of Udayarpalayam, however, refused to give up Varadarāja, claiming he had become too devoted to part with it. Lāla Ṭoḍaramala, general of the nawab of Carnatic's army, had to march in force to Udayarpalayam and compel the recalcitrant chieftain to return Varadarāja to his earlier home in Kanchipuram.[22]

Raṅganātha's Pilgrimage Tour

Actual flights could become the basis for narrative development, engendering stories of adventure, heroism, sacrifice, and miracles that would enhance the status of the image, as well as that of its protectors. There are two such narratives of Raṅganātha's departures from Sri Rangam. Both involve the main processional deity of the temple. One story is probably grounded on events during Malik Khān's raid of 1311, and the other seems to derive from the Muḥammad bin Tughluk invasion of 1327–1328.

The seventeenth-century Śrīvaiṣṇava hagiographical text *Prapannāmṛta* of Anantasūri contains the fullest account of Raṅganātha's travels following the Tughluk conquest.[23] The story begins at the time of the annual river festival, where Raṅganātha (in the form of his processional image) goes out from the temple and bathes in the Kaveri River. While Raṅganātha is relaxing there, a spy arrives and informs Pillai Lokācārya, leader of the Śrīvaiṣṇava community, that the "Yāvana" armies of the Delhi Sultanate are coming. "There is a very powerful Yāvana coming here along with his army," says the spy, "looking like Kālayāvana himself. That Yāvana has destroyed all the territories along with their gods and brahmins, just as the demon Kaṁsa once did" (120.43–44). Throughout his narrative Anantasūri draws analogies with the legendary stories of Kṛṣṇa, as if these events were reenactments of those famous acts of Viṣṇu's incarnation. Kālayāvana, the "Black Yāvana," was a demonic foe of Kṛṣṇa and the Yādavas who gathered a huge army of mlecchas and attacked Mathurā, Kṛṣṇa's capital. Kṛṣṇa quickly fabricated the city of Dvārakā and had Mathurā's residents transported there. Then he fooled Kālayāvana into entering the cave where Mucukunda was sleeping, and Mucukunda burned down the demon (*Viṣṇupurāṇa* 5.23). The allusion to Kṛṣṇa's divine trickery foreshadows the role subterfuge will play in preserving the temple icons.

The people of Sri Rangam are not sure what to do. Fear and apprehension vie with their desire to complete the ceremony. They place two signs before the image bearing the words "Go" and "Stay," and ask the deity to decide. Raṅganātha selects the one that says "Stay." The priests continue the festival, and then another informant arrives. The Yāvanas are moving quickly. This time the leaders decide they have to depart. Vedānta Deśika directs Pillai Lokācārya to remove Raṅganātha and his two wives Lakṣmī and Earth and take them south. Vedānta Deśika then lights a single lamp by the throne of the image, and heads northwest toward Tirunarayanapura (modern Melkote) near Mysore.

The troops from Delhi arrive and strike down many of the Vaiṣṇavas there. Despite the general catastrophe, however, the later texts record how Viṣṇu's servants prevent the invaders from completely destroying the temple and its most important images. One Raṅgarāja, evidently a local headman, bricks in the main sanctum, then constructs a false altar in front of the closed entrance and places some lesser images there. The iconoclasts destroy them, little suspecting that the central deity of the temple is relaxing peacefully on the other side of the wall. One of the dancing girls of the temple becomes concubine to the Turkic commander and so beguiles him that she is able to persuade him not to destroy the temple. When the general becomes ill, he believes that it is an act of God, who must be angry at him for failing to destroy the idols of polytheism. To satisfy his need for vengeance, the dancing girl arranges to have some minor images like door guardians mutilated and brought before the general as surrogate victims.[24] Finally, a Tamil brahmin named Nārasiṃhadeva becomes adviser to the commander, just as (observes the author) Akrūra served Kaṁsa. The Indian model for subversive collaboration, Akrūra acted as minister for his demonic ruler but secretly became a devotee of Kṛṣṇa. Nārasiṃhadeva persuades the Turk general to move his headquarters from Sri Rangam to Kannanur, and has himself appointed local administrator of Sri Rangam, so he can protect the shrine from any further depredations. Through such individual acts of heroism and deceit, the narratives claim, the central core of the temple remains unviolated during its time of occupation.

Meanwhile, Raṅganātha and his entourage set out along back roads toward the hinterlands. Bandits attack them and steal all their wealth. They travel first to Alakarkoyil near Madurai, then on to Kerala where they visit the fourteen Vaiṣṇava centers of the area. Next they journey to Tirunarayanapura, the Śrīvaiṣṇava center of southern Karnataka. There the Viṣṇu icon known as "Beloved Son" pays his respect to Raṅganātha. (We will encounter Beloved Son again.) Finally the party moves on to Tirupati, in southern Andhra Pradesh, the home shrine of Viṣṇu Veṅkaṭeśvara. Here too, the poet observes, the lord of the temple treats the visiting deity with all due respect. Fatigued by his travels, Raṅganātha rests happily at Tirupati for some time. His flight from Sri Rangam has turned into a lengthy pilgrimage tour of the major Vaiṣṇava centers of southern India.

Years later, a righteous brahmin named Gopaṇa ruling in Gingee has a dream.[25] Raṅganātha appears in his sleep, explains that he is now at Tirupati, and gives Gopaṇa a command: "By my order you must defeat the mleccha army with your own forces and restore me, the Lord of Raṅga, to the temple of Sri Rangam" (*PA* 122.3). Amazed by the divine summons, Gopaṇa immediately goes to Tirupati to worship Raṅganātha. A priest there tells him the story of the alienated image. Gopaṇa first takes Raṅganātha along with the two consorts Lakṣmī and Earth back to his capital, Gingee. Spies bring him reports on the Turkic armies, and when the time is right Gopaṇa's forces attack them at night and defeat them. Then, fulfilling the divine edict, Gopaṇa restores Raṅganātha to his temple.

Vedānta Deśika, the story concludes, returns from his exile to perform an auspicious ceremony for Raṅganātha. He composes two Sanskrit verses to honor Gopaṇa's victory, which can still be seen on an inner courtyard wall at Sri Rangam, dated 1371–1372.

> From Collyrium Mountain [Tirupati] which delights all the world with the lustre of its dark blue peaks, that mirror of fame Gopaṇa brought Lord Raṅganātha to Gingee and worshiped him there for some time. He destroyed the Turks who had raised their bows, and then installed Raṅganātha along with his wives Lakṣmī and Earth in Raṅganātha's own city, Sri Rangam, and once again worshiped him in the proper manner.
>
> The brahmin Gopaṇa took Raṅganātha, Lord of Everything, from Bull Mountain [Tirupati] to his own capital. When he had defeated the proud Turkic army with his own forces, he installed Raṅganātha, Lakṣmī, and Earth, and thereby reunited the ground of Sri Rangam with the Golden Age. Like lotus-born Brahman, that virtuous man now dutifully worships Raṅganātha. (Hultzsch 1900–1901)

The contemporary inscription reminds us that Raṅganātha's return to Sri Rangam was a historical event. It is difficult to judge how much Anantasūri bases his narrative on fact. The characters in the story are historical figures of the period, and stories of Raṅganātha's sojourn at Tirupati also appear in the chronicles of that temple. What is significant for our purposes is the retelling of the story, remembering and thematizing events of the fourteenth century, in a text composed several centuries later.

The narrative of flight recognizes a real threat: images are vulnerable to destruction. Yet the tale shows how concerted action by temple servants and the image itself could preserve both image and temple from destruction. Such stories recount and overcome real disjuncture by assertions of essential constancy. When Kampaṇa reopens the closed doors of the temple at Madurai, another retrospective account tells us, everything is exactly as it had been when the sanctum was bricked in, fifty years earlier. "Things were found precisely as on the day when the temple was shut: the lamp that was lighted on that day, the sandal wood powder, the garland of flowers, and the ornaments usually placed on the morning of festival days, were now found to be exactly as it was usual to find them on the evening of the same festival days. The general saw this miracle and was overjoyed. He struck his eyes and with great piety made the customary offerings" (Taylor 1835: 1.35). In late medieval south India the old order could be recovered. At its innermost sanctuary, the narratives argue, the lamp had never even gone out.

Underneath this imagery of continuity, significant historical changes were occurring in the temple, just as they were in the late medieval south Indian political order. In a careful comparison of Sri Rangam inscriptions prior to 1344 with those recorded after 1370, Leslie Orr (1995a) points to several new features of temple culture that emerge only after the temple's restoration: the āḻvārs and preceptors (or their images) have taken on greater roles in worship, goddesses receive grander shrines, and temple ritual becomes increasingly complex, with a new liturgical system providing for the redistribution of temple "honors" to important donors and political figures. At the same time, the administration of the temple takes on a clearer, more hierarchical and bureaucratized form, caste becomes a more pronounced marker of status, and rulers intervene more actively in temple affairs. If the temple lamp did not go out, then it certainly burned with new ghee.

Viṣṇu in the Sultan's Court

Vaiṣṇava stories of image loss and return, like the Indo-Muslim anecdotes of Maḥmūd at Somanātha, often follow the rhetorical form of peristrophe. An initial setting of stability is disturbed by an outside force. Invasion leads to the apparent loss of a significant icon, which suggests that the image may indeed be as impotent as the opponent avers. At a critical moment, however, the image-deity acts, to overturn the opponent's view and to reassure the audience of the continuing power of icons. The deus ex machina is not simply a plot device, but rather the central theological point.

The denouement takes the image back to its starting point, and the story ends with the image in state, honored by its devotees and honoring those who helped in its recovery.

The most elaborate narrative of Raṅganātha's exile and return is preserved in the temple chronicles at Sri Rangam, the *Koyil Oluku*.[26] This tale again follows the main processional deity of the temple on a journey away from and back to its home temple. In this story, however, Muslim invaders gain possession of the image, and it spends time in the sultan's palace in Delhi. While there Viṣṇu manages to seduce the sultan's daughter, who becomes one of Raṅganātha's most devout followers. Śrīvaiṣṇava hagiographies also relate a parallel story centering on Rāmaprīya, also known as "Beloved Son" (*sampatkumāra*), the processional icon of the temple at Tirunarayanapura in Karnataka. Here too the icon is taken to Delhi and becomes the prized plaything of the Turkic princess, but in this version it is the theologian Rāmānuja who journeys to Delhi to recover the lost image.[27]

The *Koyil Oluku* begins its account with the Turkic ruler of Delhi defeating the Kākatīya king Pratāparudra and invading Tamilnad. (The mention of Pratāparudra's defeat correlates the story with the historical campaign of Malik Khān in 1311.) At Sri Rangam the invaders plunder the treasury and take away the main processional icon, A̲lakiyamaṇavāḷa Perumāḷ. As the invaders return to Delhi, a woman from Karambanur village near Sri Rangam follows their camp. When they reach Delhi the Turkic leader locks up the appropriated idols in the palace storeroom. The woman manages to disguise herself and enter the women's quarters of the palace. The sultan's daughter sees the image of Viṣṇu in the storeroom and takes it to her own bedroom. Believing it unsuitable for Viṣṇu's image to be treated as a doll, the Karambanur woman returns to Sri Rangam and informs the temple authorities what has happened.

The Sri Rangam elders close up the temple, suspend all festivals, and travel in a party of sixty to Delhi. Once again the Karambanur woman enters the harem and sees A̲lakiyamaṇavāḷa in the princess' chambers. The god, she observes, is "playing with daughter of the the Turkic sultan during the day in the bodily form of an icon (*arcāvigraha*), and at night in the full splendor of a human incarnation (*vibhavāvatāra*)" (*KO* 20). The temple text is too discrete to elaborate the nighttime sports of the princess and her living doll. The temple singers and dancers then entertain the sultan and he is so pleased by their performance that he offers them a boon. They ask for their image. The king orders his servants to bring the image from the storehouse, but it is not there. The visitors inform him that his daughter has it in her room. Rather than allow them to enter the harem, he challenges them: "You yourselves will have to call back your God." The temple singer invokes A̲lakiyamaṇavāḷa. The Viṣṇu icon puts the princess to sleep and leaves her chambers. The king is so amazed by the animate image that he allows the Vaiṣṇava party to depart with their treasure. They head toward Sri Rangam as quickly as they can.

The Tirunarayanapura version treats the confrontation in the sultan's court more dramatically. After Rāmānuja constructs the Tirunarayanapura temple for the Viṣṇu Nārāyaṇa statue he finds at Yadava Mountain, he discovers that the temple lacks a processional icon. Viṣṇu appears to Rāmānuja in a dream and informs him that the movable image called Rāmaprīya, which belongs in the new temple, is currently in Delhi. Rāmānuja and a band of followers go to Delhi, where the sultan receives him respectfully and asks why he has come. Rāmānuja asks for the Rāmaprīya image. "Previously during his conquest of the quarters (*digvijaya*) the king had appropriated all the Vaiṣṇava and Śaiva images, and now he showed them all to the great ascetic" (*PA* 47.63). But Rāmaprīya is not among them. Rāmānuja asserts that there must be other images in the palace, but the sultan taunts him. "If this Viṣṇu Rāmaprīya is your god, and if you have summoned him, why has he not come back to you?" (47.68) Rāmānuja is silent in the face of this challenge and he leaves the palace full of anxiety and despair.

That night Viṣṇu Rāmaprīya appears to Rāmānuja in a dream. "Why are you so despondent?" asks the image. "The king's daughter is honoring me well. I am in her bedchamber. Come there and fetch me" (47.71). Next morning the king escorts Rāmānuja to the princess' room, and there indeed stands Rāmaprīya visible to all. The princess has dressed the statue in yellow, rubbed musk on his forehead, and adorned him with beautiful jewelry, just as if she were performing pūjā to the idol. Overcome with love for the icon, Rāmānuja exclaims, "Beloved Son!" and the image jumps into Rāmānuja's lap. They embrace. The king is so amazed by all this that he presents the statue to Rāmānuja and grants him permission to depart.

The sultan's challenge and Viṣṇu's response form the peripeteia of the story. Rather like an Islamic prophetic miracle, the icon's movement in a public contest of faith transgresses the expected order of things—certainly the sultan's expectations—in order to demonstrate Viṣṇu's power and the sincerity of his servants such as Rāmānuja. The image also indicates its preference for its own temple community of Sri Rangam, even over the sumptuous attentions of the sultan's daughter. However, according to this story, the power of the image extends beyond its own community of admirers. Viṣṇu's seduction of the princess reminds the audience that his appeal is not parocial but potentially universal.

The subsequent fate of the princess clarifies this point. When the sultan's daughter learns that the object of her affections has been taken, she is heartbroken. Her father sends troops to catch the Sri Rangam party on their way south, and allows her to accompany them. The temple servants learn they are being pursued, however, and manage to elude the troops. They send the image into hiding in the hills around Tirupati. Finally the princess reaches Sri

Rangam, finds that her iconic beloved is not there, and dies from the pain of separation (*viraha*). Her devotion is more fruitful in the Tirunarayanapura version of the story. There, she catches up with Rāmānuja and Beloved Son and joins the troupe of temple servants. Along the way she enters the palanquin of the image to pay her respects, and then merges into the icon. The Muslim princess has followed the devotional path of illustrious female devotees such as Āṇṭāḷ and the Cera princess.[28] In this case, however, Viṣṇu's bride comes from outside the normal Vaiṣṇava community, and her acts of devotional attention have been undertaken without realizing the true state of affairs.

At both sites shrines were set up in the temple complex to make the princess' devotion permanent. At Tirunarayanapura the shrine is at the foot of the hill facing the temple.[29] In Sri Rangam the sanctum of the sultan's daughter is in the fourth enclosure of the temple comple. There is no image of the Muslim princess (as there would be of a prominent Hindu female devotee like Āṇṭāḷ), but rather a painting depicting her modestly covered with a shawl. A divan stands before the painting. When the portable image of Raṅganātha makes his daily visit to the shrine, he is treated to a Muslim-inflected form of pūjā, to which he became accustomed during his stay with the princess in Delhi. Raṅganātha wears a lungi, and he is served the roti, chappati, cold milk, and green gram dal typical of a north Indian breakfast. His betel leaf is smeared on the front side, in the Muslim style.[30] As in many stories of devotion, the form the offerings take is less important than the spirit with which they are offered. Viṣṇu, the Lord of Creation, will accept all.

The story humanizes and normalizes the Turkic ruler of Delhi. Rather than destroying images, he appropriates them on his digvijaya, much as a Hindu conqueror would do. He treats his visitors respectfully and appreciates south Indian music. He is no Rāvaṇa or Kaṁsa here, but just another Indian sovereign. Although it does not demonize the Turks on cultural grounds, the story does convey a covert critique of Muslim aniconic worship. The implicit antonym here is the unrepresented and unrepresentable divinity of Islam: one cannot imagine the Muslim princess playing dolls with Allāh. Aniconic forms of religiosity fail to meet human emotional needs for a loving personal relationship with God. In the iconic body of a "handsome bridegroom," Viṣṇu does meet those needs, even for the daughter of an Islamic ruler.

Recovery and Authenticity

The journey is not over for Aḻakiyamaṇavāḷa, however. He is still not back where he belongs. The *Koyil Oluku* provides a lengthy denouement to the image's visit to Delhi. More acts of devotion need to be performed, and when the image finally does make it back to Sri Rangam after its lengthy absence, its authenticity must still be proven.

When they learned that the sultan's army was chasing them to get back the image, the sixty temple servants from Sri Rangam split up. Three of them took Aḻakiyamaṇavāḷa to Tirupati. But the Delhi troops found this out and followed. The temple servants retreated into the hills and hid the image. "Placing his brother-in-law and nephew on top of the hill," the chronicle relates, "the uncle tied himself to Viṣṇu with the help of roots and herbs and asked the two on the top to let him down into the declivity by means of a creeper fastened to a promontory of the mountain, jutting out like the hood of a serpent" (Hari Rao 1961: 27). In this suspended bivouac the uncle ministered to the image until he died. His brother-in-law climbed down the slope, cremated his uncle's body, and continued caring for Aḻakiyamaṇavāḷa. He died too, and the nephew then took over the task. The image spent over fifty years like this.

Meanwhile the temple of Sri Rangam had reopened. Temple officials made an extensive search for Aḻakiyamaṇavāḷa but were unable to find him, and so they had a new processional icon known as Māḷikaiyār installed in his place. Likewise they could not find the image of the Goddess, Viṣṇu's consort, which they had buried under the bilva tree. They fabricated a new Goddess and installed her beside Māḷikaiyār.

Fifty-nine and a half years after Aḻakiyamaṇavāḷa had been taken from Sri Rangam temple he was found again. "Two huntsmen saw an eighty-year-old brahmin at a spring at the foot of Tirumalai hill," reports the *Koyil Oluku*. "Hair grew wildly atop his head. He wore a creeper around his waist. His loincloth was made of areca bark and his cloak of teak leaves. He had made a sacrificial thread from the *kattan* creeper. With him they saw a divine auspicious image (*vigraha*)" (1976: 24). The disheveled octogenarian brahmin was of course the nephew, last remaining member of the trio, still caring for the icon. He explained who he was and asked the huntsmen to inform their headman, since he was too old to move the image by himself. The local ruler of nearby Candragiri escorted Aḻakiyamaṇavāḷa and his aged retainer back to Sri Rangam.[31] When they arrived, though, the temple servants refused to allow the deity to enter the sanctum. After such a long time there was no one left who could recognize the old image.

The problem of establishing authenticity was just as important for the keepers of Raṅganātha temple as it would be for a modern art dealer or collector. How can one determine whether claims to antique status are accurate? At first the temple servants suspected the old brahmin of trying to pass off a fake. However, the next morning the buried image of the Goddess started to emerge from the ground under the bilva tree, and the officials began to reconsider. Perhaps the old man was telling the truth. They asked the Cola ruler to help resolve their quandary, and he employed a unique curatorial method. The king searched the town for elderly witnesses who might remember the old image, and found a ninety-three-year-old temple washerman. Unfortunately the old man was blind. However, the washerman informed the king, there might still be a way he could identify the image as A̲ḻakiyamaṇavāḷa. In the old days he used to drink the liquid from the wet clothes of the image as a form of holy water (*tīrtha*), before he washed them. If the king would have both images, Māḷikaiyār and the putative A̲ḻakiyamaṇavāḷa, bathed and give him the wet garments from each, he would identify the old image by taste. The king did as he wished, and when the old washerman sipped the holy water from A̲ḻakiyamaṇavāḷa's bath he exclaimed, "He is our God! A̲ḻakiyamaṇavāḷa!" The washerman lost himself in love, shed tears, and went into a trance.

The washerman's decision was confirmed that night, when A̲ḻakiyamaṇavāḷa appeared to the Cola king in a dream and recounted all his perigrinations. The *Koyil Oluku* ends the episode with A̲ḻakiyamaṇavāḷa reinstalled on his former throne distributing titles and honors to all those who had served him during his exile: the temple musicians, the eighty-year-old brahmin, the old temple washerman, and the deceased princess from Delhi.[32]

The Cult of Autochthony

The narratives of Viṣṇu's flight during the fourteenth century follow a trajectory that leads the image inexorably back home. Working together, the Vaiṣṇava devotees and the god himself insure that the sacred image comes to no harm during its exile and that it returns safely to its original home. The stories suggest that a special connection exists between the image and the place it resides, which even the most determined iconoclasts could not sever.

This connectedness is explored more fully in one of the most abundant genres of late medieval south Indian religious literature, the temple hagiography (*māhātmya*, literally the "greatness" of a particular temple) or site history (*sthalapurāṇa*). The great majority of the works in this genre were composed during the sixteenth and seventeenth centuries, a veritable golden age of purāṇic composition in Tamilnad.[33] The genre of temple hagiography, observes David Shulman (1980: 32–33), was primarily pilgrimage literature. The authors were most often religious scholars residing at temple centers, the target audience consisted of visitors to particular temple sites, and the purpose of the literature was to justify and eulogize the shrines as particularly sacred and efficacious. Each hagiography treated a standard series of topics: the discovery and history of the site, the important divine and human figures who had worshiped there, the main features of the sacred topography, and the legendary background to any local idiosyncrasies in icons or liturgy.

Overall the genre contains a rich, detailed, locally inflected corpus of the narratives of divine deeds and explanatory tales that Western scholars generally term "myth."

In his survey of *Tamil Literature*, Kamil Zvelebil characterizes the temple hagiography as "the most typical product of totally non-empirical and a-historical patterns of thought" (1974: 171). The temple hagiographies do speak the language of myth, but it is wrong to view them as simply another ahistorical product of the Indian myth-making consciousness. Although they do not provide us with factual historical narratives, they are certainly the products of a historical moment, Tamilnad in the sixteenth and seventeenth centuries, and they articulate the categories and concerns of their cultural world just as much as the epics of conquest and of resistance do theirs. The impetus to compose comprehensive biographies of important sites, I would argue, grows out of the experience of disruption, and much of the thematic complexion of these site biographies results from the attempt to overcome disjuncture and to assert an overarching stability.[34] The projection of these issues into mythical time, therefore, forms part of a strategy to remove sacred sites from historical contingency.

A key argument the temple hagiographies make is that the sacred is autochthonous. Divinity inheres in particular places and objects, outside human volition. As Shulman puts it, "A divine power is felt to be present naturally on the spot. The texts are therefore concerned with the manner in which this presence is revealed and with the definition of its specific attributes" (1980: 48). The temple may begin with Śiva liṅgas or shrines arising out of the earth. Often the icon already exists but is hidden from human eyes, until the devoted attendance of a cow or the dream of a holy man reveals it. The hagiographies present this inhering divinity as invulnerable to outside attack. Attempts to remove the deity from its selected spot are doomed to failure. At Ramesvaram the powerful monkey god Hanumān wraps his tail around a liṅga formed of sand, but for all his might he cannot budge it. The marks of his tail are still visible on the liṅga, notes the text. Likewise, many temple biographies claim that their icons or shrines have survived the great deluge. As sole survivor of the cosmic dissolution, the icon or shrine then acts as the locus from which the new creation arises.

In its narration of how Viṣṇu Raṅganātha first came to be worshiped at Sri Rangam, the *Śrīraṅgamāhātmya* illustrates this notion of autochthonous divinity. The story commences with a typical Vaiṣṇava portrayal of creation linked to Viṣṇu's main iconic form at Sri Rangam: Viṣṇu lies on the milk ocean, a lotus emerges from his navel, and seated atop the lotus, Brahman carries out yet another renewal of the cosmos. After he has completed his task, Brahman sits on the shore of the milk ocean and solicits Viṣṇu's help. A shrine immediately arises from the ocean where Viṣṇu has been reclining.

The shrine flies through the air and lands in front of Brahman. Brahman enters and sees Viṣṇu lying inside.

Viṣṇu tells Brahman that this is a "self-manifested" (*svayambhuva*) shrine. Others shrines, by contrast, are created, and in the scheme of things, a self-manifested object is always more sacred than one which is fabricated. Viṣṇu explains to Brahman how to perform worship in this new shrine. When Viṣṇu has finished his disquisition, he immediately turns into an icon. Brahman remains there to honor the image of Viṣṇu.

After much time and several transfers, the shrine turns up in Ayodhya during the reign of King Daśaratha, future father of Rāma. When Daśaratha performs a sacrifice to gain offspring, one of the visiting dignitaries is the Cola king Dharmavarman. The Cola ruler sees the shrine in Ayodhya and longs to have it in his own country. After the ceremony Dharmavarman returns south and performs austerities on Sri Rangam island to gain the shrine. Sages there inform him that penance is not necessary, since Viṣṇu has already made his decision to live there.

Meawhile, Rāma is born and all the events narrated in the epic *Rāmāyaṇa* transpire. Rāma defeats the demon Rāvaṇa and conquers Lanka, then returns to Ayodhya to perform the imperial Horse Sacrifice. Rāvaṇa's brother Vibhīṣaṇa, a virtuous demon who has aided Rāma in his struggle, accompanies the victor. Also attending the great ceremony is Dharmavarman. At the conclusion of the ritual Rāma distributes valuable gifts and war booty to those who have assisted him. Rāma gives Vibhīṣaṇa the sovereignty over Lanka that his deposed brother had held, and also presents the demon with the Viṣṇu shrine to take back to Lanka with him. Dharmavarman immediately returns to Sri Rangam, where he constructs a temple in anticipation of the shrine's arrival. As Vibhīṣaṇa is returning to Lanka he stops at Sri Rangam to rest. He sets the shrine down and worships there. The Cola ruler and the local anchorites welcome the shrine, and together they celebrate a grand nine-day festival.

When Vibhīṣaṇa is ready to resume his journey, he tries to lift the shrine. It will not budge. Vibhīṣaṇa laments, but Viṣṇu appears and tells him to continue to Lanka without it. Viṣṇu has decided to remain right where he is. The Kaveri River has been doing austerities to keep the shrine within her bounds. Besides, he wishes to extend his blessings to men, not to demons.

In its story of origins, the *Śrīraṅgamāhātmya* redefines the central image of the Raṅganātha temple for a new community of worshipers. The text identifies the Viṣṇu icon not as an object made by humans and entered by divinity, as the earlier liturgical texts did, but as a direct reification of Viṣṇu himself as he appears before Brahman at the dawn of creation. The shrine itself is "self-manifested," outside human volition, and in that way superior to all created shrines.[35] As in the more historical narratives, the temple myth recognizes the possibility of displacement, for the icon makes a journey from the milk ocean to the island of Sri Rangam. Yet the final position of the image results from Viṣṇu's own choice (albeit helped along by the attentions of a Cola king and the austerities of a sacred river). And once Viṣṇu has chosen his new place of repose, no one can dislodge him, not even a wealthy, virtuous, and powerful demon like Vibhīṣaṇa. More than earlier, argues the temple hagiography, the manifestation of divinity depends on the preservation and veneration of those particular sites and icons where Viṣṇu presents himself eternally.

Subtle Returns

Lest we overly value the authentic original object, preserved in the face of threat through various strategems, it will be good to conclude this chapter by observing that Vaiṣṇava devotees had other resources for overcoming loss and destruction. Even when important images were physically destroyed, narratives provided ways to assert that new images were in fact old ones.

In 1568, the Afghan general Kālāpahār, acting on orders of the Islamic sultan of Bengal, finally defeated and deposed the Gajapati dynasty of Orissa. Kālāpahār was a vigorous iconoclast, and he was well aware of the role that Viṣṇu Jagannātha had played in Orissan politics. Apparently an informant told him where the Jagannātha images were concealed. The *Kaṭakarāja-vaṃśāvali* tells us: "Kālāpahār seized the four main images from the sanctum and took them away by elephant. He looted the Lord's temple treasury. He broke the upper portion of the big temple. He had the surrounding divinities pulverized into lime powder. He cut down the kalpa tree and burnt it. Then he took the principal images, went to the bank of the Ganges, and burned them in a pile of wood."[36] After this public display of incineration, the burnt remnants of the idols were tossed into the river.

These actions did not go unobserved, of course. A temple servant named Visara Mahānti had disguised himself as a Vaiṣṇava ascetic and followed Kālāpahār to the Ganges. The loyal servant dove into the water, rescued some charred scraps of wood from the water, concealed them in his *mṛdaṅga* drum, and took them quickly away to the village of Khandaita Kalua, in an out-of-the-way part of Orissa. In this burnt residuum of the old images, the chronicles insist, was contained their animating essence, the *brahmapadārtha*. For years Vihara Mahānti maintained Jagannātha's subtle essence with his own modest offerings to the wood scraps, much as south Indian priests would support the animating spirit of buried images by worshiping a bundle of sacrificial grass.

Soon after, an ambitious provincial warrior named Rāmacandra established a new kingdom in the peripheral region of Khurda and formed an alliance with the Mughal ruler Akbar, who had his own reasons for wishing to oust the Afghans from Orissa. After receiving a directive from Jagannātha himself in a dream, Rāmacandra went to Khandaita Kalua and laid claim to the charred residue of the old Jagannātha temple images. Then he had new images fabricated, following all the proper procedures, and inserted the wood remnants into them. Initially he set up the images in his own provincial capital, Khurda fort. Two years later, with the support of the Mughal, Rāmacandra was strong enough to take control of Puri, and there he immediately established the new Jagannātha images on the lion throne of the big temple and reinstituted worship. The temple brahmins accepted Rāmacandra as the new Gajapati, and even declared him to be a "second Indradyumna," reincarnation of the temple's legendary founder.

Here it was not the statue of Jagannātha as an integral whole, but only his subtle essence embodied in a small piece of burnt wood, that survived and served as the object of continuity, allowing the desecrated temple to restore liturgical activity and a new provincial warrior to gain legitimacy as the preserver of the former imperial dynasty of Orissa. In Puri, Vaiṣṇava worshipers today still replicate the transfer of Jagannātha's essence every twelve or nineteen years (depending on the lunar calendar) in a ceremonial replacement of images known as *navakalevara* or "new embodiment." Wooden images such as Viṣṇu Jagannātha erode naturally when subjected the rigors of almost constant ceremonial bathing, and so new ones must be made periodically. At night, with all lights extinguished, a blindfolded priest removes the *brahmapadārtha* from the old wooden images and places it into newly made ones. The retired images are then buried in a nearby graveyard, while the newly consecrated Jagannātha celebrates a grand inaugural festival by touring the city in a huge chariot.[37]

The traditional anecdotes and narratives of the late medieval south Indian Vaiṣṇava dispensation likewise stress the recovery and essential continuity of Viṣṇu icons, temples, and the social order surrounding them, despite the threat posed by the fourteenth-century Turkic invasions from Delhi. Rising from his cosmic sleep on the snake Ananta, went the mythical paradigm, Viṣṇu would act through his existing image-bodies or through new human incarnations to uphold and restore the world order as Śrīvaiṣṇavas understood it. Celebrating this successful preservation, the hagiographies of important temples like that at Sri Rangam claimed them as self-manifested sites of Viṣṇu's hierophany, impervious to all assault.

Yet underneath the narrative emphasis on continuity, changing circumstances required that Viṣṇu return in new forms. He might find it necessary to reincarnate himself in a parvenu warrior lineage, rising to supplant the old defeated ruling elites of early medieval times, just as he periodically required new Jagannātha images to replace dilapidated ones. Even where Viṣṇu's old images survived, through the adventures and maneuverings retold in late medieval devotional texts, those images were asked to take on new roles and a new political importance. The new Vijayanagara rulers had no connection with the venerable ruling dynasties of Tamilnad, like the Colas and the Pāṇḍyans, and the temples themselves came to be run by new, more complex and hierarchical organizations. The survival of these veteran images and their connection with an earlier time helped to provide the moral sanction for the new social and political order taking shape in late medieval Tamilnad and to validate the claim that this was actually a re-creation of the past.

5.
Indian Images Collected

ON 12 MARCH 1683, William Hedges (1632–1701), governor of the East India Company in Bengal, took a boat trip down the Hoogley River to the island of Sagar (Gaṅgāsāgara-saṃgama, where the Ganges joins the ocean). "We went in our Budgeros," he recorded in his diary, "to see ye Pagodas at Sagor, and returned to ye Oyster River, where we got as many Oysters as we desired" (Barlow and Yule 1887: 68). Sagar Island was an important Bengali pilgrimage center. In J. C. Harle's dry comment, "it is most likely that Hedges combined sightseeing on that day with a little collecting" (Harle and Topsfield 1987: 40). Evidently Hedges acquired on this trip a large siltstone stele carved, to judge by its sculptural style, in the eleventh century, depicting the god Viṣṇu flanked by the goddesses Śrīdevī and Sarasvatī (Figure 18).

Hedges had only arrived in Bengal in July 1682, but already his abrupt and tactless manner had made him enemies among the other Company officials, and in December 1683 his commission was formally revoked. He returned the next year to England with the Sagar Viṣṇu in tow, and in 1685 he presented it to the newly founded Ashmolean Museum in Oxford. According to a catalogue entry of that year, Hedges gave to the museum an "idol" (Latin *idolum*) called "Gonga" that had been acquired from a "pagoda" on "the island of Seagur" at the mouth of the Ganges.

The Sagar Viṣṇu is the first significant piece of Indian religious sculpture acquired by a Western museum that we can clearly identify, and also the earliest case of mislabeling.[1] However, it was not quite the first Indian religious image to inhabit the United Kingdom. That title goes to an object listed in Abraham van der Doort's 1638 inventory of the collection of King Charles I: "Item in the same windowe an east Indian Idoll of black brasse which was by my lord Denby taken out of there Churches from there alter" (Millar 1960: 94).

William Feilding, Earl of Denbigh (1582–1643) and courtier to Charles I, was one of the first English tourists to visit India. Unlike the Company merchants of the early seventeenth century, who sought profits above all, Feilding's trip to the subcontinent in 1631–1633 appears to have been motivated primarily by curiosity. As former "master of the great wardrobe,"

FIG. 18. The Hedges Viṣṇu, Ashmolean Museum. Siltstone image from Sagar Island, West Bengal, eleventh century. Given by William Hedges to Ashmolean Museum, 1686–1687. Printed by permission of Ashmolean Museum, Oxford.

Feilding enjoyed close relations with the king, and Charles employed his influence with the East India Company to provide Feilding passage on one of its ships. Not a great deal is known of what Feilding saw or did while he was in India, though he did arrange a meeting with the Mughal emperor Shāh Jahān (Foster 1910: xvii–xix). Feilding must have been proud of his voyage, for in the portrait he had painted by Anthony Van Dyck, he appears as a huntsman in semi-Indian costume, attended by an Indian servant, in a lush tropical setting (C. A. Bayly 1990: 73–74). At some point during his trip he managed to hunt down a souvenir, the black brass "Idoll" removed from inside an Indian temple, to present to his royal patron back home.

The stele from Sagar Island, now more properly labeled as "Viṣṇu (the 'Hedges' Viṣṇu)," still receives visitors at the Ashmolean Museum, whereas Charles' bronze image disappeared in the 1640s, during the Civil War, when Charles was beheaded and his great royal collection of curiosities was dispersed by auction and Puritan iconoclasm.[2] But these seventeenth-century newcomers to England mark the beginning of a new mode of life for certain Indian religious images and other objects. They were removed from their homelands as curiosities, souvenirs, or art objects, transported abroad to be sold or presented as gifts, maintained in private collections or placed on display in public institutions, and viewed by Western audiences as variously bizarre, curious, heathenish, picturesque, spiritual, or beautiful. Gradually they became incorporated into the larger world of Western art and its institutions, the market, the museum, and the scholarly discipline of art history.

Although museum display provides one of the primary ways most viewers in the West encounter South Asian art, the activities of collecting, transporting, and displaying Indian art objects that make this encounter possible have generally been overlooked in accounts of Indian art history.[3] Nor do I propose to give a general account of Western collecting of Indian religious art in one chapter. Rather, following the biographical method used throughout this book, I will focus here on a single famous work of Indian sculpture that traveled from India to England during the colonial period, and use the story of its appropriation, its redisplays, and its encounters with new audiences in London to explore issues raised by its relocation. The object chosen, "Tipu's Tiger," is not a religious image, as are the other images discussed in this book, nor is it particularly esteemed as a work of sculptural art. However, over the course of its almost two centuries in London it may well have been the most famous Indian sculpted object outside the subcontinent. Its reputation assures that a wealth of documentation surrounds the Tiger, and this enables one to retrace its peregrinations and the ways viewers have responded to it. Moreover, the fact that it does not fit easily into the category of "Indian art" as this has been defined in the twentieth century provides a useful vantage point for reconsidering the ways in which Western scholars, collectors, and audiences have defined and constructed the objects they do designate as art.[4]

FIG. 19. "Tipu's Tiger." Painted wood effigy, with mechanical organ. Made in Sri Rangapattana, Karnataka, eighteenth century. Taken by British forces in 1799, presented to East India Company Board of Directors, displayed in India Museum, and later transferred to Victoria and Albert Museum. Printed by courtesy of the Board of Trustees of the Victoria and Albert Museum, London.

THE TIGER IN TIPŪ'S COURT

In the newly renamed Jawarhalal Nehru Gallery of Indian Art in the Victoria and Albert Museum, London, safely enclosed within a glass case, resides an impressive six-foot effigy (Figure 19). A tawny male tiger, all claws extended, crouches atop a wooden man lying stiffly. The light-complexioned man wears a red coat and a black, wide-brimmed hat, clearly marking him as a European of the eighteenth century. His eyes are wide open in distress. The tiger meanwhile sinks his teeth right into the man's throat. On the left flank of the tiger, a hinged wooden flap has been let down, allowing viewers to see within the tiger a row of eighteen buttons with musical pipes behind each—for the Tiger is, at the same time, an organ. Also from the tiger's left

FIG 20. "Tipu's Tiger" on Display at the Victoria and Albert Museum.

shoulder protrudes a crank handle. When one turns the crank the man raises his left arm in futile supplication, and the apparatus emits sounds of a tiger roaring and a human groaning.

Joining "Tipu's Tiger" in the glass case is a variety of other objects that represent and evoke the eighteenth-century south Indian court of Tipū Sultān (Figure 20). Viewers see a beautiful cotton floor spread embroidered in silk flowers and tendrils, a burgundy velvet saddle cloth embellished in silver-gilt thread, a white muslin full-length court coat from Tipū's wardrobe, a steel curve-bladed sword with Persian inscription in gold lettering identifying it as a personal sword of Tipū, and sundry other objects including a helmet, a walking cane, a telescope, and a pocket watch of European manufacture. Three small paintings depict Tipū, a soldier of his guard, and a scene from his palace at Sri Rangapattana (Anglicized as Seringapatam). Almost lost among the larger objects, one may also detect a small gold medal, on which the British lion is shown overcoming a prostrate tiger (Figure 21). The medal, with its totemic representation of British victory, was awarded to those who served in the Sri Rangapattana campaign.[5] Overturning the iconography of "Tipu's Tiger," this small medal evokes the event that made the entire display possible, for virtually all the objects in the case were taken

FIG. 21. Seringapatam Medal. Gold. Designed by C. H. Kuchler, 1799, and struck at the Birmingham Mint to commemorate British victory at Sri Rangapattana. Medal presented to Lord Cornwallis, former governor-general of India, in 1800. Now on display at Victoria and Albert Museum, on loan from current Lord Cornwallis. Photographed at the Victoria and Albert Museum by permission of Lord Cornwallis. Printed by courtesy of the Board of Trustees of the Victoria and Albert Museum.

by British military forces as loot after their victorious storming of Sri Rangapattana in 1799.

Of course the Tiger was not made with museum display in mind, and it has not always been in the Victoria and Albert Museum. The Tiger was fabricated in the late eighteenth century for the Islamic ruler of Mysore, Tipū Sulṭān Fath ʿAlī Khān (r. 1782–1799), probably by local Indian artisans working with a French instrument maker. Quite possibly they were following the iconographic instructions of the sultan himself.

Tipū's father, Haidar ʿAlī Khān, was an enterprising general who took control of the kingdom of Mysore from its Wodeyar ruler, Kṛṣṇarāja II, in 1761. Both Haidar ʿAlī and his son and successor Tipū were vigorous, inventive, and ambitious rulers who sought to expand the personal powers of the sovereign within their state and to extend its boundaries without. In the latter aim they took advantage of the declining ability of the Mughal center to control subordinate rulers throughout the subcontinent during the eighteenth century. Within a few years, Mysore's expansionist policies and increasingly effective military capacities brought it into conflict with another expanding south Indian polity, the British East India Company based in Madras. Between 1767 and 1799 Haidar ʿAlī and Tipū Sultān fought four wars with the British. During the first Anglo-Mysore war of 1767–1769, Haidar ʿAlī reached the gates of Madras and forced the British to accept his proposals for a truce. In the second war of 1780–1784, the Mysore forces decisively defeated the British at Pollilur and besieged Madras by controlling and denuding the surrounding territories, until the British general Eyre Coote led the British to victory at Porto Novo in 1781. Haidar ʿAlī died of an illness during this war in 1782.

Both Haidar ʿAlī and Tipū Sultān were parvenu Sunnī Muslim rulers of a predominantly Hindu south Indian kingdom. The current Mughal emperor in Delhi, primary legitimating source of authority still in the eighteenth century, did not acknowledge the new Mysore rulers, but because Mughal power was declining Tipū was able to declare himself "Pādshāh" and take on most of the defining marks of this status without suffering Mughal retribution. Nevertheless, Haidar ʿAlī and Tipū needed to establish themselves as legitimate and proper sovereigns within the complex society of southern India. To do this they employed many of the traditional incorporative strategies of new rulers in India, such as patronizing the religious institutions of all significant communities within their territories and conducting inclusive rituals that involved subordinate rulers and local elites. They also selected ruling symbols with a keen sense of rhetoric. It is in this context, as Kate Brittlebank argues in her recent revisionist studies of Tipū Sultān's cultural politics, that Tipū's choice of the tiger as a personal and dynastic insignia appears most significant.[6]

Iconography of the tiger permeated Tipū's court. Tipū's soldiers wore uniforms decorated with tiger stripes. Royal weaponry showed the mark of the tiger: swords had tiger hilts, muskets had brass tigers for their gunlocks, and mortars were cast with tiger-head muzzles. Tipū's coins showed tiger stripes, and the ceremonial staffs reserved for high officials were mounted with silver tiger heads. His green silk banner of state was decorated with a calligraphic design in the form of a stylized tiger face, spelling out "The Lion of God is Conqueror." Tipū's magnificent throne stood on tiger legs, and featured at its front a massive tiger with head of gold and teeth of crystal, surrounded by smaller tiger heads.

British observers at the time understood this promiscuous reiteration of a single symbolic motif to be a matter of Tipū's personal choice, unique and idiosyncratic. They believed Tipū identified himself as a tiger, and to support this they often repeated a statement ascribed to him: "in this world he would rather live two days like a tiger, than two hundred years like a sheep" (Beatson 1800: 153–54). Perhaps Tipū did see his own life of ferocious exertion and constant military campaigning as similar to that of a tiger. However, as Brittlebank shows, in the late medieval south Indian dispensation within which Tipū operated, the tiger was a multivalent signifier, and Tipū's choice would have been prompted more by strategic concerns than personal predilection.

Ruling dynasties in medieval India regularly chose distinctive insignia. The tiger is recurrently associated with royalty in India. More specifically, two prominent dynastic predecessors of Tipū had employed the tiger as their insignia—the Colas who ruled much of southern India from the late tenth through early thirteenth centuries, and the Hoysalas of Dvārasamudra who supplanted the Colas and Cālukyas in Karnataka in the late twelfth through early fourteenth centuries. By his reuse, then, Tipū implicitly aligned himself with two earlier Hindu (and mainly Śaiva) imperial formations of south India. Significantly, the Wodeyars did not use the tiger as an emblem. Their royal iconography leaned toward Vaiṣṇava symbols, such as the boar, the discus, the garuḍa, and especially the double-headed eagle. Tipū had one of his guns decorated with a heel plate depicting two tigers devouring a double-headed eagle, to convey Haidar ʿAlī's and Tipū's usurpation of Wodeyar rule in Mysore in clear totemic code (Wiginton 1992: 73; Figure 22).

At the same time, the tiger linked Tipū within an Islamic context to ʿAlī, cousin and son-in-law of the Prophet Muḥammad and fourth caliph of the early Islamic community. Honored by all Muslims as a great warrior, ʿAlī is particularly venerated by Shīʿas as Muḥammad's true successor. ʿAlī is known as the "lion of Allāh" (*asad allāh*), but most Indian languages do not draw a strong linguistic distinction between "lion" and "tiger," so it was not incongruous for Tipū's banner to spell out "lion of God" with the visual form of a tiger mask. For Tipū the words *asad allāh* would equally have meant

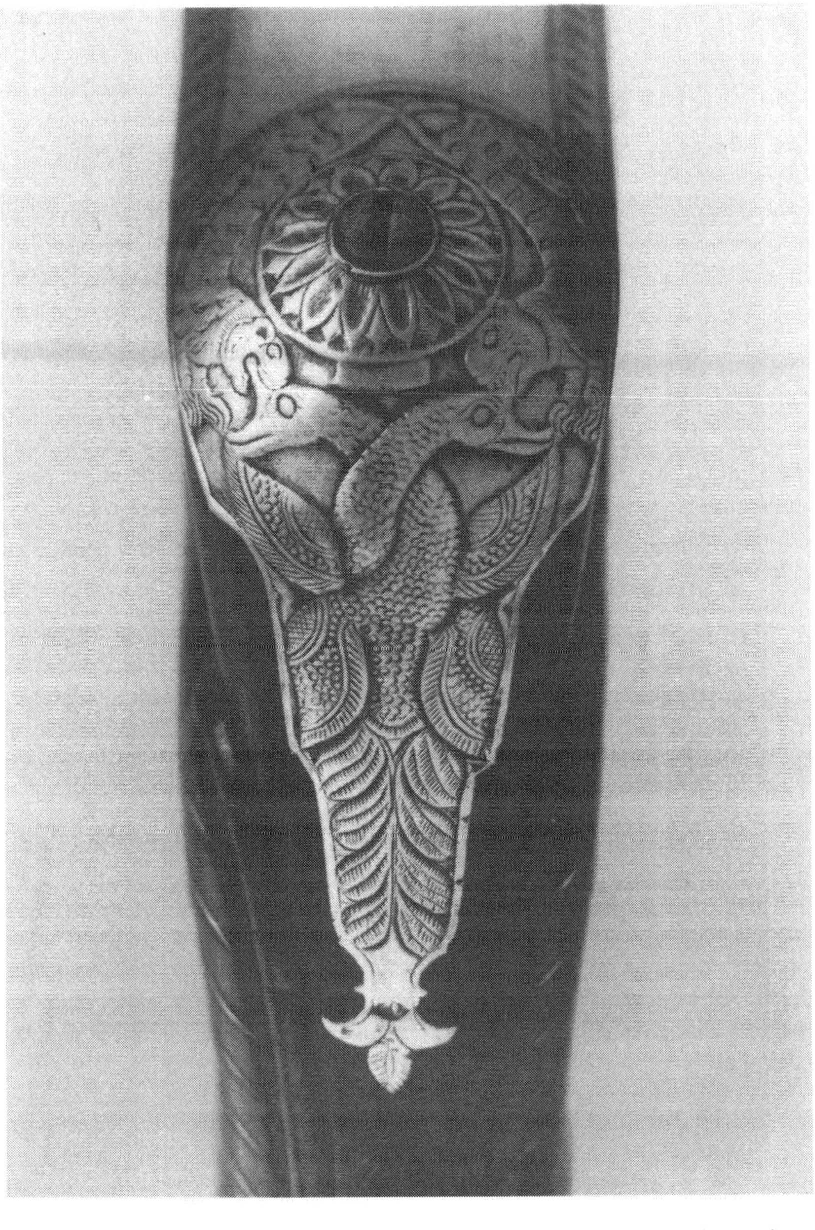

FIG. 22. Tigers Devouring Eagles, Heel Plate on Tipū's Gun. Detail from silver-mounted flintlock sporting gun, made for Tipū Sultān, 1792–1794. After fall of Sri Rangapattana, presented to Lord Cornwallis in 1799, and later passed to Earl of Pembroke at Wilton House. Photograph courtesy of Robin Wiginton.

"tiger of God." A devoted Muslim warrior, Tipu took ʿAlī as "the guardian genius, or tutelary saint, of his dominions; as the peculiar object of his veneration, and as an example to imitate" (Beatson 1800: 155). Not coincidentally, the name of Tipū's father, Haidar, the title Muḥammad bestowed on ʿAlī, also means "lion" (or tiger), so Tipu's devotion also connoted filial piety as well.

Moreover, Brittlebank argues, both Hindu and Muslim traditions in medieval south India associated the tiger with a religious notion of divine power. As we have seen, medieval Indian political theory understood that the power of kings to rule their earthly dominions was fundamentally drawn from divine sources. In late medieval south India, divine power (*śakti*) was most directly instantiated for Hindus in the form of fierce warrior goddesses such as Durgā, Kālī, and the many local goddesses referred to as Amman or Māriamman. Durgā rides a lion (or tiger) as she goes into battle against the demon Mahiṣāsura, and many of the village goddesses in the Mysore region are known as Huliamman, the "tiger goddess." Within a south Indian Indo-Muslim setting, divine power (*barakat*) manifested itself through the figure of the martial *pīr*, the saint-martyr. Like their Hindu goddess counterparts, Sufi pīrs frequently rode lions (or tigers) as their mounts, and as zoomorphic extensions of their inhering energies. In practice the cults of Hindu goddesses and Muslim pīrs were not clearly divided. They employed a shared vocabulary of symbols and common ritual strategies, and both sought to gain access to the divine energy of śakti or barakat on behalf of their worshipers. By his choice of the tiger, Tipū surrounded himself with the animal form of divine power common to the two most prominent communities of his realm.

In its iconographic composition, "Tipu's Tiger" referred back most immediately to the genre of hunting pictures common to both Islamic and Hindu court traditions in late medieval India. Typically these paintings depict rulers in the act of pursuing or slaying powerful wild animals, most often tigers. Representing the potency of the ruler in his (or her) moment of triumph, such paintings not only illustrated the popular royal pasttime, but also figured as allegories of dominion.[7] But in Tipū's version, it would appear, positions are reversed. The hunter gets captured by the game. The tiger now denotes the royal patron, overturning the conventional iconography to assume a victorious crouch atop the suppine British soldier.

With his Tiger, then, Tipū adeptly employed an insignia that would speak to the various communities that constituted his kingdom. Within his symbolic universe, the musical Tiger effigy he kept in his hall of music represented a clear iconic expression of the victory he envisioned of himself, his polity, and the forces that acted through them over his most inveterate opponent, the British.[8] Unfortunately for Tipū and his Tiger, symbolic representations of the future do not always bring about their own fulfillment.

Colonial Styles in Collecting and Display

After three inconclusive Anglo-Mysore wars, it was the ambitious Richard Wellesley, arriving as governor-general in 1798, who initiated the fourth campaign, which would lead to Tipū's decisive defeat and the annexation of most of his territories under effective British control. Claiming evidence of negotiations between Mysore and France, Wellesley ordered British forces against Tipū's fortress capital of Sri Rangapattana in 1799. Tipū died during the siege. Wellesley's victory not only solidified British control in southern India, but also created a sensation back in England, involving as it did a dramatic victory over a famously fearsome Indian potentate as well as an indirect defeat of the enemy closer to home, Napoleonic France. In addition, the British defeat of Tipū set the Tiger and many other objects from Tipū's palace along a course that would lead them to new homes in the colonial capital.

The Looting of Sri Rangapattana

After the British troops had successfully stormed the fortress, and the body of Tipū Sultān himself was found, the night of May 4 was given over to a general rampage and pillage of the city. One estimate places the value of the pillage during the night at Rs 45 lakhs. The next morning it was left up to young Colonel Arthur Wellesley, the future duke of Wellington, to restore some semblance of order and military discipline, and he did this with zeal.

> Nothing could have exceeded what was done on the night of the 4th. Scarcely a house in the town was left unplundered and I understand that in the camp jewels of the greatest value, bars of gold, etc. etc., have been offered for sale in the bazaars of the army by our soldiers, sepoys, and followers. I came in to take the command on the morning of the 5th, and by the greatest exertion, by hanging, flogging, etc. etc., in the course of that day I restored order among the troops, and I hope I have gained the confidence of the people. (Wellington 1858: 212)

So reported Col. Wellesley in a dispatch to his older brother Richard, the governor-general.

The treasures that survived this initial pillaging of Sri Rangapattana were classified as "prize," and with all the army eager to partake, a Prize Committee of seven officers was quickly formed to collect, evaluate, and apportion the captured booty. The agents were astonished by what they found: they collected the equivalent of 600,000 pounds in coins, jewels valued at 360,000 pounds, along with richly worked cloth, inlaid furniture, Persian carpets, ornamental weaponry, and much else. The total value of the prize came to something on the order of 1,600,000 pounds.

These two movements in the emptying out of Tipū's palace illustrate nicely the distinction that the British sought to draw between "plunder" and "prize." As we have already seen in medieval Indian settings, looting may be a common activity among many wartime victors, but it is also a social practice deeply imbricated with cultural premises and values. Various looting parties organize their activities differently within their differing dispensations. For the eighteenth-century British, the Mutiny Act and the Articles of War enacted by Parliament after the Restoration classified individual plundering not only as a form of theft but also of desertion, since undisciplined looting might disrupt the integrity of troops during battle. Unregulated plunder could be punished by a maximum sentence of death (Gregorian 1990: 66). Therefore it was not out of line for Col. Wellesley to hang four subaltern pillagers in the interest of stopping the plunder of Sri Rangapattana.

Prize was a different matter. With victory attained, the commanding officer was instructed to appropriate the property belonging to the defeated opponent; this was "booty," not "pillage." Following an organized procedure of assessment and usually an on-site auction, booty was transformed into "prize money" for distribution to the troops, in proper order according to ranks. If plundering involved individual, disorderly, and predatory activity subverting the terms of disciplined military arrangements, prize involved collective, orderly, hierarchical distribution rearticulating the established social order of the military itself.

Aside from its symbolic value, official looting provided a convenient method of motivating and rewarding troops. It was even an effective informal recruiting device. Major David Price, for example, recalled in his memoirs how he had first come to join the army of the East India Company. One night he found himself "listening to the tales of some old soldiers who had already served in India, under Clive and Coote—embellishing their statements with the most gorgeous stories of captured treasures. On the following day I was conducted to the India-house; where, with perfect indifference, I suffered myself to be enrolled a recruit for the service of the East India Company" (Price 1839: 11). Price later served on the Prize Committee at Sri Rangapattana and enjoyed the opportunity to distribute some of those "captured treasures" himself.

In acquiring prize, British armies also sought to observe cultural codes concerning what *not* to loot. Prize should not be expropriated from religious institutions, for example, in accord with British premises assigning church and state to separate domains. As far as I can tell, there is no evidence that the British did loot the temples or mosques of Sri Rangapattana, wealthy as they must have been. Not only did they leave the tomb of their old adversary Haidar ʿAlī intact, but they also allowed the locals to perform an elaborate funeral ceremony there for Tipū Sultān the following day. This was a way of signaling their concern not to interfere in native religious customs. There were, however, reports that British armies might have broken another implicit injunction by plundering Tipū's harem, and these reports inspired an immediate flurry of investigations and denials by the political and military authorities (Price 1839: 446–47).

The preferred target for official prize was the direct personal possessions and regalia of defeated rulers. This made the Tiger a particularly apt item for British appropriation. It was clearly not religious, and the British believed it to be closely associated with Tipū himself.

The British also had a theory about the distribution of booty. Theoretically all prize automatically belonged to the Crown, who could then redistribute it as it saw fit. Arthur Wellesley's understanding, stated in an 1803 dispatch, serves as a fair description of the process in theory:

> But as well as I can recollect, His Majesty has reserved to himself the disposal of the property in all forts captured in India, in the operations against which his troops may be employed with those of the Company. . . . His Majesty has been graciously pleased, from time to time, to grant this property to the troops employed in the capture of the fort in which it might be found, and occasionally the Supreme British authority in India has taken upon itself to anticipate His Majesty's intention, and to give the property to the troops; and this is the claim which the troops have to prize property. (Gurwood 1842: 102–3)

At Sri Rangapattana the Prize Committee was therefore acting as the agent of Governor-General Wellesley, who himself was "anticipating the intention" of King George III.

This theoretical understanding, however, was not shared by all. In practice it was more complicated. In a colonial army, with the king on the other side of the world, troops expected to receive their shares of booty, and soon. Their theory was that they were entitled to such booty through their own exertions, not just as passive beneficiaries of royal favor. Wellesley and other officials might be able to reserve a few highly prized items of booty to present to the Crown and the Company, but most of the prize had to be distributed quickly, to prevent an uprising of angry subalterns.

In contrast to the relatively egalitarian Ghaznavid distribution of booty, the British allocated prize in steeply graded rations, ranging from a share of twelve star pagodas for low-rank native soldiers ("naigues, sepoys, black doctors, pioneers, gun lascars, and authorized puckalies") through eighteen star pagodas for the lowest ranking Europeans, 1,080 for subalterns, 10,800 for colonels like Wellesley, and on up to a share of 324,907 pagodas (one-eighth of the total) for the commander-in-chief, General Harris (Wellington 1858:

223). Not surprisingly, the distribution of the prize led to considerable dispute over shares, and particularly over the assessed value of jewels, which many field officers had to accept as prize in lieu of cash (Price 1839: 438–43).

British officers held two conflicting notions concerning the most proper utilization of prize. Some valued it for its symbolic value, while others saw it primarily as a means of paying troops. Some British officials—particularly the brothers Wellesley—recognized that certain objects closely associated with the person of Tipū Sultān, such as his robes, his ceremonial weaponry, and his throne, could act as especially appropriate signifiers for their victory over Tipū and their incorporation of his territories into the British domain. The governor-general, aware of the political basis of his appointment, hoped to circulate such objects upward in the colonial chain of authority. Insofar as possible he attempted to reserve them as "presents" for the Crown and the London officers of the East India Company. The Prize Committee, on the other hand, felt primary responsibility to the troops outside its tent, and wished to monetize all.

So it was with the palace wardrobe, which included the honorific robes that in Tipū's post-Mughal Islamic court would have served as primary signifiers of sovereignty: the Prize Committee proposed to auction it off until prevented by the timely intervention of Col. Wellesley. "The prize agents," he reported, "have got a large quantity of clothes belonging to, and worn by, the late Sultaun, which, unless prevented, they will sell at public auction and which will be bought up as relics by the discontented Moormen of this place. This will not only be disgraceful, but may be very unpleasant" (Wellington 1858: 290). Wellesley recognized how charged these items of clothing might appear to potential claimants to Tipū's sovereign legacy, and successfully thwarted their recirculation within India. His brother subsequently presented them to the Honourable Court of Directors of the East India Company.[9] Wellesley's trepidations proved to be well founded, for another item of Tipū's auctioned regalia, his flag of green stripes on a red field with a sun in the center, was later hoisted to rally the rebellious native troops who carried out a short-lived mutiny against their British officers at the garrison of Vellore in 1806 (Hayavadana Rao 1930: 2.2748–50).[10]

Tipū's throne, a most impressive ruling object, was not so fortunate. Tiger legs supported the octagonal frame of the throne, surrounded by a railing decorated with smaller bejewelled tiger heads. In the middle was affixed a pillar, supporting a canopy fringed with pearls, crowned by the legendary huma bird. The entire throne was covered with pure gold, decorated with tiger stripes, and inscribed with Arabic calligraphy (Beatson 1800: 154). Despite the governor-general's directive to appropriate it intact or put it back together for presentation to the king, the iconoclasts of the Prize Committee broke the throne up into parcels equal to one-third of a subaltern's share in the prize and distributed the pieces to the troops (Price 1839: 444). Officials did manage to retain a few significant parts for royal presentation. Wellesley sent the tiger head from the base of the throne to the East India Company, and later recommended that the Company present it to King William IV. The richly jewelled huma bird, initially allocated to Colonel Gent of the Engineers, was bought back from Gent for £1,760, sent by Wellesley to Queen Charlotte, who bequeathed it to her four daughters, who in turn transferred it to their brother King George IV, stipulating that it "never be separated from the Crown of Great Britain and Ireland."[11]

The object that would turn out to have the greatest symbolic resonance for the British public, however, was not a traditional item of regalia, and it was never presented to royalty. Perhaps the fact that "Tipu's Tiger" was not made of precious materials spared it from the Prize Committee. Wellesley circulated it upward in the colonial chain of command, to the Board of Directors of the East India Company. In the memorandum accompanying the effigy, Wellesley noted that Tipū Sultān "frequently amused himself with a sight of this emblematical triumph of the Khoudadaud [Tipū's 'God-given domain'] over the English Sircar" (East India Company 1800b: 344), making clear that the object should be viewed in a symbolic or "emblematic" manner.

Wellesley had suggested that the Tiger should be sent to the Tower of London, presumably for some emblematic imprisonment, but the Company Board had other ideas. In 1799 the directors decided to set up an Oriental library and museum in their impressive new building, the East India House on Leadenhall Street. This is where "Tipu's Tiger" was put on display in 1808. It quickly became the most celebrated object in the building.

Hindoo Stuart and Other Early Collectors

Not all objects making their way from India to the United Kingdom in the late eighteenth and early nineteenth centuries were acquired through wartime looting, of course. British individuals bought some things, received others as gifts, and stole still others. This was a period of growing British economic and political power in the subcontinent, and also of a shift in the way the British viewed their role. Governor-General Wellesley understood this shift and articulated it precisely when he proposed establishing a new college in Bengal for training new British colonial officials: "The Civil Servants of the English East India Company, therefore, can no longer be considered as the agents of a commercial concern; they are in fact the ministers and officers of a powerful Sovereign; they must now be viewed in that capacity with a reference, not to their nominal, but to their real occupations."[12] Wellesley urged his new British officers to think of themselves not as lowly traders, but as participants in an imperial endeavor.

Even as British administrators were turning themselves into bureaucrats, and beginning to withdraw from participation in activities they considered "indigenous," they were also starting to construct India as a suitable object for Western knowledge. Colonial administrators struggled to understand the forms of organization of the local societies they now ruled, as a practical measure intended to bring about more efficient control and prosperity. British Orientalists studied and translated ancient Indian texts, reconstructing an ancient past for a civilization that previous British traders had approached strictly in the present tense. In initiating their work of conversion, Christian missionaries learned vernacular languages, composed dictionaries and grammars, and contributed some of the first ethnographic studies of living Indian religious practice. British artists traveled to India to find work among a new class of wealthy patrons, created a new visual portrayal of the subcontinent, and distributed their picturesque renderings of India back home. Though they had very different practical agendas, all these British students of India saw themselves as "unveiling" a previously unknown and mysterious civilization, and they viewed this project as a necessary part of their efforts to bring order, to rule, or to convert the natives.

The power and wealth of Company officials in India made acquisition of luxury items increasingly possible, and the beginnings of study and appreciation of India as a civilization with a culture and a history provided a motivation for acquiring objects that might represent and inform. Moreover, the shift in wealth and power away from the previous elite of northern India, the class of former Mughal officials, engendered a supply of collectible items, as displaced nobles sold off their collections of paintings, manuscripts, and jewelry. Within this new setting, conscious acquisition of Indian art objects by British collectors was a different matter from the haphazard appropriations of curiosity collectors like Hedges and Lord Denbigh, and different as well from the official and unofficial looting carried out at Sri Rangapattana.

Among the first deliberate collectors of what we now call Indian art, many were associated with the Calcutta circle of Warren Hastings, governor-general of India from 1772 to 1785. An administrator with scholarly predilections, Hastings is famous for his encouragement of Orientalists such as William Jones, Nathaniel Halhead, Thomas Colebrooke, and Charles Wilkins, and for his involvement in establishing the Asiatic Society of Bengal. He also patronized British artists working in India such as William Hodges and Johann Zoffany, and he personally collected Indian miniature paintings. Others around him, including William Jones, John Elliot, and Jonathan Scott, Hastings' Persian secretary, all collected paintings. The most avid collector in the group was Richard Johnson, who served as Hastings' assistant in Calcutta before being posted to Lucknow, then Hyderabad. Johnson took advantage of each of his new posts to add to his vast collection, which later became the largest part of the painting collection in the India Library at the East India House.[13]

What motivated men like Hastings and Johnson to collect the artistic productions of the society over which they ruled? Within their Enlightenment outlook, scientific curiosity about the world and its varied products was taken for granted. They also understood this curiosity to have practical benefits. When Johnson sold his collection of books and painting to the East India Company Library, he offered this description of its subject matter and purpose: "The Pictures contain portraits of the kings and most eminent nobles, warriors and men of learning, while others are explanatory of the Hindoo mythology, with their singular personifications of their musical modes, others exhibiting costume of the country, the whole forming a very numerous collection greatly contributing to the clearer understanding of the history and religion of that important country of which a larger proportion is now under the sovereignty of the Company than ever was held by their most successful Emperors" (quoted in Archer 1987: 10–11). Here Johnson describes the acquisition of Indian objects not as the representation of rule through the appropriation of royal objects, but as a means of "clearer understanding," and more specifically knowledge that would contribute to the exercise of British sovereignty in the Indian colony. British officers recognized the linkage between Orientalist knowledge and the project of colonial rule from an early period.

The majority of this first generation of collectors acquired manuscripts and paintings. Miniature paintings were available and portable. They were in most cases secular in subject matter and did not require detailed knowledge of iconography for their interpretation and appreciation. British observers of the late eighteenth century could readily perceive their workmanship and artistry, particularly in the paintings of the Mughal court.

Indian religious images were another matter. They could not be easily transported. They were not readily available in detached form. There was no tradition among Indians of collecting icons as autonomous works of art, separate from liturgical usage, and so there were no agents in place to mediate the purchase of religious imagery. Much of it was in religious use and most British officials tried not to offend Hindu religious sensibility. Moreover, the primary British cultural category for such objects was that of "idols": they were not of intrinsic interest as artistic fabrications, but they were worthy of disapprobation on religious grounds. Even the scholarly Orientalists, generally more sympathetic to Indian culture, figured Hindu idolatry as the product of a historical degeneration from a purer religious past. As a result, very few eighteenth- or nineteenth-century British residents in India showed any interest in acquiring Indian religious sculpture.

Prominent among those few were British missionaries. They commissioned and purchased Hindu religious images, and occasionally acquired them as byproducts of successful conversions. In his biography of Reverend Alphonse Lacroix, Joseph Mullens (1862: 66–70) narrates a dramatic example of this.[14] One of Lacroix's fellow missionaries, Reverend Samuel Trawin, was preaching one day near the Kalighat temple south of Calcutta when he was challenged by a "sturdy-looking farmer" and two companions. A discussion on the relative merits of Hinduism and Christianity ensued, and the Reverend found that Ramjee Pramanik, the largest landholder in Rammakal Chowk, an area then eight miles south of Calcutta, was an eager student. Finally, after many further conversations, Ramjee and his two friends accepted baptism on October 18, 1825. Trawin began preaching in Rammakal Chowk and decided to build a chapel there. The new convert Ramjee decided to help the project along.

> On one portion of his land stood a small temple of Shiva; it was a kind of family-temple, and the brahmin in charge received more support from the family than from anyone else. As it was his own property Ramjee determined to pull it down and give its materials for a place of Christian worship. . . . On a certain day in the presence of a great crowd who manifested much excitement, Ramjee brought out the idol, and flung it to the ground. The brahmin exclaimed in horror, almost in the language of Micah: "Ye have taken away my god, and what have I more?" (Mullens 1862: 68)

The missionaries recycled the temple materials to construct their new Christian chapel, and they dispatched the image of Śiva, weighing several hundred pounds, to the home office of the London Missionary Society, where it would be placed on display as a heathen idol.[15]

The first significant collection of Indian religious sculpture to reach the British Isles was acquired not through British victory and looting, but as the result of a British retreat. James Forbes, educated in classics at Hadley, was appointed writer in Bombay at the age of sixteen, and spent the next twenty years abroad. While in India, Forbes wrote prolifically, eventually compiling 150 volumes and 5,200 pages with his observations and commentary; it was, he admitted, "the principal recreation of my life." Distilled, selected, and abridged, they were published in 1813 in four folio volumes, *Oriental Memoirs*.[16] Forbes was a scholarly observer of India, interested in flora and fauna, religion, social customs, and history, and he was a talented amateur draftsman with a good eye for picturesque scenery, ruins, and natives.

During the Second Maratha War, British forces under Col. Goddard briefly captured the old fortress town of Dabhoi (ancient Darbhavatī) southeast of Baroda in Gujarat, and Forbes was appointed collector there of a small district comprising eighty-four villages. Formerly a frontier city of the medieval Solaṅki and Vāghela dynasties, Dabhoi was filled with magnificent ancient

FIG. 23. "The Gate of Diamonds at Dhuboy." Original drawing by James Forbes, 1780, engraved by J. Grieg, and printed in *Oriental Memoirs* (1813). Photographic reproduction by permission of Yale Center for British Art, Paul Mellon Collection, New Haven.

remains of fortifications and Hindu temples built in the twelfth and thirteenth centuries (Burgess and Cousens 1888; Figures 23, 24). Forbes spent several pleasant years there, and worked to restore some of the dilapidated walls and buildings, but in the Political Settlement of 1783 Dabhoi and surrounding areas were ceded back to the Marathas and he was required to surrender the district to a Maratha official. It was a sad parting for Forbes. He even composed a poem of 120 lines to express his regret.

As Forbes recounts it, when the time for his departure approached a delegation of eminent inhabitants came to his durbar to offer him their condolences and presents. Forbes refused all their material offerings. They kept pressing him to accept something, until finally he made a most unusual request: "as Dhuboy contained many remains of Hindoo antiquity, in broken columns, mutilated images, and remnants of basso-relievo scattered among dilapidated buildings in the city, I requested they would allow me to select a few of the smallest specimens from their exterior fragments, which I would

FIG. 24. "Specimen of Hindoo Sculpture on the Gate of Diamonds at Dhuboy." Original drawing by James Forbes, 1781, engraved by J. Shury, and printed in *Oriental Memoirs* (1813). Photographic reproduction by permission of Yale Center for British Art, Paul Mellon Collection, New Haven.

bring with me to Europe, and erect a temple for their reception in my own garden" (1813: 3.361). The locals wondered why a Christian would wish to possess "Hindoo idols," but Forbes answered them that his countrymen would be curious to see "specimens of oriental sculpture." Unlike most of his countrymen at the time, Forbes saw that one could remove Indian images from their religious setting, as "idols," and resituate them as distinct works of "oriental sculpture." After a night's consultation the elders of Dabhoi agreed to his desire.

Like many other nabobs, Forbes purchased an estate upon returning to England. He constructed a sculpture garden in back for his Indian souvenirs. "In eight groups," he described it, "[the sculptures] now adorn an octagon building at Stanmore-hill, erected for that purpose, under a linden-grove on the margin of a lake profusely adorned by the nymphea lotos, which, when its snowy petals and expanded foliage are gently agitated by the southern breeze, reminds me of the sacred tanks of Guzerat" (3.362). For Forbes, the Indian images he brought home from Dabhoi were valued most for their personal resonance, their capacity to evoke a picturesque Indian environment in which the retired officer had spent some of his most satisfying years.[17]

Personal collections of Indian memorabilia no doubt provided solace and remembrance to many other retired India hands as well, but as Mildred Archer notes, they did not necessarily meet with enthusiastic approval from other viewers. Archer quotes Joseph Banks, the eminent naturalist and president of the Royal Society, who was forced to endure a visit with one Mr. Newton, recently returned from the colony. "I was obliged," commented Banks, with asperity, "to admire drawers full of Indian weapons, Fly flappa pictures of the nabob & his Court, Letters from him to Mrs. Newton in Indian Language & Closets full of China defend me I say from a Nabob's collection" (1987: 16). Another tradition began here: that of the "India bore."

The most extensive and consequential collection of Indian religious sculpture by a European during this period was assembled by an unconventional military man, Charles Stuart.[18] Enlisted as a cadet in the Bengal Army in 1777, Stuart gradually rose through the ranks until he was appointed major general in 1814, even though he had little or no battle experience. Like Forbes, Stuart took a keen and sympathetic interest in native culture and Hinduism. In 1808 he anonymously published a lengthy pamphlet entitled *Vindication of the Hindoos from the Aspersions of the Reverend Claudius Buchanan*, which as the title indicates was a defense of traditional Hindu religious values directed against those missionaries like Buchanan who argued the need to convert Indians to Christianity. The general was sardonically known as "Hindoo Stuart," and rumors of his enthusiastic participation in Hindu rituals, his construction of a temple on Sagar Island, and his maintenance of an Indian wife and family led many to believe that he had "gone native." In his *Vindication* Stuart admitted to being anti-Christian, but he also assured his readers that he was not a convert to Hinduism.

While in India over nearly fifty years, Stuart acquired a vast and extraordinary collection of Indian things. His will listed "Indian Statues of Stone, Alabaster, Copper, Brass etc., Indian Spears Swords daggers Pictures of India and other Curiosities" and also mentioned an extensive library.[19] Of this hoard the most significant items for our purposes, and for Stuart's place in the history of collecting, are the Indian statues. He accumulated hundreds of them. Many were huge, weighing up to one and a half tons. A large number were ancient, dating primarily from the Pāla and Sena periods of the eighth through twelfth centuries in eastern India. And for one collecting at a time before the discipline of Indian art history had attempted to establish stylistic chronologies and criteria of quality, and long before most Westerners would ascribe the term "art" to them, Stuart obtained many objects of remarkably high artistic merit. His was arguably the greatest collection of Indian sculpture ever put together by an individual collector.

Although Stuart did not maintain any acquisition records, anecdotes reported elsewhere give some sense of his vigorous methods of collecting. The Baptist missionary John Chamberlain recorded in his diary on 20 November 1817 a conversation he had with an elderly brahmin.[20] The brahmin abruptly asked the missionary, "How is it that your countrymen steal our gods?" He then went on to explain, "Sir, a gentleman whose name I do not remember, came to me to let him take the image of Lukshmee away, which stood on the point where the river and rivulet meet; and he said he would give me a sum of money if I would consent to it. I told him that I could not take any money for it; that she was worshipped by all the people around, and that several times a year the people assembled from the country at a distance to see the goddess, and to bathe: at which time much was offered to her." The gentleman persisted. He returned four or five times, offered ample remuneration, and even took the brahmin by boat to see the assemblage of gods in his Calcutta house, but still the brahmin refused to sell. Finally, continued the brahmin, the gentleman "got his people together, and took away the goddess by night. There the tree stands, Sir, but the goddess is gone!"

Of course missionaries like Chamberlain viewed Stuart as an enemy to their cause, but others who had no motive for impugning Stuart related similar stories. The scholar James Prinsep described how two large inscribed slabs Stuart donated to the Asiatic Society of Bengal in 1810 turned out to have been cut from temples in Bhubanesvar, and recommended they be returned. Yet when Lieutenant Kittoe attempted to return the stones to their original location, he was surprised that the local priests did not appear deferential and grateful. "On the contrary," reported Prinsep, "they brought him a long list of purloined idols and impetuously urged him to procure their return as he had done that of the inscriptions."[21] Writing a few decades later, Rajendralala Mitra singled out Stuart as foremost of those who had separated the religious statuary from the temples of Bhubanesvar and defaced them (Mitra 1880: 2.84, 90).

In his later years Stuart turned his home in Chowringhee, Calcutta into a kind of museum. Two brahmin servants ushered visitors around when Stuart was out. Judging from Chamberlain's anecdote, Stuart apparently also used his collection, much as a modern museum curator might, to stimulate further donations. Yet the Stuart museum was hardly a sensation as far as early nineteenth-century British colonial society was concerned. In the mild condescension of one obituary, "In this collection there are many curious things; but there is reason to suppose that the general himself set a higher value upon it than might by others be accorded to it."[22] Contemporary Calcutta writers, notes Jorg Fisch, do not speak of the museum.

Upon Stuart's death, several of his Indian religious images were incorporated into the tomb he had built in South Park Street Cemetery, constructed on the model of a Hindu temple. An arched doorway, evidently appropriated from a Śaiva temple of the Pāla period, featured standard images of the river goddesses Gaṅgā and Yamunā at the base, and atop the lintel was a serene head of Śiva (Figure 25).[23] Invading a Christian place of burial with the idolatrous forms of a Hindu temple was perhaps Stuart's parting provocation to his old enemies, the missionaries, and they did raise a futile protest (Cotton 1923: 175). Some objects also remained in Stuart's house, which ironically was purchased by the London Missionary Society and occupied by Reverend Alphonse Lacroix in 1829.[24] Most of his collection, however, was dispatched back to England in 143 large cartons. Stuart donated fifteen items to the East India Company for its museum, and the largest portion went to his heirs, who had it auctioned off at Christies in June 1830.

The subsequent trajectory of Stuart's collection provides a striking index of the value that Indian religious imagery enjoyed in nineteenth-century England. At the Christies auction there seems to have been only one major bidder. James Bridge directly acquired about one-third of the 154 lots, while someone named Reynolds, apparently acting as Bridge's agent, bought much of the rest. Bridge had many of the sculptures installed in his home at Shepherd's Bush. Upon the death of his heir, George Bridge, the collection was again put up for auction. Again there was only one bidder: Augustus Wollaston Franks, keeper of British antiquities at the British Museum. "The auctioneer objected," narrates Marjorie Caygill, "but Franks insisted and the collection was knocked down for a nominal sum said to be five pounds. The house was about to be sold, the sculptures had to be removed quickly and Franks persuaded the family that they might at least benefit from the glory

FIG. 25. Charles Stuart's Tomb, South Park Street Cemetery, Calcutta. Constructed c. 1828. Photograph taken in 1935 by Lady Betjeman. Photograph courtesy of Theon Wilkinson and the British Association for Cemeteries in South Asia, London.

FIG. 26. Śiva and Pārvatī Panel in the British Museum. Black stone sculpture, perhaps from inside of temple, Orissa, twelfth or thirteenth century. Acquired by Charles Stuart, later donated by Bridge family to British Museum.

of making a presentation, which they did" (Caygill 1985: 77). For this reason Stuart's great collection, much of it now exhibited in the new Hotung gallery of the British Museum, is misleadingly labelled as the "Bridge Collection" (Figure 26).

The nineteenth-century British community of response assigned virtually no aesthetic or economic value to the objects Stuart had so carefully and aggressively amassed. Franks was nearly the lone exception. Things would change only in the twentieth century.

The Tiger in the East India House

During the early nineteenth century, as the British solidified their colonial control in India, the quantity of Indian objects present in England increased markedly. There were many places in London where the English public could satisfy its curiosity by viewing the world of objects made available through the British imperial endeavor. As Ray Desmond (1982: 33–35) has shown, captured arms and armor were on display in the Royal Asiatic Society museum and in the Tower of London; the Royal United Services Institution displayed armaments also, and had Tipū's uniform. The Linnean Society museum featured natural history specimens from South Asia. The London Missionary Society maintained a "Missionary Museum" on Blomfield Street, which displayed, as trophies of conversion, "the idols given up by their former worshippers from a full conviction of the folly and sin of idolatry." One could see there the image of Śiva that Ramjee Pramanik had flung down from its temple in Rammakal Chowk. Temporary dockside displays popped up regularly as East Indian merchant ships unloaded new cargoes. Of all these sites for Indian display, however, the India Museum, or "Oriental Repository," in the East India House was by far the most comprehensive. "Tipu's Tiger" was the best-known object of the India Museum, and indeed, in Richard Altick's judgement, "one of the most famous individual exhibits in London show history" (1978: 299).

Museum buildings act as frames for objects displayed within. Responses to particular objects are guided, enhanced, and contained within the parameters of expectation and possibility structured by the building itself and the organization of its exhibitions. So, to understand the response of the nineteenth-century British public to a work like "Tipu's Tiger," it is important also to consider its new home. As a site where objects appropriated from defeated opponents were redisplayed, the India Museum of East India House differed markedly from the Cola temple at Gangaikondacolapuram built by Rājendra and from Maḥmūd's great mosque in Ghazna. The British seldom if ever placed wartime loot on display in what they considered religious buildings, just as they did not officially plunder the religious institutions of those they defeated. Yet the India Museum also differed markedly from the modern museums to which we have become accustomed.

East India House was primarily a secular place of business, which also contained a museum and library. The East India Company expanded and virtually rebuilt the old India House on Leadenhall Street in 1796–1799, to reflect the increased scale of Company operations and wealth. The new building was an imposing neoclassical structure with classical style porch and pediment (Figure 27). John Bacon designed the tympanum frieze, an allegorical depiction of King George III in Roman costume defending Britannia and its commerce with the East. Inside, the main downstairs rooms were devoted to the business of the East India Company. The museum and library were located in peripheral quarters, initially in the east wing and later in rooms upstairs.[25]

The implicit hierarchy of business over learning, and of Western form over Indian substance, was reinforced by the decorative scheme employed in the downstairs rooms. An allegorical chimney-piece by Michael Rysbrack showing Britannia receiving the riches of the East dominated the Grand

FIG. 27. East India House, Leadenhall Street. Wood engraving, published in Charles Knight, *London* (1841–1844). Photographic reproduction by permission of Yale Center for British Art, Paul Mellon Collection, New Haven.

Court Room. The Revenue Committee Room featured a ceiling painting executed by Spiridion Roma, again representing Britannia receiving riches from the East. Here Britannia sits elevated on a rock, denoting the firmness of the Empire, guarded by a lion. Female allegorical figures of India and China approach her from below, holding out their offerings for Britannia's delectation. India presents a crown surrounded by pearls and rubies, while China offers porcelain and tea. Behind them two other Asiatic figures bring their presents. In the background an Indian merchant ship signifies the commercial source of these riches (Figure 28). In the same room was Benjamin West's historical painting of Robert Clive receiving the grant of *dīwānī* from the Mughal. Mustered around the niches of the General Court Room were sculptural figures of East India Company heroes, such as Clive, Stringer Lawrence, and George Pocock, decked out in Roman military costume.

As a reflection of taste, the art on display in the business rooms in East India House confirmed the "solidly British image" maintained by the Company directors. Mildred Archer points this out: "Although their profitable

FIG. 28. "The East Offering Its Riches to Britannia." Ceiling painting by Spiridion Roma, 1778. Originally in Revenue Committee Room, East India House, later relocated to ceiling over southeast staircase in New India Office, now the Foreign and Commonwealth Office, London. By permission of the British Library (Shelfmark Foster 245).

dealings were all with the East, there was no whiff of 'the exotic' in their House—no Indian miniatures, no inlaid furniture or textiles were on view, no export wares such as Chinese porcelain or wall-papers. . . . In the public rooms and offices of their own 'House', as in its architecture, the Directors preserved a 'safe' British image" (1986: 4). More than this, these works by European artists presented an iconographical validation and naturalization of the British colonial enterprise in India. The repeated analogy with Imperial Rome provided the British Raj its proper historical antecedent. The artworks reminded their viewers of the tremendous profitability of the relationship for England. Jewels simply overflow the basket offered by India as Britannia inspects one of the pearl necklaces. Yet the artists did not illustrate rule or riches as things taken from Indian subjects; India gave these things to Britannia, as if these were simply her due.

The more curious of Britannia's colonial acquisitions were on display in the museum. Established when the Leadenhall Street house was expanded in 1799, and first directed by one of the great scholars of British Orientalism, Charles Wilkins, the India Museum was a secular site in which the people of England could visually encounter the multitudinous and bizarre objects of the world made available through their empire-building adventures. Its collection was truly heterogeneous:

> a long-nosed tapir and birds with exotic plumage from Java; cases crammed with iridescent insects; the "Babylonian Stone" and five bricks which a label credulously described as being "the original bricks which the Israelites were compelled to make without straw"; a fragment of a Roman tessellated floor; an Oriental opulence of gold and silver ornaments, pearls and gems; spun and woven silks and woolens, canopies, carpets and rugs hanging and draped everywhere; and a glimpse of some of the plunder from the battle of Seringapatam—the golden tiger's head footstool from the throne of Tipu Sultan and, most popular exhibit of all, his musical mechanical Tiger. (Desmond 1982: 2–3)

In the clear dualism of the East India House, where the downstairs business rooms envisioned British sovereignty, the upstairs museum offered a synecdoche of India as colony (Figure 29). England's most comprehensive repository of Indian objects portrayed India as exotic, miscellaneous, opulent, ahistorical, and subordinated.

Audiences bring with them their own ideas and understandings of the world, their own wishes and fantasies, when they view objects in a museum. This mental set also frames the way those objects are seen and received. Due to its great popularity, "Tipu's Tiger" figures in a large number of early nineteenth-century guidebooks, travel sketches, and literary works, so we can gain a good sense of how its new English audience in the Indian Museum responded to the Tiger.

The primary descriptive term British observers used for the Tiger was "curious." The term reminds us of earlier European "cabinets of curiosities," and the Indian Museum with its zoological collections, exotic manufactured products, and odd bits and pieces of all sorts certainly was a culture-specific descendent of those sixteenth- and seventeenth-century forerunners of the modern museum. In early nineteenth-century usage, though, "curious" also had the more condescending connotation of bizarre, unintelligible, or infantile. The Tiger was treated as a toy, a "childish piece of musical mechanism," worthy only of condescension and perhaps amusement. In Barbara Hofland's 1814 novel *A Visit to London*, for instance, the young heroine Emily visiting the India House is momentarily frightened by the "harsh, moaning sound" emanating from the Tiger. The calm, mature librarian tries to reassure her that it is only a toy, but Emily asks to be taken home immediately (Desmond

FIG. 29. The Museum, East India House. "Tipu's Tiger" shown on left side. Wood engraving published in Charles Knight, *London* (1841–1844). Photographic reproduction by permission of Yale Center for British Art, Paul Mellon Collection, New Haven.

1982: 26). John Keats, who most likely saw the Tiger when he was turned down for a job by the East India Company, incorporated the "man-tiger-organ" into his satirical poem "Cap and Bells": the odd object here belongs to the emperor of the faeries, Elphinon (Mann 1957).

If it were seen only as a childish mechanism from India, however, there would have been no reason for the Tiger's great fame. The object had two other things going for it. The musical Tiger resonated with associations to recent events the British public knew well, and the clear "emblematic" composition of the effigy made it a particularly appropriate figure for symbolic and ironic reinterpretation.

All observers reinscribed the Tiger into the well-known narrative of Tipū's ferocious, tigerlike opposition to the British and his eventual subjugation by heroic British forces. Throughout the Anglo-Mysore Wars, and especially after the fall of Sri Rangapattana, England was deluged with memoirs, poems, dramatizations, and paintings retelling the story of Tipū's obstinacy and his demise. In Anne Buddle's term, a veritable "Tipū-mania" took hold of London. At least six plays dramatized the story of Tipū. British participants in the Mysore Wars related their experiences in volume after volume, and Tipū himself appeared in fictional versions by Meadows Taylor and Walter Scott. British painters in India, and those who had never set foot there, rendered the great scenes of British victory. By far the most grandiose representation was a "Great Historical Picture" of the "Taking of Seringapatam" painted by Robert Ker Porter, then nineteen years old. In a frenzy of work Porter covered more than 2,500 square feet of canvas with his epic subject in just six weeks' time, and placed the panorama in the Lyceum.[26]

Bringing this as part of their cultural literacy, British audiences saw Tipū's own identification with the tiger and his alleged attachment to the musical Tiger as material evidence of his audacity, treachery, and cruelty, a "proof of the tyrant's ferocity" (Mogridge n.d.: 152). As James Forbes (1813: 4.185) commented, "A human being, who could pass his hours of relaxation and amusement in this savage manner, may be easily supposed to have enjoyed the death of a European who unhappily fell into his power, whether effected by poison, sword, or bowstring." Not only Tipū was implicated here, however. The infantilism and crudeness of Tipū's toy Tiger could also be generalized to represent the character of *all* Oriental despots who opposed British rule: "Whether made for Tippoo himself or for some other Indian potentate a century and a half earlier," commented one observer, "it would be difficult to convey a more lively impression of the mingled ferocity and childish want of taste so characteristic of the majority of Asiatic princes than will be communicated at once by an inspection of this truly barbarous piece of music" (Society for the Diffusion of Useful Knowledge 1835: 319–20). In the late eighteenth and early nineteenth centuries, the notion of "Oriental despotism" as the characteristic mode of Indian governance served as an important justification for the imposition of British rule. Here, it would seem, was the material embodiment of an Oriental despot's mentality.[27]

In Tipū's music room, the Tiger devouring the redcoat no doubt signified an anticipated future victory over his primary south Indian rival. British observers of the time liked their allegorical compositions clear and unambiguous, and they could easily project how Tipū himself would have interpreted the iconography of the effigy. Appropriated and domesticated upstairs in the East India House, however, its signification shifted for British viewers. "Tipu's Tiger" could stand as an ironic representation of the Indian despot's imagined victory overturned by British forces. British soldiers who fought at Sri Rangapattana received medals depicting the British lion overcoming the Tiger of Mysore, but the Tiger in the museum offered a way to participate vicariously in the activity of empire building. Those back home could playfully turn the crank of "Tipu's Tiger" and, more courageous than little Emily, overcome all fears of this now-subdued enemy. At the same time, the Tiger confirmed the moral judgement of Asiatic character and Indian political culture that justified British conquest.

Exhibits may evoke different responses among differing audiences, of course. As a "community of response," British visitors to the India Museum in the first half of the nineteenth century were remarkably consistent in their responses to and comments about "Tipu's Tiger." But what about other viewers? Fortunately, one Indian visitor, Rakhaldas Haldar, kept a diary while studying in London during 1861–1862. Homesick, he visited the India Museum often during his year abroad, but with decidedly mixed emotions: "I am just returning (3½ p.m.) from a visit to the India Museum; my 6th or 7th visit. It was painful to see the state chair of gold of the late Lion of the Punjab with a mere picture upon it; shawls without Babus; musical instruments without a Hindu player; jezails and swords without sipahis and sawars; golden ornaments without wearers; and above all hookahs without the fume of fantastic shapes" (1903: 57). Haldar does not speak in his journal of the Tiger, but the golden state chair he observed had a similar background.

The empty throne formerly belonged to Maharaja Ranjit Singh (r. 1792–1839), "Lion of the Punjab," the talented leader who had united the Sikh community into an effective kingdom centered in the Punjab and its capital, Lahore. It had been constructed by Ḥafiz Muḥammad of Multan in 1818, when the Sikh army captured that city, and it was probably commissioned to commemorate the conquest (Figure 30). In the early nineteenth century Ranjit's kingdom was the only serious remaining rival to the British for dominance over north India. Ranjit succeeded in maintaining peaceful relations with the British, but in the struggle for succession following his death the British saw their opportunity to acquire the fertile lands of the Punjab. Two Anglo-Sikh wars ensued, and upon British victory in 1849 the new governor-general, J. A. B. Ramsay, marquess of Dalhousie, helped himself to the treasures of the Lahore palace as official prize. Among the Sikh regalia were the famous diamond Koh-i-noor and Ranjit's throne. Dalhousie presented the latter to the Company directors, and it went on display in the India Museum in 1853 as a trophy of victorious war.

The historical resonance of the Tiger for nineteenth-century English audiences led them to a narrative of British victory and a moral condemnation of native Indian rulers. For an Indian visitor like Rakhaldas Haldar, however, objects in the India Museum like the Sikh royal throne with only a picture on it evoked the life of home, yet by their very incompleteness and detachment from human usage they also reminded him painfully of his own separation from that living reality.

Post-Colonial Relocations

Did the Tiger ever bite back? During the Victorian period we learn of discontented jewels, looted objects in Britain that demand their own repatriation. The best known of these is Wilkie Collins' "Moonstone." In Collins'

FIG. 30. Ranjit Singh's Throne. Wood and resin core covered with embossed gold. Made by Ḥafiẓ Muḥammad of Multan, 1818 or later. Acquired by East India Company around 1849, during Anglo-Sikh Wars. Later transferred to Victoria and Albert Museum. Printed by courtesy of the Board of Trustees of the Victoria and Albert Museum, London.

1868 novel, the English officer John Herncastle appropriates for himself a huge yellow diamond in Tipū Sultān's dagger during the sack of Sri Rangapattana. A dying brahmin points to the dagger and curses him, "The Moonstone will have its vengeance yet on you and yours." Nevertheless, the obstreperous Herncastle persists in carrying off the diamond and takes it back with him to England. And the looted object, an alien presence in the home country, does indeed extract its revenge on all who come into contact with it in England, until it is finally restored to its original Indian home, adorning the forehead of an image in the temple of Somanātha.

The Moonstone is of course a fiction, but Collins admitted that he based his story on two actual royal gems: the Orlov diamond adorning the top of the Russian imperial scepter, which was supposed to have been taken from the eye of the idol at Sri Rangam, and the famous Koh-i-noor, which had been subject to a prediction of misfortune to anyone diverting it from its ancient usage.[28] Koh-i-noor, the "Mountain of Light" diamond, has quite likely the longest biography of any extant gem. It had belonged to the Mughals, the Persians under Nadir Shāh, the Afghani kingdom established by Ahmad Shāh, and the Sikh kingdom of Ranjit Singh. The British acquired it when they defeated Dalip Singh, Ranjit Singh's successor, in 1849. Characterizing the gem as "a historical symbol of conquest in India," Governor-General Dalhousie compelled Dalip Singh and the maharani of Ranjit Singh to give it as a royal presentation to Queen Victoria, and it was later incorporated into the British Crown itself, the literal analogue to India as the "jewel in the crown."[29]

Such legends did not grow up around particular Indian images, whether religious or not, in nineteenth-century Britain, as far as I am aware. "Tipu's Tiger" bit more subtly, by posing certain quandaries and ambivalences for its twentieth-century audience. These reflect two broader twentieth-century developments bearing upon Indian objects relocated to the United Kingdom during the colonial period, one taxonomic and the other political. The first is the incorporation of Indian sculpted objects such as religious images into the Western category of "art," and the second is the political breakup of the British empire and the creation of an independent Republic of India within a post-World War II international order.

Taxonomic Shift: Idols into Art

Discussing a controversial exhibition juxtaposing non-Western "tribal" objects and artworks of European modernism held at the Museum of Modern Art in 1984–1985, the anthropologist James Clifford argues that the show documents not so much an essential affinity between "primitive" art and modern Western art as it does a "taxonomic moment." "The fact that rather abruptly, in the space of a few decades, a large class of non-Western artifacts came to be redefined as art," Clifford observes, "is a taxonomic shift that requires critical historical discussion, not celebration" (1988: 196). African objects that were formerly called "fetishes" abruptly became works of "sculpture" or examples of "material culture" (199). Whether or not we wish to celebrate such classificatory changes, we do need to agree with Clifford that they take place within larger cultural contexts. According to Clifford, the recognition by European artists of an "elemental power" residing within African sculpted masks and figures occurred in a setting—avant-garde Paris, primarily, in the 1910s and 1920s—where a growing *negrophilie* brought enthusiastic responses to American jazz and the dancer Josephine Baker as well. At the same time, this taxonomic shift engendered significant alterations in the way audiences viewed the newly identified objects of art, and in the material practices of collecting, selling, and displaying them.

Something quite similar, indeed parallel, took place among Indian religious images in the West during the first half of the twentieth century. Objects that had been termed "idols" in 1900 found themselves metamorphosed into works of art. One can specify endpoints to this transformation. The taxonomic shift began with the writings of E. B. Havell and A. K. Coomaraswamy in the 1910s, and was institutionally completed with the great show of "The Art of India and Pakistan" held at the Royal Academy of Arts in London, 1947–1948. This shift grew out of a larger intellectual movement that we might call, by analogy, *indophilia*. Certain aspects of Indian culture were selected and given a positive valence as embodying "spiritual" values, and these were contrasted with the negatively valued "materialism" of late Victorian British culture. In India this movement was an important part of the gathering nationalist, anti-colonial movement, particularly through spiritual politicians such as Vivekananda, Aurobindo, Sister Nivedita, Annie Besant, and the Tagore circle.[30] In England indophilia provided a focus for the cultural critique of industrial society, and found natural allies among the William Morris circle, and others.

Robert Skelton has suggested a still more precise moment of genesis for this shift, which dramatically brought into conflict old and new ways of viewing Indian religious sculpture.[31] On the afternoon of 13 January 1910, E. B. Havell addressed the Royal Society of Arts in London on the subject "Arts Administration in India." Havell had recently returned from Calcutta, and in his recently published writings he set out to "redeem" Indian art by overturning the "prejudiced" attitudes held by most British observers and inculcated among many educated Indians as well. The chairman of the society was George C. M. Birdwood, an old India hand. Through his positions as curator of the India Office Museum, organizer of the Indian displays at the annual South Kensington exhibitions, and referee for the Indian section of the South Kensington Museum (which in 1902 became the Victoria and Albert Museum), Birdwood had been a key arbiter of taste concerning Indian art in London for some forty years. His revised *Industrial Arts of India* served as an official handbook for the India section of the Victoria and Albert Museum. He was also a prime spokesman for the "prejudices" Havell criticized. Warming to his rebuttal of Havell's address that afternoon, Birdwood pointed to a photograph of an Indonesian Buddha image and remarked: "This senseless similitude, in its immemorial fixed pose, is nothing more that an uninspired brazen image, vacuously squinting down its nose to its thumbs, and knees, and toes. A boiled suet pudding would serve equally well as a symbol of passionless purity and serenity of soul!" The gauntlet was laid down. Keeper of the category of "fine art," Birdwood would never allow Indian images entry. Havell, Coomaraswamy, the painter William Rothenstein, and other disagreed strongly. The outrage following upon Birdwood's line-drawing led to the founding of the Indian Society, dedicated to the promotion of "Indian Art" in the United Kingdom.

To redefine Indian religious images as "fine art," Havell began by identifying its "fundamental character": "Indian art is essentially idealistic, mystic, symbolic, and transcendental" (Havell 1908: 25). This spiritual essence, he went on, links it with Gothic art, which had already been rehabilitated as "art" in European taste. Yet Indian art differs from Gothic as well. "But while the Christian art of the Middle ages is always emotional, rendering literally the pain of the mortification of the flesh," Havell distinguishes, "Indian art appeals more to the imagination and strives to realise the spirituality and abstraction of a supra-terrestrial sphere" (25–26). Havell's notion of a unitary Indian artistic tradition, of course, required great selectivity. He advanced certain iconic figures (meditating Buddhas, dancing Śivas) as central to the tradition, while other types (erotic, secular, or female) ended up on the periphery. More important, Havell set up Indian art as an Other, as based on a fundamentally different aesthetic "ideal" from the standard Western canons, but nevertheless as worthy of inclusion within an expanded category of "fine art." To appreciate Indian art properly, European audiences would be required to understand and empathize with this alternative artistic intentionality. From 1910 through the 1930s, Havell and Coomaraswamy would be the main instructors.

As select Indian sculpted objects turned into art, museum practices shifted as well. Museums made space for religious images like those collected by Charles Stuart and acquired by Franks for the British Museum. The Hedges Viṣṇu, after a long stay in the Pitt-Rivers ethnographic collection, returned to display as a work of art in the Ashmolean. By 1947, the year of Indian independence, the British Royal Academy of Arts could put on a show of "Art of India and Pakistan" without apology, justification, or the late Victorian condescension of Birdwood. In his introduction to the commemorative catalogue for this exhibition, K. de B. Codrington (1948) offered an alternative way of apprehending Indian sculpture as art, which deemphasized the "spiritual" qualities and otherness that Havell and Coomaraswamy had stressed. Codrington instructed his readers to "concentrate upon the thing itself," to attend to significant form, to view Indian sculpture with much the same visual attentiveness one would devote to any other works of sculpture from other cultural traditions.

"Tipu's Tiger" appeared at the Royal Academy exhibit, but it posed something of a problem. Although it was inescapably an Indian object and had enjoyed a certain notoriety during its 140 years in London, it could not really be accommodated within either Havell's or Codrington's way of defining Indian art. British observers could not take it as representative of a spiritual reality. The Tiger had an iconography, admittedly, but it was not a religious one. As a unique and unprecedented piece it did not fit into any art historical sequence. One could not argue that it embodied an "elegant" or "sensuous" or "voluptuous" or "realistic" realization in plastic form. (These were the terms art critics used to praise other sculptural works in the exhibition.) The Tiger also lacked the prestige of age, at a time when the dominant scholarly narratives of Indian art history were tales of early cultural brilliance followed by gradual medieval decline. Not surprisingly, Codrington left the Tiger to itself and focused his introduction on early works like the Didarganj yakṣī and the friezes from Amaravati.

The old India Museum, former home of the Tiger, had been dispersed not long after the East India Company itself was disbanded following the Indian Rebellion of 1857, and the Tiger had eventually found its way into the collections of the Victoria and Albert Museum. During World War II, the Tiger suffered serious damage from a bombing, but after the war conservation workers skillfully repaired it. After its appearance in the Royal Academy exhibition, the Tiger also traveled in 1955 to New York, to appear at the Museum of Modern Art in a show of Indian textiles and ornaments. Presumably the Tiger had by then at least advanced from a "childish curiosity" to the category of "ornament." Its status apparently perplexed the curators of the Victoria and Albert Museum at that time. Mildred Archer relates that in 1956, when the Imperial Institute was demolished and the India collection needed to squeeze into smaller quarters in the main Museum building, "a stringent selection of Indian masterpieces was made" (1959: 2). The Tiger was no curator's idea of a masterpiece. However, Archer continues, "so great was the 'tiger's' general appeal" that it had to be included among the select few. However much they might wish to dismiss its value as a work of art, the Museum keepers had also to take the Tiger's public celebrity into account. This fame evidently continues to the present, for tour guidebooks to London routinely single the Tiger out (usually as the only Indian object so distinguished) for special mention within the Victoria and Albert collection.

The Politics of Repatriation

In Wilkie Collins' fiction, a mysterious trio of dedicated brahmin temple servants pursue the Moonstone during its peregrinations in England and finally carry it back to its original temple in India. In reality, I know of no such successful repatriation quests during the colonial period. The Moonstone's curse would have to wait for independence and for the development of the legal concept of "cultural property" to find its allies.

Just as Indian objects in the United Kingdom were gaining a new identity, with the imprimatur of the Royal Academy, as "art," India itself became an independent nation state. At the same time another way of defining those objects appeared. With the breakup of the old colonial empires and the establishment of a new world order in the years following World War II, new international organizations set out to develop guidelines for defining and protecting objects of particular cultural value, and in some cases for returning them to their original communities or nations.[32] Objects that the British had formerly taken from India as "prize" in colonial warfare could now be reclaimed as the India's cultural property, the patrimony of the new nation.

Theoretically all items appropriated under duress during colonial conditions might be viewed as the cultural property of India. In practice, however, reclaiming national heritage is a selective and difficult procedure. Most resolutions stress that only property of great historical or artistic importance to a nation qualifies for consideration. And of course the current holders of such treasures, the former colonial powers, are not eager to return them. The massive cultural repositories like the British Museum and the Victoria and Albert Museum in London, with their comprehensive, world-spanning collections, have their own interests to protect. Likewise, the British government would be loath to watch its premier national institutions denuded of their colonial acquisitions. Within the circles of international diplomacy, requests for repatriation of cultural treasures more often create conflict than they do good will among the states involved. Only when a larger symbolic or political point is at stake does it seem warranted to expend the necessary diplomatic capital. So, from among the great wealth of objects that passed from India to the United Kingdom during British colonial control, the Indian government has pressed claims on only a small handful.

The most frequent and fitting target for attempts at repatriation has been the Koh-i-noor diamond, which Governor-General Dalhousie described as a "historical symbol of conquest in India" when the East India Company defeated the last major indigenous power in the subcontinent in 1849. If really a symbol of conquest, then when that conquering regime departs would it not be appropriate that Koh-i-noor return to its former home? The Government of India requested the diamond's repatriation in 1947, and again in 1953 during Queen Elizabeth's coronation. Pakistan made its claim in 1976. Arguing that the British had appropriated the famous diamond from the maharaja of Lahore, a city now in Pakistan, Prime Minister Zulfikar Ali Bhutto addressed a formal request to the British prime minister, James Callaghan. Indian newspapers immediately responded that the diamond was completely Indian in origin. Even in the Mahābhārata war, went the press coverage, the Pāṇḍava warrior Bhīma fought with the jewel tied to his right arm, and subsequently it had belonged to a series of Indian rulers. Within India, the Sikh community asserted a special claim on the gem, since Dalhousie had taken it from a ruler of the Sikh kingdom. Farther afield, newspapers in Iran argued that it should return there, since the name "Koh-i-noor" is Persian and the diamond once belonged to Nadir Shāh, who looted it from Delhi in 1739. Even Afghanistan weighed in with a request, since the rulers of Kabul had held it for a time during the eighteenth century.

Thanks to the flurry of claims on the jewel, Callaghan could refuse them all on grounds that the history of the diamond was altogether confused and therefore England had clearest proprietary right to it. He pointed out that the defeated Sikh ruler Dalip Singh and the maharani formally gave it to the East India Company as a gift (though he did not add that it was a coerced gift). The British Government wished to take a firm line on these requests, the *Times* of London reported, to insure that "a queue of foreign representatives did not form outside the British Museum and other treasure houses."[33] The case of Koh-i-noor illustrates the difficulties that new nations often have in asserting unambiguous claim to objects with complex individual histories, and where precolonial regimes do not coincide with postcolonial national borders. Again in 1983 the Indian high commissioner to the United Kingdom made an unofficial request for the return of Koh-i-noor, but the diamond remains in place on the front of the Maltese crown among the British crown jewels, and the only queues now are those of tourists who file past it daily in the jewel house of the Tower of London.

Indians have pursued other appropriated objects in the United Kingdom as well, and the objects selected often reflect regional political concerns. Another of the items Dalhousie picked up during his annexation of the Punjab, Ranjit Singh's throne, came into dispute in 1983. The demand was initiated by the Akali Dal, a regional political party representing Sikh interests in the Punjab, and the central government acquiesced, no doubt in part to maintain good relations with an important regional constituency.[34] Likewise, regional politicians in Maharashtra have initiated sporadic attempts to regain the sword of the seventeenth-century Maratha warrior and ruler, Śivajī Bhonsle. These efforts have also been unsuccessful so far, largely because the mysterious sword cannot be located. If in exists at all, the current proprietor is not about to publicize its whereabouts.

Despite its fame and the clear documentation of its appropriation as colonial booty, "Tipu's Tiger" has never been target of an official repatriation request. Most likely this is due to the ambiguity of Tipū's own historical image in India. He was an Islamic ruler of a predominantly Hindu region, and so there has been no powerful local constituency to make claims on his behalf. Although some have tried to promote Tipū as a secularist and patriotic freedom fighter, Hindu nationalists have countered that he was a Muslim zealot, and cited British colonial accounts to back their accusations.[35] Yet as historical reputations change in India (as they do everywhere), and as regional and national political alignments shift (as they do everywhere), it is

FIG. 31. Dhruva Mistry's "Tipu." Painted sculpture of iron, fiberglass, and plaster, 1982. Photograph courtesy of Dhruva Mistry.

by no means implausible that "Tipu's Tiger" could be given new life as an object of significant historical and cultural value. Another relocation back to its Indian homeland might once again reverse the Tiger's significance. (In Chapter Seven, we will see how one successfully repatriated icon became temporarily transvalued as a symbol of Indian cultural autonomy.)

While the Tiger rests safely, at least for now, in its glass case in the Victoria and Albert Museum, it also presents itself for a different sort of reappropriation. At least one South Asian artist working in the United Kingdom has reemployed the imagery of the Tiger within his own work, to serve his own expressive purposes. Fresh from India, Dhruva Mistry was a student in 1981 at the Royal College of Art, near the Victoria and Albert Museum, when "Tipu's Tiger" first struck him with its powerful presence. The following year Mistry made his own adaptation of a sleek, powerful hunting cheetah, which he named simply "Tipu" (Figure 31). He sought to create a sense of intensity and presence, more powerful than the animal itself, and to call upon the range of associations viewers might have with the figure of Tipū and his well-known Tiger.[36]

Resonance, Wonder, and History

How does "Tipu's Tiger" appear to us now?

Stephen Greenblatt distinguishes between two models for exhibiting works of art, centering around notions of "wonder" and "resonance" (1991: 42). Wonder, writes Greenblatt, denotes the power of an object on display to stop viewers in their tracks, to induce an exalted attention to the object in itself. Indian sculptural images of particular formal power or elegance, such as the Didarganj yakṣī and the Śiva Vṛṣabhavāhana of Tiruvengadu, elicit that kind of intense, attentive viewing, and the mode of display in which these icons presented themselves in the 1985 "Sculpture of India" show (as described in Chapter One), isolating each as a self-contained sculptural whole, aimed precisely at enhancing the audience's response of wonderment. When the curators of the Victoria and Albert Museum made their "stringent selection of masterpieces" in the 1950s, and nearly consigned "Tipu's Tiger" to the warehouse, they probably held the power to provoke wonder as their implicit aesthetic criterion.

Wonder, however, is not the only response objects in museums may engender. Resonance, by contrast, Greenblatt defines as the power of an object to reach out beyond its formal boundaries to a larger world, and thereby to suggest or evoke the cultural forces from which it has emerged (and, I would add, occasionally also the cultural forces that have brought it to its current location). Objects of resonance help summon up history. They participate with viewers in reimagining other cultures in other times.

Despite its undoubted power, "Tipu's Tiger" has always primarily been an object of resonance. For Tipū and his court, the Tiger in the music hall of the palace referred outwardly to multiple historical predecessors and divine sources of power that Tipū wished to invoke in his struggle with the British. For London viewers who encountered the Tiger in the India Museum during the early nineteenth century, the Tiger's resonance rested upon its ability to suggest the distinctive personality of a paradigmatic oriental despot, to remind viewers of the historical events that had brought it from Mysore to London, and to embody moral judgments and colonial rationalizations. Yet resonance, much more than wonder, is a complex response that draws upon the knowledge, values, and political premises an audience brings to its encounter with the resonant object. When the audience's frame of assumptions and understandings changes historically, so too may the way a particular object resonates change as well.

The Tiger's current installation in the Victoria and Albert Museum recognizes and reflects its altered resonance. Crowded together in its display case with many other items from Sri Rangapattana, the Tiger stands not as a self-sufficient art object, but as part of an ensemble that collectively represents both the late medieval court of Tipū Sultān and the British capture of Sri Rangapattana in 1799. Yet viewers now are far removed, both spatially and temporally, from that event. Unlike the Tiger's viewers at the old India Museum, we can no longer turn its crank to hear its resounding roar. Too precious and too fragile to risk contact, the Tiger in its glass case reminds its viewers that they can no longer vicariously participate in the colonial enterprise. Even the room in which it stands, the Jawaharlal Nehru Gallery—an ironic name for an exhibit of objects acquired during England's colonial heyday—conveys something of the distance we have come from the time of Wellesley and Tipū. The heroic moment of Indian colonization that the seige of Sri Rangapattana once so vividly embodied for British audiences is now nearly two hundred years past, and the English colonial adventure has shifted from the setting within which the Tiger is viewed to become part of the display. Observing "Tipu's Tiger" juxtaposed with the small golden Seringapatam medal presented to British soldiers, modern viewers are led to explore not just a moment of creativity, but also of conflict, the violent encounter of indigenous Indian rulers with the expanding colonial dominion of the East India Company. And our responses are inextricably bound up with our own evaluations and moral judgments of British colonialism itself, the historical force that has enabled us to view the material remnants of Tipū's court in London.

For some contemporary museum goers, no doubt the Tiger remains the exotic, bizarre, childish icon that it once was to nineteenth-century British observers. In a brief recent article on the Tiger in *Antique Machines and Curiosities*, for instance, an observer urges his readers: "next time you are in

South Kensington you should certainly go and goggle at this bizarre, painted monument to anglophobia" (Parsons 1979: 48). For others of us, more cognizant of the historical forces that have deposited the Tiger in South Kensington and of the postcolonial world that we and this looted Indian object both now occupy, the Tiger must evoke a more complicated, ambivalent response.

6.

Reconstructions of Somanātha

THERE IS a myth, recounted as early as the *Mahābhārata*, that explains the origin of Prabhāsa in Gujarat as a sacred place (*MBh Śalya* ch. 34). Once King Dakṣa cursed the Moon god Soma with tuberculosis for paying exclusive attention to only one of his twenty-seven daughters, all of whom had been married to the Moon. Day by day the Moon began to fade away. Along with him the plants and herbs started to languish, and the creatures that depended on them grew emaciated. Finally the gods, who were also beginning to suffer, went to Dakṣa and asked that he remove the curse. Dakṣa replied that his curse could not be undone, but he could recommend an antidote: if the Moon would bathe in the holy spot where the Sarasvatī River flows into the Western Ocean, he could restore his glow. And so the Moon regularly wanes for half a month from Dakṣa's curse, then regains his effulgence by bathing there on each new moon day. For that reason the place is named "Prabhāsa," "brilliance."

This myth clearly relates the seaside tīrtha to the cyclic disappearances and reappearances of the moon, and suggests also the restorative powers that later pilgrimage guides would attribute to Prabhāsa. When worshipers of the god Śiva took over the site some time before the seventh century, they simply inserted Śiva into the existing narrative. In Śaiva versions, the Moon not only bathes at Prabhāsa, but also worships Śiva as his lord there.[1] Thus the tīrtha is also named Somanātha, Śiva as "Lord of the Moon." The myth also seems to prefigure the distinctive historical career of the Śaiva temple at Somanātha, for that temple too has periodically disappeared as a site of worship and then reappeared, starting with its famous destruction by the Ghaznavid sultan Maḥmūd in 1026. We have already seen in Chapter Three how later Indo-Muslim texts transformed Maḥmūd's victory over the Somanātha idol into an archetypal encounter of Islam with Hindu idolatry. In this chapter I shall take up the subsequent history of the site, and show how Somanātha has waxed and waned as a symbolic site around which various other parties have also sought to articulate their own claims upon religious and political authority in changing historical settings.[2]

Somanātha the Shrine Eternal

I first became interested in Somanātha several years ago, in 1988, when I came across a three-rupee site guide for tourists and pilgrims that had found its way into the stacks of the Yale University library. This little work by Shambhuprasad Harprasad Desai (1975), a retired officer of the Indian Administrative Service and native of Prabhāsa, told a fascinating story of repeated struggle over the site. Following Maḥmūd's raid, the guide claimed, local Hindu rulers soon rebuilt the temple, which was later desecrated by armies of the Delhi Sultanate. At least nine more times, according to Desai, Muslim invaders desecrated the shrine and just as often intrepid Hindus reconsecrated it. Checking around, I found that many other sources told much the same story. The historical details were often fuzzy, the number of desecrations varied, and the references to primary sources were hard to track down. Nevertheless, from the 1870s or so on, almost every author who wrote of Somanātha confidently asserted that the site had been repeatedly contested by the Muslim and Hindu communities over six or more centuries. By 1990 the Muslim desecration count had apparently climbed to twenty-one, at least according to one letter printed in the *New York Times* (26 November 1990).

The best known and most comprehensive work on Somanātha, I found, is *Somanātha, The Shrine Eternal* written by Kanaiyalal Maneklal Munshi and first published by Bharatiya Vidya Bhavan in 1951 to commemorate the reconstruction of the temple. In this popular work Munshi argues that the worship of Śiva and the sanctity of his Somanātha shrine are prehistoric, part of India's primordial tradition. In historical times, Munshi goes on, Śiva served as a "guardian of national resurgence" in the early centuries C.E. Munshi postulates a "first temple" established at Prabhāsa by the beginning of the Common Era, and a "second temple" supposedly destroyed by Arab Muslim armies from Sind in the eighth century. The author then retells Maḥmūd's destruction of the temple, and many subsequent rebuildings and redesecrations. "Somanātha was the shrine beloved of India," he concludes. "An ancient race subconsciously felt that it was Somanātha which connected it with the past and the present; it was the eternal symbol of its faith in itself and its future. As often as the shrine was destroyed, the urge to restore it sprang up more vividly in its heart" (Munshi 1976: 89). Munshi identifies Somanātha with both the national and the racial identity of India.

So fixed in historical memory has this story become that Hindu nationalist groups—the Visva Hindu Parishad (VHP) and the Bharatiya Janata Party (BJP)—pointedly chose Somanātha as the starting point for their 1990 Rath Yatra ("chariot procession"; Figure 32). The example of Somanātha seemed to add historical weight to their more questionable claim that another Mus-

FIG. 32. The Rath Yatra at Somanātha. Organized by the BJP-VHP, 1990, with chariot in foreground and Somanātha temple in back. Photograph courtesy of *Frontline*, Madras.

lim invader, the Mughal Babur, had constructed the Babri Masjid in Ayodhya after destroying a Hindu temple that allegedly marked the site of Rāma's birth.[3] In Hindu nationalist rhetoric, Somanātha figured prominently in a broader historical vision of barbaric foreign invasions by Muslims and the continuous struggle of indigenous Hindus to maintain their religious and cultural heritage, of which the nationalists placed themselves as the current instrument. In the BJP's official "White Paper" on the subject, they observe: "Here was an ancient temple which had been ravaged, looted, and ransacked repeatedly by foreign invaders from Sultan Mahmood Ghaznavi to Emperor Aurangzeb. Every time the Temple was razed to the ground and a mosque put in its place by the marauders, it sprouted again—only to be pulled down again" (Bharatiya Janata Party 1993: 16). The BJP's use of an organic metaphor, the ever-sprouting temple, renders Somanātha and its restoration part of nature itself, the irresistible expression of the "urge" (as Munshi had put it) of the Hindu "race."

Few people nowadays, I am sure, think of Somanātha in terms of the waxing and the waning of the Moon. It has instead become firmly embedded in a communalized historical narrative that speaks of continuous, essential animosity between two religious communities. For me, too, what began as an investigation into the intriguing history of a site and its icon became engaged with the contemporary politics of the Hindu past.

I was initially drawn to studying Somanātha by the stark, agonistic portrait of the site in works by Desai and Munshi, pitting iconoclasts and rebuilders as two clear-cut communities of response toward a Hindu icon. While I was looking into Somanātha's history, however, leaders of the VHP and the BJP were using their version of that history to support an iconoclastic mobilization of their own. As the Ayodhya campaign illuminated powerfully for me how a selective recounting of the past could be effectively redeployed in the present, it pushed me to ask new questions. I became concerned not just with the events that physically affected Somanātha and its icon, but with the narratives and memories of those events. I began to focus on the situations and agendas of those who have retold the stories of Somanātha.

Accounts of Somanātha like those of Desai, Munshi, and the BJP suggest that the collective memory of Muslim iconoclasm in India is a fixed, unchanging quantity, engendering a single continuous grievance among Hindus, and that the impulsion to rebuild temples at places like Somanātha and Ayodhya is an ahistorical, constant, and necessary desire within the Hindu psyche. When we examine the history of Somanātha, however, a more complex picture emerges. We find not simply a history of acts, the oft-cited alternation of Islamic desecrations and Hindu reconstructions. There is also a history of rememberings.

Memory does not exist by itself. It must be given form, narrated and renarrated by humans to themselves and others, in order to persist or return.

Those who formulate and articulate collective memories do so in their own times, alive to their own situations. So the memory of iconoclasm, I will argue, has been periodically reembodied in new narratives, and these narratives have never been transparent renderings of fact nor innocent of larger agendas. In this chapter I examine the historical moments in which the temple of Somanātha and its history of destruction and reconstruction have been remembered, and some of the uses to which these reevoked memories have been put.

Medieval Rememberings

As we have seen in Chapter Three, the Ghaznavid ruler Maḥmūd attacked and destroyed the Solaṅki temple in 1026, and from that very moment his court eulogists began to extol his act as exemplary. A hyperbolic literature grew up around this confrontation of a prominent Islamic ruler with an Indian idol. Indo-Muslim authors depicted Maḥmūd as a warrior of miraculous powers, and they tried to identify Somanātha as the cultic center of all Indian idolatry. Apocryphal incidents came to embellish the story: the idol flies, Maḥmūd strikes the belly with his mace, Maḥmūd grinds the idol into lime paste and feeds it to the brahmins, and many more. Collectively, Indo-Muslim authors advanced Maḥmūd's act of iconoclasm as a model for zealous Muslim rulers bringing new Indian territories under sway.

ʿIṣāmī Remembers Maḥmūd

By the fourteenth century, the narrative of Maḥmūd at Somanātha reached its most elaborate form in the work of ʿIṣāmī, the *Futūḥ al-Salātīn* (1350–1351). Fakhr al-Dīn ʿIṣāmī was an unemployed and disgruntled poet when the chief qāẓī of ʿAlā al-Dīn Hasan Bahman Shāh invited him to attend court at Daulatabad. The Muslim elite of Daulatabad had recently rebelled against the Delhi Sultanate of the Tughluks and successfully declared its independence, and Hasan Bahman Shāh was proclaimed ruler of the Bahmani Sultanate in 1347. Seeking the new sultan's patronage, ʿIṣāmī proposed to write an epic poem that he claimed would rival Firdawsī's *Shāhnāma*. He would take as his subject the conquest of Hindustan by Turkish Muslim rulers, from the time of Maḥmūd of Ghazna up to the reign of Hasan Bahman Shāh himself. It is not surprising that Hasan supported the proposal. As a renegade ruler breaking away from the Tughluk regime in Delhi, without clear royal antecedents of his own, Hasan would welcome the legitimizing effect of the epic lineage that ʿIṣāmī proposed to construct for him.[4]

In the *Futūḥ al-Salāṭīn* ʿIṣāmī advances most of the themes we have already outlined. Maḥmūd is an exemplary hero, the first conqueror of India. Destruction of "idol-houses" is a central aspect of Islamic conquest in India, and Somanātha is the supreme Hindu temple, so the raid on Somanātha is the crowning event in Maḥmūd's career.

ʿIṣāmī stresses to his royal listener that Maḥmūd should serve as a model for action. "All the deeds that he performed in this country yesterday, have become, one and all, a story to-day. The achievements that you make to-day will also become a story to-morrow" (Husain 1967: 67). Carving out a new Islamic polity in the middle of the subcontinent, Hasan Bahman Shāh would certainly have comprehended the parallels between his situation and Maḥmūd's. However, rulers are free to accept advice and apply historical analogies selectively. Although Hasan did emulate Maḥmūd in vigorously mounting military campaigns against other regimes on all sides of his, apparently he did not adopt ʿIṣāmī's recommendations concerning "idol-houses" literally. The earliest Persian chronicles of Hasan's career make no mention of any significant symbolic acts of temple destruction as he brought most of the Deccan under Bahmani control.[5]

Other Islamic conquerors, however, did take the Maḥmūdian model of directed idol destruction seriously. As we have seen, Solaṅki rulers rebuilt Somanātha twice after Maḥmūd's raid. When the Delhi Sultanate sought to bring Gujarat under its imperial control in the late thirteenth century, the general Ulugh Khān, acting on the orders of ʿAlā al-Dīn Khaljī, desecrated Kumārapāla's imperial temple around 1298. "The idols . . . were broken to pieces in pursuance of Abraham's tradition," related the Khaljī court poet Amīr Khusraw, describing the raid. "But one idol, the greatest of them all, was sent by the *maliks* to the Imperial Court, so that the breaking of their helpless god may be demonstrated to the idol-worshipping Hindus. It seemed as if the tongue of the Imperial sword explained the meaning of the text: 'So he (Abraham) broke them (the idols) into pieces except the chief of them, that haply they may return to it'" (Habib 1931: 36). Salvaging the principal idol for public desecration in the imperial capital, Ulugh Khān's actions at Somanātha certainly recalled those of Maḥmūd, but the poet reaches further back for his paradigm, not just to Maḥmūd or Muḥammad, but to the man credited as the founder of monotheism itself, Abraham, the first man to struggle against idolatry.

Padmanābha Remembers Kānhaḍade

The Khaljī invasion disrupted the existing ruling order of western India and provided an opening for ambitious young Rajput warriors to make names for themselves. One such warrior was Kānhaḍade, a Cāhamāna prince of the Sonagira clan governing the area around Jalor fort, one of nine forts in the Marwar region of southern Rajasthan. In the aftermath of Ulugh Khān's campaign in western India, Kānhaḍade set up an autonomous city state and, through his resistance to Delhi's control, established himself as a local legend. A century and a half later, in 1455, Padmanābha, a brahmin of the Jalor court, composed an epic account of his deeds, the *Kānhaḍade Prabandha*, at the request of the local ruler Akhairāja, a direct descendent of Kānhaḍade.[6] Here too Somanātha figures as a central character.

Padmanābha begins his epic of resistance by recounting the circumstances that brought about the Khaljī attack, and then describes Ulugh Khān's victory over the Gujarati ruler at Anahilapataka and the sack of Somanātha. Like demons (*asuras*) the armies of the Delhi Sultanate pound on the stone images with hammers and use iron crowbars and wooden beams to uproot the Śiva liṅga in the sanctum. Padmanābha observes that it is Kali-yuga: "Such strange and improper happenings were taking place: the *kaliyuga* was, no doubt, showing its true temper: Lord Śiva, leaving the earthly abode, went away to Kailāsa" (Bhatnagar 1991: 10). Just as images might retreat from threatened temples, so apparently deities could abandon their icons under duress. But the poet views this as an act of divine cowardice and addresses Śiva directly to remember past deeds where he had shown greater fortitude:

> Earlier, O God, Rudra (Śiva), in the fire of your anger, all the demons (*daityas*) were burnt! You fostered righteousness again on this earth and removed the fear in the *Devaloka* [Divine World]. Your anger reduced Kāmadeva to ashes and destroyed Tripurāsura, as easily as a strong gust of wind blows away a piece of cotton. I, Padmanābha, ask you plainly, Lord Somanātha (Somaiya), "Where is your trident now?" The poet's heart aches, as he remonstrates with the Lord (10–11).

Padmanābha's retrospective pleading with Śiva to defend his earthly images highlights the need for human action and human heroes to rescue the divine icon.

Ulugh Khān orders that the idol be returned to Delhi and crushed into lime. His troops load the liṅga onto a huge cart pulled by three pairs of bullocks, and off they go. As the armies of the sultanate return through the Marwar region on their way back to Delhi, Ulugh Khān taunts the local ruler Kānhaḍade with his captured idol. At dawn the two consorts of Śiva, Pārvatī and Gaṅgā, appear to Kānhaḍade in a dream. The goddesses reveal that the Turks have captured Śiva. "Wake up, O immortal one!" they urge him. "The Asapati (i.e. Emperor) is taking away Somanātha through your territory. Earlier also, Rāma had Rudra freed from the demons. Again, Bali, son of Virochana, displayed his intense devotion and got Śiva freed. Now, on this third occasion, you must come forward, O Kānhaḍadeva! O brave one, delay not in this." (12) Like the goddess who appears to Kampaṇa in *Madhurāvijaya*, Śiva's two female companions here have selected their instrument of recovery, and they cite the example of an earlier incarnation of Viṣṇu to urge him into action.

After receiving expert dream interpretation from the royal priest, Kānhaḍade "shakes off his lethargy" and makes a vow not to eat until he has defeated the foreigners (*mlecchas*) and freed Somanātha from them. He gathers warriors from the thirty-six Rajput clans and leads a night raid on the Turkish camp. He routs the confused warriors and recaptures the icon. Kānhaḍade escorts Somanātha into Jalor, where all rejoice that he has defeated the Turks and liberated Śiva. People begin to recognize Kānhaḍade as an incarnation of Kṛṣṇa.

Rather than return the Somanātha liṅga intact to its original site, as one might expect, Kānhaḍade orders it divided into five new embodiments (*mūrtis*). He sends one back to Saurashtra, presumably for reinstallation at Somanātha temple, but the other four he has installed in temples around the Marwar region, in Lohasing, Mount Abu, Saivadi, and his fort capital Jalor. For Kānhaḍade, evidently, the goal of this reappropriation is only partly to restore Somanātha as an eternal sacred site. He is more concerned to borrow the prestige of Somanātha in gaining Śiva's manifest presence for the newly autonomous "little kingdom" he is establishing in Marwar. "In all the nine divisions of the earth," proclaims the poet, "Kānhaḍade's fame spread for achieving what many regarded as an impossible task" (28).

Unlike Gaṅgādevī's story of Kampaṇa recovering Madurai, however, Padmanābha does not end his narrative with this successful recovery. The temporary defeat of the sultanate forces and reestablishment of the traditional order in Jalor is only the first chapter in this more tragic epic of resistance. Padmanābha goes on to recount ʿAlā al-Dīn's growing anger and determination to subdue the recalcitrant Rajput ruler. The sultan mounts several campaigns against Jalor, each resisted by Kānhaḍade and his fellow Rajputs with great heroism. The sultan's daughter comes to believe that Kānhaḍade is the tenth incarnation of Viṣṇu, and she urges her father to end his war on the Rajput kingdom. She falls in love with Kānhaḍade's son, Vīramade. The sultan proposes to end the hostilities through a marriage alliance and offers to make Kānhaḍade governor of all Gujarat, but Vīramade refuses the marriage proposal as shameful. The war goes on until finally ʿAla al-Dīn succeeds in overcoming the renegade state. Kānhaḍade dies in battle.

Throughout his poem, Padmanābha praises *puṇya*, meritorious action, as the highest value. Kānhaḍade is able to defeat the foreigners due to his past acts of puṇya, Padmanābha asserts, and in turn Kānhaḍade earns through his current deeds great puṇya for himself and his entire clan. Puṇya renders value and reward even upon actions that are ultimately futile, like Kānhaḍade's doomed resistance against the greatly superior forces of the Delhi Sultanate.

In praising this warriors' code of action, Padmanābha spoke to his own patron as well, for the setting in which the poet remembered and recounted the tale of Akhairāja's ancestor was quite similar. In 1455 Jalor was again relatively independent of Delhi's rule, but the recent establishment of the Lodi dynasty brought the threat of renewed attempts to bring Marwar under control of the sultanate. Padmanābha promoted the virtues of resistance to a local ruler who might soon have the opportunity to follow Kānhaḍade's example.

The poems of ʿIṣāmī and Padmanābha exemplify well the medieval genres of literature that I, following Ahmad, have discussed in Chapters Three and Four as as Indo-Muslim "epics of conquest" and Hindu "epics of resistance." Both center around acts of iconoclasm and recovery of the now-famous Śiva liṅga of Somanātha. However, the poems do not remember these acts as the spontaneous expressions of some popular religious will. Rather, the two poets clearly present them as actions of rulers or claimants to rule, which are undertaken in "frontier" political circumstances of contested rule as ways of constituting authority (Richards 1974). This is not to say, however, that they were therefore portrayed as "nonreligious" actions. In both cases the poets carefully ground the acts of their heroes within the moral systems of value provided by their respective religious cultures. Maḥmūd's destruction of Somanātha is linked to the Prophet Muḥammad, whereas Kānhaḍade's recovery of the liṅga results from the directive of two goddesses. For both authors, a ruler must base his moral and political authority within a shared religious ideology, and the authors place themselves in a position to articulate and remind their royal audiences what those values are.

Jain Tales of Somanātha

Śaivas of the Pāśupata school appropriated Prabhāsa tīrtha from its earlier cultic usage and renamed it Somanātha. Maḥmūd of Ghazna broke the liṅga and transported its fragments back to his capital, and so Somanātha became a figure in Indo-Muslim discourse. Kānhaḍade recaptured the Somanātha liṅga from Ulugh Khān and reconsecrated its parts throughout his own domain. Likewise, the Śvetāmbara Jains of western India sought to appropriate Somanātha. They never actually took over the site or seized the Śiva liṅga. However, in Jain narratives revolving around the famous Śiva temple they adapted Somanātha to their own rhetorical purposes. Jain authors of the late medieval period remembered Somanātha as the icon that Maḥmūd devastated while their own image stood impervious to assault, and they remembered Kumārapāla's rebuilt Śiva temple as the place where the Solaṅki emperor converted to the Jain faith.

Jain temples of western India also suffered during the invasions of the Ghaznavids, Khaljīs, and others. Images were forced into retreat and exile, while others were destroyed. Like the Hindus of south India, the Jain community developed its own literature of recovery, in which images reappear wondrously, more powerful than ever. In the fourteenth century Jinaprabhasūri filled a book, the *Vividhatīrthakalpa* ("guide to the various Jain holy places"), with accounts of Jain pilgrimage spots that had survived or revived miraculously. The Jain literature of recovery reaffirmed the power of Jain images and by extension the Jain community of faith. As Phyllis Granoff comments, "Despite the temporary reversals suffered by the Jain community with the destruction of their holy places, the texts seem to be saying, the attacks by the Muslims would seem ironically to have provided a perfect opportunity for continued proof of the greatness of Jainism. Images broken could be miraculously restored, offering an occasion for all to behold the wondrous power of the Jain deities."[7] As we have seen with the stories of Viṣṇu Raṅganātha, survival and miraculous recovery in the face of iconoclastic threat here offer a testimony of Jain images' power, fortitude, and essential connection with its place and its worshipers.

Jain authors did not question the efficacy of images as such, but they were concerned to establish the relative powers of different icons. Maḥmūd's famous sack of the liṅga at Somanātha provided an opportunity for narrative juxtaposition with one of their own. In his *Satyapurīya Mahāvīra Utsāha*, the court poet Dhanapāla describes Maḥmūd's campaign in Gujarat. After successfully destroying Somanātha, Maḥmūd heads on to Satyapura (modern Sanchor in southern Rajasthan), site of a celebrated image of the Jain tīrthaṅkara Mahāvīra. Here too he decides to demolish the idol, but this time it is not so easy. As his elephants pull on ropes to topple the image, the ropes break and the elephants go tumbling. Soldiers strike the body of Mahāvīra with maces, but their blows only bounce back at the strikers. They leave marks on the image but they cannot budge or break it.[8] The Jain image thus demonstrates his resilience by withstanding the worst that Maḥmūd can mete out, and at the same time proves his superiority over the icon of Śiva, which could not.

The Jains also insert themselves into the Śaiva scene when Kumārapāla later rebuilds Somanātha as an imperial-scale temple. More than just taking Somanātha as a setting, though, the Jain authors also adapt a conventional form of Śaiva miracle story to Jain usage with an ending that altogether shifts the message of the story. Śiva appears in bodily form from the liṅga to deliver a Jaina message.

In his fourteenth-century *Prabandhacintāmaṇi*, Merutuṅga relates an anecdote concerning Hemacandra, the great Jain author and polymath who was one of Kumārapāla's religious instructors.[9] Like many traditional Indian sovereigns, Kumārapāla maintained proponents of various religious schools of thought at his court. As the reconstructed Somanātha nears completion, Kumārapāla invites Hemacandra to accompany him on a pilgrimage to the vast new Śaiva temple. To the surprise of the courtiers, Hemacandra agrees, and at the temple he evokes even more amazement by entering the sanctum and worshiping Śiva according to proper Śaiva liturgical practice.

After Kumārapāla has made his own offerings, he dismisses all the other courtiers and temple officials and remains in the inner sanctum with Hemacandra to ask an important question. Different schools of thought all advance differing gods as the highest one, Kumārapāla observes. He asks Hemacandra to declare to him, in this holiest place, who is the god that can give salvation. In reply Hemacandra proposes to invoke Somanātha himself so that Kumārapāla may receive the answer from a divine mouth. He tells Kumārapāla to throw black aloe wood incense onto a flame, while he enters into meditation. The room fills with thick smoke. The candles go out. "Suddenly," narrates Merutuṅga, "a light burst forth, brilliant as the sun. The king rubbed his eyes excitedly, and when he looked again he saw above the water pitcher an ascetic, shining like pure gold from the Jambu River. The ascetic's form was without compare, his nature was beyond comprehension, and he was difficult for human eyes to view" (Muni 933: 85). The astonished king feels the apparition from its toes up to its twisted locks of matter hair and confirms that it is a real manifestation of Śiva. Then he falls to the ground and prays to the god to honor his petition.

Śaiva narratives of divine manifestation follow certain conventions, as Phyllis Granoff has pointed out (1989: 365–67). The appearance of the deity usually occurs in response to the fervent prayers of a devotee, who is often in a state of hardship or uncertainty. Śiva emerges directly out of a liṅga in the form of an emanating light or an anthropomorphic form of himself, and then rescues the acolyte from his or her difficulties. In his Jain story, Merutuṅga adopts all the conventional motifs from the Śaiva literature, but the salvation Śiva Somanātha offers Kumārapāla is assuredly not one a Śaiva audience would expect. Referring to the Jain teacher Hemacandra, Śiva says, "King, this great sage is an incarnation of all the gods. Because he sees the highest *brahman* directly, he has understood the past, present, and future as if he held them like pearls in the palm of his hand. There is no doubt about the path to liberation that he teaches" (85). Kumārapāla finally has all his doubts removed, and there in the privacy of the Somanātha sanctum he takes the vow of the Jain lay convert to abstain from eating meat and drinking wine until the end of his life.

British Interventions: The Gates Episode

As the British began to gain a political presence in western India during the late eighteenth century, Somanātha temple stood unused and dilapidated. The twelfth-century temple of Kumārapāla had been desecrated one time more than it had been reconsecrated. A Persianate dome had been erected atop the sanctum, probably in the fifteenth century, and the Śaiva temple had been temporarily turned into a makeshift mosque. (Doming of former temples turned into mosques was not an uncommon architectural alteration of the period. One of the best-known examples is the Jñāna Vāpī mosque of Aurangzeb, formerly the temple of Śiva Viśveśvara, in Benares; see Figure 33.) In the late eighteenth century Ahalyā Bāī Holkar, queen of Indore, apparently inquired about restoring Somanātha. The local brahmins advised her that the old temple was ruined beyond re-vivification, so the pious queen instead built a new and much smaller shrine nearby, where Somanātha's new liṅga was cautiously placed in a secret underground vault (Figure 34).[10] Theologically, Ahalyā Bāī's advisers were correct: Śiva can manifest himself anywhere. There is no metaphysical reason he would prefer an ostentatious royal temple over a subterranean retreat.[11] More than this, Ahalyā Bāī's construction of a substitute Somanātha, with its royal acceptance of the demise of Kumārapāla's old structure, represented an effort to put an end to the long conflict over the site.

Ahalyā Bāī's strategic evacuation appears to have achieved its aim for a long time. For many decades, as far as we can tell, both Hindus and Muslims abandoned Somanātha temple as a site for worship or for confrontation. The temple was still useful for other purposes, though. One British visitor observed in 1838, "as proof of the wonderful solidity of this structure," that the temple roof had recently been used for artillery in defending the nearby port from pirates (Postens 1838: 868). But Ahalyā Bāī could not have anticipated the modern methods of historical reconstruction with which British and Indian observers of the succeeding two centuries would revivify Somanātha once again.

It was through Persian texts that the British became aware that Somanātha had a significant past. In 1770 Alexander Dow translated Firishta's chronicle, *Gulshan-i Ibrāhīmī*, with its dramatic account of Maḥmūd striking the belly of Somanātha with his mace to release a jackpot of gold and jewels hidden inside, and this served as primary source for widely read historians such as Edward Gibbon (1783) and James Mill (1826). Mill's *History of British India* was the first European account to divide Indian history into three chronological periods arranged in ascending order of civilization: Hindu, Muslim, and British. In Mill's scheme, as in Firishta's chronicle, the career of Maḥmūd

FIG. 33. Śiva Viśvanātha Temple with Dome, Varanasi. Original engraving printed in James Prinsep, *Benares* (1831). Photograph courtesy of American Institute of Indian Studies, Center for Art and Archaeology, Varanasi.

Fig. 34. Ahalyā Bāī's New Somanātha Temple. Constructed 1783–1788 under the patronage of Ahalyā Bāī Holkar, queen of Indore. Recent renovation (1995) reveals the two levels of the temple, with the most important Śiva liṅga inside the lower chamber.

FIG. 35. "Mosque and the Tomb of the Emperor Sooltaun Mahmood of Ghuznee." The "gates of Somanātha" form the entrance to the tomb. Lithograph by R. Carrick, originally published in James Rattray, *The Costumes of the Various Tribes . . . of Afghaunistaun* (1848). Photographic reproduction by permission of Yale Center for British Art, Paul Mellon Collection, New Haven.

and his confrontation at Somanātha was framed as an exemplary moment in the transition from one political and cultural order to another. By the early nineteenth century, other British travelers and administrators had been collecting other accounts of Maḥmūd at Somanātha (Prinsep 1838b, Tod 1839).

Somewhere along the line, the British also gained the idea that Maḥmūd had looted some ancient sandalwood gates from Somanātha and transported them back to Ghazna. I have not been able to trace the origin of this notion, but by the 1830s it was accepted as fact by virtually all British observers and some Indian sovereigns as well. Itinerant European travelers and spies visiting the ruins of Ghazna identified the old ornamental gateway still standing at Maḥmūd's tomb as the "Gates of Somanātha" (Masson 1842: 2.219–20; Vigne 1840: 128; Figure 35). The British notion that the destruction of Somanātha was a marker of the historical transition from Hindu to Muslim civilization in India, and their belief that an important physical object taken from India by Maḥmūd was still intact in Ghazna formed the basis for the first British attempt to enter into the symbology of Somanātha and use it to their own purposes.

Let us begin with the event itself, in which the British governor-general sought to reappropriate the gates on behalf of India, and then consider why this action proved to be so problematic.

Ellenborough's Plan

After British forces suffered a humiliating defeat in their invasion of Afghanistan, the Conservative prime minister, Robert Peel, sent Edward Law, earl of Ellenborough, in 1841 as the new governor-general of India, with a charge to repair the damage caused by the ill-conceived adventure. Ellenborough had opposed the campaign initially, and he now decided against continuing any effort to annex Afghanistan as a buffer against the supposed threat of Russian expansionism. As he saw it, the main problem was to withdraw British troops from Afghanistan back to the earlier borders of British India without giving the appearance of weakness or defeat. He needed, in brief, to make retreat look like victory. Here is where the memory of Somanātha could prove useful.

Ellenborough issued orders for his commanding general, William Nott, to retreat by way of Ghazna, and there to appropriate the Gates of Somanātha and Maḥmūd's mace. Formerly they had been taken as trophies from India by Maḥmūd, he asserted, and now they would be returned to India as trophies of a successful campaign. A great victory celebration would be held when the army crossed the Sutlej River into Firozpur, with triumphal arches, a "street" formed by 250 caparisoned elephants, gun salutes, military parades, and medals for the returning soldiers (Kaye 1851: 2.664–65). The gates would then be passed from hand to hand among local north Indian rulers, until they finally reached Somanātha. Through this dramatic ceremony and restoration, Ellenborough would rearticulate the boundaries of "British India" and demonstrate British concern for the well-being of its Indian subjects within those borders.

General Nott's troops were not able to find the apocryphal mace, even though General Keane had reported seeing it a few years earlier hanging over Maḥmūd's grave. They did remove the ancient gates from Maḥmūd's tomb, taking all possible precautions not to desecrate the shrine any further than was necessary, and carefully transported them back toward India.[12]

Meanwhile, in November 1842, Ellenborough issued his "Proclamation of the Gates," translated into both Persian and Hindi, and addressed to "all the

Princes and Chiefs, and People of India."[13] Declaring the gates a "glorious trophy of successful war," Ellenborough asserted that by returning them the "insult of 800 years is at last avenged." Ellenborough's introduction of the idea that Indians would harbor a grievance continuously over eight centuries was consonant with developing British ideas about Indian society as unchanging and timeless. Moreover, he situated the British as the unbiased observer to Indian religious disputes, able to maintain justice and restore the ancient order of things even after eight hundred years. However, in the public rhetoric of the proclamation, Ellenborough did not figure the gates within the frame of conflicts between Hindus and Muslims, who together composed the Indian people over whom the British ruled. Rather, he portrayed the looted gates as a matter of foreign invasion, and wished his deed to be seen as an act of love and identification with the "people of India." "You see how worthy it [the British government] proves itself of your love," he proclaimed, "when, regarding your honour as its own, it exerts the power of its arms to restore to you the gates of the temple of Somnauth, so long the memorial of your subjugation to the Afghans." Ellenborough read nineteenth-century nationhood—India, Afghanistan—back into the actions of the eleventh century, and projected Somanātha's restoration in the nineteenth century as a matter of concern to the entire Indian people. Ellenborough spoke not just to the people of India, but also for them, in his desire to demonstrate British interest in what he imagined to be the "feelings of the people."

However, several problems soon emerged in Ellenborough's grand symbolic gesture. The guards at Maḥmūd's tomb wept over their loss, asking, "Of what value can these old timbers be to you; while to us they are as the breath of our nostrils?"[14] But for other Afghanis the loss of the gates failed to create much of an impression. More disappointing still, the restoration of the gates did not seem to have any great effect upon its intended Indian audience. Evidently Ellenborough was making a symbolic statement in an outdated vocabulary, and no one in Afghanistan or India seemed greatly to care. With the advent of British overlordship, Somanātha was perhaps no longer remembered as an appropriate marker of regional political authority, let alone national honor.

The restoration did have an unintended and intense effect upon English observers, however. Some worried that Ellenborough's restoration scheme would turn the Muslim population of India against British rule. Others ridiculed the pompous style of the proclamation and observed that it was rhetoric worthy of an "Oriental Despot." Whigs were angered by Ellenborough's public criticism of their Afghan policies. Most important, Ellenborough alienated an important sector in his own party. Conservative Evangelicals were outraged because Ellenborough was participating in what they considered "idolatry."

Idolatry and Its Others

Ellenborough should have known better. Throughout the early nineteenth century, the issue of involvement by East India Company officials in the affairs of Hindu temples was debated repeatedly in Parliament, and as head of the Board of Control Ellenborough had participated in many of those debates. He remained confident that experienced "India hands" would understand and support his symbolic gesture (and some did), but since he was a political appointee of the Company's Court of Directors, overseen by Parliament, the India hands were not his only or most important constituency. As it turns out, the episode of the Somanātha gates serves as a good marker, the last British attempt to gain legitimacy within existing Indian systems of authority by interacting with Hindu deities in their temples.

In the late eighteenth and early nineteenth centuries, as the East India Company had taken control over major portions of the Indian subcontinent, British officials were aware of the important role certain Hindu images and temples played in the indigenous culture and the construction of political authority. Accordingly, colonial officers actively placed themselves within the ambit of Hindu temples. They collected and redistributed temple revenues, arbitrated disputes over ritual prerogatives, administered religious endowments, renovated decrepit structures, gave presents to the deity, and participated publicly in major temple festivals. In short, they vigorously adopted the traditional role of Indian sovereigns (Figure 36).

When invading new territories, the British were generally careful to show proper respect to the most important deities of the area, even to the point of securing divine complicity before undertaking military operations. When Lt. Col. Campbell prepared to invade Orissa in 1803, Governor-General Wellesley sent a dispatch outlining etiquette for Jagannātha of Puri. "On your arrival at Juggernaut," ordered the governor-general, "you will employ every possible precaution to preserve the respect due to the Pagoda, and to the religious prejudices of the Brahmins and Pilgrims. You will furnish the Brahmins with such guards as shall afford perfect security to their persons, Rites and Ceremonies, and to the sanctity of the Religious Edifices, and you will strictly enjoin those under your Command to observe your orders on this important subject with the utmost degree of accuracy and vigilance."[15] Just before the British troops reached Puri, the temple priests informed them that Jagannātha himself had responded positively to this British solicitousness. As one military officer reported back, "The Brahmins at the holy temple had consulted and applied to Juggernaut to inform them what power was now to have his temple under its protection, and that he had given a decided answer that the English government was in future to be his guardian."[16] With Jagannātha's sanction British forces entered Puri without resistance.

FIG. 36. "The Idol Juggernaut on his Car during the Ruth Jattra in 1822." The British attendants at the festival are not identified. Anonymous Company School watercolor, presented to Col. Ramsey Phipps, 1820–1822. Now in collection of the Victoria and Albert Museum. Printed by courtesy of the Board of Trustees of the Victoria and Albert Museum, London.

In southern India, Company officials anticipated that their support and renewal of significant temples and festivals would contrast their sovereignty favorably with that of previous native rulers, and particularly with the period of devastating Anglo-Mysore wars during the reigns of Haidar ʿAlī and Tipū Sultān. When Lionel Place became collector of the jagīr (modern Chingleput District in Tamilnad) in 1794, he worked diligently to restore the Viṣṇu Varadarāja temple of Kanchipuram. Military troops had repeatedly occupied the temple during the wars, and Place rebuilt the structures that soldiers had torn down (Irschick 1994: 79–85). Place even presented the deity with a jeweled head ornament. At Sri Rangam the new collector, John Wallace, carried out much the same project of temple restoration and reform of administration. After Tipū's final defeat at Sri Rangapattana in 1799, British officials placed the current heir of the Wodeyar dynasty previously overthrown by Haidar ʿAlī back on the throne. They moved the court back to Mysore, to be near the dynastic temple of Cāmuṇḍā, a form of the goddess Durgā. They made extensive land grants to Hindu and Jain institutions in the area, and reinstituted the Duhsehra (Daśaharā) festival (C. A. Bayly 1988: 113).

British officials thus placed themselves in direct relationship with living Hindu temple deities. This was altogether different from the collecting of (mostly) disused temple sculptures carried off by men like James Forbes and Charles Stuart, and to British observers of the time it was more deeply problematic. Company officials believed that, as modern rational Christians, they could interact with Hindu images in a purely instrumental manner, without accepting any of the native "prejudices" that informed the operations of the Hindu temple. They argued in terms their directors in London would readily understand—profits. Active temples were lucrative. However, when officers at the East India Company sponsored temple reconstruction, engaged in ritual exchanges with Hindu temples, and presided over Hindu festivals, were they not implicitly accepting the premises of temple Hinduism? In a practical sense, they were placing themselves in the role of royal devotee to a Hindu god. It was this apparent complicity with the Hindu dispensation that opened Company officials to attack on their Christian flank, as participants in "idolatry."

"Idolatry" is not principally a positive religious practice, but a category of discourse. Etymologically it derives from the Greek term for "adoration of images," but the term has historically been used in a polemical and pejorative manner as a way of classifying and censuring the presumed beliefs and practices of others. Adherents of other religious communities may worship physical objects or fabricated icons in the belief that they are in some way divine, but the charge of "idolatry" firmly asserts that these are false gods, nothing but vanity, deceptions. The discourse of idolatry involves a profound denial of livelihood to the images of others. At the same time, it dialectically affirms a community of faith that is distinct from and superior to those it classifies as idolaters.

The discourse of idolatry has its historical origins in the polytheistic setting of the ancient Near East, and in the successful efforts of the leaders and prophets of the Hebrew tribes to create a unified religious community by renouncing all tangible representations of the divine. The Hebrew prophets denounced the religious icons of other surrounding cults as "insubstantial puffs of wind," as "corpses," as "dunghills," and claimed that their own God forbade them to make images supposed to represent or embody Him.[17] Later the early Christians, and subsequently the founders of Islam adopted similar critiques of the religious practices of their neighbors, and likewise repudiated attempts to give physical form to their God. In each case the discourse of idolatry proved useful as a polemical strategy within a pluralistic religious setting where the worship of images was common or predominant. Founding fathers of the new religions used the charge of idolatry to create a community of response toward the cultic practices of surrounding cultures, and so to help engender a new and distinct religious formation. Crucial as it was at the moment of foundation, however, the discourse of idolatry was not a continuous feature in any of the three historical religions, least of all within Christianity. Although it is beyond the scope of this chapter to retrace the history of idolatry as a Christian polemical tactic, it is important to view the discourse of idolatry as an ideological resource within the tradition, which may be adapted strategically within specific situations.

The anthropologist A. M. Hocart long ago argued that charges of idolatry, and the acts of iconoclasm that often accompany them, are regularly linked with programs of religious and political centralization (1970: 246–48). In ancient Palestine, he observed, local icons meant power dispersed, whereas a central cult in Jerusalem meant power concentrated at headquarters. So too in the colonial situation the discourse of idolatry appears as part of the consolidation of colonial control.[18]

In the early nineteenth century, Christian missionaries working in India and their Evangelical supporters in England began to level the charge of idolatry not only against the vast population of Hindu image worshipers they wished to convert, but also against any British colonial official associated with Hindu temples. Missionaries argued that Christian Englishmen could not have any intercourse with Hindu idols without polluting themselves. British collectors became, in missionary pamphlets, "dry nurses to Vishnu" and "Churchwardens of Juggernout" (Mudaliar 1974: 17). (Considered by the British to be the preeminent temple of India, Jagannātha became, in Ronald Inden's apt phrase [1987: 3], the "anti-hero of Hinduism" in nineteenth-century missionary writings.) Missionary tracts accused British officials of promoting pagan practices. As the missionary Alexander Duff facetiously wrote of Lionel Place, "Probably no one bearing the honoured name of 'Christian,' has left behind him so distinguished a reputation for his services in the cause of idolatry as Mr. Place."[19]

Evangelicals in London mounted pressure on the East India Company to alter its policies toward temples, and through the 1830s they initiated a series of proposals and consultations aimed at severing all Company connection with Hindu religious institutions. In his treatise on *The State in Its Relation with the Church*, William Gladstone argued against any involvement in or even acceptance of Hindu religion by British officials serving in India, and his book became a rallying point for the Evangelical critique of colonial policy (Imlah 1939: 208). Finally in 1841, the Court of Directors issued orders for Company officers to withdraw from all "interference" in native religious establishments.

Abandonment had its consequences. To south Indian Hindus, the new policy of disengagement appeared as an abdication of responsibility by a sovereign authority. Riots broke out in south Indian towns, and community leaders collected mass petitions denouncing the colonial government's abandonment of royal duty (C. A. Bayly 1988: 114). For British colonial society, withdrawal from temple activities was another step in its self-transformation into a ruling caste, remote and isolated but secure in its conviction of racial superiority. Yet it also left them without clear means of articulating and symbolizing their authority to rule India. Bernard Cohn (1983: 173) speaks of "an incompleteness and contradiction in the cultural-symbolic constitution of India" under British colonial rule in the first half of the nineteenth century, and this abdication of any divine warrant they might receive from Hindu temple images only exacerbated the incompleteness.[20]

Ellenborough's grand plan to restore the Gates of Somanātha in 1842, then, came too late. British audiences perceived it as yet another misguided attempt to involve England in the idolatrous practices of temple Hinduism. Whigs and Evangelicals moved to censure Ellenborough's actions in March 1843 (Figure 37). This gave Thomas Macaulay an opportunity to make one of his most pungent speeches on Indian affairs in the House of Commons. With characteristic rhetorical flourish, Macaulay accused Ellenborough of insulting his own national religion "in order to pay honour to an idol." "The great majority of the population of India consists of idolators, blindly attached to doctrines and rites which, considered merely with reference to the temporal interests of mankind, are in the highest degree pernicious," he went on. "In no part of the world has a religion ever existed more unfavourable to the moral and intellectual health of our race" (1871: 632–33). After cataloging all the hideous, grotesque, and immoral features of Hindu religiosity that European scholarship had up to then unveiled, Macaulay pointed out that, since Somanātha temple was currently disused, a restoration of the gates would only make sense if Ellenborough intended to have the temple rebuilt and reconsecrated. Moreover, Macaulay reminded the Members of Parliament, that temple would feature as its central icon the liṅga, which the British understood to be a phallus. "Lingaism is not merely idolatry, but idolatry in its most pernicious form" (636). By this logic Ellenborough stood accused of phallic worship. The motion to censure was defeated, but not long after this the Court of Directors of the East India Company elected to recall their controversial governor-general.

In the end, the gates also turned out to be inauthentic. That is, they could not have been the ones Maḥmūd supposedly appropriated from India. The Somanātha gates were said to be sandalwood; these were deodar. The inscriptions were examined, and turned out to be strictly Islamic in origin. Likewise, the decorative style of the gates was most like that found in eleventh-century Egypt and Syria, not that of Hindu India. Accordingly, art historians now ascribe the workmanship of the gates to itinerant Fāṭimid craftsmen traveling east, rather than gates traveling west (Rogers 1973: 243–44).

FIG. 37. "The Modern Sampson Carrying Off the Gates of Somnauth." Caricature of Lord Ellenborough by John Doyle (HB), 1842. Printed by permission of the British Museum.

Even at the time the gates were appropriated from Ghazna, Major Henry Rawlinson (later to become a distinguished philologist and Assyriologist) examined the inscriptions and decided they had not come from medieval Gujarat, but he did not publicize his doubts. "As the Governor-General's orders were imperative, and the effect would be the same whether the gates were genuine or were only believed to be genuine, their removal was determined upon" (Rawlinson 1898: 132). Here Rawlinson was partially correct. For ceremonial restorations, actual authenticity is less important than putative authenticity. However, once it was revealed publicly that the gates had not come originally from Somanātha, the entire symbolic enterprise deflated. The gates were abandoned in Agra fort, where they took on a new significance linked to their more recent historical role. For many years they were shown to visitors as "Ellenborough's Folly."

Nationalist Reconstructions

Through Ellenborough's time, British historical memory of Somanātha centered primarily around a single event, Maḥmūd's raid of 1026. Shortly after this, though, British writers began to construct a more extensive longitudinal history of the site. The most significant step in this project was the vast work of Henry Elliot assisted by John Dowson, the seven-volume collection of Indo-Muslim translations entitled *History of India as Told by Its Own Historians*, which began to appear in 1849. Medieval Persian literary texts, including those of Amīr Khusraw and ʿIṣāmī, were sifted for "historical facts," and historians were able to postulate a whole series of medieval desecrations and reconsecrations, from Maḥmūd through Aurangzeb (Campbell 1896, Cousens 1931). In effect, Somanātha was no longer simply the site of a single famous invasion, but rather a place of ongoing struggle between two religious communities.

This new way of remembering Somanātha was consonant with the new predominance of communal conflict in British colonial narration of India's past. As Gyanendra Pandey has argued, "By the end of the nineteenth century, the dominant strand in colonialist historiography was representing religious bigotry and conflict between people of different religious persuasions as one of the more distinctive features of Indian society, past and present—a mark of the Indian section of the 'Oriental'" (1990: 23). For nineteenth-century British writers, this vision of medieval India rived and weakened by religious difference enabled them to contrast their own rule favorably with that of the Muslim sovereigns they had supplanted. Ironically, it also formed part of the historiographical legacy that Indian nationalist historians of the early twentieth century accepted from their British teachers. Distinguished Indian historians such as Jadunath Sarkar and M. S. Commissariat picked up and elaborated the narrative of Somanātha, and it continues to reappear today in such works as Desai's site guide, Munshi's souvenir volume, and BJP speeches.

Munshi's Historical Fiction

The next symbolic (and actual) reanimating of Somanātha came about largely through the efforts of one man, Kanaiyalal Maneklal Munshi. A Bhargava brahmin whose father was a member of the Indian Civil Service, Munshi trained to become a lawyer, as his family hoped. When he was fifteen Munshi attended the 1902 Congress session in Ahmedabad, where he was inspired by the oratory of Surendranath Banerjee, and soon after he involved himself in independence activities. He also began to write fiction, and his second work, *Patan-ni Patan* in 1916, gained him widespread recognition. By the early 1920s, Munshi was a leading lawyer at the Bombay Bar and also the leading novelist in the Gujarati language, a founder of Sahitya Samsad Literary Academy and editor of a literary journal, *Gujarat*. Throughout his life Munshi energetically juggled a successful legal practice, public service, political activities, and a prolific literary output. He served as cabinet minister and state governor, founded the important cultural organization Bharatiya Vidya Bhavan, and found time to write some fifty works of fiction, history, current affairs, and autobiography.

Munshi made his first visit to Somanātha in December 1922, at a time of personal crisis. Later he described the sight of Kumārapāla's ancient temple as one of the decisive moments in his life: "Desecrated, burnt and battered, it still stood firm—a monument to our humiliation and ingratitude. I can scarcely describe the burning shame which I felt on that morning as I walked the broken floor of the once-hallowed *sabhamantap* littered with broken pillars and scattered stones. Lizards slipped in and out of their holes at the sound of my unfamiliar steps, and—Oh! the shame of it—an inspector's horse, tied there, neighed at my approach with sacrilegious impertinence" (Dave et al. 1962: 4.89–90). Into this retrospective account, Munshi deftly weaves the humiliations of Muslim iconoclasm, the negligence of Hindus toward their own religious and cultural heritage (which nevertheless "still stands firm"), and the laconic mode in which the British liked to deprecate Indian sacred sites, using them for obviously profane purposes like armories, stables, and picnic grounds. From this visit Munshi took on the reconstruction of Somanātha as something of a personal mission.

Like other nationalist writers and historians of his generation, Munshi sought to give historical grounding to the independent nation state they were attempting to bring into being, and to counter the divisive and pejorative characterizations of the Indian past that the British had taught them and their fellow Indians. From early in his career, Munshi became convinced that Gujaratis were not adequately aware of the "greatness of their ancestors," and so he made the reconstruction of a Gujarati golden age an important part of his literary agenda. He located this primarily in the early medieval period, in the centuries prior to ʿAlā al-Dīn Khaljī's incorporation of Gujarat into the Delhi Sultanate. In his first three historical novels, *Patān-ni Prabhuta* ("the greatness of Patan," 1916), *Gujarāt-no Nāth* ("Lord of Gujarat," 1918–1919), and *Rājādhirāja* ("King of kings," 1922–1923), Munshi attempted to reanimate the period he considered the very pinnacle of regional glory, the early twelfth century, when the Solaṅki ruler Jayasimha Siddharāja, Kumārapāla's predecessor, brought all of what we now call Gujarat within a single consolidated dominion.

Munshi's novelistic remembrance of a golden age effectively cast the Delhi Sultanate as the disrupter of Gujarat's glory. He was not the only Indian writer of the period to do so. The preeminent nineteenth-century Bengali novelist and nationalist Bankim Chandra Chatterjee likewise pushed the period of colonial subjugation back before the onset of British rule, to the first Muslim invasions of Bengal. For Chatterjee, India had been a subject nation for seven centuries (Chatterjee 1986: 56). Similarly, nationalist historians of Munshi's time, in contesting the historiography of the colonial British, looked primarily to pre-Muslim India for the fundamental and positive ground for their depiction of a unitary India, as Gyan Prakash has argued.[21]

In 1937, while staying in a Kashmiri hill station, Munshi wrote his most famous historical romance, *Jaya Somanātha*, centered around Maḥmūd's raid of 1026.[22] Munshi opens the novel with an extended description of the great annual festival at Somanātha temple, held on the full moon of Kārttika month. Hundreds of brahmins chant, hundreds of dancers dance, hundreds of thousands of pilgrims arrive from all over India. Bhīma, the Solaṅki king of Gujarat, attends with his royal retinue. All assembled watch the maiden dance of Chaula, who expresses in ecstatic steps her sublime devotion (and by extension that of all present) to the Lord Śiva. Shortly thereafter news arrives of Maḥmūd's latest Indian campaign, evidently directed this time toward Gujarat and the temple at Somanātha. Munshi tells a story of intrigue and romance, negotiation and battle, which culminates with the heroic but unsuccessful defense of the temple by the Solaṅki armies and Maḥmūd's definitive breaking of the idol with his mace. King Bhīma, fortunately, has fallen unconscious from his wounds during the battle, and the temple priest places him in a boat, which enables him to escape the final Ghaznavid assault. After Maḥmūd's armies take their plunder and head back toward Afghanistan, Bhīma returns to reorganize life in Gujarat, and as quickly as possible he begins to rebuild the temple. Munshi closes the novel with another great festival at Somanātha. This time it is the ceremonial installation of a new Śiva liṅga. Kings and pilgrims again assemble, and Chaula again dances, so profound in her devotion that she falls dead at the close of her performance.

Like medieval epics of conquest and resistance, the romantic historical novel of the nineteenth and early twentieth centuries was a genre well suited to revivify the past in ways consonant with modern premises and purposes. The historical novels of European authors like Walter Scott contributed to the rise of nationalism in places such as Scotland, and the first modern Indian practitioner, Bankim Chandra Chatterjee, played an important role in articulating and nurturing feelings of Bengali national pride and self-assertion at the inception of the nationalist struggle against British colonial control. Munshi's father had given a set of Scott's novels to his twelve-year-old son, who became a devoted reader of historical romances; during his college years Munshi also imbibed Chatterjee's Indian historical novels through traveling performances and translations. As an adult, Munshi became the most important writer to adapt the genre to Gujarati.

In his novels as well as his other writings, Munshi portrays Somanātha not simply as a religious site and place of devotion sacred to Śiva, but also as a symbol closely identified with the integrity of Gujarat as a social and political unity. Yet he often shifts from region to nation. He accepts Ellenborough's rhetorical conceit that Maḥmūd's raid was not just the looting expedition of a medieval Turkish ruler, but a calamity that echoes within the Indian (not just the Gujarati) psyche down through time: "That is why for a thousand years Maḥmūd's destruction of the shrine has been burnt into the Collective Sub-conscious of the race as an unforgettable national disaster" (Munshi 1976: 89).

In the hands of an Indian nationalist author, however, the signification of this alleged continuing grievance was different from what it was for the British governor-general. Munshi remembered the tale of Somanātha as an analogy, with the British cast this time not as restorers of order but as its disrupters. In the nationalist homology, British imperialists were the modern Ghaznavids and the troops of freedom fighters, like the courageous Solaṅki defenders of Somanātha, were offering "national resistance to the invader." Yet the story suggested other readings as well, and Munshi's audience could just as easily identify the Ghaznavids with the present-day Muslim population of Gujarat, seen as their religious descendants. By centering his anti-imperial novel around the invasion of a Muslim regime, Munshi allowed it to cut both ways.

Evoking a mythic narrative structure of golden age, fall, and restoration, Munshi's novelistic treatment of *Jaya Somanātha* also suggested the proper denouement for modern-day Somanātha. Another reconstruction of the temple could symbolize successful resistance to British invaders and restoration of a preexisting order of society. Perhaps Munshi could find another Bhīma to fulfill his novelistic vision in the real world.

Rebuilding the Temple

The Bhīma he sought turned out to be Sardar Vallabhbhai Patel, and the setting in which Munshi saw his dream realized was more complex than this nationalist homology might suggest.[23] Somanātha was situated in the princely state of Junagadh, where a population 82 percent Hindu was ruled by a Muslim nawab. As the British retreated on the eve of independence, the nawab announced that Junagadh would join Pakistan. A revolt ensued, and the local Congress party set up a parallel government of "Free Junagadh." The nawab was forced to flee with his jewels, wives, and dogs to Pakistan. The situation became increasingly chaotic until Shah Nawaz Bhutto, the Muslim divan (and father and grandfather to future Pakistan rulers), invited the Indian Army to quell the disturbances. Munshi was with Sardar Patel when the latter received information about Bhutto's invitation. "When [Patel] finished the telephone conversation," Munshi related, "his face was beaming. He told me what the message was and smiled. My first thought, I expressed in these words: 'So it is JAYA SOMANĀTHA.' Sardar smiled" (Munshi 1976: 71). As minister of the states in charge of integrating former princely states into the new India, Patel quickly visited Junagadh in November 1947, and on Dīpāvali day he held a public meeting at Queen Ahalyā Bāī's temple, the substitute Somanātha, where he announced a plan to reconstruct the original Somanātha. Patel's declaration evoked great excitement—it was "just like Independence Day," recalled one observer—and some of the crowd that day engaged in a little spontaneous demolition of the old temple before officials put a stop to it (Figure 38). A group of Muslim fakirs who had taken up residence at the site were quickly chased out.[24]

Even with the powerful minister promoting the plan, it still met with opposition. First to argue against the reconstruction of Somanātha were the archeologists. The remains of Kumārapāla's twelfth-century temple would have to be torn down and removed before construction could begin, and even in its disused, mosquified state the old temple was still a significant historical and artistic monument. The archeological community therefore made a counterproposal that Somanātha be turned into a "protected archaeological site." This category was another legacy of the colonial British. As part of their interest in controlling and conserving the Indian past, British Orientalists and antiquarians had instituted an Archaeological Survey of India. One of the Survey's greatest promoters, George Nathaniel Curzon, British viceroy of India from 1899 to 1905, spoke of its purpose as a comprehensive project of knowledge: "It is . . . equally our duty to dig and discover, to classify, reproduce and describe, to copy and decipher, and to cherish and conserve."[25] One of the Survey's primary tasks was to identify and preserve neglected sites of historical or artistic merit, as veritable museums.

FIG. 38. Dīpāvali at Somanātha, 1947. After Sardar Patel's speech on 13 November 1947, the crowd begins to disassemble the old Somanātha temple. Photograph courtesy of Shantilal Nanjibhai Bhatt, Bhatt Art Studios, Junagadh.

Ancient Hindu temples that had fallen out of worship could find new life, even without living images and without worshipers, protected as archeological displays for tourists and students of India's past. This, argued the Survey, was the proper role for Kumārapāla's Somanātha to play in modern India.

Munshi held firm to his position that Somanātha was not merely an ancient monument. "It lived," he asserted, "in the sentiment of the whole nation and its reconstruction was a national pledge. Its preservation should not be a mere matter of historical curiosity" (Munshi 1976: 75). When he was accused of the "vandalism" of historical remains, he shifted the issue into one of past and future, death and life. Those who opposed the project, he said, were "more fond of dead stones than live values." As for himself, he added, "I am fond of history, but fonder still of creative values." Protected sites were dead legacies of the past. Munshi sought a living monument that would honor the past, by following as closely as possible the twelfth-century architectural plan, but would at the same time serve as the living center and symbol of cultural resurgence in the new India. In addition to the usual amenities for visiting pilgrims, he argued, Somanātha ought to include an All-India Sanskrit University, to maintain and promote traditional forms of

FIG. 39. The Somnath Trust Consults Plans for the New Somanātha. Members of the board and others present include Moraji Desai, Samaldas Gandhi, K. M. Munshi, and Brijmohan Birla. Bending over and hidden from view is Prabhashankar Sompura, the architect. Photograph courtesy of Shantilal Nanjibhai Bhatt, Bhatt Art Studios, Junagadh.

Hindu learning in a contemporary institutional format. Patel weighed in with his opinion that the "Hindu sentiment" was strongly in favor of a restoration of the Śiva liṅga, and that the Hindu public would not be satisfied with mere preservation of the dilapidated temple (Munshi 1976: 76).

The reconstructionists buried the archeologists. The Somnath Trust commissioned Prabhashankar Sompura, a prominent and erudite member of the Sompura community of traditional western India architects, to carry out the reconstruction (Figure 39).[26] The archeologists received one important concession, though. Munshi asked the Department of Archaeology to conduct excavations at the site over the course of two months, September and October 1950, just before the bulldozers moved in. B. K. Thapar's archeological report, providing physical evidence for the historicity of Maḥmūd's raid, appeared in Munshi's volume, *Somanātha, the Shrine Eternal*. The Archaeology Department set up the many pieces of sculpture they unearthed, together with many sculptures from Kumārapāla's deconstructed temple, in a new Prabhas-Patan Museum, some two hundred meters north of Somanātha.[27]

FIG. 40. Sardar Vallabhbhai Patel Statue at Somanātha. Erected 1970 by Sardar Patel Memorial Hall Committee. Patel faces the eastern Digvijaya Gate to Somanātha Temple.

Patel died in December 1950 and Munshi lost his most potent political patron. (Twenty years later the Sardar Patel Memorial Hall Committee would commemorate Patel's role in the reconstruction of Somanātha by erecting a large statue depicting him with arms crossed and an expression of firm resolve on his face, situated directly on the main temple axis to the east of the entryway; see Figure 40.) Shortly after this the Somanātha scheme met with renewed opposition. This time secularists suggested that the temple reconstruction was an exhibition of Hindu revivalism. Criticism came to a head over a plan of Digvijaya Singhji, the jam saheb (local ruler) of Nawanagar, who was both Rajpramukh of the Saurashtra government and chairman of the Somanātha Board of Trustees. As board chairman, the jam saheb took on the royal role of *yajamāna* (patron) in the rituals of establishment necessary for construction of the new temple. The jam saheb wrote letters to Indian diplomats serving as ambassadors of the new nation state around the world, asking that each send him soil, water, and twigs from the countries in which they were stationed, to be used in the installation ceremony of the new Śiva liṅga. He requested the ambassador in China, for example, to collect and contribute water from the Hoang Ho, Yangtse, and Pearl Rivers and twigs from the Tien Shan mountains. In this way, the jam saheb hoped, the installation might symbolize "the unity of the world and the brotherhood of man."

The jam saheb's intention to make this major installation ceremony as encompassing as possible was nothing new in Hindu ritual practice. In the early medieval royal consecration (*rājyābhiṣeka*) outlined in the *Viṣṇudharmottarapurāṇa*, for instance, the king-to-be was daubed with mud from all parts of the earth, bringing about his symbolic marriage with the earth, and later washed with the waters from every type of source, including rivers, tanks, wells, the four oceans, waterfalls, and springs (Inden 1978: 43–45, 50). As we saw in Chapter One, medieval establishment rituals for images likewise aimed at concentrating all categories of being, all powers, onto the divine icon. What was new was the post-World War II world order, with its worldwide networks of diplomatic missions, which enabled the jam saheb to envision a consecration ceremony more comprehensive and international than any ever before it. Śiva Somanātha could become the most universal of all India's icons.[28]

However, not all Indian diplomats were eager to participate by proxy in the consecration. The ambassador in China, K. M. Panikkar, wrote Prime Minister Jawaharlal Nehru to express his dismay and embarrassment. Nehru had his own reservations about the Somanātha restoration and he raised them in Cabinet meetings and in a series of letters to Munshi, the jam saheb, Panikkar, and others (Nehru 1994: 603–12). He worried that any appearance of government involvement in the construction of a huge Hindu temple would contradict the vision of India as a modern secular nation state that he was working to promote. And he feared that enlisting the Indian diplomatic corps in the ritual collecting of water and sprouts on behalf of a giant liṅga could be misunderstood abroad. It might reinforce old colonial-era stereotypes about Indian superstition. "I fear there is no realisation here," he chastised Munshi, "of how other people react to some of our ways of thinking and action."

More than this, the hoopla over the temple at Somanātha seemed to bring the gates back to life. A story broadcast on Radio Pakistan announced that independent tribes had decided to prevent the Afghanistan Government from returning to India the gates of Somanātha formerly carried off by Maḥmūd. Nehru had to complain to Liaquat Ali Khan, the prime minister of Pakistan, insisting that there was "not an atom of truth" in the story. In fact, he went on, nobody even knows if there are any such gates anywhere. Nevertheless, such "news" enabled the Pakistan press to suggest that India was not after all such a secular state.

Munshi replied to Nehru in a long letter dated 24 April 1951. He argued that the government had been centrally involved in the project from the

FIG. 41. The Jam Saheb Acting as Yajamāna. Digvijaya Singhji, the jam saheb of Nawanagar, presides at the ceremonial laying of the foundation for the new Somanātha. Photograph courtesy of Shantilal Nanjibhai Bhatt, Bhatt Art Studios, Junagadh.

beginning and should continue to be (1976: 180–86). He also claimed to speak for the "collective subconscious" of India in pushing the reconstruction: "You know well that my historical novels have brought the ancient history of Gujarat vividly before modern India, and my novel *Jaya Somanātha* has had a great appeal in the country. I can assure you that the "Collective Sub-conscious" of India today is happier with the scheme of reconstruction of Somanātha sponsored by the Government of India than with many other things that we have done and are doing" (184). For Munshi, the rebuilding of the temple was both a religious enterprise and also part of the project of

FIG. 42. Somanātha Today.

nation building. "This temple once restored to a place of importance in our life," he asserted, "will give to our people purer conception of religion and a more vivid consciousness of our strength, so vital in these days of freedom and its trials" (186). Nehru might not accept Munshi's religious aims, but he could certainly comprehend the need for national consciousness during freedom's trials.

The reinstallation of Somanātha took place in November 1951 (Figure 41). Rajendra Prasad, president of India, presided over the ceremony. Nehru had objected to this too, but Prasad observed that he would do the same for a mosque or church if invited. Munshi himself was not present. He was then Union minister for food and agriculture, and was in Burma negotiating the sale of rice. Yet he could still imagine the event, and write: "With the dawn of a new era, the new temple has risen like the phoenix, from its own ashes" (1976: 48; Figure 42).

The rebuilding of Somanātha in the immediate post-Independence period had a double valence. Munshi characteristically portrayed the endeavor as responding to a "national urge": "This national urge was reflected when Sardar, with uncanny insight, saw that we would never genuinely feel that freedom had come, nor develop faith in our future, unless Somanātha was

FIG. 43. Digvijaya Gate, Somanātha. Constructed to commemorate the Jam Saheb by his wife.

restored" (1976: 90). The "we" in Munshi's statement is left unspecified, so that his readers could view Somanātha as a symbol of India's new nationhood. It had required the extended efforts of a popular author and man of affairs to link the ancient temple site with the movement for national independence, but Munshi sought to characterize it in terms of an undifferentiated and natural national urge. More restrictively, however, the "we" could also signify the Hindu public of former Junagadh state. The rebuilding made for them a dramatic statement of the Hinduness of the area and a decisive visual reiteration of Junagadh's accession to India (Figure 43).

CONCLUSION: THE USES OF MEMORY

With Munshi's use of Somanātha both as a symbol of nationhood and an assertion of Hindu majority power in Gujarat, we come full circle to the rhetoric of Hindu nationalists of the 1990s. Hindu nationalist rhetoric, like Munshi's historical fiction, takes religious sites like Somanātha and the Ayodhya site they call "Rāma's birthplace" as constant and eternal foci of

Hindu devotion. Recalling instances of alleged Islamic destruction of these sacred shrines, Hindu nationalists evoke a schematized, Manichean historical vision of ancient harmony, foreign invasion and disruption, and brave indigenous resistance eventually overcoming the invaders to restore order. Like Munshi, they claim that the restoration of a long-abandoned temple site is essential to the integrity of Hindu society, and have mobilized toward this end. Evoking Munshi's successful project, the BJP has portrayed its mobilization to build a Rāma temple atop the site of the Babri Masjid as a "continuation of the spirit of Somanātha."[29]

This historical outline of the later history of Somanātha, however, tells a more complicated and varied story. There is no unitary "spirit of Somanātha." From the mid-tenth century when the Solaṅki ruler Mūlarāja defeated the chieftain of Junagadh, Somanātha has been a recurrent figure in the discourse of political rule in western India and, more recently, in India as a whole. But that does not mean its significance has been stable or uncontested. Over time many parties have laid claim to the pilgrimage site where the Moon regained his effulgence, to the icon of Śiva Somanātha, and to the memory of what has taken place there. Each party has had its own agenda. Like the Rajput prince Kānhaḍade situating the fragments of the Śiva liṅga around his own incipient kingdom, each has sought to appropriate some of the accumulated prestige of Somanātha for its own claims to authority.

If the Hindu nationalists' appropriation of Somanātha brings us full circle, the origin myth of the site—with its assumption of periodic fading and resurrection—should remind us that the completion of such cycles also act, according to long-standing Indian cosmological premises, as starting points for new ones. When I visited Somanātha in August 1995, security guards and metal detectors inside the Digvijaya Gate controlled entrance to the temple. The BJP use of Somanātha as the starting point for their Rath Yatra in 1990 had once again brought the temple into public consciousness. The destruction of the Babri Masjid in 1992, the reports of at least some compensatory attacks on Hindu temples in Islamic countries, and the VHP's continuing campaign to liberate other mosques erected on former Hindu temple sites had created a renewed sense of alarm. Now, with the BJP ruling Gujarat state, local authorities feared that Somanātha, with its high profile as a place of past communal struggle, might once again be made a target for Muslim iconoclasm. Though it is difficult to imagine a modern-day Maḥmūd attacking the temple, the apparatus of modern security stationed in the temple gateway made its own statement in visual rhetoric, of a threatened religious heritage and the need for still greater surveillance in order to defend it.

7.

Loss and Recovery of Ritual Self

"We are those whom Christmas overthrew
Some centuries after Pheidias knew
  How to shape us
  And bedrape us
And to set us in Athena's temple for men's view.

"O it is sad now we are sold—
We gods! for Borean people's gold,
  And brought to the gloom
  Of this gaunt room
Which sunlight shuns, and sweet Aurore but enters cold.

"For all these bells, would I were still
Radiant as on Athena's Hill."
  "And I, and I"
  The others sigh,
"Before this Christ was known, and we had men's good will."

(T. Hardy 1976: 927–28)

IN THOMAS HARDY'S "Christmas in the Elgin Room," we are privileged to overhear the after-hours conversation among the Greek gods removed from the Parthenon, otherwise known as the "Elgin Marbles," one Christmas eve in the British Museum. Hardy portrays these ancient works of the sculptor Phidius as being still alive, just as their original Greek audience might have understood them to be, but depressed. Through Hardy's triumphalist conceit, we hear them reflect on their own loss of power, and learn of their historical observation that it was Christ who was finally responsible for their now disempowered position.

In the 180-year debate over the repatriation of the Parthenon friezes, the animate character of the sculptures has never to my knowledge been used as an argument for their return (Hitchens 1987). No one supposes that these old Hellenic deities are still alive; they have been truly and irrevocably supplanted in their homeland by Christ, as Hardy's talking friezes recognize. However, another repatriation case, involving a twelfth-century south Indian bronze image of Śiva Naṭarāja, has recently raised the issue of continued life among expropriated icons (Figure 44). This image from Pathur, a small village in Tamilnad, was smuggled abroad in 1977, sold to a collector, confiscated from the British Museum as stolen property, tried in a British court, and finally returned to its homeland in 1991. What makes this case more striking (and the Hardy poem more relevant) is that the god Śiva himself appeared in court as a plaintiff, acting as a "juristic person" to sue for the return of his image. Śiva is much more alive in contemporary India than the old Greek gods are in modern-day Greece, and in the postcolonial world his domain of activity appears to have reached even into the old imperial capital.

In this chapter we follow the Pathur Naṭarāja on its journey from rural Tamilnad to London and back again.[1] Retracing its travels will provide an exemplary view of the system through which the art market in urban centers of the West acquires its raw materials from other parts of the world, and of the resistance some Indians offer to expropriation of their cultural heritage. The case of the Pathur Naṭarāja illustraes the potential conflict between collectors and worshipers of Indian icons, and the problematic legal issues concerning the return of stolen religious objects. Finally, the biography of this Naṭarāja enables us to consider the limits of a divine image's ritual life. To what extent can a dispossessed icon recover its divine livelihood?

Early Life of the Pathur Naṭarāja

Although there is little documentation pertaining directly to the early life of the Pathur Naṭarāja, it is not difficult to reconstruct. Pathur is a small village on the bank of the Vettar River in the Kaveri delta area, east of Thanjavur. A Śiva temple called Viśvanāthasvāmi was constructed in the latter part of the twelfth century, judging from the architectural style of its remains. Art historians believe that one Viśvanātha, a prominent local headman, sponsored its construction and incorporated his own name into that of the temple. There is no evidence of an earlier structure on the site. The Naṭarāja would have been made as part of a suite of bronze images, at the same time the temple itself was built. This was standard procedure for new temples in medieval south India. The temple, the central Śiva liṅga, and the bronze images would all have undergone parallel rituals of establishment (*pratiṣṭhā*), to constitute them as suitable supports for the presence of Śiva.

The Pathur Naṭarāja depicts Śiva in one of his most familiar aspects, that of the Lord of Dance. When Śiva dances it is no ordinary dance, as Śaiva literature makes abundantly clear. Śiva recurrently dances the material cosmos into being, he maintains it in its dynamic equilibrium through his dance,

FIG. 44. The Pathur Naṭarāja. Bronze image of Śiva Naṭarāja, fabricated in the twelfth century for the Viśvanāthasvāmi temple, Pathur, Tamilnad. The icon was buried, dug up in 1976, and now resides in the Icon Centre, Tiruvarur, Tamilnad. Photograph courtesy of Susan Borden.

and he periodically dances it back into destruction. For his medieval worshipers, Śiva was the animating instigator of all movement in a dynamic, ever-changing cosmos, and his dance was a central metaphor for comprehending the multiple ways he acted upon the world and all sentient beings within it.

In the tenth century, stone and bronze sculptors in Tamilnad developed a new way of depicting Śiva's cosmic dance, which iconographic texts would later label *Ānandatāṇḍava* (the "fierce dance of bliss") and *Bhujaṅgatrāsita* (Śiva "frightened by a snake"). Śiva's right leg firmly suppresses the demon Apasmāra ("ignorance"), who holds a small snake. His left leg is raised and thrown across his body. In his two rear hands he holds the drum of creation and the fire of destruction. One fore-hand offers a gesture of *abhayamudrā* ("fear not"), while the other points to his raised left foot of grace. Dancing within a circle of flames that represents the material cosmos, Śiva appears dynamic and forceful in his activity, yet his expression is one of elegant serenity, as if he remained ultimately aloof from all this furious motion.

By all indications, the powers that be of medieval south India found this a compelling iconographic form. From 970 C.E., the ruling Cola family began to feature Śiva Naṭarāja on the outer walls of the Śaiva temples they patronized, and portable bronze Naṭarāja images served as processional icons for virtually every Śaiva temple in Tamilnad. It appears that the Colas regarded Naṭarāja as their special family deity and they heavily patronized Cidambaram, a Śaiva temple particularly associated with Śiva's dance, as the central religious institution of their kingdom. Other subordinate rulers, headmen, and village assemblies within the Cola dominion followed the lead of the royal family, and so Naṭarāja became the most ubiquitous iconographic representation of Śiva in Tamilnad throughout the Cola period, from the late tenth through the thirteenth centuries. So Viśvanātha and the village elders of Pathur took a customary path in making the bronze Naṭarāja the largest and no doubt the most prominent portable icon in their new temple.

The early life of the Pathur Naṭarāja centered around the Viśvanāthasvāmi temple. After it was ritually established as part of the retinue of images in the Pathur temple, it played a role in the regular liturgical patterns of an active Śaiva temple. Much of the time it would have stood by, a secondary image representing one aspect of Śiva's active presence in the world, while the Śiva liṅga served as ritual center. During processions, however, it would have become the mobile icon of Śiva's complete presence in Pathur, acting as the physical means through which Śiva could extend his grace beyond the restricted sphere of the inner sanctum.

This liturgical pattern of the Pathur Naṭarāja, we must presume, followed a regular repetitive course until some major disruption changed its life. Temple officials removed the bronze image from the sanctum and ceremonially buried it outside. They dug a large pit in the temple courtyard, and on the bottom placed various ritual implements and a trident, Śiva's special weapon. The officials covered these over, probably with sand, and atop them placed eight bronze icons, lined up face down: images of Śiva Somāskanda, Caṇḍeśvara, Gaṇeśa, Śiva Bhairava, the two Nāyaṉār saints Appar and Sambandar, and two images of Pārvatī. When these were covered, they placed Naṭarāja face down on top, and then covered the entire cache with hay and filled in the pit. The images were obviously handled with care, and they may have been wrapped in cloth. As we have seen in Chapter Four, burial of temple images in times of threat was a common defensive strategy to protect consecrated objects from those who might steal them for their valuable raw materials or damage them as idols of another faith. Such burials were performed as ritual acts, following procedures laid out in priestly handbooks.

It is not certain just when the disruption took place in Pathur. One possibility, repeatedly suggested during the London court hearings, is that it occurred in the early fourteenth century, when the armies of the Delhi Sultanate led by Malik Khān carried their southern campaign into Tamilnad as far south as Madurai. Contemporary accounts of this campaign, we have seen, indicate that the desecration or destruction of at least some major Hindu temples and icons was part of the conquerors' agenda, and even a peripheral village like Pathur certainly could have feared invasion. However, the one surviving inscription from the Viśvanāthasvāmi temple in Pathur, recording a dispute over land between the local Śiva and Viṣṇu temples, dates to 1346, so it is doubtful that the temple images were already buried at that time. Other subsequent periods of military disruption in the Kaveri delta, such as the coastal raids of the Portuguese in the sixteenth century or the wars between the British and Mysore of the eighteenth century, might equally well have dictated the wisdom of temporarily hiding the images underground.

Whatever the instigating cause, the images remained buried for a long time. Something above ground happened that prevented their timely disinterment. Meanwhile the Viśvanāthasvāmi temple also went out of worship and fell into disrepair. By the 1970s the old temple was a ruin. Though still recognizable as a former temple, it was too decrepit to allow for worship or reconsecration. Nearby, the Pathur Naṭarāja and its fellow bronzes hibernated underground, forgotten, until a landless laborer named Ramamurti chanced upon them in 1976.[2]

Naṭarāja Enters the International Art Market

In 1976 Ramamurti was a thirty-eight-year-old "coolie" or landless laborer. He and his brother Pancanathan lived in a thatched hut they had built on what they considered unoccupied waste land. In August or early September of that year, Ramamurti began to build a cowshed. He dug a pit

FIG. 45. Ramamurti's Pit and Viśvanāthasvāmi Temple Ruins, Pathur. The pit where Ramamurti found the Pathur bronzes is in the foreground, the temple ruins in back. Photograph courtesy of Gary Schwindler.

to get soil for the walls of the shed. The pit was within the old brick walls of the temple, though the temple itself was in ruins and the brick walls so eroded they were barely visible (Figure 45). At a depth of a "man's height" his spade struck metal. Digging away the dirt, Ramamurti found nine metal images all lying face down. Nobody was around. He hastily reburied his find, until he could decide what course of action to take.

Ramamurti's Choice

Ramamurti faced a choice. It was an economic and moral decision, involving a calculation of possible returns and of potential punishment, of rights to property and of the identity of the objects he had uncovered. He had to make his choice with very limited knowledge. The repercussions of his choice, which Ramamurti could never have foreseen or imagined, would ultimately involve the legal systems of India and Great Britain, several million dollars in court costs, and bring great celebrity to one of the objects in the pit.

The Indian Treasure Trove Act, VI of 1878, outlines the proper legal procedure for one who finds buried treasure in India. According to this act,

> Whenever any treasure in amount or value ten rupees is found, the finder shall, as soon as practicable, give to the Collector notice in writing (a) of the nature and amount or approximate value of such treasure; (b) of the place in which it was found; (c) of the date of the finding; and either deposit the treasure in the nearest Government treasury, or give the Collector such security as the Collector thinks fit, to produce the treasure at such time and place as he may from time to time require. (Kennedy, pp. 111–12)

The owner of the property on which the treasure is found must also notify the collector. The district collector then holds an inquiry, to determine the facts of recovery and, insofar as possible, the circumstances under which the treasure was initially hidden. If he determines that the treasure has been hidden for more that a hundred years, he may declare the treasure "ownerless," and give it to the finder or divide it between the finder and the owner of the property. Conversely, a person who finds buried treasure and fails to report it becomes liable to prosecution for criminal misappropriation, and may be imprisoned for up to a year or fined or both.

The Treasure Trove Act conflates buried religious images with all other forms of buried wealth as property, which can be assigned an owner and a monetary value, and can be partitioned among more than one recipient. In practice, district collectors and other officials often choose to redefine buried images as "art," as cultural heritage that is the collective patrimony of the Indian people, and assign them to museums or other public institutions. This was the option exercised by the Thanjavur collector in the case of the Śiva Vṛṣabhavāhana and other Tiruvengadu bronzes, as discussed in Chapter One.

A different alternative, respecting the religious integrity and continuity of buried images as ritual objects, is exemplified in the case of Esalam, another village in Tamilnad. While some residents were renovating the local Śiva Rāmanāthasvāmi temple in August 1987, they discovered a buried hoard containing twenty-three bronze images, an inscription engraved on fifteen copper sheets fastened with a Cola royal seal, and assorted ritual paraphernalia. After reporting the find to the local officials, they placed all the objects inside the temple and made provisional preparations for their worship, clothing and garlanding them and offering camphor. Soon after, news of the find reached the attention of R. Nagaswamy, then director of the

FIG. 46. Esalam Bronzes Returned to Worship. Bronze images disinterred near Śiva Rāmanāthasvāmi temple, Esalam, Tamilnad, have been prepared for reintegration into temple worship. Photography courtesy of the Institut Français d'Indologie, Pondicherry.

Tamilnad State Department of Archaeology, who quickly set out for the site. "On seeing us," he reports, "the entire village over 2000 people—both men and women—thronged to the temple. I had the privilege of explaining to them a brief account of the copper plates, the history of the temple, etc. The entire village as one man was overwhelmed with joy and in one voice wanted to arrange for their worship" (Nagaswamy 1987: 7). Nagaswamy does not describe just what those arrangements for worship were, but clearly the residents of Esalam considered the long-buried images still suitable for worship (Figure 46).

All over India one encounters found images or fragments of old images that worshipers have reincorporated into the liturgies and devotional practices of their active temples and shrines. Sometimes there is a reasonable historical continuity of identity, as at Esalam, but just as often a recovered image is assigned a new identity in accord with the current dispensation of the community into which it is integrated. To take one among many examples, the broken images that turn up during construction projects in and around Varanasi these days are often reconsecrated as Bīr Babas, local "heroes" or semi-divine guardian figures especially associated with the cowherding Ahir caste. The physical appearance of a found image, Diane Coccari points out, may determine the name of the Bīr it represents: "Naṅgan Bīr ('naked hero') of Bhadaini has the body of a Jain Tīrthaṅkara, and the well-known Mur Kata Baba ('head-cut baba') on Durga Kund Road is a decapitated sculpture of, many think, the Buddha" (1989: 133). However, "the original identity of the piece is unknown and unimportant."[3] It is the new identity that is significant to the new worshipers. Only those of us who accept the historical fixity of original identity would say that the locals of Varanasi have "misidentified" the objects they are worshiping.

Not surprisingly there are times when the values of cultural heritage and ritual integrity come into conflict. This was the case of the Didarganj yakṣī in 1917, as we saw in the Introduction. There, British authorities had to persuade the locals of Didarganj, who had begun worshiping the river find as a goddess, to cede their icon to the Patna Museum.

Ramamurti did not know all the provisions of the Treasure Trove Act, nor had he ever heard of the Didarganj yakṣī. In later court testimony he did admit that he was aware at the time that he ought to inform the authorities of his find. He understood that the images were "ancient statues of deities," though he did not know their names. He was aware that the land he was digging on belonged to the old temple, even though it was in ruins. Of course, with the temple beyond repair there could be no restoration of the images, as at Esalam, and, as a landless laborer, Ramamurti probably did not feel the pious investment in the local religious establishment that higher caste villagers might have felt.

Ramamurti was aware, if only vaguely, of another option. Objects like the ones he had discovered were worth money, if the right buyer could be found. "I did not tell [the authorities]," he testified, "because I thought I could get good money if they are sold. I have been hearing that they fetch a lot of money" (Kennedy, p. 109). He also knew that he could not sell them in the open bazaars of nearby cities like Thanjavur or Trichi; the sale had to be clandestine. Of course he could never have known the full dimensions of the international art market, nor the value an object like the Naṭarāja might have to an art dealer or collector in London. As a supplier, he needed only to know that his objects could be transformed into cash.

Ramamurti made his decision. On 20 September or so he went with his family to Trichi, ninety miles from home, where he contacted his wife's uncle Dorai. Dorai agreed to locate a buyer who could give Ramamurti cash for the bronzes he had found. The Pathur Naṭarāja made its entry into the international art market.

Ramamurti would suffer for his choice. The police arrested him and, Ramamurti claims, beat him during his interrogation. He was later taken to a foreign country and required to answer questions in a legal ritual that must have frightened and mystified him. Nevertheless, Ramamurti persisted in distinguishing his actions from theft. "You cannot define it as stealing," he testified in London, "I was poor and I kept them. It was not stealing" (Kennedy, p. 109). Justice Kennedy concurred that Ramamurti's misappropriation differed in degree from the direct theft of images from an active temple, which would be a "much wickeder thing." The landless laborer seems to have taken recourse in the fatalism of the habitually oppressed. At the court hearings, Kennedy observed, "Ramamurti was quite expressionless, and displayed neither anxiety or concern: his demeanor was entirely in keeping with the fatalism displayed in his answers" (22).

The Art Market and Indian Images

With Ramamurti's choice to gain some cash through his find, the Pathur Naṭarāja entered a new stage of life, in which it would be treated as a commodity in the international art market. As we have seen, a taxonomic shift in the first half of the twentieth century transformed Indian religious images from "idols" into "art" for Western viewers, and they began to acquire desirability and exchange value as a corollary to this cultural revalorization. Before following the Naṭarāja's passage through this journey, it will be useful to sketch out a few aspects of the system it was entering.

Let us start with the cultural approach to commodities proposed by anthropologist Igor Kopytoff in his essay on "The Cultural Biography of Things" (1986), supplemented by the introductory comments of Arjun Appadurai (1986). "From a cultural perspective," Kopytoff begins, "the production of commodities is also a cultural and cognitive process: commodities must be not only produced materially as things, but also culturally marked as being a certain kind of thing. Out of the total range of things available in a society, only some of them are considered appropriate for marking as commodities." Commodity status is not an essential aspect of an object's being, Kopytoff observes. "The same thing may be treated as a commodity at one time and not another" (1986: 64). The Pathur Naṭarāja was not created as a commodity, but was turned into one through Ramamurti's choice. Following a distinction Appadurai (1986: 16) draws, the Naṭarāja was not a "commodity by destination," but a "commodity by diversion." It was created for another purpose and later diverted from that setting into commodity status. Nowadays in southern India many fine Naṭarāja bronzes, often closely replicating antique Cola style, are fabricated specifically for sale to tourists in the handicrafts emporia of Madras, Bangalore, and other cities; these are commodities by destination. Diversions of objects from other cultural settings into commodity status, Appadurai observes, are often symptomatic of moments of human crisis—warfare and plunder, theft, or (as in Ramamurti's case) economic hardship.

Just as things may enter commodity status, so too they can leave it, temporarily or permanently. Kopytoff calls it "terminal commoditization" where further exchange of an object is precluded by legal or cultural fiat. For a commoditized art object like the Pathur Naṭarāja, terminal commoditization might come about through purchase by a museum. When it becomes part of a museum's "permanent collection" the object is effectively taken out of circulation. Moreover, conventions of museum display and labeling tend to erase all signs of its previous status as a commodity. Often only the accession number in small print at the bottom of the label, alluding in numerical form to the event of acquisition, remains to remind the alert viewer that the object has not always been in the museum from its inception. The nonsalability of the museum object, says Kopytoff, imparts singularity and uniqueness, "a special aura of apartness from the mundane and the common" (1986: 69). However, the occasional museum practice of "deaccessioning," the museum world's euphemism for returning objects to the market, indicates that even terminal commoditization need not be altogether final.

For the Pathur Naṭarāja an alternative possibility of terminal commoditization opened up. As a stolen and illegally exported antiquity, the Naṭarāja could be repatriated and returned to its singular existence as a temple icon. Here too cultural and religious rules would effectively prohibit any recommoditization of the image, and it would partake of a "special aura of apartness" not only through nonsalability but also through sharing in a divine reality.

The small dramas of individual objects passing in and out of the "commodity situation" reflect their participation in larger cultural systems of meaning and practice. Appadurai usefully distinguishes between the "cultural biography" of a specific individuated thing and the "social history" of a class of things. One important chapter in the social history of Indian religious images is the Western revaluation of these objects as artistic, collectible, and valuable, and the corresponding incorporation of this class of things within the international art market. The international art market, and more specifically the trade in South Asian art and antiquities, has its own complex social organization, its own customs and forms of etiquette, its own institutions and arenas of exchange, even its own way of seeing.

In her book on *The Return of Cultural Treasures*, Jeanette Greenfield provides an overview of the modern trade in stolen art and antiquities. Accurate figures are difficult to come by, since much of this economic market is necessarily underground, but Greenfield shows that the trade is huge, active, and increasing. This trade affects countries with rich archeological treasures most profoundly, since they offer the most abundant sources for the materials of exchange. Further, since commodities in the art trade tend to move from poor to rich nations, the market exerts its greatest pressure on countries that are economically poor but rich in cultural products of the past, like India. They become primary suppliers of raw materials.

Because the trade is clandestine, statistics are necessarily imprecise, but a few estimates can give a sense of the scale of the market. During the *India v. Bumper* trial, K. K. Rajasekharan Nair, inspector general of police in Tamilnad, reported that between eight hundred and one thousand idol thefts had taken place in the state of Tamilnad alone over the previous ten years, and twenty or twenty-five of those cases had involved Naṭarājas (Kennedy, p. 18). Between 1977 and 1979 three thousand thefts of antiquities were reported in India, and only ten cases solved. UNESCO estimated that more than 50,000 art objects were smuggled out of India in a ten-year period (Greenfield 1989: 239–40). These figures presume the growth of a delivery system, an informal network of thieves, smugglers, compliant officials, dealers, auctioneers, and buyers who transfer the objects from their sources to their final destinations, and who transform them into commodities and works of art.

The development of a demand and a market for ancient Indian religious images has not gone unchallenged. In India and elsewhere, individuals and agencies have begun efforts to block or diminish the wholesale commoditization and expropriation of objects of religious and cultural value. Kopytoff and Appadurai would call this "commodity resistance." District collector Palaniappan's efforts to preserve detached images like the Cālukyan door guardian from expropriation by creating a local museum, discussed in Chapter Two, provides one example.

Since World War II, with the emergence of the postcolonial nations, the notion of "cultural property" has entered the lexicon of international diplomacy. The underlying assumption is that modern nation states exercise a claim upon the historical products of their geographical and cultural predecessors, and that they have some moral responsibility to maintain it on behalf of their citizens. The trade in illegal antiquities directly challenges national claims on cultural property since it threatens to appropriate all detachable, movable, salable objects for market exchange, leading them by an invisible hand toward the richer nations of the West. Many non-Western countries have accordingly restricted the export of culturally significant art and antiquities. India passed its "Antiquities and Art Treasures Act" in 1972. However, enforcing these provisions poses extraordinary difficulties. The antiquities are too widely dispersed, the profits to be made are too tempting, the national borders are too porous, and the preservation of cultural heritage does not have first claim on India's scarce enforcement resources.

The art market is transnational, however, and international organizations such as the International Criminal Police Organization (Interpol), the International Organization for the Protection of Works of Art, and the International Council of Museums also contribute in efforts to control the illegal traffic in smuggled antiquities. Most notably, UNESCO has over the past forty years issued a series of conventions and recommendations aimed at protecting cultural property.[4] A 1954 convention established international guidelines for preserving cultural property during armed conflict. Looting was no longer an acceptable practice. Most significant for the art trade was the 1970 "Convention on the means of prohibiting and preserving the illegal import, export and transfer of ownership of cultural property." However, UNESCO recommendations do not impose any legal obligations on the participating nations. They only indicate a preferred course of action. Implementation is left up to individual nations.

The wealthy nations that form the primary consumers of non-Western antiquities have taken various stances toward UNESCO conventions. The United States, Canada, and India have all accepted the 1970 convention, and have enacted legislation in accord with it. For Switzerland, by contrast, the trade in art treasures is a major source of income, estimated at $2 billion per year, and the Swiss government has placed no restrictions on the market. The British government was also in a difficult position due to its great wealth of cultural property acquired during the colonial period, and it took a voluntaristic approach. It asked the art trade to comply on its own with a code of practice by which illegally imported art objects would not be bought or handled. No doubt some scrupulous dealers did observe this code, but this approach left the major auction houses in London virtually unregulated (Greenfield 1989: 245–47).

Passage from Pathur to London

With Ramamurti's choice, the Pathur Naṭarāja was sent on a journey that would lead it from its village in Tamilnad to London. There is perhaps nothing especially remarkable about this image's particular voyage, except the specificity with which it can be recounted. Large numbers of antique art objects make similar trips from India to the West every year, but their itineraries remain concealed, since the art market supply network is largely clandestine. With the Pathur Naṭarāja, by contrast, the police investigation in Tamilnad and the subsequent trial in London made public the system of expropriation and the motley cast of characters by which the art market gains its materials of exchange, at least in this one case.

When Ramamurti decided to convert his trove into cash, he contacted his relative Dorai in Trichi. Dorai first came alone to Pathur to inspect the hoard, then a few days later came back in a taxi with two other persons, Papanasam Pillai and R. Meivel. Meivel was acting as an informal agent for his friend Chandran. Pillai and Meivel wanted to take the Naṭarāja image back with them to Trichi, but Ramamurti wisely held out for cash. Two days later the same group returned, this time with Chandran as well. Chandran gave Ramamurti Rs. 200, about $15 by 1976 exchange rates, for the Naṭarāja, and promised to give him more after the image was sold. Ramamurti never received any subsequent payment.

Chandran ostensibly worked in the film industry. Other witnesses at the trial however, who were no paragons of virtue themselves, described him as a "big rowdy" and a "man of bad character." Even his henchman and "very dearest friend," Meivel, admitted that Chandran "does plenty of offensive things" (T. 6: 15). He was charged with attempted murder in 1978 and convicted of rioting with a deadly weapon. In short, he was a small-scale hoodlum.

Chandran did not give testimony at the trial in London. His friend Meivel did. Meivel was twenty years old at the time of the initial sale. Justice Kennedy characterized him as a "happy-go-lucky rogue" and a "cheerfully unthinking" young man, but Meivel did not portray himself as so carefree. He did not have a father, and his mother did manual labor as a coolie. He had been without a job for two years when Chandran suggested he help out with the images deal, and Meivel saw it as a quick way to alleviate his poverty. "I just wanted to get things right in my life. I did not think about anything else," he recalled (T. 6: 16).

Chandran and Meivel put the Pathur Naṭarāja on the seat beside the taxi driver and returned to Trichi, where they kept it first at Chandran's home, then at Meivel's, and even reburied it when the object was attracting too much neighborhood curiosity. To see if the image was made of gold they broke off a piece from Naṭarāja's flame and a piece of the pedestal. If it had turned out to be gold, presumably they would have reduced the image to its raw material, but since it was not they decided to sell it as an antique. Pillai located a potential buyer named G. Magbool Hussain from Thanjavur. Hussain in turn brought in another buyer, R. M. Balraj Nadar from Madras.

Magbool Hussain was a beedi (tobacco) merchant in Thanjavur, with various other business enterprises. He made good money of around Rs. 6,000 per month. As a successful businessman, Hussain had also served as municipal councillor in Thanjavur up through 1976. He also dealt in antiquities as a sideline. Though he had never previously been convicted for this, he well understood that he was engaging in criminal activities. When they later arrested him, police found two other stolen images he had hidden in a steel trunk. Hussain also understood the need to compartmentalize his life. "This is a sort of dealing," he observed of the antiquities trade, "that what the right hand would not be known to the left" (T. 7: 7).

For Balraj Nadar, handicrafts and antiquities were his primary business, and he had been in the business more than ten years. He said he earned around Rs. 4,000 or 5,000 per month at it. He dealt primarily in wood carvings, mainly for local customers, but sometimes he also traded in metal sculpture, and sometimes he sold directly to foreign customers. The police had charged Balraj Nadar with illegal trafficking in stolen antiquities several times, but until then he had escaped conviction.

Magbool Hussain and Balraj Nadar arrived in Trichi and carefully inspected the Naṭarāja image. Chandran initially asked Rs. 300,000, but Hussain pointed out that the image was damaged and made a more realistic counteroffer of Rs. 10,000. Hussain and Balraj conferred outside as Hussain escorted Balraj to the bus stand, and Balraj agreed to give Hussain Rs. 20,000 if Hussain delivered the image to him in Madras. When Hussain returned, Chandran and Meivel agreed to the price of Rs. 10,000, since (as Meivel remembered) it was Dīpāvali season and they had expenses. They wrapped the image with hay and old paper, placed it in a crate, wrapped the crate with newspaper, bound it with nylon thread, and carted it off to the railroad station, where it was sent off to Madras labeled as household goods. Hussain, Meivel, and Papanasam Pillai all accompanied the package to Madras. As Justice Kennedy noted facetiously, the size of the Naṭarāja's retinue no doubt reflected the trust the smugglers had in each other. Hussain picked up the package of household items at the station and took it to a lorry shed, where Balraj Nadar met them. Balraj could not inspect the contents of the crate since there were other people working in the shed, but he paid Hussain Rs. 10,000 at the time and the remaining Rs. 10,000 six months later. Hussain in turn gave Meivel and Pillai a partial payment, and made a second payment to Chandran when Hussain returned to Trichi, but he never gave the full Rs. 10,000 they had agreed on.

Balraj Nadar immediately dispatched the crate by lorry to Bombay, under the name of Mr. Sami, the south Indian equivalent of John Doe. Ten days later he traveled by train to Bombay, picked up Mr. Sami's cargo, and took it to a dealer he knew, Valar Prakash. He initially asked for Rs. 50,000, but Prakash pointed to the damaged state of the image and would only give Rs. 30,000. Balraj agreed to the sale.

At this point the trail of the Pathur Naṭarāja goes cold. The police never located Valar Prakash. However, at some point between November 1976 and June 1977 the image made its way from Bombay to London. Despite its weight of over 150 pounds, it passed through customs unrecorded. No one can now say whether officials were negligent or paid off. The trail picks up again in London, where the Naṭarāja soon became the possession of Julian Sherrier. Before following it, though, we need to go back to Tamilnad to see what became of Ramamurti's other disinterred images.

Two weeks after Ramamurti had sold the Naṭarāja, another vanload of buyers from Trichi arrived in Pathur. This time it was Dorai, Papanasam Pillai, and Magbool Hussain. Hussain was evidently coming directly to the source in order to bypass Chandran as middleman. Ramamurti was eager to deal, since he too had Dīpāvali expenses, and so he sold six of the remaining statues to Hussain and his cohorts. He held back two, claiming that he had promised them to someone else. They gave him Rs. 600 on the spot and promised to buy him a piece of land in the village after they resold the images. Needless to say, Ramamurti never received any land. Hussain and his cohorts wrapped the images in bundles of beedi leaves and loaded them into the beedi van. To conceal the images as best they could, they removed the gasoline tank from the van and lodged four of the deities there. In place of the tank they used a metal can of gasoline and fed the fuel directly into the carburetor. The plan was to proceed directly to Bombay to sell the images there, but they soon discovered the van was not in shape to make the 750-mile trip. They garaged it in Pudukkottai. When Hussain returned a month later, the police were waiting for him.

It is not entirely clear just how the Tamilnad police learned of the Pathur images. One of Justice Kennedy's hypotheses seems most plausible: Meivel and Chandran may have tipped off the police after finding themselves cut out of the second deal. Meivel escorted the police to Pathur in December 1976 and showed them the pit where Ramamurti's two remaining images were still buried. The police arrested Ramamurti and extracted a lengthy statement from him. At this time, Ramamurti claimed, the village policeman Mardhumuttu beat him up. Eleven days later the police arrested Magbool Hussain in Pudukkottai and recovered the six images from the beedi van. Only the Naṭarāja remained at large. Hussain told the police that he had sold the image to Balraj Nadar, but it took them many months to track Balraj down. In 1977 Balraj petitioned the High Court in Madras to prevent arrest. He alleged that the police were harassing him, that he had no connection with Hussain in the Naṭarāja affair, and that he was a heart patient who would be gravely endangered by arrest. By the time Balraj Nadar did talk to the police it was too late to catch up with Valar Prakash, or to prevent the Naṭarāja from leaving the country.

Meanwhile in London, Julian Sherrier, an art dealer and part-time Indologist, had acquired a Cola-period Naṭarāja that he wanted to sell. He had an Oxford laboratory perform a metallurgical analysis of the bronze in July 1977, and he asked Mrs. Doreen Barkat Ram living in Lahore, Pakistan, to write a letter attesting to its sale. In her letter dated 9 October 1977, Mrs. Barkat Ram claimed that she had inherited the image as family property through her marriage with Seth Barkat Ram, scion of a very wealthy north Indian family, and had owned it for several decades prior to selling it to Sherrier. In the trial it quickly emerged that Mrs. Barkat Ram was Sherrier's mother. Two other members of the Barkat Ram family declared that the family had never possessed any south Indian religious images. Evidently Sherrier and his mother were constructing a new "history" for the object he was trying to sell. A recently smuggled antique bronze would of course be less appealing to the big-money buyers Sherrier hoped to attract, and so Sherrier gave it a safer provenance.

Sometime in the late 1970s Sherrier approached Michael Dollard, an art and antiquities consultant based in New York, and asked for assistance: did Dollard know anyone who would be interested in buying a Cola Naṭarāja? At the time Sherrier was asking an inordinate 1.5 million pounds for the bronze, and Dollard knew of no client who would spend such a sum. However, by 1982 Sherrier's financial situation had worsened. For a time Barclays Bank held the Naṭarāja as security on a loan Sherrier had taken there.

Sherrier was dropping his asking price for the image dramatically, and Dollard had become art adviser to a potential customer, Robert Borden, executive officer of the Bumper Development Corporation based in Calgary, Canada.

Robert Borden had begun purchasing Asian antiquities in 1973. Over the next decade he became a serious collector. He estimated that he had bought forty to fifty Hindu and Buddhist objects, most of which he lent out to various museums in Canada, primarily the Glenbow Museum in Calgary and the Edmonton Art Gallery. For Borden, collecting Asian art had a moral dimension. In his testimony he spoke of his "deep concern for the understanding of cultures" and his conviction that exhibiting works of art can aid this understanding by demonstrating the quality and depth of other civilizations past and present (T. 19: 57). Borden met Dollard in 1980 and was impressed with Dollard's judgment and integrity. He placed Dollard on retainer to advise upon and procure works of art for Borden and the Bumper Corporation.

In the spring of 1982 Dollard took Borden to Julian Sherrier's apartment to take a look at the Naṭarāja and several other Indian antiquities Sherrier was offering. A Barclays guard and a conservator from the British Museum were present as well. Borden inspected the Naṭarāja closely to make sure it was not a fake, but he did not bother to ask Sherrier where the image had come from. Borden was aware that Sherrier was in financial difficulties and believed that it would be an opportune time to negotiate a good deal. On 10 June 1982, Borden authorized Dollard to purchase the Naṭarāja for the Bumper Corporation. Dollard bought this and three other, less valuable works of art from Sherrier for 411,111 pounds.

The Transactional Network

All persons involved with the Pathur Naṭarāja's passage, from Ramamurti to Robert Borden, were linked within a single chain of transactions. All participated in a system by which Indian antiquities are dislodged from their native localities and made available to wealthy purchasers in the West. The system is grounded upon a disparity of wealth and driven by demand. Some persons and institutions, primarily in the West but also increasingly in urban India as well, wish to acquire South Asian objects they consider beautiful ancient artworks of another culture. This demand is not "natural," as we have seen in Chapter Five, but originates historically from the taxonomic shift in cultural systems of classification and valuation of the early twentieth century. In the late eighteenth and early nineteenth centuries, when James Forbes and Charles Stuart formed their collections of medieval Indian sculpture, there was no network of Indian suppliers. They expropriated directly at the source, and the objects they acquired had virtually no value to others in nineteenth-century England. Without the persuasive intellectual work of art historians such as Havell and Coomaraswamy and their successors, a Canadian oil executive like Borden would not be purchasing medieval Indian religious icons.

Based squarely on the profit motive, the network of suppliers has grown to meet the demand, as even Ramamurti understood.[5] For the chain of suppliers the image is regarded solely as a commodity, purchased only to be sold again, and the physical status of the object is directly related to its resale value. Greenish patina, as Magbool Hussain and Robert Borden both understood, indicates age and therefore enhances value. Only at the upper end of the chain, with Borden, Dollard, and perhaps Sherrier, does a more disinterested concern for the aesthetic properties of the work of art appear. For all participants good profits are indeed available. Hussain's quick 100 percent profit of Rs. 10,000 is not at all unusual, commented dealer Balraj Nadar, "because they are ancient articles." Because trafficking in ancient stolen articles is illegal, however, participants must balance the possibility of high profits against the high likelihood of loss and the danger of arrest in all such underground economic pursuits. At the lower end of the supply chain, in this case the sellers had difficulties in collecting the agreed-upon prices, and several of them were ultimately arrested and charged with unlawful activities.

The chain of supply here was not an organized one. There was no controlling agent, but rather an ad hoc string of mutually suspicious persons. Robert Borden could not call up a Tamilnad supplier and ask to be sent a Cola-period bronze Naṭarāja. Rather he employed an agent to be on the lookout for worthy Cola bronzes surfacing in London or other Western centers of the art trade. For this reason the trajectory of Indian antique objects is highly contingent, determined at each stage by the limited knowledge and acquaintanceship of the trader.

As a clandestine economic system, a key feature of this transactional chain was knowledge, or more often the lack of it. Prior to the trial, no participant in the Naṭarāja case had an overview of the entire network, and most of the participants stressed in their testimonies that they deliberately did not ask questions about the others. Sherrier consciously created false knowledge about the image's provenance, in the form of the spurious letter from his mother, but more often the suppliers practiced a kind of willed ignorance. Hussain's metaphor was that of one hand deliberately not knowing what the other did, as if not knowing too much would protect one.

Even Borden, a collector who portrayed himself at the trial as a man of upright moral conduct and social conscience, practiced willful ignorance. Justice Kennedy did not question Borden's good faith in purchasing the Naṭarāja. "In a case where few witnesses have escaped charges of dishonesty, inaccuracy and bias no such suggestion has been made against him," Kennedy concluded (p. 9). However, in order to preserve his good faith Borden also consciously disregarded all questions of provenance when purchasing the Naṭarāja. As he himself put it, "I have bought enough objects to know that one simply doesn't ask those questions" (T. 19: 61). Of course, if he had asked he would have received the false pedigree Sherrier had already concocted.

Once this purchase was concluded, the transformation in the identity of the Pathur Naṭarāja appeared complete. From its former life as a divine image of the god Śiva in a Tamil temple, the Naṭarāja had passed through a liminal stage as a commodity. Much as in the human rites of passage made famous by Arnold Van Gennep and Victor Turner, this bronze Śiva was repeatedly covered and concealed during its passage. It was kept in almost constant motion, and it was maintained largely apart from any public participation in a larger social world, whether temple, market, or museum. It was handled by a variety of unsavory characters. With Borden's purchase, though, the Pathur Naṭarāja left its commodity situation to rejoin the public sphere as an Indian art object in a Canadian museum.

Borden planned to lend the Naṭarāja to the National Gallery in Ottawa or some other Canadian institution, where it would do its part "to improve the quality of understanding between people from where I live and people in other places" (T. 19: 57). The bronze just needed a little cleaning up before it made its next journey. To this end Borden gave the image to Miss Enderley, a conservator at the British Museum who was acting in a private capacity. While the Naṭarāja was at the British Museum someone became suspicious that it was a stolen bronze and alerted the authorities. The Indian High Commission had by now received information concerning the Pathur Naṭarāja case, and they asked for assistance from the London Metropolitan Police. The police seized the Naṭarāja from the custody of Enderley at the British Museum on 25 August 1982. Once again the Pathur Naṭarāja was sent on a new course. It now entered the British legal system as a contested property.

The Pathur Naṭarāja in Court

When the police seized the Naṭarāja, the Bumper Corporation issued a writ for the image's return. Bumper claimed that it had purchased the object properly from Julian Sherrier and held valid title to it. The Government of India then interpleaded between the police and Bumper, claiming that the seized image was the one illegally sold by Ramamurti and smuggled from India to London. When the various claims and counterclaims were sorted out, the Indian Government became the plaintiff seeking the return of the Naṭarāja it held was stolen property, while the Bumper Corporation became the defendant seeking its renewed possession. Solicitors and barristers were engaged, and the case came to trial before Justice Ian Kennedy, Queen's Bench, on 17 November 1986.

The court case rested essentially on two key issues. The first, an "issue of fact" as Kennedy put it, involved the identity of the image. Was the "London Naṭarāja" sold by Sherrier to the Bumper Corporation the same as the "Pathur Naṭarāja" dug up by Ramamurti and purchased in turn by Chandran, Magbool Hussain, Balraj Nadar, and Valar Prakash? If the plaintiff could not establish this identity to the judge's satisfaction, its case collapsed. The second was an "issue of law." Who or what could legitimately sue for return of the Naṭarāja? Even if the Indian Government proved that the London Naṭarāja had come from Pathur, it also needed to establish that some plaintiff possessed a claim upon the image superior to that of Bumper's claim. The Government of India, as we will see, did not have such a claim, and it enlisted four other plaintiffs to assert their own claims. It was in this context that Śiva himself became involved in the proceedings, as a "juristic personality" suing for the return of his material embodiment.

The court case would decide more than just the next place of residence for the Naṭarāja image. The decision would also determine its future status and mode of livelihood. The choice lay between the two stations I contrasted in Chapter One, the museum and the temple. Robert Borden of the Bumper Corporation made clear that he would place the Naṭarāja on display as an art object in a Canadian museum. The Government of India, by contrast, repeated as a principle, "once a religious object, always a religious object." The plaintiffs intended to restore the Naṭarāja as a liturgical icon in its original home, the Viśvanāthasvāmi temple in Pathur, Tamilnad.

India and the Recovery of South Indian Images

The Indian Government made a decision to pursue the Pathur Naṭarāja aggressively. The court case would consume forty-four court days and involve legal costs far above the market value of the bronze in question, but the government never backed off. They turned down at least one proposal for an out-of-court settlement (Raghunathan and Parthasarthy 1991). Prime Minister Rajiv Gandhi took a personal interest in the case and let officials in Tamilnad state government know that the central government would bear all necessary costs in litigating the case and transporting the image back to India.

The government's primary aim, no doubt, was part of a larger effort to stem the illegal antiquities trade. The central government defines antiquities as part of the "cultural heritage" of the Indian people and assumes a moral and legal responsibility for protecting them. For the Indian government, winning a well-publicized legal battle over a religious image like the Pathur

Naṭarāja in a Western courtroom would send a cautionary message both to India's internal network of smugglers and also to those abroad who dealt in or purchased Indian art. Justice Kennedy recognized this larger agenda. "I am sure," he wrote, "that the real energy behind the present claim is that of the Government of the Union [of India] which . . . wants to stop, and if possible reverse, the outward flow of a precious part of the nation's cultural heritage" (Kennedy, p. 114).

This was not the first time the Indian government had pursued expropriated south Indian religious images in foreign lands. A similar case involved another Cola-period Śiva Naṭarāja image, purchased in 1979 by the Kimbell Art Museum in Fort Worth, Texas, from an art dealer in London. The bronze had been stolen from the Maṇavāḷeśvara temple in Tiruvilakkuti (Thanjavur District), Tamilnad in February 1978. Tamilnad police diligently investigated the case and eventually arrested one C. V. Raman as the head of a gang of antiquities thieves. He admitted that he had sent the bronze to the United Kingdom. The police passed the information on to Interpol and Scotland Yard, and they managed to locate an Indian dealer residing in Middlesex, who had over two hundred antiquities in his possession. To verify the identity of three bronzes stolen from Sembanarkoil, the temple priest Shri Muthiah Gurukkal was brought to London. "I could recognise the idols," the priest later claimed, "just as a mother could recognise her missing children when they are traced and brought back to her" (Rajasekharan Nair 1082: 8). The dealer, however, was unable to tell police the current whereabouts of the Tiruvilakkuti Naṭarāja, and the trail appeared to be lost until Tamilnad police inspector K. K. Rajasekharan Nair spotted it dancing in an advertisement for the Everest Art Gallery in the art periodical *Apollo*. Scotland Yard raided the home of the former proprietor of Everest, where they found forty-one other stolen Indian antiquities but not the Tiruvilakkuti image. With this new lead, the police were able to trace the image to Fort Worth. Somewhere along the line the Naṭarāja had been given a new biography, so when the Kimbell Museum bought the image it was accompanied by affidavits attesting that it had left India prior to 1947. The museum nevertheless decided to cooperate with the Indian government in resolving the matter out of court, and the Tiruvilakkuti Naṭarāja returned to India in 1984.[6]

The Indian government also chased the Sivapuram Naṭarāja, a spectacular tenth-century statue that many connoisseurs consider among the very finest Cola works of bronze sculpture. The *New York Times* dubbed this the "tale of the trouble-making idol," as if the image had brought its vicissitudes upon itself (Glueck 1974). The tale begins in 1951, when villagers uncovered the Naṭarāja in a treasure trove in Sivapuram (Thanjavur District), Tamilnad. The government claimed the image as its own property, but the locals objected. They did not want the image sent off to a museum, and the authorities finally turned the image over to the temple in Sivapuram where it was returned to worship. The image had become corroded from its long hibernation underground, however, and it was sent out to a bronzemaker for restoration. The artisan surreptitiously made a copy of the image, returned the shiny new copy to the temple, and sold the original to an art dealer in 1957. A series of sales eventually took it to New York, where the dealer Ben Heller sold it to the Norton Simon Foundation in 1973 for $1 million.[7] Meanwhile a British art historian, Douglas Barrett, researching Cola-period bronzes in Tamilnad, discovered that the Naṭarāja and two other bronze images in worship in Sivapuram were modern fakes. Police were able to trace the original Naṭarāja to Norton Simon. The Government of India claimed ownership of the image, but Simon resisted India's demands to return the disputed object. In December 1974 India brought a $2.5 million suit against Simon, his foundation, and the dealer who had sold it to him.

Simon admitted that the Naṭarāja had been smuggled out of India. "Hell yes, it was smuggled," he told a *Times* of London reporter, "I spent between $15 million and $16 million over the last year on Asian art, and most of it was smuggled" (Hopkirk 1973). Nevertheless, he argued that it had not been stolen. The temple authorities, he believed, had rightfully sold it to a dealer. Simon viewed the lawsuit as a form of intimidation, and when Ambassador Daniel Moynihan involved himself in an effort to negotiate a settlement, Simon accused him of trying to gain political favor in Tamilnad. "Things were going well until Mr. Moynihan intervened," he complained. "The Indians have problems in Madras, and Madras wants the Naṭarāja back. I know they have problems, but I say to Mr. Moynihan, don't push me around" (Glueck 1974). Finally the two disputants did come to an agreement before the suit came up for decision. The Sivapuram Naṭarāja was required to spend ten years in the United States, visiting various museums as an art object, before it could return to its home in Tamilnad.

Norton Simon presented himself as an aggrieved and combative art collector, but his brusque comment about "problems in Madras" points to a secondary motivation of the Indian government in pursuing the Sivapuram and Pathur Naṭarājas. As we have seen in cases like that of the Sikh throne, a seemingly unitary category like "cultural heritage" is in fact a complex historical product in the large, multiethnic, regionally diverse nation state of India. Constructing and defining cultural heritage is a complicated, often highly politicized process. Likewise the selective pursuit of expatriated items of cultural heritage involves political negotiations and calculations. The central government has committed considerable resources to the recovery of south Indian images and, as Simon suggests, this does reflect tensions within the relationship between Tamilnad and the Center. In the mid 1980s, when Rajiv Gandhi pledged the Center's full support in recovering the Pathur Naṭarāja, he was trying to maintain the fragile allegiance of the regional political party ruling Tamilnad, the ADMK led by M. G. Ramachandran and Jayalalitha, as part of his tenuous ruling coalition. The national government may pursue repatriation strategically for internal political purposes, to demonstrate to particular regions and communities that it is concerned with their specific interests.

Identification: The London and Pathur Naṭarājas

To consider the first key issue in *India v. Bumper*, we must examine more closely the assumption I have been making thus far in this chapter, that we are dealing with only one image, not two. It will be useful to adopt two names, as was done in the trial. Ramamurti dug up one Naṭarāja bronze, the "Pathur Naṭarāja," and it was sold in succession to Chandran, Magbool Hussain, Balraj Nadar, and Valar Prakash. This image disappeared in Bombay in December 1976, probably on route to the West. There was also a Naṭarāja bronze in the possession of Julian Sherrier in London, certainly by July 1977, which he sold to Robert Borden and the Bumper Corporation in 1982. The Metro Police seized this image and it appeared in court. We will call this the "London Naṭarāja."

The central question, then, was simply: are the Pathur Naṭarāja and the London Naṭarāja one and the same object? The Indian government had to prove that they were one. Bumper needed only to establish that the London Naṭarāja was not from Pathur. They did not need to prove that the London Naṭarāja had not been smuggled. Considering the scale of the antiquities trade it was not unlikely that more than one Cola-period Naṭarāja was circulating in London in the late 1970s.

The legal argument over identification was complex. As Kennedy outlined it in his decision, the argument involved the testimony of eyewitnesses (both Indian smugglers and London viewers), the art-historical analysis of style, and scientific evidence of several sorts. Both sides retained expert witnesses in the fields of metallurgy, entomology, and geomorphology, as well as art historians. In the annals of Indian art history there has perhaps never been so much concentrated attention, involving so many types of expertise, paid to identifying the provenance of a single sculptural work. For our purposes, it is necessary only to summarize these arguments briefly.

To make their case that the London Naṭarāja was the Pathur Naṭarāja, the plaintiffs presented the Indian history of the image. Four witnesses who had been directly involved in the Indian chain of transactions gave testimony—Ramamurti, Meivel, Magbool Hussain, and Balraj Nadar. They recounted the itinerary of the Pathur Naṭarāja, and also compared the image in court with the image they remembered handling. The barristers asked them in detail about their observations, particularly about any damage or missing features they may have noticed at the time.

All four witnesses identified the London Naṭarāja as the object they had smuggled. However, their testimony was not as compelling as it might have been, for several reasons. In light of the multiplicity of Cola Naṭarājas, the witnesses were asked to make a very precise comparison involving an object that they had seen eight years earlier, in conditions less than optimum for viewing. In 1976 they had mostly viewed the Pathur Naṭarāja, still covered in dirt, in the dim glare of a flashlight. None was especially trained in the discipline of examining art objects, though Hussain and Balraj Nadar did handle sculptures regularly. More subversive still to the Indian case were the characters of the witnesses. Three of the four appeared habitually and occupationally dishonest; only Ramamurti seemed a reliable witness, and he was terrified. Moreover, since all the witnesses had been arrested and still faced possible charges in connection with the case, they had a definite motivation to cooperate with the Indian authorities.[8] Justice Kennedy largely discounted the possibility that they had been coached, but concluded with only faint confidence that some of the witnesses' testimony was "capable of belief."

To counter the evidence of the Indian smugglers, the Bumper side could present an alternative history for the London Naṭarāja. Unfortunately for them, the fictitious pedigree for the image concocted by Julian Sherrier was quickly shattered. Even so, they could try to establish that the London Naṭarāja had already resided in London prior to September 1976 when Ramamurti dug up the Naṭarāja in Pathur. Bumper presented one witness, Allain Prescencer, who testified that he had seen the Naṭarāja in Sherrier's apartment in May 1976. While less suspect than the smugglers, Prescencer had been a good friend of Sherrier's and may have wished to help him out with his testimony. Justice Kennedy discounted Prescencer's evidence as having "an air of unreality." During the appeal in 1990 a second witness, the American art dealer Robert Ellsworth, also testified to seeing the London Naṭarāja in Sherrier's flat in early 1976, but this new evidence did not prove decisive.

Other persons who were supposed to have seen Sherrier's image did not testify. For example, Prescencer claimed that John Irwin, keeper of the Indian Art and Antiquities Department at the Victoria and Albert Museum, had inspected the London Naṭarāja with him that evening in May 1976, but during the trial Irwin turned out to be away lecturing in India. Because the Government of India was taking such a keen interest in the case, it may be that other potential witnesses for Bumper decided not to jeopardize their personal and institutional relations with Indian officialdom. Nevertheless, in Kennedy's judgment, the Bumper side failed to present an alternative narrative of how and when the London Naṭarāja arrived in London, and Prescencer's uncertain testimony was not sufficient to prove that the object had been in London before September 1976.

The Indian government's second line of argument involved an analysis of sculptural style and thus brought art historians into the courtroom as expert witnesses. By comparing the London Naṭarāja with the eight images recovered from Pathur (which had also traveled to London to appear in court), India set out to prove that together they formed part of a coherent suite of temple images, a group of bronzes presumably fabricated together at the same time the Viśvanāthasvāmi temple was built, and they therefore exhibited a stylistic similarity. Going a step further, the plaintiffs argued that one of the Pārvatī images from the Pathur trove had originally been the female companion of the Naṭarāja. They were reuniting a couple. The plaintiffs' expert was R. Nagaswamy, then the director of the Tamilnad Department of Archaeology.

The defendants made the counterargument that the Pathur images and the London Naṭarāja did not form a cohesive group at all. All the images in question were from the Cola period, they admitted, but their dates extended from the early eleventh through the early thirteenth centuries. This dissimilarity in style and date, the Bumper side argued, would undermine any attempt to join the London Naṭarāja with the Pathur images. Gary Schwindler, associate professor of art at Ohio University and author of an excellent Ph.D. dissertation on "The Dating of South Indian Metal Sculptures," was witness for the defense.

Faced with the testimonies of dueling art historians, Justice Kennedy was called upon to render art historical judgments, and more, to decide what constitutes the most effective method for dating south Indian bronzes. Schwindler's primary method involved a close visual comparison of bronze sculptures with stone sculpture intact on temples, where chronological information is much more abundant. Nagaswamy suggested a more comprehensive approach, using bronzes dated by inscription, bronzes dated by association with temples, comparisons between bronze and stone sculpture, and paleography to build an overall sense of stylistic sequence among Cola bronze images. Generally Kennedy found Nagaswamy's method more persuasive, but he also found it necessary to take into account the particular experience and interests of the experts. As state archaeology director, Nagaswamy had overseen the registration of some 25,000 metal images in Tamilnad. Though Nagaswamy undoubtedly had vast experience with bronzes, his "passionately held views" led Kennedy to be somewhat cautious. As the justice wrote of Nagaswamy, "he was clearly a devout Hindu, and I sensed that he was deeply offended at the thought that idols of his Gods should be the subject of commerce" (Kennedy, p. 37). In Kennedy's judgment, Schwindler lacked Nagaswamy's deep background, but also appeared more impartial. At the end of the art historical arguments, though, Kennedy decided that there was no compelling reason not to believe that the London Naṭarāja, the Pathur images, and the Viśvanāthasvāmi temple had been created at the same time.

Kennedy classified three types of scientific evidence as "subsidiary grounds of proof." First, both sides carried out metallurgical comparisons of the London Naṭarāja with the Pathur images and other Cola-period bronzes in court, and the metallurgy testimony consumed four and a half long days in court. This method presumes that the composition of the *pañcaloha* (five-metal) bronze mixture used in casting south Indian images may vary over time, and the plaintiffs hoped to show a similarity in composition between the London and Pathur images. It is a promising method of material analysis, but still very much in its infancy with regard to south Indian bronzes, and Kennedy decided that a lack of established chronological standards vitiated any valid conclusion. Metallurgy did not contribute to his conclusion.

Entomologists got into the act because the images had "termite runs" on them. Evidently a nest of termites had lived beneath the Pathur burial pit. Hay strewn above the images attracted foragers, and as the termites made their way past the buried images they left black marks, "as if a dark liquid had trickled over part of the surface and then dried." The fact that similar termite runs appeared on the London Naṭarāja and the Pathur images supported the Indian argument that they came from the same pit. It was not conclusive, though, since the methods of ceremonial burial in south India might often involve potential termite food—not only hay, but also cloth wrapping or wooden caskets. Many disinterred bronzes could have similar black markings; no one has ever made a survey of this.

Finally, geomorphologists were asked to compare particles of soil found on the images with the soil in and around Ramamurti's pit. Here the defense seemed to gain an advantage, for their expert witness, Rita Gardner, was able to demonstrate that the dirt on the London Naṭarāja differed distinctly from the soil surrounding the burial pit in Pathur. However, this finding was undermined by the likelihood that those who originally buried the temple images in Pathur did not use the natural soil of the pit when they covered the images, but instead introduced some foreign, free-running material like sand. In sum, none of the scientific methods of analysis proved conclusive to Kennedy's judgment.

Was the London Naṭarāja, then, the Pathur Naṭarāja that Ramamurti dug up? It is certainly possible to envision other scenarios. The London Naṭarāja, all agreed, was an illegal immigrant to the United Kingdom, but that is not sufficient to prove it came there from Pathur. No doubt there were more than one smuggled Naṭarāja circulating in London in the mid-1970s. It is possible that Sherrier did have the object prior to November 1976, the earliest the Pathur Naṭarāja could have reached London, and that those who did see it at Sherrier's apartment before then felt it would be disadvantageous to admit this publicly. If this were the case, what then happened to the Pathur Naṭarāja? Perhaps it did not make it out of Bombay. If it was exported it may still be hidden away by a dealer or collector, awaiting the informal statute of limitations by which most stolen art objects gain respectability through the passage of time.

Nevertheless, like Justice Kennedy, I find the argument and evidence of the Indian side more persuasive. Kennedy concluded: "I am entirely persuaded that the London Naṭarāja is the Pathur Naṭarāja" (63), and "I am satisfied that the [London] Naṭarāja has been proved to be that found and sold by Ramamoorthi in about September 1976, and so proved to a high degree of probability" (64).

Whether or not the London Naṭarāja in truth did come from Pathur, Kennedy's decision and its reaffirmation in subsequent appeal defines the object appearing in court as the Pathur Naṭarāja. That decision forms the basis for the next phase in the life of the image. But first we must see who had a valid claim upon the object in question.

Śiva's Juristic Personality

Even when the courts had established that the London Naṭarāja was identical with the one illegally taken from Pathur, a significant legal issue remained. The Indian side had to show that someone or something had a claim upon the Naṭarāja image superior to that of the Bumper Corporation, which had at least purchased the object from Sherrier in good faith. This proved to be unexpectedly difficult.

The Union of India was undoubtedly the effective agent in seeking return of the Naṭarāja. The Indian government, acting through the Indian High Commission, hired the lawyers and paid the bills. Yet the central government had no legal claim upon the object itself. Although there is Union legislation protecting the nation's artistic and cultural heritage in general, Kennedy pointed out, no provision enables the Union to assert ownership of any particular work of art or antiquity (64). India could act as a "technical plaintiff" and guarantor of court costs, but it could not legally claim the Naṭarāja on its own behalf.

The Indian side therefore put forward claims of other plaintiffs. Initially there were three additional plaintiffs: the state government of Tamilnad, R. Sadagopalan as executive officer of the Viśvanāthasvāmi temple, and the temple itself. The state could make a claim based on the provisions of the Treasure Trove Act of 1878, which allows government officials to take custody of ownerless treasures, and of the Hindu Religious and Charitable Endowments Act, which provides for state intervention to limit abuse of charitable endowments like temple properties. In Tamilnad, the plaintiffs argued, a Hindu temple is an institution that acts legally as a "juristic person."

Later in the case the Indian side introduced still another plaintiff, Śiva. The god Śiva, acting as a "juristic person," would claim ownership of the Śiva Naṭarāja image that had originally resided in the Viśvanāthasvāmi temple. Śiva's participation in the case gained publicity and engendered the best headline: "Sueing Shiva Dismays Dealers" (Beckett 1988). And rightly so, for when Hindu gods begin suing in British courts, this is newsworthy. Might not Śiva and his other divine cohorts from India begin seeking all sorts of objects that had once belonged to them? Anthony Gardner, an antiquities dealer with Spinks, expressed this concern: "Anyone contemplating buying a Shiva Nataraja in future is going to think very carefully about its history, or else risk a writ from Shiva" (Beckett 1988). Indeed, Śiva's appearance in English court is also symbolically problematic, for—as the defense argued in their appeal—the United Kingdom is a Christian kingdom ruled ultimately by the queen under the Christian God, and this ought to preclude other foreign gods from bringing suit. We need to examine more closely just what Śiva's juristic personality comprises and how it came into being.

As we have seen, the fundamental premise underlying Hindu temples and image worship in medieval and modern south India is that a god comes to inhabit a properly consecrated physical icon and makes himself or herself present and accessible to human devotees. The icon lives and has a personality through the deity's presence within it. The animated deity icon is referred to as *svāmin* (or Tamil *uṭaiyār*), "lord" and "owner" of the temple and its property. Medieval south Indian inscriptional records articulate this assumption clearly and repeatedly. Donors make their gifts of land, money, jewelry, animals, and the like directly to the god, named as the lord of the temple. The recipient, then, is the god embodied in the central icon of the temple, which in the case of medieval Śaiva temples is the Śiva liṅga. In the medieval Hindu universe, Śiva is owner of all temple property not as a juristic personality but as a divine person.

Complications with Śiva's divine proprietary rights to Śaiva temple property arose historically when this right was translated out of its original dispensation, the cosmic and moral order of medieval temple Hinduism from which it arose. The first translation took place in the literature of Dharmaśāstra, the corpus of classical and medieval Sanskrit "legal" literature. Dharmaśāstra grows out of an intellectual tradition whose primary sources, Veda-based Smārta literature and Mīmāṃsā, were aniconic and anti-theistic in orientation. Dharmaśāstra authors paid primary religious allegiance to Vedic sacrificial ritual, in which gods do not embody themselves, rather than to the image-centered liturgy of Hindu temples. Early Mīmāṃsā authors, we have seen, strenuously argued against the cult of images by attempting to deny any corporeality for divine beings. Dharmaśāstra writers did need to recognize gift-giving practices pertaining to Hindu temples within their legal formulations, but in light of Mīmāṃsā principles a deity could not be capable of receiving such gifts. The Dharmaśāstrins took recourse in such interpretive qualifiers as "imaginary" or "figurative" ownership and "secondary" reception of gifts. A gift presented to a god is really given to the brahmins who minister to the rituals, and it is only in a secondary or nonessential sense that one might call it a "gift to god." As Gunther-Dietz Sontheimer points out, in medieval India a basic discrepancy had already appeared between the practical understanding of temple donors as reflected in inscriptions and the legalistic formulations of the Dharmaśāstra scholars.[9]

A second translation occurred when British colonial administrators, starting from the time of Warren Hastings, attempted to employ and enforce Dharmaśāstra literature as a legal code for India. Attempting to apply Dharmaśāstra principles in ways they had never before been exercised, colonial British jurists set in motion a new dynamic reformulation of what came to be called "Hindu law." This label is something of an historical misnomer. The legal system that developed out of British application of Dharmaśāstra was not a simple outgrowth of indigenous legal literature, but a complex dialogic construction during the colonial period, involving Dharmaśāstra, British and Roman legal concepts, Muslim legal traditions, British and Indian jurists, and the Indian litigants whose disputes supplied the instigation for the development of new legal principles.

The earliest Anglo-Indian formulations concerning temple property in the early nineteenth century, Sontheimer points out, accepted the notion that a deity could be recipient and owner. In the late nineteenth and early twentieth centuries, however, Indian jurists revised this understanding by looking back to Dharmaśāstra formulations and interpreting them through the Roman legal concept of "judicial personhood." Again the belief that a divine being could incarnate himself or herself in physical form was ruled out of court, and the jurists shifted their focus from the deity to the intention or motivation of the gift giver. What must be legally honored was the "pious or benevolent idea" embodied within a gift to the deity. The deity holds property solely in an "ideal sense," since it, as a "merely artificial person," only personifies the pious intention of the donor. Roman law allowed the postulation of exactly such artificial or ideal entities, calling them "juristic persons." Indian jurists adopted this concept, and transformed the temple deity from a divine person into a personification.

It was this Anglo-Indian tradition of case law and legal formulations that the Indian plaintiffs presented as the basis for the claim of Śiva as a juristic person, and that Kennedy relied upon in formulating his judgment. Following the principle of "comity of nations," whereby "each nation respects the laws and usages of every other, so far as may be without prejudice to its own rights and interests," Kennedy based his decision primarily on two authoritative summaries of Hindu law, D. F. Mulla's *Principles of Hindu Law* (1929) and especially B. K. Mukherjea's *The Hindu Law of Religious and Charitable Trust* (1952).

Following Mukherjea, Kennedy discerned three propositions that form the basis for Indian law concerning temple ownership (Kennedy, p. 73). First, "neither God nor any supernatural being can be a person in law." Mukherjea argues that the Supreme Being of which the idol is an image cannot own temple property according to law. If it did, the Supreme Being in one temple could lodge a claim against the Supreme Being in another. Second, "property dedicated by the founder of a temple is disposed for the pious spiritual purposes of that founder." In establishing a Hindu temple, the sponsor must have intended that the public would benefit from worshiping the god or gods in that building. Third, the pious aim of the founder continues to reside in the physical idol as representing and symbolizing that aim. At this point, we may say that the Śiva liṅga of Pathur owned the properties of the Viśvanāthasvāmi temple, including the Naṭarāja image, but Mukherjea cautions that such ownership could be attributed to the deity "only in a secondary or ideal sense." Divine ownership is "a fiction but not a mere figure of speech." "The deity as owner represents nothing else but the intentions of the founder" (Mukherjea 1952: 46). To Mukherjea's three propositions, Kennedy added a fourth of his own, that "any juristic person must be capable of identification." To be juristic persons, Hindu icons must have names and descriptions.

In his decision Kennedy ruled that Śiva, embodied in the liṅga at Viśvanāthasvāmi temple, as a juristic person embodying the temple founder's pious intention, did have a claim to the Naṭarāja image superior to that of Bumper's claim. Śiva was not the only successful plaintiff, though. Kennedy also concluded that the temple itself, suing through its custodian Sadagopalan, had a superior claim. The state of Tamilnad likewise had a claim under the provisions of the Treasure Trove Act and local legislation. The Bumper Corporation and Robert Borden would have to return the Naṭarāja to India, without compensation. Even though Kennedy held that Borden had acted in good faith when he purchased the Naṭarāja, the decision also required Borden to pay the Indian court costs of over 300,000 pounds sterling.[10]

The divine person Śiva could not appear in an English court, since Supreme Beings are precluded. However, as Hindus well know, Śiva has always been adept at assuming other forms and strategic manifestations to carry out his purposes on earth, and in this case it would seem he adopted the relatively subtle incarnation of a juristic personality as a way of regaining the Pathur Naṭarāja image. This local manifestation may represent a considerable intellectual detour from the understanding Viśvanātha would have held when he established the Pathur temple. Nevertheless, modern-day Hindus could still view this as Śiva seeking a just recompense through the best means available. As one Tamilnad state official put it, "I can only say that lord Nataraja himself won the case appearing before courts in the form of the idol" (Vidyasagar 1991).[11]

Recovery of Ritual Selfhood

Throughout the case, Indian and Tamilnad officials announced their intention to return the Pathur Naṭarāja along with the other Pathur images to the temple in Pathur, which they would renovate and return to worship. All can accept this as an honorable aim, respectful toward the "pious intention" of the twelfth-century sponsors and toward the religious welfare of the present-day local population. However, this plan raises questions about the capacities of these religious objects to regain sacrality. After all, the Pathur Naṭarāja had been buried for centuries, damaged by smugglers, handled by all sorts of miscreants, and taken abroad. For Śaivas, what are the limits of ritual recuperation? Indian officials held to the simple principle, "Once a religious image always a religious image." Yet the lives of Indian images we have looked at in this book suggest that matters are never so simple. Likewise, medieval priestly texts developed more complex guidelines for assessing whether alienated images could recover their divine selfhood.

Although the issue of ritual recovery was not germane to the *India v. Bumper* case, the Sanskritist and scholar of Śaivism, Alexis Sanderson, filed a report on behalf of the defense concerning the matter.[12] From Śiva's point of view, the Latin adage "ars longa, vita brevis" needs to be reversed. While Śiva himself is by definition eternal, the fabricated embodiments he inhabits on earth are inescapably subject to the entropic forces of decay and destruction that are the lot of all matter. As we have seen throughout this book, icons may deteriorate through the normal effects of ritual erosion, they may suffer inadvertent pollution, and they may become targets for the more drastic seizure, mutilation, and destruction of human agents motivated by political or economic ends. Any such loss posed a grave concern for the temple priests and worshipers of these embodied divinities, for it threatened to erase the divine presence for which they had extended such elaborate ritual effort.

To help deal with such cases, medieval priestly texts recognized the various ways images could become unsuitable for worship, set out criteria for determining whether they were recoverable, and specified ritual procedures for revivifying them. How strictly priests actually followed these provisions is impossible now to determine, but the texts do provide guidelines by which Hindus thought about the reanimation of abused icons.

Medieval Śaiva texts like *Somaśambhupaddhati* (*SP*) and *Mayamata* (35: 15–18) begin their discussions by listing the different ways icons could become degraded. They might, for example, become broken, burned, split, defaced, or worn out. They might have been made improperly in the first place, or made by unsuitable persons. They could be dislocated in a flood. They might be attacked violently by enemy armies or stolen by thieves, and they might be handled by impure persons. Even temporary suspension of regular worship could cause an idol to lose some of its animating energy. All these required some ritual recuperation, varying according to the degree of injury.

In certain cases, the texts consider damage to the image to be so great that it must simply be abandoned. Most texts agree that an image which has lost its distinguishing features (*lakṣaṇa*)—as when an invader has hacked off its arms—is no longer fit to embody the god. Images of god should be complete and whole, just as Śiva himself is. Some texts take a stronger line and urge that worshipers abandon all abused icons. For example, *Īśānaśivagurudevapaddhati* (*kriyā* 64: 1–4) rules:

> A Śiva liṅga that is broken, cracked, split, moved, fallen, seized, burned, worn out, one that has lost its limbs, one damaged or fallen down along with its sanctum, a human liṅga made incorrectly by someone without proper knowledge or qualifications, one established for bad purposes, or a liṅga threatened by river or ocean—such a liṅga is abandoned completely by its animating mantras and its divinity. One should discard a liṅga that has been forsaken by its mantras and divinity like a stone, since that liṅga may become a home to goblins and demons.

One should dispose of such images as quickly as possible, say the texts, since they are effectively dead as supports for divinity. Clay images are thrown into the water, metal images are melted down, and wooden ones are cremated in fire, much as human corpses are consigned to flames on the funeral pyre.

Sometimes, too, images deteriorate irrevocably in more predictable fashion. Receiving regular baths of water, milk, honey, cow urine, and various other materials will over time wear down even the best-quality bronze or stone, and they will require replacement. At Jagannātha temple in Orissa, wooden images are used as the central icons of Viṣṇu and his cohorts. As one local text, the *Bhuvanaprakāśa*, admits, this choice of material entails a major disadvantage: stone images need to be replaced only after ten thousand years, metal ones after one thousand, while wooden ones require replacement every ten years (Tripathi 1978: 223). As described in Chapter Four, the temple holds a regular ceremony of replacement, entitled *navakalevara* ("new embodiment"), every twelve or nineteen years (depending on the lunar calendar), during which new wooden images are manufactured and carefully consecrated, and the deceased images are buried in a nearby graveyard.

Generally, Śaiva texts consider moderately worn, displaced, or untended images to be recoverable, provided they remain intact and recognizable. *Mayamata* (35: 39–40), for example, clearly distinguishes between images that have lost "major limbs" and must hence be abandoned, and those that have lost such minor appendages as "hands, nose, ornaments, ears, or teeth," which "should be rendered complete by restoring these things."

The flame of an untended fire diminishes to coals, though, and likewise a divine presence becomes less intense in any unworshiped image. If a priest fails to worship a liṅga daily, the *Īśānaśivagurudevapaddhati* recommends that he perform a reparation involving additional offerings and recitation of the expiatory mantra. If he fails to worship for more than twelve days, however, an elaborate ritual of reconsecration becomes necessary. Likewise, before returning to ritual life a damaged or displaced icon must first undergo a reconsecration (*jirṇoddhāra*, literally a "rescuing of what is worn out"), since "a worn liṅga that does not undergo the ritual of jirṇoddhāra may become a refuge for demons" (*SP* 288). The reduced intensity of divine presence in an untended image creates a vacuum that undesirable spirits may exploit.

Jirṇoddhāra largely follows the pattern of the original ritual of establishment, described in Chapter One, without the initial rites of selection and fabrication but with an additional pacification rite (*śāntihoma*) necessary to expiate any beings or forces that may have entered the object while its guard was down. Before performing this pacification, the priest requests Śiva to remove himself temporarily from the object: "This liṅga has become spoiled, O Pervasive One. To rescue it there must be a pacification rite. That is your command. Therefore, O Great Lord and Creator, please remain here, in me [for the duration of this rite]" (*SP* 289). Śiva's animating energy is transposable. The priest moves it from the liṅga or damaged image into his body. After the pacification has purged all obstructive forces from the object, he returns the energy to its icon and reenacts the rites of animation, purification, and affusion that initially established the object.

The premises underlying jirṇoddhāra, then, cohere with the Śaiva notion of varying levels of divine presence. In icons that have, for whatever reason, gone out of service without suffering grievous physical injury, Śiva remains present but only at a general level. The basic identification of image and deity established during initial rites of consecration is not undone, yet mistreatment, erosion, or ritual inattention have brought about a diminishment in Śiva's participation. To regain its full ritual status, the image must be subjected to ritual procedures that reestablish Śiva's special presence in it.

In light of these provisions from Śaiva ritual texts that are still followed, in principle if not in detail, by most south Indian Śaiva temples, it is clear that serious ritual work would be needed to restore the Naṭarāja and its temple in Pathur.

By the reckoning of *Mayamata*, the Pathur Naṭarāja is certainly salvageable as an icon, for physical damage to it was confined to peripheral iconographic detailing. Only the snake on Śiva's right hand and the flame in his left hand, along with parts of his scarf and his whirling locks, were broken. Ritual burial, even over a period of centuries, need not be an impediment to resto-

Fig. 47. Pathur Ruins and Śiva Liṅga. The central Śiva liṅga displaced outside the Viśvanāthasvāmi temple ruins. Photograph courtesy of Gary Schwindler.

ration. There does not appear to be any statute of limitations where Śiva is concerned. Although the medieval Śaiva texts do not make any explicit rulings, there are several modern precedents whereby south Indian villagers have returned treasure-trove images to worship, such as the twenty-three bronzes of Esalam. A strict follower of the priestly texts might oppose restoration of the Naṭarāja because it has been handled during its travels by untouchables and foreigners, but in twentieth-century India, priests and worshipers have generally softened or abandoned older strictures excluding untouchables. Overall, there is no compelling reason to suppose that Śiva's presence has entirely abandoned the Naṭarāja, but the image would certainly require a complete ritual jirṇoddhāra to rekindle that presence and regain its ritual selfhood.

The Śiva liṅga of Viśvanāthasvāmi temple, however, was a different matter. Not only had the liṅga not received any offerings of worship in some time, but it had also been displaced from its usual spot in the center of the sanctum. Displacement is not a serious detriment in the case of bronze images, which are intended as mobile (*cala*) icons for processions, but temple liṅgas are meant to be stable and immobile (*acala*). The Pathur liṅga had been separated from its foundation stone, the *brahmaśila*, and the middle pedestal (*pīṭha*) section was dislocated. The topmost cylindrical section had become lopsided (Figure 47). Sanderson concluded: "Given the condition and position of the liṅga it conforms to the characteristics of one which not only has been abandoned by the deity but is unable to be reinstalled" (8). The ruined condition of the liṅga and temple evidently did not preclude Śiva's appearance in court as a juristic person, but it would prohibit any salvaging of the old liṅga for ritual purposes. From the perspective of the Śaiva liturgical texts, the only acceptable procedure would be to build the temple and liṅga anew, and to follow the full course of ritual establishment for each.

Ceremonial Return and Its Aftermath

After its court case in London, the Pathur Naṭarāja had certainly attained greater celebrity as a litigated commodity than it had ever possessed as a consecrated temple image. And so, when it returned to Tamilnad on 9 August 1991, it was honored with political ceremonial suitable to its new status as an icon in the cultural politics of art repatriation.

The new Indian high commissioner in the United Kingdom, Dr. L. M. Singhvi, personally accompanied the image on its flight home from London. The official presentation took place at the Secretariat in Fort St. George, Madras, seat of the Tamilnad state government, and all the English-language newspapers covered the event. Singhvi handed over the Naṭarāja image, decked out in flower garlands and a silk robe, to the Tamilnad chief minister, Ms. Jayalalitha. She lit two brass oil lamps before it to mark its grateful acceptance by the government and people of Tamilnad. A plate of fresh pūjā offerings, the first the image had enjoyed in many centuries, stood before the Naṭarāja (Figure 48).

Both Singhvi and Jayalalitha spoke of the importance of the case. Singhvi praised the cooperation between India and Britain during the lawsuit, and thanked the London police, the British Museum, and British authorities and experts for their assistance. He claimed that the court ruling had established important legal principles by which India could assert its right to its priceless heritage, and he asserted that recovery of the Pathur bronze would help deter "international gangs of idol lifters."[13] Jayalalitha remembered Rajiv Gandhi's personal interest in the case and portrayed the legal victory as a historical turning point. The restoration of the Pathur Naṭarāja, she proclaimed, marked the end of an era in which "our priceless cultural treasures have been plundered by foreign countries and we have been forced, through circumstances, to bear all this in silence."[14] The chief minister also presented "Naṭarāja" mementos to fifteen officials who had participated in the effort to retrieve the image, including barrister Bhaskar Ghorpade, inspector general of police K. K. Rajasekharan Nair, and expert witness R. Nagaswamy.

Jayalalitha also announced plans for the Naṭarāja's future. It would return to Pathur as soon as workmen completed a renovation of the temple. The temple required substantial rebuilding and it would also need a consecration

FIG. 48. The Ceremony of Return. The Pathur Naṭarāja, properly decorated, flanked by the Tamilnad chief minister, Jayalalitha, and the Indian high commissioner to the United Kingdom, L. M. Singhvi, during a ceremony held at the Tamilnad secretariat, Madras, August 1991, to celebrate the return of Śiva. Photograph courtesy of *The Hindu*, Madras.

renewal ceremony, a ***kumbābhiṣeka***. After its long sojourn outside its temple environs, the image also would need a ritual reanimation. "A stolen image that has been a show-piece abroad and produced in court as an exhibit," commented one newspaper, "has to be deified through prescribed religious rituals before it is accepted for temple worship."[15] The medieval Śaiva texts had not exactly anticipated this form of abuse, but the reporter seems to offer a valid extrapolation from āgama guidelines. Jayalalitha hoped the work could be completed in six months, and would cost around Rs. 700,000.

I would like to be able to close this chapter by describing a dramatic reconsecration of the Viśvanāthasvāmi temple in Pathur and restoration of the Pathur Naṭarāja to worship. This would make a satisfying conclusion to the Naṭarāja's biography, bringing its long circle of travels to a gratifying completion. But the world does not always submit to the requirements of narrative, and matters like the restoration of a small temple in rural Thanjavur District are easy to neglect. When I tried to visit the image in August 1995, the Pathur Naṭarāja had taken another detour, to the Icon Centre at Tiruvarur.

Responding to a rash of thefts from rural temples, the Tamilnad government established the Icon Centre in the 1980s. Police cannot possibly guard

FIG. 49. The Icon Centre, Tiruvarur. Constructed in the outer enclosure of the Śiva Tyāgarāja temple, Tiruvarur, during the 1980s to house vulnerable religious icons. The current home of the Pathur Naṭarāja.

all the myriad local temples of Tamilnad containing valuable images against art thieves, and the Icon Centre would provide a centralized safe haven for valuable endangered bronze images. Situated in the outer precincts of the Tyāgarāja temple at Tiruvarur, the Centre is a vault with two reinforced concrete walls and doors with double locks (Figure 49). Armed police guard it around the clock. When the Pathur Naṭarāja arrived in 1991, about a thousand religious icons resided there. Other celebrated repatriated images such as the Tiruvilakkuti Naṭarāja and the Sivapuram Naṭarāja were already there, and many images from small ancient temples around Tamilnad had taken refuge in the Icon Centre.

Safety to one, though, can be detention to another. On the same day that *The Hindu* newspaper devoted front-page coverage to the ceremonial return of the Pathur Naṭarāja, another journalist in the same paper reported that priests and officials of several small rural temples in Thanjavur District felt that their gods were in jail, held without freedom to leave the Icon Centre.[16] The Centre was not consecrated, it was not a temple, and the public was not admitted. In deference to the wishes of devotees, a priest was allowed to enter the Centre once a week to perform a special collective pūjā for the images. The atmosphere inside was stiflingly hot, humid, and stale. The valuable icons were in danger from metal fatigue and diseases. The reporter called it a "death trap for idols."

It is a sad irony that, after so much effort was expended by so many to regain the image for India, Tamilnad, and the "pious intention" of the twelfth-century donor, the Pathur Naṭarāja should end up in a concrete vault, virtually unworshiped, safe from the international art market but now in danger of suffocation and heatstroke. After its difficult life, it deserves a better retirement.

FIG. 50. Viṣṇu Veṅkateśvara, Tirupati. Calendar print, artist unidentified.

Conclusion:
Identities and Manifestations

THERE ARE TIMES when Indian religious images must specify their own identities. According to the Śrīvaiṣṇava hagiography *Ārāyirappati-kuruparāmparaprapāvam*, the image of Viṣṇu Veṅkaṭeśvara at Tirupati once made such a choice (Figure 50). It seems that the temple had been neglected for some time, and worshipers of Śiva attempted to claim the site as theirs, arguing that the black image in the sanctum was in fact an icon of Śiva in his dual form as Harihara ("half Śiva, half Viṣṇu"). The local ruler intervened to mediate and called upon the famous Vaiṣṇava preceptor Rāmānuja to help solve the dispute. Rāmānuja proposed that the two parties allow the icon to decide. They would place before the image a trident and a *ḍamaru* drum, the distinctive insignia of Śiva, and a discus and conch, Viṣṇu's special signs. "Whichever ones it chooses," advised Rāmānuja, "will indicate its selection of identity" (*svarūpa*). They closed the doors of the sanctum and waited. The next morning, when they reopened the doors, the image was holding the discus and conch, while the trident and drum lay beneath its feet. The image was Viṣṇu.[1]

In one sense, most religious images in India do articulate their identities through the special insignia they bear. Iconography, the examination of those signs, is the first line of reconnaissance when archeologists and art historians seek to identify a newly uncovered Indian religious object. But throughout this book I have argued that, in a broader sense, the identities of these icons are never so fixed or permanent. As Hindus recognize, divine images enter into a host of complex ritual, personal, material, and spiritual relationships with the human devotees who worship and attend to them. Even as the images hang on to their distinctive insignia, they may find themselves carried off to new places, where they encounter new audiences, who may not know or appreciate their earlier significances. Or, even staying in their original locations, the images may take on new roles and new meanings in response to the changing world around them. The objects we have looked at have been repeatedly relocated, reframed, and reinterpreted by new communities of response in new historical settings.

And the reconstruction of identity continues today. Take, for example, the Didarganj yakṣī, exhumed in 1917 and quickly the subject of a skirmish between local worshipers and Patna museum officials, which introduced this series of biographies. As scholars continue to argue over her date of origin and her original identity (should we call her a yakṣī, a chowry bearer, or a goddess?), the icon has taken on a new occupation as a traveling emissary of ancient Indian art and culture. From the 1947 exhibition at the Royal Academy, London, through the succession of Festivals of India put on in the 1980s in London, Washington, Paris, and Moscow, the yakṣī has appeared at nearly every significant exhibition of Indian art outside India. On view in these world capitals, the yakṣī and her cohorts are called upon to help people of other nations recognize and appreciate India's cultural achievements and ways of thinking. Proponents of the festivals hope that these sculptural goodwill tours can help stimulate further exchange programs and continuing dialogue between the nations involved.[2]

When the yakṣī returned from her travels with a new chip on her cheek, however, she also became the most visible figure in a series of public debates in India between central government officials and archeologists over questions of compensation and control. At least twenty-seven objects suffered noticeable damage during the American and French festivals, and the curators of state and local museums where many of the objects normally resided wanted remuneration. The state government of Bihar demanded Rs. 62,500,000 for the damage to the Didarganj yakṣī, while the committee set up by the Centre to evaluate damages offered less than one-hundredth that amount. As the controversy escalated, others raised issues of preservation of cultural heritage and the propriety of sending national treasures abroad, national prestige and postcolonial pride. Some archeologists maintained that irreplaceable masterpieces of Indian art should never be exposed to the dangers of international travel. "If France did not allow the Mona Lisa out of the Louvre," argued the archeologists, "then why should India despatch its precious lady [the Didarganj yakṣī] to impress a handful of art enthusiasts abroad" (Reynolds 1989)? Exhibition officials replied that India needed to put its best art forward if it hoped to make a "splash" in the cosmopolitan capitals. This apparently even included objects still in worship. When festival organizers laid claim to some rare Cola bronzes in Tamilnad, the locals took them to court and succeeded in blocking the official appropriation by arguing that they were actively worshiping the bronzes as divinities. A chastened festival official offered as explanation, "We were doing it for the greater glory of Indian art."[3]

It is not just political forces that lead to renegotiations of identity. Scholarly practices also contribute to the process. We have seen in this book how the scholarly recovery of Somanātha's past by British colonial and Indian nationalist historians helped reanimate the abandoned temple site as a living symbol of medieval Islamic depredations, and led to its 1950 reconstruction as a symbol of Indian nationhood and the "Hinduness" of Gujarati culture. We have also seen how the scholarly advocacy of Havell and Coomaraswamy in the early twentieth century helped bring about a taxonomic shift whereby ancient Indian religious "idols" were transformed, for Western viewers, into "art." With this shift, objects from India could be incorporated into the larger Western world of art, with its methods of supply and exchange, its institutions of collection, its conventions of display, its ways of seeing, and its own ongoing discourse of scholarly commentary. This present study, of course, also forms part of that discourse.

Most art historians and religious historians writing about Indian religious icons and temples focus primary attention upon the moment of creation. This too casts identity in a particular mold. Knowledge of the iconographic form of an object and the date and place of its fabrication come to be seen as the constitutive knowledge of the object. In its focus on material creation, this perspective has the effect of restricting our sense of the meaningful possibilities of an object and it draws our attention away from the object's participation in the ongoing social life of its communities.

In this book I have not sought to deny the validity or interest of the traditional art historical concern with origins. Following the anthropologist Igor Kopytoff and the literary critic Stanley Fish, I suggest a shift in scholarly attention, toward the circumstances—religious, cultural, political, and economic—within which the identities of religious icons are constructed and reconstructed. I argue that the subsequent livelihoods of particular objects, especially ones inhabited by gods, are just as worthy of interest and disciplined inquiry as the setting of birth. The lives of the Indian images we have followed through history are made and remade through their encounters with differing audiences, who reciprocally bring with them different ways of seeing and acting toward the images they encounter.

By making this argument the organizing thread, I propose an expanded frame for viewing Indian religious objects, one that accepts contingency, instability, and plurality in the identities of images. Like the other "frames" we have examined, this grows out of a particular intellectual dispensation, which is often called "postmodernism," a term whose own instability of definition reflects the epistemological attitude it seeks to designate. But perhaps it is not so new at all. In its recognition of change and situatedness, and in its attempt to ground the identities and significances of images in their shifting encounters and relationships with human audiences, this frame also coheres with the views of devout Hindus, medieval and modern, who optimistically acknowledge that their gods may manifest themselves in countless diverse ways, in response to ever-changing realities. With this in mind, we can eagerly await further manifestations.

Notes

Introduction

1. A. K. Coomaraswamy's 1928–1931 monograph, *Yakṣas*, is still the best single source on early Indian cults devoted to these nature divinities. The most recent statement on the subject, by Frederick Asher and Walter Spink (1990), seeks to remove the Didarganj yakṣī from the Mauryan period and move it several centuries forward in time, to the Kuṣāṇa period.

2. Diane Coccari (1989: 133) discusses a similar process of integrating found images into contemporary modes of belief and worship in present-day Varanasi. Ancient Buddhas and Jinas turn into "Bīr Babas," local guardian divinities. I discuss this more fully in Chapter Seven.

3. In his catalog entry for the 1985 "Sculpture of India" show in Washington, D.C., where the Didarganj yakṣī was a featured attraction, Pramod Chandra observes that Spooner was not altogether correct: "As a matter of fact, the fly whisk is a common attribute of this type of divinity, but this, fortunately, was unknown to the donors" (1985: 49). Chandra's ironic aside, "fortunately," addresses an audience of art appreciators who, he is confident, will value the international display of this great work of art above its ritual usage for the local residents of a hamlet in Bihar. It was not so fortunate for the latter group. If they were "donors," they were certainly unwilling participants in the benefaction.

4. Other biographical treatments of Indic objects that have been useful to me in thinking about my approach are Victor Goloubew's 1932 account of the Buddha-tooth, Stanley Tambiah's comments on the Emerald Buddha (1976), and Samuel Parker's unpublished study of Aśoka's Sarnath Pillar (1987).

5. An important stimulus for this study has been the powerful art-historical synthesis of David Freedberg, *The Power of Images* (1989), who proposes a universal theory for human response to images. I share Freedberg's recognition of the recurrent "power" that images exercise over humans, but I attempt here to locate the sources of this power differently. My project might be seen as a culture-specific, and culturalist, reply to Freedberg, which aims to delineate what I see as a profound plurality of responses even to the same objects, based on the different theological premises and cultural values that human viewers bring to their encounters with images.

6. The *Oxford English Dictionary* offers as definitions of dispensation: "ordering, management; esp. the divine administration or conduct of the world," and "an arrangement or provision of Providence and of Nature." Christian theological usage also recognizes dispensations as malleable: "a religious order or system, conceived . . . as a stage in a progressive revelation, expressly adapted to the needs of a particular nation or period of time." If one removes the teleological implication, this provides a useful way of designating different regimes of value based on distinctive sets of theological, cosmological, and moral premises about how the world is and ought to be.

Chapter One

1. Descriptions of the image may be found in Nagaswamy 1983: 52–57 and Chandra 1985: 196–98.

2. The relevant inscriptions are *ARE* 456 and 457 of 1918. Altogether ninety-three inscriptions were copied from the temple in 1896 and 1918, and many have been published in *South Indian Inscriptions*, vols. 5, 13, and 19. See Thomas 1986: 138–39 for a list of published inscriptions of Tiruvengadu. I thank Leslie Orr for advice concerning these and other Cola inscriptions.

3. For the 1951 find, see Ramachandran 1956–1957 and Rathnasabapathy 1982: 133–34. Twelve more images were unearthed when building a new shrine to Vīrabhadra within the temple complex in 1960. Two are now in the Government Museum, Madras, and the rest were returned to the temple for worship (see Nagaswamy 1959–1960). In 1972, sixteen more images were found; these are now in the Thanjavur Art Gallery. I thank R. Nagaswamy for discussing the Tiruvengadu finds with me.

4. Western museums do sometimes display the type of Śiva-liṅga known as *mukhaliṅga*, in which one or four visible faces of Śiva appear to emanate outward from the cylindrical shaft, giving the icon greater sculptural value. No mukhaliṅga appeared in the "Sculpture of India" exhibition. According to Śaiva liturgical texts, the mukhaliṅga is considered somewhat inferior to the more unmarked plain liṅga, and the faceless liṅga is far more common as a central icon in south Indian temples. See Davis 1991: 121–22.

5. Through the excavated images, inscriptions, medieval Śaiva āgama texts, and present-day temple arrangement, it is possible to be relatively precise about the eleventh-century temple. For accounts of āgama prescriptions concerning the arrangement of images in a temple, see Dagens 1984: 130–49 and Davis 1991: 60–72.

6. On the devotional uses of cāmipaṭams, see Smith 1995: 35–41. The continuity of sacrality from liturgical object into mechanically reproduced copy goes against the predictions most notably of Benjamin's famous essay, "The Work of Art in the Age of Mechanical Reproduction." See also Inglis 1995 for a discussion of the evolution

of this artform, primarily as seen through the career of one master, C. Kondiah Raju (responsible for Figures 7 and 17 in this volume).

7. Although the "Sculpture of India" show made little attempt to recreate the setting or atmosphere from which the pieces originally came, other special exhibitions of Indian religious art in the United States have occasionally tried to structure display in a manner consonant with its original religious location. For examples, see Michael Meister's (1981) review of the "Manifestations of Shiva" curated by Stella Kramrisch at the Philadelphia Museum of Art, and Vishakha Desai's (1993) discussion of the "Gods, Guardians and Lovers" show at the Asia Society.

8. For an invigorating critique of the language and premises of aesthetic connoisseurship, especially as it regards non-Western arts, see Price 1989.

9. Among the most noteworthy early texts, dating to the fifth and sixth centuries, that prescribe pūjā directed toward anthropomorphic images are *Viṣṇusmṛti* 64–65 and *Baudhāyanagṛhyapariśiṣṭasūtra* 2.14 and 2.17. On the general shift from the earlier Vedic liturgical program to a theistic system centered primarily on icons of Viṣṇu and Śiva, see Inden 1979 and 1992. For a brief résumé of temple Hinduism, see Davis 1991: 3–21.

10. *Viṣṇusmṛti* 1.1–65. The *Viṣṇusmṛti* belongs to the Kāṭhaka school of the Yajurveda, one of the oldest Vedic schools. In an early form the text may have served as the Kaṭha Dharmasūtra; later it was extensively reworked by Vaiṣṇavas. Its final redaction was probably completed around the sixth century.

11. *Svayambhuvāgama vidyā* 4.3, quoted in Vedajñāna, *Śaivāgamaparibhāṣamañjarī* 1.2 (Dagens 1979: 56–57).

12. In this section I rely primarily on the formulations of the Vaiṣṇava Pāñcarātra and Śrīvaiṣṇava and the Śaiva school of Śaiva siddhānta. For the Śrīvaiṣṇavas, I am particularly indebted to the works of John Carman (1974), Vasudha Narayanan (1985, 1987), and their joint study (1989). For Śaiva siddhānta theology as it relates to pūjā, see Davis 1991: 122–36. As always, I am indebted to my teachers in India, S. S. Janaki, N. R. Bhatt, and Sri Sabharatna Sivacarya, and to the scholars Hélène Brunner and Bruno Dagens, for my understanding of Śaiva siddhānta.

13. I follow David Freedberg 1989: 161–67 here. The views of Aquinas and Bonaventure, he asserts, are central and recurrent in Christianity. Freedberg traces their mainstream position back to earlier Christian figures like Pseudo-Dionysius, Gregory of Nyssa, and Gregory the Great.

14. Thus Freedberg's apt comment on Bonaventure's theory of the image: "Here too are the real origins of a general theory of signs" (1989:166).

15. Pope 1900: xxxii. Pope draws his recounting of Māṇikkavācakar's hagiography from the modern poem *Vathavurarpurāṇam*, which is based on the *Tiruviḷaiyāṭarpurāṇam*, a Tamil *sthalapurāṇa* of the seventeenth century celebrating the deeds of Śiva at Madurai.

16. For this outline of the general ritual format of *pratiṣṭhā*, I rely on several early (fifth- and sixth-century) textual discussions (*Baudhāyanagṛhyapariśiṣṭasūtra* 2.13,

Bṛhatsaṃhitā 49–50, and *Matsyapurāṇa* 252–70), on later Śaiva siddhānta treatises (especially the *Kāmikāgama*), and on south Indian *śilpa* texts (*Mayamata*, *Sakalādhikāra*). I have also benefitted from Shantanu Phukan's unpublished essay on early *pratiṣṭhā* texts (1989).

17. The procedure for bronzes is outlined in *Padmasaṃhitā kriyāpāda* 19.33–46, in Smith, 1969: 46–47.

18. There is equally a rich recent literature of translations and analysis of Tamil bhakti poetry. For this brief discussion I have relied primarily on Ramanujan 1981, Cutler 1987, Peterson 1989, Carman and Narayanan 1989, and Shulman 1990.

19. For an analysis of the various connections established within Tamil bhakti poetry and the rhetorical strategies employed to make these connections, see Cutler 1987: 19–38.

20. Phyllis Granoff points to the same feature in medieval Jain hymns and literature (1994: 10–11).

21. *Bhāgavatapurāṇa* 10.8.32–43. On the composition of this text and its relation to poetry of the Āḻvārs, see esp. Friedhelm Hardy 1983. The episode was not in earlier versions of the Kṛṣṇa story, such as in *Harivaṃśa* and the *Viṣṇupurāṇa*.

22. *Kūrmapurāṇa* 1.25.67–101. This purāṇa, originally a Vaiṣṇava text of the late sixth or seventh century, was appropriated and recast as a Śaiva treatise by the Pāśupata school, probably in the early eighth century. Similar versions of the story are told in other purāṇas.

23. Extant images from Tiruvengadu date from the early Cola period of the tenth and eleventh centuries, and result from the rebuilding and reoutfitting of the temple in the mid-tenth century and its expansion over the next hundred years.

24. For Basavaṇṇa's treatment of image worship, see Ramanujan 1973: 84 and 88. Likewise, the more mystic Vīraśaiva saint Allama Prabhu treats the worship of stone images as redundant and unnecessary (Ramanujan 1973: 153). Ravidās's satiric views appear in Hawley and Juergensmeyer 1988: 26–27. Other later devotional poets who satirized or criticized the cult of images include Kabīr (Hess and Singh 1983: 42) and Rāmprasād Sen (Nathan and Seely 1982: 61, 63). Granoff 1993: 81–89 discusses narratives from the *Padmapurāṇa* and *Skandapurāṇa* that challenge and satirize the early medieval temple cult.

25. The best guide to this critique in Sontheimer 1964. Sontheimer describes the Mīmāṃsā as an "intellectual" brahminic opposition against the "popular" image-worshiping practice. He goes on to show how the Mīmāṃsā position was later modified and adopted within the legal literature of Dharmaśāstra, and the way this conditioned British colonial and post-Independence Indian legal understanding of the status and prerogatives of temple images. We will return to this issue in Chapter Seven.

26. The key passage here is *Mīmāṃsāsūtra* 9.1.6–9 on the question of "divine agency." See Nyayaratna 1889: 136–46 and Jha 1936: 1429–37.

27. The key passage here is Śaṅkara's commentary on Baudhāyaṇa's *Brahmasūtras* 1.3.26–33. I follow Sontheimer 1964: 53–58 in reading this as a direct response to

Śabara. However, Sontheimer takes Śaṅkara's argument here to indicate "full scholarly recognition" of the popular beliefs concerning image animation, and fails to place this within Śaṅkara's larger systematic demotion of image worship. For a fuller treatment of the position of image worship in Śaṅkara's Advaita, see Venkatarama Iyer 1964: 195–205.

28. For a brief treatment of Rāmānuja's theology as a response to both Mīmāṃsā and Advaita positions, see Carman and Narayanan 1989: 34–42.

Chapter Two

1. The materials of this essay have been presented at the American Committee on Southern Asian Art conference, Richmond, Virginia in 1988, at the American Institute for Indian Studies conference on "Perceptions of India's Past" in Varanasi in 1989, and at the Association for Asian Studies conference in Washington, D.C., in 1992. I would like to thank all those who pointed me to additional examples and made interpretive suggestions at these conferences.

2. *BS* 46.1–17 contains Varāhamihira's full discussion of image portents (Kern 1865: 206–9; Kern 1873: 57–59). Granoff 1994 refers to similar examples in *Mahābhārata* (6.2.26; 6.108.11), *Viṣṇudharmottarapurāṇa* (2.135; 3.117), and several other texts.

3. Bharatiya 1993. Granoff 1994: 8. The genealogical history of the Chamba kingdom, in the western Himalayan region of present-day Himachal Pradesh, describes a similar tale of kingship and image acquisition associated with Sahilavarman, the tenth-century founder of Chamba town. See Vogel 1911: 78–95. In Asian Buddhist settings, the foundation of new Buddhist polities was frequently linked with the arrival of new Buddha images (or relics), supposed to have come from India or other Buddhist centers. For some examples, one may compare the travels of the Emerald Buddha in Southeast Asia (Tambiah 1976: 76–77), the images brought to Tibet from China and Nepal during the reign of Song-tsen-gam-po (Snellgrove and Richardson 1980: 73–74), and the medieval Chinese traditions concerning the rediscovery of "Aśoka images" (Shinohara 1994).

4. The Jagannātha temple chronicle *Mādaḷā Pāñji* relates that Anangabhīma III (r. 1211–1238) dedicated everything—including his kingdom—to Lord Jagannātha and remained as his deputy. Anangabhīma did not even receive a royal affusion ceremony (*rājyābhiṣeka*), adds the chronicle, because the true king Jagannātha ordered it so. Starting from January 1230, Anangabhīma's inscriptions refer to him as "son" and "deputy" of Jagannātha. Later inscriptions no longer speak of the "prosperous and victorious reign of King Anangabhīma," but rather the "prosperous and victorious reign of Puruṣottama." Kulke 1986a: 139–55 offers the best historical account of Jagannātha's royal cult during the medieval period. Other examples of temple images exercising sovereignty include the brief overlordship of Śiva Virupakṣa over the formative Vijayanagara empire in the fourteenth century (Nilakanta Sastri

and Venkataramanayya 1946: 44–45), and that of Viṣṇu Padmanabhasvāmin in Trivandrum over the Travancore kingdom, beginning in December 1749 and continuing until the princely state of Travancore was absorbed into the Republic of India in 1947 (Sreedhara Menon 1962: 202–3).

5. On the famous encounter of Picasso and his cohorts with "primitive" art, see Rubin 1984. For a discussion of Elgin's intentions in appropriating the marbles that now bear his name, see Appendix 2: The Commons Debate 1816, in Hitchens 1987: 127.

6. See for instance, Sivaramamurti 1964: 19. I am indebted to R. Nagaswamy for first pointing out these stylistic developments to me.

7. The earliest inscriptional example of image appropriation in India is the "Jina of Kaliṅga" that the second-century B.C.E. ruler Kharavela of Orissa regained from the Māgadha ruler whose predecessor had taken it away (Jayaswal and Banerji 1983: 71–89). An early literary reference may be found in the *Akanānūru* (149), a collection of the classical Tamil Cankam (dated c. 100 B.C.E. to 250 C.E.), describing a king who conquers a city and takes an image (Hart 1975: 25). I thank John Cort, Ginni Ishimatsu, and others who brought these examples to my attention.

8. The solid gold Buddha was most likely destroyed in the 1017 Cola raid carried out by Rājendra on Anurādhapura. The chronicle account of this raid is *CV* 55.15–21, translated later in this chapter. There is no report of the golden Buddha image in Cola sources. The Jewel Palace was also probably devastated during this raid. See Hocart 1924: 1–17.

9. The English term "loot" derives from the Hindi *lut*, which may in turn come from the Sanskrit root *lup* ("to seize, rob"), although Sanskrit writers most often employ other terms to refer to the activity we think of as looting. The term seems to have enjoyed colloquial usage in Anglo-Indian circles from at least the mid-eighteenth century, but it did not become widely used back home in England until the mid-nineteenth century (Yule and Burnell 1903: 519–20; *Oxford English Dictionary*, s.v.).

10. Other Dharmaśāstra treatments of wartime plunder, not differing much from that of Manu, may be found in *Gautamadharmasūtra* 10.20–30 and *Kāmandakīyanītisāra* 19.18.22.

11. As an illustration of presentation to temple deity, the Cola king Rājarāja announces in the inscriptions of his imperial temple at Thanjavur: "These are the gold insignia (Tam. *cinna*, Skt. *cihna*) and the sacred gold ornaments that I, Lord Rājarāja, gave to the Highest Lord Rājarājeśvara [Śiva, dwelling in the temple built by Rājarāja] from my own treasuries and from the treasuries that I pillaged from the Ceras and the Pāṇḍyas, beginning with the twenty-third year up to the twenty-ninth year of my reign" (Hultzsch 1892: 1–14). As an illustration of the second type of donation, another inscription from Rājarāja's time, at a much less ostentatious Śaiva temple in Tiruppalanam, records that one Kampan-Maniyan, a headman of Tonur, set up for worship an "Emerald Deity." Kampan had accompanied Rajaraja on his invasion of the Western Ghats and distinguished himself there. Upon returning he requested

that the king present him with an idol from the plunder he had acquired on the campaign, and he was given the Emerald Deity, which he duly consecrated in a temple near his home (*ARE* 135 of 1927–1928).

12. On the role of regalia in *rājyābhiṣeka*, see Inden 1978: 46. Geiger 1960: 116 and 124–27 describes the role of regalia in Sinhalese war and royal ceremonial, on the basis of Ceylonese chronicles.

13. For example, inscriptions of the Eastern Cālukyas, a collateral branch of Cālukyas, contemporary with the Cālukyas of Kalyāṇī, who ruled from Vengi (Andhra Pradesh), traced the origins of their dynasty through many generations of legendary kings. After a temporary loss of autonomy, the dynasty was reestablished by Viṣṇuvardhana, who reacquired the Cālukya royal insignia.

> When his mother had explained the history of the lineage, Viṣṇuvardhana went and worshiped the Goddess Gaurī on the Cālukya Mountain, and gratified also the gods Skanda, Viṣṇu, the Mothers, and Śiva's troops. There he received the insignia of overlordship (*sāmrājyacihna*) that came to him through lineal succession and had only been, as it were, placed on deposit with those divinities: namely, the white parasol, the singular conch, the five great sounds, the *pālidhvaja*, the kettle drum, the emblem of the boar, the peacock tail, the spear, the lion throne, the crocodile gateway, the golden scepter, the Gaṅgā and Yamunā, and others as well. (Hultzsch 1896–1897: 239)

With sovereignty restored through these regalia, the inscriptions tell us (albeit hyperbolically), Viṣṇuvardhana went on to defeat his dynastic opponents and rule the entire Deccan from the Narmada River to Rāma's Bridge. Inscriptions of the Orissan Gaṅga dynasty similarly link the inception of rule with Kāmārṇava's pilgrimage to Mahendra Mountain, where he worships Śiva as Lord Gokarṇasvāmin and receives the boar insignia, and then returns with all the insignia of overlordship (including the singular conch, the kettledrum, the five great sounds, the white parasol, and the golden yak-tail fan) to establish the kingdom. See Fleet 1889.

14. On the role of dvarapālas, see for instance the eleventh-century south Indian *śilpa* text *Mayamata* 36.310–14. See Dagens 1976: 2.478–79 and n. 276, based on a passage from *Kāraṇāgama*.

15. Balasubrahmanyam 1975: 96–102 accepts the local tradition at face value. The Tamil devotional epic *Periyapurāṇam* describes Parañjyoti's actions at Vātāpi, for he subsequently became a great Śaiva saint and changed his name to Ciṟuttoṇṭar. However, there is good reason to doubt that the Gaṇeśa image now identified with the Pallava victory of the seventh century was actually taken from the Cālukya capital, for in appearance the image resembles Cola-period productions of the tenth and eleventh centuries. See Catlin 1991: 142–44 for a more circumspect discussion of the Vātāpi Gaṇeśa. For our purposes, it is more significant that local tradition would persist in identifying a later icon with a well-known act of royal conquest and looting.

16. On the political significance of this temple, see Desai 1992. The image currently enshrined in the temple is a three-faced stone Vaikuṇṭha of a typical tenth-

century Candella style. It lacks the fourth face referred to in the foundation inscription and lacks also the stylistic features characteristic of the Himalayan region where the golden Vaikuṇṭha originated. Desai argues that this stone image "formed the backdrop of the main image of Vaikuṇṭha," which has since disappeared. It is not possible now to trace how or when the golden Vaikuṇṭha was removed from the temple.

17. The Bālakṛṣṇa from Udayagiri was disarmed and thrown from its pedestal, perhaps in 1565 when armies overran Vijayanagara city. Such desecration and mutilation would have barred the object from further ritual use. The archeologist A. H. Longhurst found the image lying among the debris of its disused temple in the early twentieth century, and sent it off to join the collection of the Government Museum, Madras. Here the Udayagiri Bālakṛṣṇa that once signified Gajapati subordination to Vijayanagara sovereignty now takes it place as a representative of the "Vijayanagar Period (1300–1600)."

18. The work of Ronald Inden is particularly pertinent to this section. See especially his discussion of the Rāṣṭrakūṭa imperial formation (1990: 228–62).

19. Gupta 1961–1962: 131. Gupta believes that the *nāman* that Govinda claims to have taken from the Sinhala ruler refers to the two Buddha images that Aggabodhi VIII sent him, and that the Tārā acquired from the Bengali ruler Dharmapāla was likewise an image offered as a gift of surrender. Sircar 1961–1962: 135–40 disputes Gupta's conclusions. As for the Gurjāra board bearing the doorkeeper, see below.

20. Goyal 1967 stresses the connection of the Guptas with Prayāga, whereas Williams 1982: 45–46 argues for the dynastic significance of the two river goddesses to the identity and art of the Guptas.

21. The Pallavas of Kāñcīpuram also began to incorporate the imagery of Gaṅgā in the seventh century, most notably in the cave temple of Trichi. Here the image of Śiva as Lord of Gaṅgā in a shrine overlooking the Kaveri River homologizes the Pallava king Mahendra I with Śiva and refigures the Kaveri as the southern Ganges. The Pallavas never made it as far north as the Ganges-Yamuna doab, but their iconographic innovation may well be linked to a victory over the Gaṅga dynasty based in southern Karnataka. See Rabe 1995: 235–43 and Von Stietencron 1977: 373–74.

22. See for examples Balasubrahmanyam 1975, Nagaswamy 1970, and Pichard et al. 1994: 1.149–56. I thank Françoise l'Hernault for keeping me informed of recent finds of appropriated objects at Gangaikondacolapuram.

23. Bhandarkar 1925–1926: 235–57. The pun on the other name of the Gurjāras, Pratihāra, was no doubt intended.

24. A parallel example of the political semantics of door guardianship concerns the famous twelfth-century Rajput hero Pṛthvīrāja III of the Cāhamāna dynasty, and is recounted by Chand Bardai in his *Pṛthvīrājaraso*, as well as several other late medieval sources. The Cahamana ruler, goes the story, fell in love with Samyogitā, daughter of Jayacandra, king of Kanyakubja and the most powerful ruler in northern India at the time. Jayacandra, however, refused to countenance his political rival as his daughter's suitor, and at Samyogitā's bridegroom-choice ceremony (*svayamvara*) he

forebade Pṛthvīrāja to attend. Instead he installed a statue to represent the absent prince and placed it as palace gatekeeper. Humiliated by the slight, Pṛthvīrāja daringly abducted Samyogitā. War followed. See Sharma 1975: 86–88 and 110–14.

25. For references, see Nilakanta Sastri 1955: 255–56. This work remains the authoritative historical narrative of the Cola dynasty, and I rely on it throughout this chapter.

26. Hultzsch 1899: 64–71. The passage is somewhat obscure, and I follow Nilakanta Sastri's interpretation in my reading. On the Cālukya *kaṇṭhikā*, see Hultzsch 1896–1897: 226–42, verses 25–26.

27. The door guardian was found not in the Airavateśvara temple at Darasuram, but in the area of the old palace, no longer extant. This indicates its continued treatment more as a political signifier rather than religious object. I thank Françoise L'Hernault for pointing its find spot out to me.

28. Kalhaṇa also narrates (*RT* 7.869–1732), with clear disapproval, the reign of Harṣa, a Kashmiri ruler of the late eleventh century. Under the influence of bad ministers, Harṣa makes a policy of systematically plundering the temples of his domain to replenish his treasury. For Kalhaṇa the moralist, Harṣa's bad turn illustrates the self-destruction inherent in monetary acquisitiveness unrestrained by proper self-discipline, a potential danger for every ruler (7.1099–1101).

29. T. K. Palaniappan, "A Year of Progress," in Rathnasabapathy 1982: 129–30. Palaniappan's remarks are reprinted from the 1953 Tanjore Arts Festival Souvenir Volume.

Chapter Three

1. Earlier versions of this chapter have been presented at the University of Texas South Asia Seminar (1990) and the Association for Asian Studies conference (1991). I am not an Islamicist and have relied entirely in this chapter on translated sources, of which there are fortunately an abundance. Arab and Persian sources are cited by translators here and in the bibliography. A chronological list of texts is in the Bibliographic Appendix. I would like to thank several specialists in Islam for their encouragement and their comments, which have alerted me to additional sources and helped me avoid many errors: John Brockopp, Richard Eaton, Jerry Ellmore, Carl Ernst, Barbara Metcalf, and Theodore Wright. Of course, none of them is responsible for any misrepresentations that may remain in this section.

2. Amir Khusrau, *ʿAshiqa*, translated in Elliot and Dowson 1867: 3.546, quoted in Ahmad 1963: 471.

3. Amir Khusrau, *Khazāʾinul Fuṭūh*, in Habib 1931: 49, quoted in Ahmad 1963: 470.

4. Earlier Islamic encounters with Indian temples and icons, such as those that took place during the Arab conquest of Sind in the early eighth century, do not seem to have engendered the same narrative development in later Indo-Muslim accounts. At Multan, for instance, the caliph ʿAbd al-Malik allowed the central temple to

remain standing, and one-third of its income from the pilgrimage trade was given over to the Muslim rulers. See Friedmann 1972.

5. For some historiographical discussions of "what really happened" at Somanātha, see Habib 1967: 51–58; Nazim 1931: 115–21 and 209–24; and Parekh 1954: 287–96.

6. There are several Islamic paradigms for this "symbolic appropriation of the land" by identifying and converting the holiest site of a conquered territory, starting with Muḥammad's conversion of the Kaʿba in Mecca. Oleg Grabar (1987: 46–64) discusses the more subtle appropriation of Mount Moriah in Jerusalem, where in 691–692 C.E. the caliph ʿAbd al-Malik had the Dome of the Rock constructed above existing Jewish and Christian structures. Since Islam was not meant as a totally new faith but rather as the continuation and culmination of the Abrahamic religions already inhabiting the area, Grabar notes, the Dome asserted the superiority of Islam while inviting adherents of the other religions to accept the overarching faith of their new overlord.

Modern Hindu observers such as K. M. Munshi have often accepted and attempted to verify the hyperbolic Muslim reports on Somanātha to suit their own agenda. I will return to the later uses of this literature in Chapter Six, which traces the roles of Somanātha up to the present.

7. Faris 1952: 43–47; Friedmann 1975: 214–21. The notion that Adam descended to Earth in South Asia, more specifically on Adam's Peak in Sri Lanka, appears in Hadīth reports, and is repeated in a number of Indo-Muslim works. At Adam's Peak, it is worth noting, the same "footprint" is identified by its various religious communities of response as being the impression of Adam, of Śiva, and of the Buddha. For an interesting compilation of Islamic traditions conerning Adam's South Asian descent, see Ernst 1995.

8. This identification dates back to Farrukhi and Gardizi, writers contemporary with Maḥmūd. See Parekh 1954: 288 for quotations. On Manāt, see Ibn al-Kalbī, in Faris 1952: 12–14. Some later authors like Badā'ūnī disputed the identification, saying it was based merely on the resemblance of names (Ranking 1898: 28).

9. For summaries of Maḥmūd's historical career, see Habib 1931 and Habib 1967. An excellent general account of Ghaznavid policy is Bosworth 1963. Bosworth 1966 discusses Maḥmūd's reputation among his contemporaries and the subsequent Islamic community.

10. My discussion of Farīd al-Dīn ʿAṭṭār is based on Bosworth 1966: 90–92, which is based in turn on the 1959 dissertation by Gertrud Spiess, *Mahmud von Gazna bei Farīdu'd-dīn ʿAttar* (Basel).

11. Some early treatments of the Mahmud-Ayaz theme include the *Chahar Maqala* of Nizam-i-ʿArudi in the early twelfth century, and Saʿdī's *Būstān*. See Schimmel 1992: 130–31. I thank Fran Pritchett and Carl Ernst for bringing this aspect of Maḥmūd's narrative personality to my attention.

12. See P. Hardy 1960: 94–110 for a general discussion of ʿIṣāmī and evaluation of his "historical value."

13. Elliot and Dowson 1867: 1.97–99. In her critical study of al-Kazwīnī's sources, Maria Kowalska (1967: 76) traces his account of Somanātha to Ibn al-Athīr's *Kitāb al-Kāmil* of 1231. Romila Thapar (1966: 233–34) quotes al-Kazwīnī's entire selection in her standard textbook, *A History of India 1*, without historiographical qualification. Wolpert, *New History of India*, also reports the floating liṅga (1993: 107), with the mild cautionary comment that "the chronicler probably exaggerated."

14. The floating image motif reappeared in an 1801 ballad by a certain "Shaikh Din," first collected by Colonel James Tod (1839: 345–50), who obtained it from "the ignorant scion of an ancient Cazi." A fuller translation is given in Watson 1879: 153–61. I thank Phyllis Granoff for this reference.

15. Nazim 1931: 221 identifies ʿAṭṭār as the first to relate this anecdote. The most influential version undoubtedly was that of Firishta, in his *Gulshan-i Ibrāhīmī* (c. 1606). See Briggs 1966: 1.40–44. Through the 1770 English translation of this work by Alexander Dow, Firishta's account became the basis of retellings by European authorities like Gibbon (1783: 10.336–38) and Mill (1826: 221–22).

16. Later Hindus, not surprisingly, developed their own interpretations for how a human conqueror could have defeated the god Śiva. For example, the twentieth-century Bengali author Tarashankar Bandopadhyay recalls in his autobiography, *Smṛtikathā*, how his father explained that Muslims were able to loot Somanātha temple and carry off its icon only because Śiva had already abandoned it, on account of corrupt priests and hypocritical worshipers. Without Śiva's presence, the liṅga carried off by the Ghaznavids was indeed an inert piece of stone, much as Muslim accounts alleged. For Bandhopadhyay's father, however, this made no impact on Śiva himself (Granoff 1991b: 4).

17. The best guide for charting the historiographical preoccupation with Maḥmūd's motivation is Hardy 1962, which chronologically surveys European and twentieth-century Indo-Muslim and Hindu assessments of Maḥmūd. Modern Muslim historians like Habib and Nazim have generally preferred the economic interpretation, seeking to rescue Maḥmūd from the religious zeal implicit in the idol-breaker episodes. Likewise, many Western narrators have confidently held that Maḥmūd simply feigned religious zeal to mask pure acquisitiveness.

18. A similar fate must have befallen a marble image of Brahman excavated by the Italian Archaeological Mission in the "palace" area of Ghazna. According to the archeological report, "Attention should be called to the fact that the face of the statue . . . is completely wiped out, destroyed, it would seem, not by iconoclastic fury but slowly worn away by passing feet, its appearance being much like those of mediaeval tombal stones in church pavements" (Scerrato 1959: 39–40).

19. Grabar (1987: 56–58) discusses the various objects sent from around the Islamic world for display in the Kaʿba in Mecca, as detailed in an accounting list maintained there. Some were tokens of notable conversions, such as a golden image seated on a baldachin throne of silver which an unnamed Tibetan king donated when he became a Muslim. Others were significant objects appropriated from defeated rulers and territories, intended "to symbolize the unbeliever's submission to Islam through

the display of his *Herrschaftszeichen*, or symbols of power, in the chief sanctuary of Islam" (58). The liṅga of Somanātha, if it did reach Mecca, would have been treated as such a symbol of power.

20. The same motif reappeared in the 1801 Shaikh Din ballad, which made communalism the motivation of Maḥmūd's invasion (Tod 1839, Watson 1879). It seems that the Muslim population of the Somanātha area was once sorely oppressed by a Hindu ruler, who would slaughter one Muslim every day before the idol for its meal. When Maḥmūd eventually learned of this oppression, he invaded Gujarat, defeated the truculent king, ground the idol into lime, and forced the defeated ruler to consume it. Maḥmūd here became server of a communal form of poetic justice: the Hindu king who fed his idol the flesh of Muslims must finally consume the idol itself.

Chapter Four

1. The identification of Amir Khusraw's "Barmatpur" here is not altogether certain. I follow Krishnaswami Ayyangar's argument (1971: 108–9), but other historians such as Hari Rao (1976: 89–92) have suggested that Amir Khusraw's Barmatpur may refer to Sri Rangam.

2. Portions of this chapter were presented as "After Iconoclasm: Hindu Narratives of Recovery," at the 1994 University of Wisconsin South Asia Conference. I thank Muzaffar Alam for his comments at that presentation.

3. The single manuscript of the *Madhurāvijaya* is missing a portion of the chapter where the goddess appears, and she is not identified in the existing text. The editor takes her as dharma personified, whereas K. A. Nilakanta Sastri (1966: 266) understands her to be goddess of the Pāṇḍyan region. Her narrative role is parallel to Rājyaśrī in *Harṣacarita* and other caritas, as in her selection of Kampaṇa in 9.38. Her gift of a divine sword also suggests the role of Durgā in later Vijayanagara Navarātri ceremonial, as discussed in Chapter Two.

4. *Manusmṛti* 1.81–86; *Viṣṇupurāṇa* 6.1–2. The *Viṣṇupurāṇa* offers the most vivid of purāṇic accounts, as H. H. Wilson noted. For another purāṇic account of Kali-yuga, compare *Kūrmapurāṇa* 1.27–28.

5. Some late medieval authors argued the converse. Reversing cause and effect, they held that Kali-yuga enabled the Turkic invasions to succeed. Phyllis Granoff 1994 quotes from Jinaprabhasūri's fourteenth-century *Vividhatīrthakalpa*: "When the Wicked Age [Kali-yuga] shows its might, all the minor deities become absorbed in their own silly games and they lose their concentration; the superintending deities, whose task it is to guard the images in a temple, falter in their responsibilities." Negligent door guardians in turn allow the sultan to enter the temple and shatter the image.

6. The most striking illustration of this point is the compilation of Avasthy and Ghosh (1936) entitled "References to Muhammadans . . . " citing fifty-one epigraphs. The irony is that there are *no* references to "Muhammadans" or Muslims. All inscrip-

tions refer to Turuṣkas, Yāvanas, Mlecchas, and Pārasikas. Likewise, Phillip Wagoner (1994: 2) observes no references to "Muslims" as a religious identity in Vijayanagara texts.

7. Venkataramanayya and Somasekhara Sarma 1957–1958: 261. Prolaya Nāyaka was a local chieftain who claimed brief autonomy shortly after the fall of Warangal, the Kākatīya capital, in 1323. The inscription is dated between 1325 and 1350. I thank Cynthia Talbot for bringing this inscription to my attention.

8. *Pṛthvīrājavijaya* 6.36, quoted in Pollock 1993: 276. Pollock discusses *Pṛthvīrājavijaya* and cites several other incarnations of Rāma during the late medieval period, narrated in inscriptions and historical narratives (270–77), in his important overview of the medieval Rāma cult and its political repercussions.

9. For instance, Nilakanta Sastri 1966: 237. South Indian historians dispute whom the brothers initially served, but most accept their Muslim flirtation followed by later apostasy. Without contradicting this tradition, Stein sees it as part of the "central mythical core of the origin of Vijayanagara" (1989: 20).

10. Krishnaswami 1964: 43–44 lists numerous inscriptions recording Kampaṇa's benefactions. Still more donations were made by Kampaṇa's officers, most notably by chief minister Somappa Dannayaka. On Somappa's gifts, see ibid. 49–51.

11. Kampaṇa was not the only fourteenth-century Hindu ruler to reopen south Indian temples. Others include the Śambhuvarāya king Venrumankoṇḍa (*ARE* 434 of 1903), Viśālayadeva of Kuraikkudi (*ARE* 119 of 1908), and Erapotuleṁka, a local chieftain of Pillalamari who acknowledged Kampaṇa as overlord (Sreenivasachar 1940: 113–14). I thank Philip Wagoner for the last reference. It is worth noting also that subsequent Vijayanagar rulers favored a "Cola revival" style as the dominant model for sacred architecture through their empire, as George Michell (1994) has effectively argued. In Tamilnad the new Vijayanagara structures most often consisted of elaborations and expansions of preexisting sacred cores, rather than foundations of new temple sites.

12. Hultzsch 1900–1901: 330. The Viṣṇu Govindarāja image Gopaṇa restored to Cidambaram serves as still another reminder that others besides the "Turks" in medieval India dislodged religious images. According to several Cola-period eulogistic poems, the Cola ruler Kulottuṅga II had the Vaiṣṇava icon taken out of the shrine of Śiva Naṭarāja, evidently to remove any iconic competition, and had it thrown into the sea. Rescued (according to tradition) by the Śrīvaiṣṇava preceptor Rāmānuja, the Govindarāja image was maintained in the Vaiṣṇava temple of Tirupati until Gopaṇa's time. The Śaiva priesthood of Cidambaram apparently was none too happy with the restoration and again removed the icon. It required the intervention of the Vijayanagara ruler Acyuta Rāya to reconsecrate the Viṣṇu image once again in 1539 (Mahalingam 1940: 325–26, n. 86).

13. Parker 1992: 113. Parker also notes that construction resumed in the 1960s, after a long hiatus, when Raṅganātha appeared in the dream of a Śrīvaiṣṇava preceptor and ordered him to undertake the project of completing the unfinished gateway.

14. Auboyer 1969 offers a useful brief guide to the architecture and history of the temple.

15. Hardy 1983: 267, 441–42. Hardy views the rise of Sri Rangam with ambivalence, for in his view it represents a confinement of the earlier Tamil Vaiṣṇava tradition, which he sees as erotic, ecstatic, and aesthetic in orientation, within a more conventional brahminic outlook.

16. The 644 inscriptions of Sri Rangam temple are conveniently collected in a single volume of *South Indian Inscriptions*, vol. 24 (Narasimhaswamy 1982). In a recent unpublished study of the early medieval Sri Rangam inscriptional corpus, Leslie Orr (1995a) observes that kings do not often appear as donors at Sri Rangam prior to the mid-thirteenth century. Only in the period of dynastic conflict and transition, with Pāṇḍyas and Hoysalas contesting control over the old Cola core territories, did Sri Rangam emerge as a significant site for royal donation and legitimation.

17. Together with his strategy of conspicuous patronage, Sundarapāṇḍya also requested Lord Raṅganātha to make some alterations in temple administration, with which Viṣṇu complied. (Narasimhaswamy 1982, nos. 203 and 257). These inscriptions identify themselves in Sanskrit as the direct orders of Raṅganātha: "This is the highest, eternal decree of the very holy Raṅganātha, who brings about the creation, preservation, and destruction of the three worlds." The same formula had been used earlier in an inscription from the reign of the Cola king Kulottuṅga II (*South Indian Inscriptions* 3 no. 88; 24 no. 140).

18. This is the only procedural guide to the ritual burial of images that I have been able to locate. Nagaswamy 1987 discusses the text briefly, in his essay on the Esalam treasure-trove bronzes.

19. There is no comprehensive listing of images discovered in south Indian treasure troves, but there have been many hundreds, probably thousands. I have already discussed in Chapter One the four separate finds of bronze images unearthed in one Tamil village, Tiruvengadu. The earliest modern account of a treasure-trove find, so far as I know, is M. Textor de Ravisi's *Memoir* of the 1856 unearthing of four Buddhist bronzes and one porcelain in Nagapattinam, now in the Madras Government Museum (Ramachandran 1954: 135–36). In the annual *Administrative Reports of the Madras Government Museum*, "treasure-trove finds other than coins" were listed in appendices from 1927–1928 on, at a rate of roughly five sites and twenty icons per year. These listings usually provide some minimal information concerning the discovery, such as "found while digging in the neighborhood of a shrine." Several reports of treasure-trove hoards remark on the care with which the icons have been laid in the ground, and some even observe the ashes scattered among the buried images, remnants of a ritual burial ceremony (see Nagaswamy 1987: 1–3). Other major hoards have been found in hidden cellars and storerooms within temple complexes, obviously intended for concealment during times of danger. Nagaswamy 1982 relates an unusually vivid account of one such chamber at Nallur, where sixteen bronzes had been hidden. Of course, many treasure-trove discoveries remain unreported, whenever a finder decides to sell his cache surreptitiously. We will consider

one such recent case in detail in Chapter Seven. I thank R. Nagaswamy, former state director of archaeology in Tamilnad, for discussing treasure-trove finds with me.

20. Kulke 1986: 322–23. Kulke provides a fascinating account of Jagannātha as a central figure in complex power struggles during the late sixteenth through early eighteenth centuries. It is useful to note that Hindu claimants were at times the ones who posed a threat to the image, while Mughal governors acted as its protector. Kulke argues that "the initial fight of the Afghans *against* the Jaganātha cult turned under the Moghuls into a struggle *for* the domination over the cult. . . . It culminated in the events during the year 1735 when a new Muslim Subahdar, against the embittered resistance of the [Hindu] Khurda Rāja, but with the obvious support of the priests of Puri, forcibly brought back the image of Jagannātha from its hiding-place in South Orissa and established the cult of Puri" (1986: 323). Jagannātha and his temple priests, it appears, valued security of rule over religious affiliation in choosing a sovereign protector.

21. The story of Śrī Nāthji's migration is told in the *Śrīgovardhannāthjī ke prākaṭya kī vārtā* by Hariray, a seventeenth-century poet. I rely on Entwistle 1987: 184. For an excellent account of the often delicate maneuverings and negotiations over the movements of Pūṣṭimārga icons during this period, see Peabody 1991. Nath 1996 retraces the complicated itinerary of an important Caitaryaite image of Kṛṣṇa, which now occupies the Śrī Govindadeva temple in Jaipur. First discovered by the eminent Gauḍīya Vaiṣṇava theologian Rūpa Gosvāmin in Vṛndāvana in 1534, the image was exiled in 1669 on account of Aurangzeb's policies and installed in at least six different temples, before it was finally consecrated as state deity by the Kacchavāha ruler Jai Singh in 1727, the same year he founded his new capital city of Jaipur. Nath notes that Jai Singh considered Govindadeva the actual ruler of his kingdom, and he acted as the deity's emissary.

22. The event is recorded in a long inscription on a slab erected in the temple, dated 1710 (*ARE* 1920, p. 122). Varadarāja's return is also commemorated in the annual "Udayarpalayam festival" of the temple. See Raman 1975: 38, 85. Susan Bayly also relates the story (1989: 57, 59–60), based on a family history of the Udayarpalayam zamindars.

23. Other versions of this narrative may be found in the Telugu history of Śrīvaiṣṇavism, *Ācāryasūktimuktāvali* of Nambūri Keśavācārya (Krishnaswami Ayyangar 1919: 40–45) and the Sri Rangam temple chronicles, *Koyil Oluku* (Hari Rao 1961: 127–33). Krishnaswami Ayyangar 1971: 157–64 examines the story for its historical content, and is particularly valuable in identifying places mentioned in the story.

24. Hari Rao 1961: 127–28. Keśavācārya's *Ācāryasūktimuktāvali* also relates the tale of the loyal courtesan (Krishnaswami Ayyangar 1919). She finally has the Turkic general thrown off one of the temple towers. According to a similar local tradition, the defenders of the temple at Sri Rangam made ten or twelve duplicate images of Raṅganātha and placed them in various places to confound the Muslim iconoclasts with Viṣṇu's divine multiplicity. This early example of mechanical reproduction, however, led to a subsequent problem for the perpetrators in ascertaining authen-

ticity. Which was the original Raṅganātha? As in the *Koyil Oluku* story discussed later in this chapter, a blind but devoted washerman was able to make the identification. I have not been able to locate a textual basis for this anecdote.

25. On Gopaṇa, see Krishnaswami 1964: 55–60. The historical figure Gopaṇa is repeatedly associated with restoration of temples and images, including the reconsecration of the Viṣṇu Govindasvāmin image in the Śiva Naṭarāja temple at Cidambaram.

26. Kirusnasvami Ayyankar 1976: 18–30. English translation in Hari Rao 1961: 24–31. Several manuscript chronicles were collected, copied, and deposited in the temple storehouse in 1800, when Sri Rangam came under East India Company control and Joseph Wallace, British administrator in Trichi, sought to use them to mediate disputes over temple prerogatives (Parthasarathy 1954: 84–86).

27. *Prapannāmṛta* 47–48. Govindacharya 1906: 185–90 retells the story. The narrative is also related in the *Guruparamparaprabhāva* (see Narayanan 1985: 56–57). Both works are comparatively late. Govindacharya attempts to provide a historical basis for the story of Rāmānuja's trip to Delhi, suggesting he may have recovered an object looted by the Ghaznavids in the early eleventh century. More likely the story grows out of the same fourteenth-century events as the Sri Rangam version and, following the hagiographic logic that conjoins great events with great persons, has been projected back onto the great Vaiṣṇava preceptor who founded the temple at Tirunarayanapura while in exile from Cola country.

28. Ramanujan 1982 succinctly outlines the pattern. In addition to Āṇṭāḷ and Kulaśekhara's daughter, the daughter of the Cola king Dharmavarman, Vasalakṣmī, also chose Viṣṇu of Sri Rangam at a *svayamvara* attended by all the forms of Śiva and Viṣṇu (Hari Rao 1976: 9, 16). This union is celebrated in the *Lakṣmīkāvya*, a fifteenth-century Sanskrit work. According to local tradition, Viṣṇu of Sri Rangam has twelve wives, including the usual ones (Lakṣmī, Earth, etc.), the Kaveri River, Āṇṭāḷ, the Cola and Cera princesses, and the princess from Delhi. Govindacharya reports a later Sanskrit poem, the *Yavanīpariṇaya*, commemorating the marriage of the Delhi princess with Viṣṇu at Tirunarayanapura, but I have been unable to locate this text.

29. C. Hayavadana Rao 1930: 5.727 quotes the observation of Francis Buchanan (*Journal* 1.342): "A monument was built for the princess, but as she was a Turc, it would have been improper to place this building within the walls of the holy place; it has therefore been erected at the foot of the hill, under the most abrupt part of the rock."

30. For a brief published account, see Somasundaram Pillai 1965: 33. I thank Prema Nandakumar, S. Sampath Kumaran, S. R. Sampath Thathachariar, and Vasudha Narayanan for descriptions of the shrine, which is located too far inside the temple complex for a non-Hindu like myself to visit.

31. At this point in the narrative the Tamil text available to me (Kirusnasvami Ayyankar 1976, based on an earlier 1909 Madras edition) diverges from the version translated by Hari Rao. In the former, the local ruler retains Aḻakiyamaṇavāḷa at

Candragiri until Gopaṇa returns the image to Sri Rangam. I follow Hari Rao's more interesting version here.

32. Although subordinated by Aḻakiyamaṇavāḷa's return, the Māḷikaiyār image was not removed from the sanctum. Nowadays the image, known as Yogabherar, stands at the feet of the reclining Raṅganātha image, as illustrated in the lithographic depiction of Kondiah Raju and Subbiah (Figure 17) (Somasundaram Pillai 1965: 29). Parallel issues of recovery, authenticity, and replacement came to the fore in a recent case involving a twelfth-century stone image of Garuḍa, Viṣṇu's divine mount, that was stolen from its temple in Puri and then dramatically recovered by the Central Bureau of Investigation just before it boarded an international air flight. When the Garuḍa first disappeared, temple officials had a replica made and installed in the shrine. However, reported Ruben Banerjee, there persisted "a nagging suspicion in the minds of the faithful that the replica has a somewhat malignant aspect" (1990: 31). Locals blamed several mishaps, including the breakdown of Jagannātha's chariot during the festival procession, on the new replacement. However, when the original Garuḍa returned, a new controversy ensued. Some argued that the replacement icon, which had been ritually consecrated and worshiped, could not simply be abandoned. Further, they held that the stolen Garuḍa had been defiled when thieves and detectives handled it. Others opted for return of the original image, hoping to avert further disasters. Unfortunately Banerjee does not report the outcome of this dispute.

33. Shulman 1980: 32. The earliest Tamil *sthalapurāṇa* dates to the twelfth century, and Umāpati composed his important *Koyilpurāṇam* (on the Naṭarāja temple at Cidambaram) early in the fourteenth century. After that, the great bulk of works were composed in the sixteenth and seventeenth centuries. See the useful list of major works and authors in Shulman 1980: 353–54.

34. Hermann Kulke has observed the same phenomenon in his study of local histories from Nepal and Orissa (1979). The production of these historical narratives came in response to attacks on temples, argues Kulke. As in the Tamil temple hagiographies, these local histories invest the divine images with eternality, and make regional rulers their earthly representatives. See Granoff 1991a: 189.

35. An interest in self-manifested icons and shrines becomes much more evident in late medieval India, I believe, after the Turkic invasions and the establishment of Islamic polities in the subcontinent. Peabody (1991: 739–41) shows how self-manifested icons (*nidhisvarūpa*) figured preeminently in the late medieval Vaiṣṇava Puṣṭimārga scheme of images, above the man-made images (*puṣṭisvarūpa*) of their own sect and the lesser icons (*mūrti*) of other groups. Śrī Nāthji of Nāthadvāra, discussed previously, is the best-known self-manifested icon of the Puṣṭimārga community.

36. *Kaṭakarājavaṃśāvali* 77. The *Kaṭakarājavaṃśāvali* is an early nineteenth-century Sanskrit work, compiled from the Jagannātha temple archives. Kulke 1986c: 321–29 reconstructs the complex events of Orissan politics during this period, based on this and several other historical accounts. The eighteenth-century Indo-Muslim *History of Bengal* of Ghulam Husain Salim ascribes miraculous powers of iconoclasm to Kālā-

pahār, worthy of Maḥmūd himself: "Of the miracles of Kālāpahār, one was this, that wherever in that country, the sound of his drum reached, the hands and the feet, the ears and the noses of the idols, worshipped by the Hindus, fell off their stone figures, so that even now stone-idols, with hands and feet broken, and noses and ears cut off, are lying at several places in that country" (*Riyaz-us-Salatin*, p. 18, quoted in Kulke 1986c: 323, n. 12).

37. Tripathi 1986 describes the ritual in detail. Celebrants do not consider *navakalevara* to be a historical reenactment of sixteenth-century events, but Tripathi argues that the unique ritual procedure may have assumed its current form during the period of recurrent threat, flight, concealment, and recovery of Jagannātha during the sixteenth and seventeenth centuries (1986: 229). See also his comments on the substance of the present *brahmapadārtha* (260–61).

Chapter Five

1. Harle 1987. The term "Gonga" was used by seventeenth-century observers to refer to all Hindu male idols or "devils," explains Harle, but later curators understood the term solely in reference to the river goddess Gaṅgā, and so failed to connect the 1685 catalogue entry with the obviously masculine Viṣṇu image.

2. Millar 1972: xi–xxv provides a detailed account of the fate of Charles' collection during the 1640s. Arthur MacGregor (1989: 417) mentions an additional "East Indian Idoll" in black touchstone that Van der Doort gave the king. I thank James Harle for passing this reference on to me.

3. For instance, Chandra 1983 traces the beginnings of Indian art history as an intellectual discipline, but does not mention the activity of collecting at all. Partha Mitter's important study (1977) tells us a great deal about the history of Western intellectual responses to Indian art, but only glancingly refers to a few important collectors and shows. Useful brief studies of early European collecting in India include those of Mildred Archer (1987), Falk and Archer (1981), and Robert Skelton (1978, 1985a, 1985b). Desmond 1982 offers an excellent description of the formation of the Indian Museum, the nineteenth-century collection amassed by the East India Company. An important attempt to comprehend collecting and redisplay as a social practice within the context of British colonial control of the subcontinent is Cohn 1992.

4. Material in this chapter has been presented at the 1994 American Committee on Southern Asian Art conference in New York, the 1995 panel on "The Cultural Biographies of Things" at the Association of Art Historians annual conference in London, and at a panel on "Historicizing the Art Historical Object" at the 1996 College Art Association conference in Boston. I am grateful to audiences at these presentations for their questions and suggestions.

5. Soldiers in the British army were awarded medals in gold, silver gilt, silver, copper, or tin, according to rank. Mayo 1897: 134–45 discusses the two types of Seringapatam medals. For illustrations, see Mayo, Pl. 16, and C. A. Bayly 1990. The medal

currently on display in the Victoria and Albert was presented to Lord Cornwallis, former governor-general who had directed the Third Anglo-Mysore War, and it was lent to the museum by the current Lord Cornwallis.

6. In this section, I rely largely on the recent dissertation (1994) and two published essays (1993, 1995) on Tipū by Kate Brittlebank. I am also indebted to her for many useful comments on an earlier draft of this chapter. As Brittlebank points out, highly partial early colonial depictions and concerns have dominated the historiography of Tipū's reign until very recently. Her research represents the best attempt so far to reintegrate Tipū and his polity within its medieval Indian social and cultural setting.

7. For an example, see "The Huntress," an early eighteenth-century Deccani painting depicting Queen Chaṇḍa Bībī of Ahmadnagar, the heroic queen who unsuccessfully defended her city against the Mughals in 1600 (Zebrowski 1983: 233). Zebrowski comments that the queen here has "the fierce folk qualities of Rajput representations of the Hindu goddess Durgā slaying the buffalo demon" (234). Images of Durgā in her act of victory form an earlier iconographic model for Tipū's tiger.

8. Mildred Archer postulates a more specific incident providing the inspiration for the tiger. In December 1792, a tiger mauled the young son of General Hector Munro on Sagar Island. A friend wrote an eyewitness report in the *Gentleman's Magazine*, and the event produced a sensation among English audiences in India and England. General Munro had commanded a division during Eyre Coote's victory over Haidar ʿAlī at Porto Novo in 1781, and Archer suggests that Tipū may have taken solace for the defeat there in the violent death of Munro's son (Archer 1959: 11–15). Whether or not Tipū used this incident as the basis for his Tiger, the death of young Munro did inspire the potters of Staffordshire to commemorate the event in ceramic. See Buddle 1990: 82–83.

9. On the role of clothing in the sharing of Mughal authority, see Buckler 1928. Cohn 1983: 168–70 describes the general eighteenth-century British misreading of this system as one of "bribes" and "tribute."

10. The banner was captured by General Gillespie, who put down the Vellore uprising. It is now in the royal palace at Windsor.

11. Forrest 1970: 355. In his Appendix V, Forrest traces a large number of Tipū relics now located in the United Kingdom.

12. Quoted from Wellesley's "Minute in Council of Fort William," 18 August 1800, reprinted in Roebuck 1819: iv.

13. Johnson's collection was first acquired by the India Museum, and is now in the India Office Library. See Falk and Archer 1981: 14–29 on Johnson and his collection. This is by far the most detailed account of any early collector of Indian art.

14. The event is also described in a contemporary letter dated 14 March 1826 from Micaiah Hill to the London Missionary Society (Christian World Mission Library Archives). I thank Rosemarie Seton for help with Christian World Mission archives at the School of Oriental and African Studies Library, University of London.

15. It is not certain where this particular image is now. In the twentieth century the London Missionary Society gradually deaccessioned its old images, many to the

British Museum and other such institutions. The C.W.M. archives contains some correspondence relating to other objects in the London Missionary Society collections, but I have been unable to find any record of a transaction involving this Śiva from Calcutta.

16. Forbes 1813. A second edition of two volumes, revised by his daughter, was published in 1834. In the second edition, his daughter also added a brief account of Forbes' life. See Godrej and Rohatgi 1989: 123–27 for a brief treatment of Forbes as an amateur artist.

17. Forbes later moved to Paris with his daughter and son-in-law. An 1816 edition of *The Beauties of England and Wales* (Brewer 1816: 10.630) mentions that one Col. Roberts now occupied Forbe's villa in Stanmore, and that "some curious specimens of Hindoo sculpture" still resided in the garden. I have not been able to track Forbes' collection of Gujarati sculpture after that.

18. Fisch 1984 offers a comprehensive account of Stuart's life and activities. A brief account may be found in Caygill 1985. I would like to thank Richard Blurton, Theon Wilkinson, and Wladimir Zwalf for discussing Stuart and his collection with me.

19. Stuart's will, established 28 August 1828, is in the India Office Library, *Bengal Wills*, 1828, Parts 3 & 4, pp. 213–24. There is a more detailed list of objects drawn up by his lawyer, Mr. Palmer, also in the India Office Library: "Particulars of the late General C. Stuart's Museum sent to Messrs. Cockerell, Trail & Co." (IOL L/AG/34/27/93, 745–96).

20. Yates 1824: 444–45 records Chamberlain's diary entry verbatim.

21. Prinsep 1838a: 558. The story has been repeated several times, including Chanda 1936: 69–70 and Cohn 1992: 323–24. Elsewhere Chanda 1935 seeks to counter the "unpleasant impression" of Stuart such anecdotes might produce, and Fisch 1984: 51–52 likewise argues against charges that Stuart was an "idol-stealer."

22. Anonymous obituary in "Asiatic Intelligence—Calcutta," *Asiatic Journal and Monthly Register* 26 (1828): 607.

23. The fullest description of Stuart's tomb is that of Chanda 1935: 54–55. Most of the original images have since been looted from the tomb.

24. Lacroix's biographer Joseph Mullens notes Stuart's "apostasy to Hinduism through the influence of the fair idolatresses who filled his dwelling," and comments on the irony: "It was strange that that house should have fallen into a missionary's hands. The apostate had done much to strengthen Hinduism, and had been a great scandal to his Christian countrymen. The missionary lived only to destroy the system, and to adorn the gospel which he proclaimed in its stead" (1862: 77–78).

25. Architectural descriptions of the East India House on Leadenhall Street, no longer extant, may be found in Britton and Pugin 1828: 2.77–89 and Platt 1843: 5.49–64. See also Miller 1852: 96–102 for a more impressionistic account. For full description of the downstairs artworks, now divided between the Foreign and Commonwealth Office in Whitehall and the India Office Library, see Foster 1906 and Archer 1986. The Rysbrack chimney-piece and Roma's ceiling painting are both now in the Foreign and Commonwealth Office.

26. For catalogues and discussions of this cultural efflorescence, see Forrest 1970: 315–27 and 346–53, Buddle 1989, and Buddle 1990. Scott's short novel *The Surgeon's Daughter* depicts the young Tipū as a lecherous monster, from whom a young Scottish girl must be saved. Altick 1978 describes Porter's great canvas, in the context of the English craze for panoramas in the early nineteenth century. After its showing at the Lyceum, Porter offered to sell it to the East India Company, but the Company turned it down. The work was destroyed in a fire, and all that remains is a smaller version published as an engraving by J. Vendramini in 1802–1803. See Buddle 1990: 70–73 for a reproduction.

27. On the development of the British notion of "Oriental despotism" and its use in both explaining and justifying British conquest, see Cohn 1987: 208–12. John Barrell discusses the role of tiger imagery and particularly that of "Tipu's Tiger" in Thomas DeQuincey's writings and in early nineteenth-century imperialist discourse generally (1991: 48–52).

28. Collins' 1868 Preface, included in Collins 1944. On the Russian imperial scepter and its diamond, see Balfour 1987: 77–80. Later examples of looted Indian treasures in detective fiction include Arthur Conan Doyle's "The Sign of Four" and "The Adventures of the 'Western Star'" by Agatha Christie. In B. M. Crocker's "The Little Brass God" (1905), a small image of the goddess Kālī brings misfortune to a new British collector and his family (Crocker 1905). In the 1930s, H. T. W. Bousefield's "The God with Four Arms" features a four-armed bronze image of Indra, acquired by disreputable methods, that leads its possessors into crime, murder, and execution (1991). I thank Jaya Mehta for bringing the latter two examples of the mini-genre to my attention. The theme still makes occasional reappearances, as in Robert Newman's 1986 mystery novel for young readers, *The Case of the Indian Curse*, as well as in recent B.B.C. television adaptations of the Doyle and Christie stories. In Davis 1994 I connect this motif with a late-Victorian discomfort with the practice of looting (especially as carried out by British troops during the suppression of the Rebellion of 1857–1858), and an attempt to displace it as the characteristic practice of racial others.

29. From Dalhousie's brief to Queen Victoria, 7 April 1849, quoted in Das 1964: 700. Much of the early life of Koh-i-noor remains controversial. For a summary by the official British keeper of the jewel house, see Younghusband 1921: 151–59. The most scrupulous recent treatment is Balfour 1987: 15–29.

30. The fullest discussion of this attitude in its Indian setting may be found in Guha-Thakurta 1992. She discusses in detail the roles of Havell, Coomaraswamy, and Sister Nivedita in the Indian swadeshi movement of the early twentieth century.

31. Skelton 1978: 303. Proceedings of the event along with subsequent letters are recorded in the *Journal of the Royal Society of Arts* 58 (4 February 1910): 273–98.

32. Greenfield 1989: 214–31 provides the most useful summary of these international recommendations, resolutions, and conventions.

33. *Times* of London, 25 September 1976, p. 1. Even Lord Ballantrae, great-grandson of Dalhousie, joined the 1976 Koh-i-noor queue (facetiously?), arguing that his ancestor had "owned" it for about a year in 1849. See Balfour 1987: 28–29 and

Greenfield 1989: 148–52. I thank John Guy of the Victoria and Albert Museum for allowing me to look through the museum's file of clippings on repatriation cases.

34. *Sunday Observer*, 24 July 1983, p. 5.

35. Brittlebank 1994: 1–2 describes the 1990 controversy that erupted when Indian national television, Doordarshan, attempted to air a serial on the life of Tipū based on Bhagwan Gidwani's popular historical novel, *The Sword of Tipu Sultan*. Doordarshan sought to portray Tipū as a "secular" ruler, and the Bharatiya Janata Party sought a court injunction to prevent the series. The BJP charged that Tipū had been a fanatical Muslim persecutor of Hindus.

36. Buddle 1990: 88–91. Dhruva Mistry's "Tipu" has been shown at the Royal Academy (1982), the Royal College of Art (1983), and the Zamana Gallery in London (1990). It now belongs to a private collector. I thank Dhruva Mistry for corresponding with me about his work, and Vishakha Desai for first informing me of this example of the "afterlife" of "Tipu's Tiger."

Chapter Six

1. A full Śaiva version of the myth is in *Ekaliṅgamāhātmya* (14.1–34), a fifteenth-century Sanskrit hagiography of Śiva Ekaliṅga in Mewar (Premalata Sharma 1976: 49–52). Most purāṇas recognize Prabhāsa as a Śaiva tīrtha. See, for examples, *Vāmanapurāṇa* 57.51–53, *Kūrmapurāṇa* 2.34.16–20, and *Varāhapurāṇa* quoted in *Kṛtyakalpataru*, Tīrthakāṇḍa, ch. 19. However, in early purāṇas it is not treated as a major holy center, of the same status as Vāraṇāsī, Prayāga, Gayā, or Kurukṣetra.

2. I presented some of this chapter at the Association for Asian Studies annual conference in 1994. I thank two respondents there, Richard Eaton and Barbara Metcalf, for helpful comments.

3. The Ayodhya mobilization and final destruction of the Babri Masjid in December 1992 has generated a large body of scholarly literature. The most convenient collections are the volumes of essays edited by Sarvepalli Gopal (1990) and David Ludden (1996).

4. ʿIṣāmī narrates the background of the poem's composition in the text itself. For a general discussion of ʿIṣāmī and evaluation of his "historical" value, see P. Hardy 1960: 94–110.

5. Sayyid ʿAlī Tabataba'i, *Burhan-i Maʾathir* (1592–1596), translated by J. S. King 1899: 119–38 and sequence.

6. The text in Old Rajastani was critically edited by Vyas (1953), and has been recently translated by V. S. Bhatnagar (1991). That it is translated now, with the parenthetical subtitle "India's Greatest Patriotic Saga of Medieval Times" (as if the Delhi Sultanate was somehow not "India") and fitted with a highly Hindu-centric introduction, is part of the modern, communalized remembering of Somanātha. For a historical reconstruction of Kānhaḍade's career, see Sharma 1975: 180–92.

7. Granoff 1991a: 196. One of Jinaprabhasūri's most interesting recovery stories

concerns the Mahāvīra image of Kannanaya, and parallels many of the motifs of the south Indian Vaiṣṇava stories of Viṣṇu Raṅganātha we looked at in Chapter Four (Granoff 1992: 3–7). Here the image is hidden and then recovered through a dream message. It sweats in anticipation of a new invasion. Muslim armies capture the image and lock it up in the treasure house in Delhi. Jinaprabhasūri then becomes a courtier at the sultan's court and is able to retrieve the Mahāvīra. In later accounts such as the *Jinaprabhasūriprabandha*, Granoff (1992: 26–27) tells us, the sultan challenges Jinaprabha to make it speak. The image bursts out in a poem wishing victory simultaneously to Jains, to the sultan and his beloved, and to Jinaprabhasūri. The miraculous and diplomatic icon so impresses the Muslim ruler that he builds a temple for the image. I am grateful to John Cort and Phyllis Granoff for urging me to look at Jain narratives dealing with Somanātha.

8. Sharma 1969: 165–66. Dhanapāla was court poet of the Paramara king Bhoja, who was ruling in Ujjain at the time of Maḥmūd's Gujarat campaign. Jinaprabhasūri retells the anecdote in his *Vividhatīrthakalpa* (p. 29). In a recent Hindi guide to Jain holy places, the *Tīrtha Darśana* (Madras: Sri Mahavir Jain Kalyan Sangh, 1980), the anonymous author relates a more extended tale of attacks both unsuccessful and successful undertaken by both Muslim and Hindu rulers. As the fame of Satyapura grew, so did the jealousy of non-Jains. In the eleventh century, a Hindu king in Malwa tried unsuccessfully to destroy the image. In 1291 a "Mughal army" failed in its attempt on the image, and again in 1299 Ulugh Khān, brother of ʿAlā al-Dīn Khaljī, could not dislodge the tenacious Jain icon. After his brother's failure, the story goes on, ʿAlā al-Dīn mounted another raid, captured the image, and took it back with him to Delhi. The narrator concludes that "nothing is known of the golden image taken to Delhi by Alauddin Khilji," but that "the present image at Satyapura is also ancient and impressive" (298). I thank John Cort for passing this modern account on to me.

9. Muni 1933: 84–86; Tawney 1901: 130–33. The anecdote is also related in Jinamaṇḍana's *Kumārapālacarita*, dated 1436. See Buhler 1936: 28–31 and Granoff 1989: 384, n. 61.

10. Cousens 1931. Ahalyā Bāī's interest in Somanātha appears to have been part of a larger (and unique) project, by which she devoted much of Indore's royal resources to maintaining and renovating major pilgrimage spots throughout India. Her iconic beneficiaries included Viṣṇu Jagannātha in Puri, Śiva Rāmeśvaram in southern India, Śiva Kedāranātha in the Himalayas, Śiva Viśveśvara in Varanasi, and many others (Thakur 1932: 139–44). There is some indication that she regarded Śiva as the actual ruler of her dominion. State activities were undertaken "by command of Śiva." John Malcolm, British political agent in Central India in the early nineteenth century, recounts her religious munificence and the ceremony with which she dedicated to treasury to charitable purposes (1823: 1.186–87).

11. Stella Kramrisch even argues that Śiva might prefer underground chambers such as the one at Somanātha and several other Gujarati sites, in accord with the metaphysical scheme of cosmic embodiment from a primordial seed Kramrisch sees

as the underlying structure of all Hindu temples (1976: 172). More likely underground shrines were primarily defensive in character.

12. For transporting the gates, elephants could not be used, since the swaying motion of their gait might open the joints. A special cart had to be fitted out. See the report of the Gates Committee, in Sanders et al. 1843.

13. India Office Library: Parliamentary Branch Records (L/Parl/1), vol. 87. "Gates of the Temple of Somnauth: Orders for Escort and Proclamation" (1843). The proclamation is printed verbatim with a scathing commentary in Kaye 1851: 2. 650–51. See also Ellenborough's retrospective interpretation of the restoration in his letter to the Secret Committee, 28 March 1843, printed in Law 1926: 53–57.

14. Henry Rawlinson's MS Journal, quoted in Kaye 1851: 2.607.

15. India Office Library: H.M. Series 59, fol. 423/4, quoted in Kulke 1986b: 346.

16. Melville to Gov.-Gen., 11.9.1803 (Parliamentary Papers, 1845/664, p. 77), quoted in Kulke 1978: 346.

17. Halbertal and Margalit 1992 provides a rich analysis of the varied discursive uses of "idolatry" within the Judaic tradition.

18. Hocart discusses a religious-nationalist dispute over idols in Fiji in 1912, where the idol-worshiping cult of the Children of Water came into conflict with the Methodism of the colonial administrators. Hocart notes the threat this posed for the colonizers: "If tolerated, it would have meant also the revival of all the local cults, the spiritual autonomy of Fiji, and an attempt to translate it into temporal independence. The worship of numerous spirits housed in sticks or clubs, and domiciled in Fiji, was incompatible with the centralized rule of the Colonial Office" (248).

19. Alexander Duff, lecture in 1850 to the Y.M.C.A., quoted by J. W. Kaye, *Christianity in India* (1859: 380), re-quoted in Irschick 1994: 85. Duff goes on to provide an interesting account of the lasting effects of Place's reforms in Kanchipuram temple culture:

> When visiting Conjevaram last year (1849), I found his name still cherished with traditionary reverence by the votaries of Brahmanism. The nomenclature which he had introduced was still in vogue. The native officers spoke of the pagoda as the "Established Church;" of the temple revenues as the "church funds;" of the Brahman keepers of the idol shrines as the "churchwardens." In the neighborhood of one of the great temples a spacious garden was pointed out as the "gift of Mr. Place to the god;" within was shown a gorgeous head ornament, begemmed with diamonds and other jewels, worth a thousand pounds, which Mr. Place had presented to the great idol. (Quoted in Irschick 1994: 85)

For a general summary of the Evangelical critique of British involvement in Hindu idolatry, see Mayhew 1988: 144–53.

20. Cohn goes on to show how British colonial administrators went about attempting to resolve this ritual incompleteness in the post-1857 period by generating their own syncretic political rituals.

21. Prakash 1990. He goes on to note that, while this rendered historical India ac-

tive and sovereign, the "Hindu chauvinism" embedded within nationalist history of this period had and still has "deadly implications in a multiethnic country like India" (389).

22. My summary of the plot here is drawn from Dave et al. 1962: 2:74–89, based on Munshi's own recounting in *Kulapati's Letters*.

23. My narration here is based largely on Munshi's own account, appended to later editions of *Somanātha, the Shrine Eternal*. Peter Van der Veer has also recounted Munshi's role in the reconstruction of Somanātha, in the context of his larger argument concerning religion and nationalism (1994: 146–52).

24. I thank architects Amritlal Trivedi and Chandulal P. Trivedi, and photographer Shantilal Nanjibhai Bhatt for their recollections of this event.

25. G. N. Curzon, quoted in Anderson 1991: 179, n. 30. Anderson comments parenthetically, "Foucault could not have said it better." On Curzon's contributions to archeology in India, see Roy 1953.

26. The plan for reconstruction also provoked dispute among Sompura architects. According to Amritlal Trivedi, who was another respected Sompura *sthāpati* at the time (and is still actively engaged in sacred architecture), the Somnath Trust invited both Prabhashankar and Amritlal to submit plans for reconstructing Somanātha. Basing himself on a *śilpa* adage that "any temple over a man's height should not be torn down," Amritlal called for a rehabilitation of Kumārapāla's old temple. He would incorporate original pieces wherever possible and reproduce the remainder in the same type of stone, maintaining the same quality of workmanship that the twelfth-century remains exhibited. Prabhashankar proposed a clean rebuilding. The new temple would occupy the exact ground plan of the old, and the elevation would follow *śilpa* prescriptions for a Kailāsa Mahāmeru (imperial-level) temple, though it would not be an exact replication of Kumārapāla's temple. Prabhashankar would use a different stone and, in the interest of speed, he would not attempt to match the medieval quality of sculptural ornamentation. It is not difficult to see why Munshi and the Jamsaheb chose Prabhashankar's plan. To maintain the symbolic value of rebuilding Somanatha it would be important to act quickly. In fact, the reconstruction took place so swiftly that many of the outside niches, which should house divine figures, remain uncarved blocks of stone to this day, giving the temple a curiously incomplete appearance.

27. The structure housing the museum had also experienced shifts in identity. Built originally during Kumārapāla's time as a temple to the Sun god Sūrya, it served as a Jāmi Masjīd in later medieval times, before being appropriated and transformed into a secular archeological site museum.

28. A similar concern with universality may be seen in the Visva Hindu Parishad brick campaign of the 1980s, when all villages in India were requested to make, sanctify, and contribute a brick for the Rāma Janmabhumi temple to be built in Ayodhya. The new Indian diaspora made it possible for the group also to collect bricks from around the world, wherever nonresident Indians supported the Ayodhya program. See Davis 1996.

29. To manifest that continued spirit more concretely, the VHP General Secretary Ashok Singhal chose as architect for the new Rāma Janmabhumi temple the grandson of Prabhashankar Sompura, Chandrakantbhai Balavantbhai Sompura. Sompura's design was widely displayed on posters during the 1990 Rath Yatra.

Chapter Seven

1. Some of the materials in this chapter have been presented at the University of Chicago (1991), the College Art Association conference in Boston (1991), Columbia University (1992), and the Center for the Advanced Study of India at the University of Pennsylvania (1995). I am grateful to Rita McCleary and Irene Winter for extensive comments on earlier drafts of this chapter.

2. Primary written sources for legal case and reconstruction of Pathur Naṭarāja biography are transcripts of proceedings and Justice Ian Kennedy's lengthy decision. I would like to thank Anne Bennett and Sunita Mainee for allowing me access to their copies of transcripts. Citations from court transcripts, abbreviated as T., give day and page number. I cite Kennedy's decision by his name; it is listed in the bibliography under United Kingdom, High Court.

3. Coccari also makes the important observation that the prohibition in śāstraic literature of the use of badly mutilated images is not applied here. "What is authoritative is the revelation of the image and the subsequent proofs of power and efficacy the deity is believed to exhibit" (133–34). Some Bīr images are established with full *pratiṣṭhā* rites, but most, she notes, are set up by nonbrahmin priests through a simpler ritual dedication.

4. Greenfield 1989: 214–31 provides a useful summary of the international agreements reached by UNESCO and others. She includes the texts of the 1954 and 1970 Conventions as microfiche appendices XVI and XVII.

5. Taminad police superintendent U. C. Chandramouleeswaran (who later investigated the Sivapuram Naṭarāja case) notes in his 1972 essay on "Idol Theft: Investigation," that the earliest police records on "idol theft as an organised offense" date back to 1936, when one Dr. Durbrains of Pondicherry smuggled many religious icons from Thanjavur District through the French colony of Pondicherry on to France. Chandramouleeswaran goes on to describe how suppliers responded to the new desire for Indian art: "The foreign tourist enamoured by the beauty of these wonderful creations went to the so called curio dealers and wanted ancient pieces and they were prepared to pay any price. This prompted our curio dealers to engage themselves in this lucrative trade" (1972: 121). He could have been thinking precisely of Balraj Nadar.

6. See Venkataramani 1984 and "Museum Preparing for Return of Indian Bronze," *Stolen Art Alert* 1984: 3. Rajasekharan Nair 1982 best describes the investigation leading to identification of the Tiruvilakkuti Naṭarāja.

7. In an odd real-life echo of the Moonstone's curse, several of the persons involved in the smuggling network soon thereafter suffered. The bronzemaker became

paralyzed in his right side, making it impossible for him to continue his craft. Another was ruined financially, and one died shortly after selling the Naṭarāja. The investigating superintendent of police, U. C. Chandramouleeswaran, commented that "right from the beginning the idol was casting a superstitious spell on all who came in contact with it," and R. Nagaswamy reported a "local tradition" that Śiva had punished all those who had trifled with his sacred image.

8. When I inquired in August 1995 in Madras about the outcome of charges against these witnesses, I learned they had all been "charge-sheeted," but the cases had not come to trial yet. In India, I was told, these things move slowly.

9. Sontheimer 1964 provides an excellent historical overview of divine ownership in Indian law. He traces the Mīmāṃsā critique of image worship and the Dharmaśāstra reinterpretation of religious endowments based on that critique. He goes on to detail the historical ramifications of the Dharmaśāstra view in Anglo-Indian law up to the present.

10. Borden appealed the decision, but the court of appeals upheld Kennedy's judgment in February 1991 (*Bumper Corp. v Commissioner of Police of the Metropolis, All England Law Reports*, 1991). Borden then petitioned the House of Lords for leave to appeal the case further, but the Lords refused to consider it ("Row over Ownership of Nataraja Ends" 1991). Even after the Naṭarāja returned to India, Borden refused to pay court costs to the Government of India. The Indian government pursued the matter to Canada, where in 1995 a Canadian court upheld the British order. Borden now has no recourse but to pay the Indian costs (Jennings 1996: 6).

11. Siva's well-publicized victory establishing his juristic personality in a British court may have some interesting repercussions for temple administration in India. When the temple trustee of the Venkatesvara Balaji temple in Banganga, Maharashtra, sought recently to sell the temple and its property to a local realty firm for a cool 13,600,000 rupees, a group of four devotees filed a suit on behalf of the temple deities Viṣṇu Venkateśvara, Garuḍa, Gaṇeśa, and Hanumān. "We are going to argue that the gods cannot be summarily thrown out or deprived of their property in this manner," explained one petitioner. "They have, after all, been living in the temple for two hundred years." Their lawyer cited the Pathur Nataraja case as precedent for the juristic personhood of the four plaintiffs (Palnitkar 1995: 40).

12. This section is based on Davis 1992: 51–53 and Sanderson 1986. I thank Alexis Sanderson for sharing his unpublished court reports with me.

13. Singhvi's hope seems to have been borne out. Since the highly publicized Pathur Nataraja case and other successful investigations of the late 1970s and early 1980s, the incidence of reported thefts of icons from Tamilnad temples has substantially declined, according to K. K. Rajasekharan Nair. I thank the inspector general for providing me with a statement of idol theft cases over the period 1990–1994 as well as the quarterly reports on "Property of Cultural Heritage" printed by the Indian National Crime Records Bureau over the same period.

14. "Pathur Nataraja restored to TN," *Indian Express*, 10 August 1991, p. 7.

15. "Nataraja's sojourn to U.K. and back," *Times of India*, 10 August 1991, p. 11.

16. "Too stuffy for gods to live in," *Hindu* 10 August 1991, p. 11.

Conclusion

1. *Ārāyirappatikuruparāmparaprapāvam* pp. 227–28. The incident is discussed briefly in Carman 1974: 43. In his *History of Tirupati*, Krishnaswami Ayyangar relates the dispute as an historical event without granting the image any agency. Rāmānuja simply meets the Śaivas in debate and persuades the king's court that the site is really a Vaiṣṇava one (1940–1941: 1.265–67).

2. Tanen 1991 offers a succinct statement of purpose for international cultural festivals by the diplomat who served as American coordinator for the 1985 Festival of India in the United States.

3. Chengappa 1986: 150. For more on the disputes over damages and compensation, see also Singh 1989.

Bibliography

Indic Language Sources (texts and translations, by title)

Aitreyabrāhmaṇa

Keith, Arthur Berriedale, trans. 1920. *Rigveda Brāhmaṇas: The Aitreya and Kauṣītaki Brāhmaṇas of the Rigveda*. Harvard Oriental Series, vol. 25. Cambridge: Harvard University Press.

Ārāyirappatikuruparamparāprapāvam

Kirusnasvami Ayyankar, S., ed. n.d. *Ārāyirappati Kuruparamparāprapāvam*. Trichi: Srinivasam Accakam.

Baudhāyanagṛhyapariśiṣṭasūtra

Harting, Peter Nicolaas Ubbo, ed. 1922. *Selections from the Baudhāyana-Gṛhyapariśiṣṭasūtra*. Amersfoort: J. Valkhoff & Co.

Bhagavadgītā

Śaṅkara. 1988. *Bhagavadgītā with Śāṅkarabhāṣya* [1929]. In *Works of Śaṅkarācārya in Original Sanskrit*, vol. 2. Delhi: Motilal Banarsidass.

Bhāgavatapurāṇa

Dutt, Manmatha Nath, trans. 1895–1896. *A Prose English Edition of Srimadbhagavatam*. 3 vols. Calcutta: H. C. Dass.

Brahmasūtras of Baudayana with Śaṅkara's *Bhāṣya*

Śaṅkara. 1964. *Brahmasūtra with Śāṅkarabhāṣya*. In *Works of Śaṅkarācārya in Original Sanskrit*, vol. 3. Delhi: Motilal Banarsidass.

Thibaut, George, trans. 1890. *The Vedānta-Sūtras with the Commentary of Śaṅkarācārya*. Sacred Books of the East. 3 vols. Oxford: Clarendon Press.

Bṛhatsaṃhitā of Varāhamihira

Kern, H., ed. 1865. *The Bṛhat Saṅhitā of Varāha-Mihira*. Bibliotheca Indica. Calcutta: Baptist Press.

———. trans. 1873. The Bṛhat-Saṅhitā; or, Complete System of Natural Astrology of Varāha-mihira. *Journal of the Royal Asiatic Society of Great Britain and Ireland*, n.s. 4: 279–338 et seq.

Cūlavaṃsa

Geiger, Wilhelm, ed. 1925. *Cūlavaṃsa: Being the More Recent Part of the Mahāvaṃsa*. Pali Text Society Text Series, no. 20. London: Humphrey Milford.

Geiger, Wilhelm, trans. 1929. *Cūlavaṃsa: Being the More Recent Part of the Mahāvaṃsa*. Pali Text Society Translation Series, no. 18. London: Oxford University Press.

Ekaliṅgamāhātmya

Premalata Sharma, D. K., ed. 1976. *Ekaliṅgamāhātmya*. Delhi: Motilal Banarsidass.

Īśānaśivagurudevapaddhati of Īśānaśiva

Ganapati Sastri, T., ed. 1920–1925. *Īśānaśivagurudevapaddhati*. Trivandrum Sanskrit Series. 4 vols. Trivandrum: Government Press.

Kāmikāgama

Swaminatha Sivacarya, C., ed. 1975. *Kāmikāgama, Pūrvabhāga*. Madras: South Indian Arcaka's Association.

Kānhaḍade Prabandha of Padmanābha

Vyas, K. B., ed. 1953. *Kānhaḍade Prabandha: A Mediaeval Epic Poem in Old Western Rājasthānī of Padmanābha*. Rajasthan Puratan Granthamala. Jaipur: Rajasthan Puratattva Mandira.

Bhatnagar, V. S., trans. 1991. *Kānhaḍade Prabandha (India's Greatest Patriotic Saga of Medieval Times)*. New Delhi: Aditya Prakashan.

Kaṭakarājavaṃśāvali

Tripathi, Gaya Charan, and Hermann Kulke, eds. 1987. *Kaṭakarājavaṃśāvali: A Traditional History of Orissa*. Sources of Orissan History. 2 vols. Allahabad: Vohra Publishing.

Kōyil Oluku

Kirusnasvami Ayyankar Svami, Sri, ed. 1976. *Kōyiloluku*. Trichi: Srinivasam Piras.

Parthasarathy, T. S., trans. 1954. *The Kōyil Olugu (History of the Srirangam Temple)*. Tirupati: Tirumalai-Tirupati Devasthanams.

Hari Rao, V. N., trans. 1961. *Kōil Olugu: The Chronicle of the Srirangam Temple with Historical Notes*. Madras: Rochouse & Sons Private Ltd.

Kṛtyakalpataru of Lakṣmīdhara

Rangaswami Aiyangar, K. V., ed. 1942. *Kṛtyakalpataru of Bhaṭṭa Lakṣmīdhara*. Vol. 8, *Tīrthakāṇḍa*. Gaekwad's Oriental Series, vol. 98. Baroda: Oriental Institute.

Kūrmapurāṇa

Gupta, Anand Swarup, ed. 1971. *The Kūrma Purāṇa*. Varanasi: All-India Kashiraj Trust.

Bhattacharya, Ahibhushan, trans. 1972. *The Kūrma Purāṇa (with English Translation)*. Varanasi: All-India Kashi Raj Trust.

Madhurāvijaya of Gaṅgādevī

Thiruvenkatachari, S., ed. and trans. 1957. *Madhurāvijayam of Gangā Devi*. Annamalai University Historical Series, no. 13. Annamalainagar: Annamalai University.

Mahābhārata

Sukthanker, Vishnu S., and S. K. Belvalkar, eds. 1933. *The Mahābhārata*. Poona: Bhandarkar Oriental Research Institute.

Manusmṛti with Medhātithi's *Bhāṣya*

Jolly, Julius, ed. 1887. *Manu-smṛti; The Code of Manu*. London: Trubner.

Buhler, Georg, trans. 1984. *The Laws of Manu*. Sacred Books of the East, vol. 25. Delhi: Motilal Banarsidass.

Kevalananda, Swami, and J. R. Gharpure, eds. n.d. *Manusmṛti with the Bhāshya of Bhaṭṭa Medhātithi*. Collections of Hindu Law Texts, no. 9. Poona: Aryasamskriti Mudranalaya.

Jha, Ganganatha, trans. 1920–1926. *Manusmṛti: The Laws of Manu with the Bhāṣya of Medhātithi*. 5 vols. Calcutta: University of Calcutta.

Matsyapurāṇa

Vasu, S. C., and others, trans. 1972. *The Matsya Purāṇam*. Sacred Books of the Aryans. Delhi: Oriental Publishers.

Mayamata

Dagens, Bruno, ed. and trans. 1976. *Mayamata: Traite sanskrit d'architecture*. 2 vols. Pondicherry: Institut Français d'Indologie.

Mīmāṃsāsūtras of Jaimini with Śabara's *Bhāṣya*

Nyayaratna, Mahesachandra, ed. 1889. *The Mīmānsā Darśana*. Bibliotheca Indica, vol. 2. 2 vols. Calcutta: Baptist Mission Press.

Jha, Ganganatha, trans. 1936. *Shabara-Bhāṣya*. Gaekwad's Oriental Series, no. 73. 3 vols. Baroda: Oriental Institute.

Mṛgendrāgama

Shastri, Madhusudan Kaul, ed. 1930. *Mṛgendrāgama, Vidyāpāda and Yogapāda*. Kashmir Series of Texts and Translations, no. 50. Bombay: Nirnaya Sagar Press.

Hulin, Michel, trans. 1980. *Mṛgendrāgama: Sections de la doctrine et du yoga*. Publications de l'Institut Français d'Indologie, no. 63. Pondicherry.

Navasāhasāṅkacarita of Padmagupta

Bharatiya, Shastri Jitendrachandra, ed. 1963. *The Navasāhasāṅkacharitam of Āchārya Parimala Padmagupta*. Vidyabhawan Sanskrit Granthamala, no. 66. Varanasi: Chowkhamba Vidyabhawan.

Padmasaṃhitā

Smith, H. Daniel, ed. 1969. *A Sourcebook of Vaiṣṇava Iconography According to Pāñcarātrāgama Texts*. Madras: Pancaratra Parisodhana Parisad.

Paramasamhitā

Krishnaswami Aiyangar, S., trans. 1940. *Paramasamhitā [of the Pāñcarātra]*. Gaekwad's Oriental Series, no. 86. Baroda: Oriental Institute.

Prabandhacintāmaṇi of Merutuṅga

Muni, Jinavijaya, ed. 1933. *Prabandha Cintāmaṇi of Merutuṅgācārya*. Singhi Jaina Series. Santiniketan: Singhi Jaina Jnanapitha.

Tawney, C. H., trans. 1901. *The Prabandhacintāmaṇi, or Wishing-Stone of Narratives, Composed by Merutunga Ācārya*. Bibliotheca Indica, no. 141. Calcutta: Asiatic Society.

Prapannāmṛta of Anantasūri

Ramanarayanacarya, Svami, ed. 1966. *Prapannāmṛta*. Varanasi: Somani Trust.

Rājataraṅginī of Kalhaṇa

Sitaram Pandit, Ranjit, trans. 1935. *Rājataraṅginī: The Saga of the Kings of Kashmir*. Allahabad: Indian Press.

Stein, M. A., ed. 1892. *Kalhaṇa's Rājataraṅginī or Chronicle of the Kings of Kashmir*. Bombay: Education Society's Press.

Śaivāgamaparibhāṣāmañjarī of Vedajñāna

Dagens, Bruno, ed. and trans. 1979. *Śaivāgamaparibhāṣāmañjarī de Vedajñāna: Le florilege de la doctrine śivaite*. Publications de l'Institut Français d'Indologie. Pondicherry.

Sakalādhikāra

Gopala Iyengar, V., ed. and trans. 1973. *Sakalādhikāra of Sage Agastya*. Tanjore Sarasvati Mahal Series, no. 141. Thanjavur: Tanjore Maharaja Serfoji's Sarasvati Mahal Library.

Somaśambhupaddhati of Somaśambhu

Subrahmanya Sastri, K. M., ed. *Somaśambhupaddhati*. Devakottai: Saivagamasiddhanta Paripalanasangha.

Brunner-Lachaux, Helene, trans. 1963–1977. *Somaśambhupaddhati*. 3 vols. Pondicherry: Institut Français d'Indologie.

Śrīvacanabhūṣaṇa of Pillai Lokācārya

Lester, Robert C., ed. and trans. 1979. *Śrīvacana Bhūṣana of Pillai Lokācārya*. Madras: Kuppuswami Sastri Research Institute.

Vikramāṅkadevacarita of Bilhaṇa

Buhler, Georg, ed. 1875. *The Vikramāṅkadevacharita*. Bombay Sanskrit Series, no. 14. Bombay: Government Central Book Depot.

Banerji, S. C., and A. K. Gupta, trans. 1965. *Bilhaṇa's Vikramāṅkadevacaritam*. Calcutta: Sambodhi Publications Pvt. Ltd.

Vimānārcanākalpa

Vimānārcanākalpa. 1923. Madras: Venkatesvara Mudralaya.

Viṣṇupurāṇa

Jalan, Motilal, ed. 1967. *Śrīśrīviṣṇupurāṇa*. Gorakhpur: Gita Press.

Wilson, H. H., trans. 1840. *The Vishnu Purana: A System of Hindu Mythology and Tradition*. London: John Murray.

Viṣṇusmṛti

Jolly, Julius, ed. 1881. *Viṣṇusmṛti: The Institutes of Vishnu*. Bibliotheca Indica. Calcutta: Asiatic Society.

———, trans. 1880. *The Institutes of Vishnu*. Sacred Books of the East, vol. 7. Oxford: Clarendon Press.

Vividhatīrthakalpa of Jinaprabhasūri

Bhandarkar, D. R., and Kedarnath Sahityabhusana, eds. 1923. *Tīrthakalpa: A Treatise on the Sacred Places of the Jains by Jinaprabha Sūri*. Bibliotheca Indica, vol. 238. Calcutta: Baptist Mission Press.

Muni, Jina Vijaya, ed. 1931. *Vividhatīrthakalpa of Jinaprabha Sūri*. Singhi Jaina Series, no. 10. Santiniketan: Singhi Jaina Jnanapitha.

Other Works

Ahmad, Aziz. 1963. "Epic and Counter-Epic in Medieval India." *Journal of the American Oriental Society* 83: 470–76.

Ali, Ahmed, trans. 1984. *Al-Qur'ān: A Contemporary Translation*. Princeton: Princeton University Press.

Alpers, Svetlana. 1991. "The Museum as a Way of Seeing." In *Exhibiting Cultures: The Poetics and Politics of Museum Display*, edited by Ivan Karp and Steven D. Lavine, pp. 25–32. Washington, D.C.: Smithsonian Institution Press.

Altekar, A. S. 1934. *The Rashtrakutas and Their Times*. Poona Oriental Series. Poona: Oriental Book Agency.

Altick, Richard D. 1978. *The Shows of London*. Cambridge: Harvard University Press.

Anderson, Benedict. 1991. *Imagined Communities: Reflections on the Origins and Spread of Nationalism*. 2nd ed. London: Verso.

Annual Report on South Indian Epigraphy. 1887–1955. Madras: Government of India.

Appadurai, Arjun, ed. 1986. *The Social Life of Things: Commodities in Cultural Perspective*. Cambridge: Cambridge University Press.

Archer, Mildred. 1959. *Tippoo's Tiger*. Victoria and Albert Museum Monograph no. 10. London: Her Majesty's Stationery Office.

———. 1986. *The India Office Collection of Paintings and Sculpture*. London: British Library.

———. 1987. "The British as Collectors and Patrons in India, 1760–1830." In *Treasures from India: The Clive Collection at Powis Castle*, edited by Mildred Archer, Christopher Rowell, and Robert Skelton, pp. 9–16. London: Herbert Press.

Asher, Frederick, and Walter Spink. 1990. "Maurya Figural Sculpture Reconsidered." *Ars Orientalis* 19: 1–25.

"Asiatic Intelligence—Calcutta." 1828. *Asiatic Journal and Monthly Register* 26: 607.

Auboyer, Jeannine. 1969. *Srī Ranganāthaswāmi: Le temple de Vishnu à Srirangam*. Paris: SHC/WS.

Avasthy, Rama Shankar, and Amalananda Ghosh. 1936. "References to Muhammadans in Sanskrit Inscriptions in Northern India—A.D. 730 to 1320." *Journal of Indian History* 15: 161–84 and 16: 24–26.

Balasubrahmanyam, S. R. 1975. *Middle Chola Temples: Rājarāja I to Kulottuṅga I (A.D. 985–1070)*. Faridabad: Thomson Press.

Balfour, Ian. 1987. *Famous Diamonds*. London: William Collins Sons.

Banerjee, Ruben. 1990. "Return of the Idol." *India Today*, 30 November, p. 31.

Barlow, R., and Henry Yule, eds. 1887–1889. *The Diary of William Hedges, Esq.* 3 vols. London: Hakluyt Society.

Barnett, Lionel D. 1921–1922. "Three Inscriptions from Hottur." *Epigraphia Indica* 16: 73–88.

Barrell, John. 1991. *The Infection of Thomas De Quincey: A Psychopathology of Imperialism*. New Haven: Yale University Press.

Barthes, Roland. 1957. *Mythologies*. New York: Hill and Wang.

Baxandall, Michael. 1972. *Painting and Experience in Fifteenth-Century Italy: A Primer in the Social History of Pictorial Style*. Oxford: Oxford University Press.

Bayly, C. A. 1988. Indian Society and the Making of the British Empire. In *The New Cambridge History of India*, vol. 2.1. Cambridge: Cambridge University Press.

———, ed. 1990. *The Raj: India and the British, 1600–1947*. London: National Portrait Gallery Publications.

Bayly, Susan. 1989. *Saints, Goddesses and Kings: Muslims and Christians in South Indian Society, 1700–1900*. Cambridge South Asian Studies 43. Cambridge: Cambridge University Press.

Beatson, Alexander. 1800. *A View of the Origin and Conduct of the War with Tippoo Sultaun*. London: G. and W. Nicol.

Beckett, Alison. 1988. "Sueing Shiva Dismays Dealers." *Times of London*, 21 February, p. 9C.

Benjamin, Walter. 1985. "The Work of Art in the Age of Mechanical Reproduction." In *Illuminations: Essays and Reflections* [1968], pp. 217–51. New York: Schocken Books.

Bhandarkar, D. R. 1925–1926. "Sanjan Plates of Amoghavarsha I." *Epigraphia Indica* 18: 235–57.

Bharati, Shuddhananda. 1968. *Alvar Saints and Acharyas*. Adyar, Madras: Shuddhananda Library.

Bharatiya Janata Party. 1993. *White Paper on Ayodhya & The Rama Temple Movement*. New Delhi: Bharatiya Janata Party.

Birdwood, George C. M. 1884. *The Industrial Arts of India*. South Kensington Museum Art Handbooks, new edition. London: Chapman and Hall.

Bosworth, Clifford Edmund. 1963. *The Ghaznavids: Their Empire in Afghanistan and Eastern Iraq*. Edinburgh: Edinburgh University Press.

———. 1966. "Mahmud of Ghazna in Contemporary Eyes and in Later Persian Literature." *Iran* 4: 85–92.

Bousfield, H. T. W. 1991. "The God with Four Arms." In *The Mammoth Book of Ghost Stories 2*, edited by Richard Dalby, pp. 79–88. New York: Carroll & Graf.

Breckenridge, Carol Appadurai. 1977. "From Protector to Litigant—Changing Relations Between Hindu Temples and the Raja of Ramnad." *Indian Economic and Social History Review* 14: 75–106.

Brewer, J. Norris. 1816. *The Beauties of England and Wales*. London: J. Harris.

Briggs, John, trans. 1966. *History of the Rise of the Mahomedan Power in India till the Year A.D. 1612* [1826]. Calcutta: Editions Indian.

Brittlebank, Kate. 1993. "Curiosities, Conspicuous Piety and the Maker of Time. Some Aspects of Kingship in Eighteenth-Century South India." *South Asia* 16(2): 41–56.

———. 1994. "The Making of a Padshah: Tipu Sultan's Search for Legitimacy in the Context of Eighteenth-Century South India." Ph. D. dissertation, Monash University, Clayton, Victoria, Australia.

———. 1995. "*Sakti* and *Barakat*: The Power of Tipu's Tiger." *Modern Asian Studies* 29(2): 257–69.

Britton, John, and A. Pugin. 1828. *Illustrations of the Public Buildings of London*. 2 vols. London: J. Taylor.

Browne, Edward G., trans. 1921. *Chahar Maqala ("Four Discourses") of Nizam-i-ʿArudi of Samarqand*. E. J. W. Gibb Memorial Publications. London: Cambridge University Press.

Buckler, F. W. 1928. "The Oriental Despot." *Anglican Theological Review* 10(3): 238–49.

Buddle, Anne. 1989. "The Tipu Mania: Narrative Sketches of the Conquest of Mysore." *Marg* 40(4): 53–70.

———. 1990. *Tigers Round the Throne: The Court of Tipu Sultan (1750–1799)*. London: Zamana.

Buhler, Georg. 1936. *The Life of Hemacandrācārya*, translated by Manilal Patel. Santiniketan: Adhisthata Singhi Jaina Jnanapitha.

Bumper Development Corp. Ltd. v Commissioner of Police of the Metropolis and Others (Union of India and others, claimants). 1991. *All England Law Reports* 4: 638–49.

Burgess, James, and Henry Cousens. 1888. *The Antiquities of the Town of Dabhoi in Gujarat*. Edinburgh: George Waterston and Sons.

Campbell, James M. 1896. *Gazetteer of the Bombay Presidency*. Vol. 1, Part 1: *History of Gujarat*. Bombay: Government Central Press.

Carman, John Braisted. 1974. *The Theology of Rāmānuja: An Essay in Interreligious Understanding*. Yale Publications in Religion, 18. New Haven: Yale University Press.

———, and Vasudha Narayanan. 1989. *The Tamil Veda: Piḷḷān's Interpretation of the Tiruvāymoli*. Chicago: University of Chicago Press.

Catlin, Amy. 1991. "'Vātāpi Gaṇapatim': Sculptural, Poetic, and Musical Texts in a Hymn to Gaṇeśa." In *Ganesh: Studies of an Asian God*, edited by Robert L. Brown, pp. 141–69. Albany: State University of New York Press.

Caygill, Marjorie. 1985. *Treasures of the British Museum*. London: British Museum.

Chanda, Ramaprasad. 1935. "'Hindoo' Stuart: A Forgotten Worthy and His Tomb." *Bengal Past and Present* 50: 52–55.

Chanda, Ramaprasad. 1936. *Medieval Indian Sculpture in the British Museum*. London: Kegan Paul, Trench, Trubner.

Chandra, Pramod. 1983. *On the Study of Indian Art*. Cambridge: Harvard University Press.

———. 1985. *The Sculpture of India, 3000 B.C.–1300 A.D.* Washington, D.C.: National Gallery of Art.

Chandramouleeswaran, U. C. 1972. "Idol Thefts: Investigation." *Tamil Nadu Police Journal* 13(3): 116–29.

Chatterjee, Partha. 1986. *Nationalist Discourse and the Colonial World: A Derivative Discourse?* London: Zed Press.

Chengappa, Raj. 1986. "Damaging Display." *India Today*, 30 November, pp. 148–50.

Chidanandamurthy, M. 1973. "The Meaning of 'Pālidhvaja': A Reinterpretation." In *Srikanthika: Dr. S. Srikantha Sastri Felicitation Volume*, pp. 85–88. Mysore: Geetha Book House.

Clifford, James. 1988. *The Predicament of Culture: Twentieth-Century Ethnography, Literature, and Art*. Cambridge: Harvard University Press.

Coccari, Diane M. 1989. "Protection and Identity: Banaras's Bīr Babas as Neighborhood Guardian Deities." In *Culture and Power in Banaras: Community, Performance, and Environment, 1800–1980*, edited by Sandria B. Freitag, pp. 130–46. Berkeley and Los Angeles: University of California Press.

Codrington, K. de B. 1948. "Sculpture." In *The Art of India and Pakistan*, edited by Leigh Ashton, pp. 3–15. London: Faber and Faber Limited.

Cohn, Bernard S. 1983. "Representing Authority in Victorian India." In *The Invention of Tradition*, edited by Eric Hobsbawm and Terence Ranger, pp. 165–209. Past and Present Publications. Cambridge: Cambridge University Press.

———. 1987. "African Models and Indian Histories." In *An Anthropologist among the Historians and Other Essays*, pp. 200–23. Delhi: Oxford University Press.

———. 1992. "The Transformation of Objects into Artifacts, Antiquities and Art in Nineteenth-Century India." In *The Powers of Art: Patronage in Indian Culture*, edited by Barbara Stoler Miller, pp. 301–29. Delhi: Oxford University Press.

Collins, Wilkie. 1944. *The Moonstone*. Garden City, New York: Doubleday, Doran.

Coomaraswamy, Ananda Kentish. 1928–1931. *Yakṣas*. Smithsonian Miscellaneous Collections. 2 vols. Washington, D.C.: Smithsonian Institution.

Cotton, H. E. A. 1923. "The Editor's Notebook." *Bengal Past and Present* 25(2): 170–76.

Cousens, Henry. 1931. *Somanātha and Other Mediaeval Temples in Kathiawad*. Archaeological Survey of India, Imperial Series, vol. 45. Calcutta: Government of India.

Crocker, B. M. 1905. "The Little Brass God." In *The Old Cantonment with Other Stories of India and Elsewhere*, pp. 51–65. Collection of British Authors. Leipzig: Bernhard Tauchnitz.

Cutler, Norman. 1987. *Songs of Experience: The Poetics of Tamil Devotion*. Religion in Asia and Africa. Bloomington: Indiana University Press.

Dagens, Bruno. 1984. *Architecture in the Ajitāgama and the Rauravāgama*. New Delhi: Sitaram Bhartia Institute of Scientific Research.

Darke, Hubert, trans. 1960. *The Book of Government, or Rules for Kings*. New Haven: Yale University Press.

Das, Manmath Nath. 1964. "Transmission of Koh-i-noor from Lahore to London." *Journal of Indian History* 42: 699–706.

Dave, J. H.; C. L. Gheewala; A. C. Bose; R. P. Aiyer; and A. K. Majumdar, eds. 1962. *Munshi: His Art and Work*. 4 vols. Bombay: Bharatiya Vidya Bhavan.

Davis, Richard H. 1991. *Ritual in an Oscillating Universe: Worshiping Śiva in Medieval India*. Princeton: Princeton University Press.

———. 1992. "Loss and Recovery of Ritual Self among Hindu Images." *Journal of Ritual Studies* 6(1): 43–61.

———. 1994. "Three Styles in Looting India." *History and Anthropology*. 6: 293–317.

———. 1996. "The Iconography of Ram's Chariot." In *Contesting the Nation: Religion, Community and the Politics of Democracy in India*, edited by David Ludden, pp. 27–54. Philadelphia: University of Pennsylvania Press.

De, B., trans. 1913. *The Tabakat-i-Akbari (or A History of India from the Early Musalman Invasions to the Thirty-sixth Year of the Reign of Akbar) of Khwajah Nizamuddin Ahmad*. Bibliotheca Indica, n.s. 225. Calcutta: Baptist Mission Press.

Desai, Devangana. 1992. "The Patronage of the Lakshmaṇa Temple at Khajuraho." In *The Powers of Art: Patronage in Indian Culture*, edited by Barbara Stoler Miller, pp. 78–85. Delhi: Oxford University Press.

Desai, Shambhuprasad Harprasad. 1975. *Prabhas and Somnath*. Junagadh: Sorath Research Society.

Desai, Vishakha N. 1993. "Beyond the Temple Walls: The Scholarly Fate of North Indian Sculpture, A.D. 700–1200." In *Gods, Guardians, and Lovers: Temple Sculptures from North India, A.D. 700–1200*, edited by Vishakha N. Desai and Darielle Mason, pp. 19–31. New York: Asia Society Galleries.

De Slane, William MacGuckin, Baron, trans. 1842–1871. *Ibn Khallikan's Biographical Dictionary*. 4 vols. Paris: Oriental Translation Fund of Great Britain and Ireland.

Desmond, Ray. 1982. *The India Museum, 1801–1879*. London: Her Majesty's Stationery Office.

Dhaky, M. A., and H. P. Shastri. 1974. *The Riddle of the Temple of Somanātha*. Indian Art Monograph 1. Varanasi: Bharata Manisha.

Dirks, Nicholas B. 1987. *The Hollow Crown: Ethnohistory of an Indian Kingdom*. Cambridge: Cambridge University Press.

Dow, Alexander, trans. 1770. *The History of Hindostan*. London: S. Beckert & P. A. de Hondt.

East India Company. 1800a. "Description of Various Articles Found in the Palace at Seringapatam, and Sent to England as Presents to the Royal Family, and to the Court of Directors of the East India Company." *Asiatic Annual Register* 2:338–44. London: J. Debrett.

East India Company. 1800b. *Copies and Extracts of Articles to and from India, Relative to the Cause, Progress, and Successful Termination of the War with the Late Tippoo Sultaun.* London: East India Company.

Edwards, A. Hart, trans. 1911. *The Bustān of Sadi.* Wisdom of the East. London: John Murray.

Elliot, H. M., and John Dowson, trans. 1867. *The History of India as Told by Its Own Historians: The Muhammadan Period.* 7 vols. London: Trubner and Company.

Entwistle, Alen W. 1987. *Braj: Centre of Krishna Pilgrimage.* Groningen Oriental Studies, vol. 3. Groningen: Egbert Forsten.

Ernst, Carl W. 1992. *Eternal Garden: Mysticism, History, and Politics at a South Asian Sufi Center.* Albany: State University of New York Press.

———. 1995. "India as a Sacred Islamic Land." In *Religions of India in Practice,* edited by Donald S. Lopez, pp. 556–63. Princeton: Princeton University Press.

Falk, Toby, and Mildred Archer. 1981. *Indian Miniatures in the India Office Library.* London: Sotheby Parke Bernet.

Faris, Nabih Amin, trans. 1952. *The Book of Idols: Being a Translation from the Arabic of the Kitāb al-Aṣnām by Hishām ibn-al-Kalbī.* Princeton Oriental Studies, vol. 14. Princeton: Princeton University Press.

Fisch, Jorg. 1984. "A Solitary Vindicator of the Hindus: The Life and Writings of General Charles Stuart (1757/58–1828)." *Journal of the Royal Asiatic Society of Great Britain and Ireland,* pp. 35–57.

Fish, Stanley. 1980. *Is There a Text in this Class? The Authority of Interpretive Communities.* Cambridge: Harvard University Press.

———. 1989. *Doing What Comes Naturally: Change, Rhetoric, and the Practice of Theory in Literary and Legal Studies.* Durham: Duke University Press.

Fleet, J. F. 1883. "Sanskrit and Old Canarese Inscriptions, No. 127." *Indian Antiquary* 12: 156–65.

———. 1889. "Sanskrit and Old-Kanarese Inscriptions [Vizagapatam Grants]." *Indian Antiquary* 18: 161–76.

Forbes, James. 1813. *Oriental Memoirs: Selected and Abridged from a Series of Familiar Letters Written during Seventeen Years Residence in India.* 4 vols. London: White, Cochrane, and Co.

Forrest, Denys. 1970. *Tiger of Mysore: The Life and Death of Tipu Sultan.* London: Chatto & Windus.

Foster, William. 1906. *A Descriptive Catalogue of the Paintings, Statues, &c. in the India Office.* 3rd ed. London: Eyre and Spottiswoode.

———. 1910. *The English Factories in India, 1630–1633.* Oxford: Clarendon Press.

Freedberg, David. 1989. *The Power of Images: Studies in the History and Theory of Response.* Chicago: University of Chicago Press.

Friedmann, Yohanan. 1972. "The Temple of Multan: A Note on Early Muslim Attitudes to Idolatry." *Israel Oriental Studies* 2: 176–82.

———. 1975. "Medieval Muslim Views of Indian Religions." *Journal of the American Oriental Society* 95: 214–21.

Geiger, Wilhelm. 1960. *Culture of Ceylon in Mediaeval Times*. Wiesbaden: Otto Harrassowitz.

Gibb, H. A. R.; J. H. Kramers; E. Levi-Provencal; and J. Schacht, eds. 1960. *The Encyclopedia of Islam*. 7 vols. so far. Leiden: E. J. Brill.

Gibbon, Edward. 1783. *The History of the Decline and Fall of the Roman Empire*. 12 vols. London: W. Strahan & T. Cadell.

Gladstone, W. E. 1841. *The State in its Relation with the Church*. 2 vols. London: John Murray.

Glueck, Grace. 1974. "Simon and India: Battle on Idol Widens." *New York Times*, 30 December, p. 36.

Godrej, Pheroza, and Pauline Rohatgi. 1989. *Scenic Splendours: India through the Printed Image*. London: British Library.

Goetz, Hermann. 1974. "The Kailasa of Ellora and the Chronology of Rashtrakuta Art." In *Studies in the History, Religion and Art of Classical and Medieval India*, pp. 91–107. Wiesbaden: Franz Steiner Verlag.

Goloubew, Victor. 1932. "La temple de la dent à Kandy." *Bulletin de l'Ecole Française de l'Extrême-Orient* 32: 441–74.

Gopal, Sarvepalli, ed. 1990. *Anatomy of a Confrontation: The Babri-Masjid-Ramjanmabhumi Issue*. New Delhi: Penguin.

Govindacharya, Alkondaville. 1906. *The Life of Rāmānujāchārya*. Madras: S. Murthy.

Goyal, Shriram. 1967. *A History of the Imperial Guptas*. Allahabad: Central Book Depot.

Grabar, Oleg. 1987. *The Formation of Islamic Art*. Revised edition. New Haven: Yale University Press.

Granoff, Phyllis. 1989. "The Biographies of Siddhasena: A Study in the Texture of Allusion and the Weaving of a Group-Image." *Journal of Indian Philosophy* 17: 329 84 and 18: 261–304.

———. 1991a. "Tales of Broken Limbs and Bleeding Wounds: Responses to Muslim Iconoclasm in Medieval India." *East and West* 41: 189–203.

———. 1991b. "When Miracles Become Too Many: Stories of the Destruction of Holy Sites in the Tāpī Khaṇḍa of the *Skanda Purāṇa*." Paper at the annual meeting of the Association for Asian Studies. New Orleans.

———. 1992. "Jinaprabhasūri and Jinadattasūri: Two Studies from the Śvetāmbara Jain Tradition." In *Speaking of Monks: Religious Biography in India and China*, edited by Phyllis Granoff and Koichi Shinohara, pp. 1–96. Oakville, Ontario: Mosaic Press.

———. 1993. "Halāyudha's Prism: The Experience of Religion in Medieval Hymns and Stories." In *Gods, Guardians, and Lovers: Temple Sculptures from North India, A.D. 700–1200*, edited by Vishakha N. Desai and Darielle Mason, pp. 66–93. New York: Asia Society Galleries.

———. 1994. "The Jina Bleeds: Threats to the Faith and the Rescue of the Faithful in Medieval Jain Stories." Unpublished essay, Macmaster University, Hamilton, Ontario.

Greenblatt, Stephen. 1991. "Resonance and Wonder." In *Exhibiting Culture: The Poetics and Politics of Museum Display*, edited by Ivan Karp and Steven D. Lavine, pp. 42–56. Washington, D.C.: Smithsonian Institution Press.

Greenfield, Jeanette. 1989. *The Return of Cultural Treasures*. Cambridge: Cambridge University Press.

Gregorian, Raffi. 1990. "Unfit for Service: British Law and Looting in India in the Mid-Nineteenth Century." *South Asia* 13: 63–84.

Guha-Thakurta, Tapati. 1992. *The Making of a New "Indian" Art: Artists, Aesthetics and Nationalism in Bengal, c. 1850–1920*. Cambridge South Asian Studies, no. 52. Cambridge: Cambridge University Press.

Gunawardana, R. A. L. H. 1979. *Robe and Plough: Monasticism and Economic Interest in Early Medieval Sri Lanka*. Association for Asian Studies: Monographs and Papers. Tucson: University of Arizona Press.

Gupta, Parmeshwari Lal. 1961–1962. "Nesarika Grant of Govinda III, Śaka 727." *Epigraphia Indica* 34: 123–34.

Gurwood, Lieutenant-Colonel, ed. 1842. *Selections from the Dispatches and General Orders of Field Marshal the Duke of Wellington*. London: John Murray.

Habib, Mohammad. 1967. *Sultan Mahmud of Ghaznin*. Delhi: S. Chand.

———, and Mrs. Afsar Umar Salim Khan. 1961. *The Political Theory of the Delhi Sultanate (Including a Translation of Ziauddin Barani's Fatawa-i Jahandari, Circa 1358–9 A.D.)*. Allahabad: Kitab Mahal.

Habib, Muhammad, trans. 1931. *The Campaigns of ʿAlāʾuʾd-dīn Khiljī, Being the Khazāʾinul Fuṭūh (Treasures of Victory) of Hazrat Amīr Khusrau*. Bombay: D. B. Taraporewala Sons.

Halbertal, Moshe, and Avishai Margalit. 1992. *Idolatry*, translated by Naomi Goldblum. Cambridge: Harvard University Press.

Haldar, Rakhaldas. 1903. *The English Diary of an Indian Student, 1861–62*. Dacca: The Asutosh Library.

Hardy, Friedhelm. 1983. *Viraha-Bhakti: The Early History of Kṛṣṇa Devotion in South India*. Delhi: Oxford University Press.

Hardy, Peter. 1960. *Historians of Medieval India*. London: Luzac and Company.

———. 1962. "Mahmud of Ghazna and the Historian." *Journal of the Panjab University Historical Society* 14 (December): 1–36.

Hardy, Thomas. 1976. *The Complete Poems of Thomas Hardy*, edited by James Gibson. London: Macmillan.

Hari Rao, V. N. 1976. *History of the Śrīrangam Temple*. Sri Venkateswara University Historical Series. Tirupati: Sri Venkateswara University.

Harle, J. C. 1987. "The Hedges Visnu." In *Investigating Indian Art*, edited by Marianne Valdiz and Wibke Lobo, pp. 121–31. Veröffentlichungen des Museums für Indische Kunst, vol. 8. Berlin: Museum für Indische Kunst.

Harle, J. C., and Andrew Topsfield. 1987. *Indian Art in the Ashmolean Museum*. Oxford: Ashmolean Museum.

Hart, George L., III. 1975. *The Poems of Ancient Tamil: Their Milieu and Their Sanskrit Counterparts*. Berkeley and Los Angeles: University of California Press.

Havell, E. B. 1908. *Indian Sculpture and Painting*. London: John Murray.

Hawley, John Stratton, and Mark Juergensmeyer. 1988. *Songs of the Saints of India*. New York: Oxford University Press.

Hayavadana Rao, C., ed. 1927–1930. *Mysore Gazetteer*. 5 vols. Bangalore: Government Press.

Hess, Linda, and Shukdev Singh, trans. 1983. *The Bījak of Kabir*. San Francisco: North Point Press.

Hitchens, Christopher. 1987. *The Elgin Marbles: Should They be Returned to Greece?* London: Chatto and Windus.

Hocart, Arthur Maurice, ed. 1924. *Memoirs of the Archaeological Survey of Ceylon*, vol. 1. Colombo: Government Printer.

———. 1970. *Kings and Councillors: An Essay in the Comparative Anatomy of Human Society*. Classics in Anthropology. Chicago: University of Chicago Press.

Hopkirk, Peter. 1973. "Siva Was Smuggled into America." *Times of London*, 14 May.

Hultzsch, E. 1892. "Inscriptions of the Tanjavur Temple." *South Indian Inscriptions* 2: 1–14.

———. 1894–1895. "Ranganatha Inscription of Sundara-Pandya." *Epigraphia Indica* 3: 7–17.

———. 1896–1897. "Pithapuram Pillar Inscription of Mallapadeva: Śaka-Saṁvat 1124." *Epigraphia Indica* 4: 226–42.

———. 1899. *South Indian Inscriptions* 3.

———. 1900–1901. "Ranganatha inscription of Goppana; Śaka-Saṁvat 1293." *Epigraphia Indica* 6: 322–30.

Husain, Agha Mahdi, trans. 1967. *Futūḥu's Salāṭīn or Shāh Nāmah-i Hind of ʿIṣāmī*. Bombay: Asia Publishing House.

Imlah, Albert H. 1939. *Lord Ellenborough: A Biography of Edward Law, Earl of Ellenborough, Governor-General of India*. Cambridge: Harvard University Press.

Inden, Ronald B. 1978. "Ritual, Authority and Cyclic Time in Hindu Kingship." In *Kingship and Authority in South Asia*, edited by J. F. Richards. Madison: University of Wisconsin South Asian Studies.

———. 1979. "The Ceremony of the Great Gift (*Mahādāna*): Structure and Historical Context in Indian Ritual." In *Asie du sud, traditions et changements*, pp. 131–36. Colloques Internationaux du C.N.R.S. Paris: Editions du C.N.R.S.

———. 1985. "The Temple and the Hindu Great Chain of Being." *Purusartha* 8.

———. 1987. "Administering the God of the Hindoos." Paper at the annual meeting of the American Anthropological Association. Chicago, November.

———. 1990. *Imagining India*. Oxford: Basil Blackwell.

———. 1992. "Changes in the Vedic Priesthood." In *Ritual, State and History in South Asia: Essays in Honour of J. C. Heesterman*, edited by A. W. Van Den Hoek, D. H. A. Kolff, and M. S. Oort, pp. 556–77. Leiden: E. J. Brill.

Inden, Ronald B., and Ralph W. Nicholas. 1977. *Kinship in Bengali Culture*. Chicago: University of Chicago Press.

Inglis, Stephen R. 1995. "Suitable for Framing: The Work of a Modern Master." In *Media and the Transformation of Religion in South Asia*, edited by Lawrence A. Babb and Susan S. Wadley, pp. 51–75. Philadelphia: University of Pennsylvania Press.

Irschick, Eugene F. 1994. *Dialogue and History: Constructing South India, 1795–1895*. Berkeley and Los Angeles: University of California Press.

Jayaswal, K. R., and R. D. Banerji, eds. 1983 [1929–1930]. "The Hathigumpha Inscription of Kharavela." *Epigraphia Indica* 20: 71–89.

Jennings, Sarah. 1996. "Buyer Beware: An International Tale for Collectors." *ARTnewsletter* 21.15 (March 19): 6.

Kaye, John William. 1851. *History of the War in Afghanistan*. 2 vols. London: Richard Bentley.

Khadduri, Majid. 1955. *War and Peace in the Law of Islam*. Baltimore: Johns Hopkins Press.

Khare, G. H. 1936. "Krishnadevaraya of Vijayanagara and the Vitthala Image of Pandharpur." In *Vijayanagara Sexcentenary Commemoration Volume*, pp. 191–96. Dharwar: Vijayanagara Empire Sexcentenary Association.

Kielhorn, F. 1892. "Inscriptions from Khajuraho." *Epigraphia Indica* 1: 121–52.

King, Major J. S., trans. 1899. "History of the Bahmani Dynasty." *Indian Antiquary* 28: 119–38, 141–55, 180–92, 209–19, 235–47, 277–92, 305–23.

Knox, Robert. 1992. *Amaravati: Buddhist Sculpture from the Great Stupa*. London: British Museum Press.

Kopytoff, Igor. 1986. "The Cultural Biography of Things: Commoditization as Process." In *The Social Life of Things: Commodities in Cultural Perspective*, edited by Arjun Appadurai, pp. 64–91. Cambridge: Cambridge University Press.

Kowalska, Maria. 1967. "The Sources of al-Qazwīnī's Āthār al-Bilād." *Folia Orientalia* 8: 41–88.

Kramrisch, Stella. 1976. *The Hindu Temple*. First published 1946. 2 vols. Delhi: Motilal Banarsidass.

Krishna Sastri, H. 1912. "The Second Vijayanagar Dynasty; Its Viceroys and Ministers." In *Annual Report, Archaeological Survey of India, 1908–09*. Calcutta: Government Printing.

———. 1920. "The Tiruvalangadu Copper-Plates of the Sixth Year of Rajendra-Chola I." *South Indian Inscriptions* 3: 385–439.

———. 1923. *South Indian Inscriptions* 4.

Krishnan, K. G. 1984. *Karandai Tamil Sangam Plates of Rajendrachola I*. Memoirs of the Archaeological Survey of India, no. 79. Delhi: Archaeological Survey of India.

Krishnaswami, A. 1964. *The Tamil Country under Vijayanagar*. Annamalai University Historical Series, no. 20. Annamalainagar: Annamalai University.

Krisnaswami Ayyangar, S. 1919. *Sources of Vijayanagar History*. Madras University Historical Series. Madras: University of Madras.

———. 1936. "The Character and Significance of the Empire of Vijayanagara in

Indian History." In *Vijayanagara Sexcentenary Commemoration Volume*, pp. 1–28. Dharwar: Vijayanagara Empire Sexcentenary Association.

———. 1940–1941. *A History of Tirupati*. 2 vols. Madras: Tirumalai-Tirupati Devastanam Committee.

———. 1971. *South India and Her Muhammadan Invaders*. New Delhi: S. Chand.

Kulke, Hermann. 1979. "Geschictsschreibung und Geschichtsbild im hinduistischen Mittelalter." *Saeculum* 30: 100–12.

———. 1986a. "Early Royal Patronage of the Jagannatha Cult." In *The Cult of Jagannatha and the Regional Tradition of Orissa*, edited by Anncharlott Eschmann, Hermann Kulke, and Gaya Charan Tripathi, pp. 139–55. South Asia Institute, Heidelberg University, South Asian Studies. New Delhi: Manohar Publications.

———. 1986b. "'Juggernaut' under British Supremacy and the Resurgence of the Khurda-Rajas as 'Rajas of Puri.'" In *The Cult of Jagannath and the Regional Tradition of Orissa*, pp. 345–57.

———. 1986c. "The Struggle between the Rajas of Khurda and the Muslim Subadars of Cuttack for Dominance of the Jagannatha Cult." In *The Cult of Jagannath and the Regional Tradition of Orissa*, pp. 321–42.

Law, Algernon, ed. 1926. *India under Lord Ellenborough, March 1842–June 1844*. London: John Murray.

Levy, Reuben, trans. 1951. *A Mirror for Princes: The Qābūs Nāma by Kai Kā'ūs ibn Iskandar*. London: Cresset Press.

Longhurst, A. H. 1916–1917. "Udayagiri Fort and Temple, Nellore District; The Krishna Temple at Vijayanagar." In *Annual Report of the Archaeological Department, Southern Circle, Madras, 1916–17*, pp. 22–30. Madras: Government Press.

Ludden, David, ed. 1996. *Contesting the Nation: Religion, Community and the Politics of Democracy in India*. Philadelphia: University of Pennsylvania Press.

Macaulay, Thomas Babington. 1871. "The Gates of Somnauth." In *The Miscellaneous Writings and Speeches of Lord Macaulay*, pp. 630–41. London: Longmans, Green, Reader, and Dyer.

MacGregor, Arthur. 1989. "Sports, Games and Pastimes of the Early Stuarts." In *The Late King's Goods: Collections, Possessions and Patronage of Charles I in the Light of the Commonwealth Sale Inventories*, edited by Arthur MacGregor, pp. 403–21. London: Oxford University Press.

Mahalingam, T. V. 1940. *Administration and Social Life under Vijayanagar*. Madras: University of Madras.

Malcolm, John. 1823. *A Memoir of Central India, Including Malwa and Adjoining Provinces*. 2 vols. London: Kingsbury, Parbury, & Allen.

Mann, Phyllis G. 1957. "Keats's Indian Allegory." *Keats-Shelley Journal* 6: 4–9.

Masson, Charles. 1842. *Narrative of Various Journeys in Baluchistan, Afghanistan and The Panjab*. 3 vols. Karachi: Oxford University Press. Reprinted 1974.

Mayhew, Arthur. 1988. *Christianity in India*. Delhi: Gian Publishing House.

Mayo, John Horsley. 1897. *Medals and Decorations of the British Army and Navy*. 2 vols. Westminster: Archibald Constable and Co.

Meister, Michael. 1981. "Display as Structure and Revelation: On Seeing the Shiva Exhibition." *Studies in Visual Communication* 7(4): 84–89.

Michell, George. 1994. "Revivalism as the Imperial Mode: Religious Architecture During the Vijayanagara Period." In *Perceptions of South Asia's Visual Past*, edited by Catherine B. Asher and Thomas R. Metcalf, pp. 187–97. New Delhi: American Institute of Indian Studies.

Michell, George, Catherine Lampert, and Tristram Holland, eds. 1982. *In The Image of Man*. London: Weidenfeld and Nicolson.

Mill, James. 1826. *The History of British India*. London: Baldwin, Cradock, & Joy.

Millar, Oliver. 1960. *Abraham van der Doort's Catalogue of the Collections of Charles I*. Glasgow: Walpole Society.

———. 1972. *The Inventories and Valuations of the King's Goods, 1649–1651*. Glasgow: Walpole Society.

Miller, Thomas. 1852. *Picturesque Sketches of London*. London: Office of the National Illustrated Library.

Mirashi, V. V. 1955. "Bilhari Stone Inscription of Yuvarajadeva II." *Corpus Inscriptionum Indicarum* 4: 204–24.

Mitra, Rajendralala. 1880. *The Antiquities of Orissa*. 2 vols. Calcutta: W. Newman & Co.

Mitter, Partha. 1977. *Much Maligned Monsters: History of European Reactions to Indian Art*. Oxford: Clarendon Press.

Mogridge, George. N.d. *Old Humphrey's Walks in London and Its Neighbourhood*. London: Religious Tract Society.

Mudaliar, Chandra Y. 1974. *The Secular State and Religious Institutions in India: A Study of the Administration of Hindu Public Religious Trusts in Madras*. Wiesbaden: Franz Steiner Verlag.

Mukherjea, Bijan Kumar. 1952. *The Hindu Law of Religious and Charitable Trust*. Calcutta: Eastern Law House Ltd.

Mulla, Dinshah Fardunji. 1929. *Principles of Hindu Law*. 6th ed. Bombay: J. M. Pandia.

Mullens, Joseph. 1862. *Brief Memorials of the Rev. Alphonse Francois Lacroix*. London: James Nisbet.

Munshi, Kanaiyalal Maneklel. 1976. *Somanātha, the Shrine Eternal*. 4th ed. Bombay: Bharatiya Vidya Bhavan.

"Museum Preparing for Return of Indian Bronze." 1984. *Stolen Art Alert* 5.2 (March): 3.

Nagaswamy, R. 1959–1960. "New Bronze Finds from Tiruvenkādu." *Transactions of the Archaeological Society of South India* 5: 109–22.

———. 1970. *Gangaikondacholapuram*. Madras: Tamilnadu State Department of Archaeology.

———. 1982. "Nallur Bronzes." *Lalit Kala* 20: 9–11.

———. 1983. *Masterpieces of Early South Indian Bronzes*. New Delhi: National Museum.

———. 1987. "Archaeological Finds in South India: Esālam Bronzes and Copper-Plates." *Bulletin de l'Ecole Française de l'Extrême-Orient* 76: 1–68.

Narasimhaswamy, H. K., ed. 1982. *South Indian Inscriptions, Vol. XXIV (Inscriptions of the Raṅganāthasvāmi Temple, Śrīraṅgam)*. New Delhi: Archaeology Survey of India.

Narayanan, Vasudha. 1985. "Arcāvatāra: On Earth as He Is in Heaven." In *Gods of Flesh/Gods of Stone: The Embodiment of Divinity in India*, edited by Joanne Punzo Waghorne and Norman Cutler, pp. 53–66. Chambersburg, Pennsylvania: Anima Publications.

———. 1987. *The Way and the Goal: Expressions of Devotion in the Early Śrī Vaiṣṇava Tradition*. Washington, D.C.: Institute for Vaishnava Studies.

"Nataraja's Sojourn to U.K. and Back." 1991. *Times of India*, 10 August, p. 11.

Nath, R. 1996. "Śrī Govindadeva's Itinerary from Vṛndāvana to Jayapura c. 1534–1727." In *Govindadeva: A Dialogue in Stone*, edited by Margaret H. Case, pp. 161–83. Delhi: Indira Gandhi National Centre for the Arts.

Nathan, Leonard, and Clinton Seely, trans. 1982. *Grace and Mercy in Her Wild Hair: Selected Poems to the Mother Goddess*. Boulder: Great Eastern.

Nazim, Muhammad. 1931. *The Life and Times of Sulṭān Maḥmūd of Ghazna*. Cambridge: Cambridge University Press.

Nehru, Jawaharlal. 1994. *Selected Works of Jawaharlal Nehru*. Second series. Edited by S. Gopal, 16: 603–12. New Delhi: Jawaharlal Nehru Memorial Fund.

Nelson, J. H. 1868. *The Madura Country: A Manual*. Madras: Asylum Press.

Newman, Robert. 1986. *The Case of the Indian Curse*. New York: Atheneum.

Nilakanta Sastri, K. A. 1955. *The Colas*. 2nd ed. Madras: University of Madras. Reprinted 1984.

———. 1966. *A History of South India from Prehistoric Times to the Fall of Vijayanagar*. 4th ed. Madras: Oxford University Press.

———. 1972. *The Pāṇḍyan Kingdom from the Earliest Times to the Sixteenth Century*. Madras: Swathi Publications.

Nilakanta Sastri, K. A., and N. Venkataramanayya. 1946. *Further Sources of Vijayanagara History*. 3 vols. Madras: University of Madras.

Orr, Leslie. 1995a. "Retrospective Realities: Community and Leadership in a Medieval Hindu Temple." Lecture, Canadian Society for the Study of Religion. 2 June.

———. 1995b. "The Vaiṣṇava Community at Śrīraṅgam in the Early Medieval Period." *Journal of Vaiṣṇava Studies* 3(3): 109–36.

Palaniappan, T. K. 1982. "An Year of Progress." In S. Rathnasabapathy, *The Thanjavur Art Gallery Bronze Sculptures*. Thanjavur: Thanjavur Art Gallery Administration.

Palnitkar, Milind. 1995. "Temple Sues on Behalf of Deities." *India Abroad*, 14 April, p. 40.

Pandey, Gyanendra. 1990. *The Construction of Communalism in Colonial North India*. Delhi: Oxford University Press.

Parekh, Mrs. Kulsum. 1954. "Some Controversial Points in the History of the Temple of Somnath." *Islamic Culture* 28: 287–96.

Parker, Samuel K. 1987. "Structure, History and Creativity in the Visual Arts: The Sarnath Asokan Pillar." Unpublished essay, University of Chicago.

———. 1992. "Contemporary Temple Construction in South India: the Srirangam *Rajagopuram*." *Res* 21: 110–23.

Parsons, Denys. 1979. "Tipu's Tiger." *Antique Machines and Curiosities* 1(2): 47–48.

Pathak, K. B. 1907–1908. "Kendur Plates of Kirtivarman II." *Epigraphia Indica* 9: 200–6.

———. 1909–1910. "Rayagad Plates of Vijayaditya." *Epigraphia Indica* 10: 14–17.

Pathak, Vishwambhar Sharan. 1966. *Ancient Historians of India: A Study in Historical Biographies*. Bombay: Asia Publishing House.

"Pathur Nataraja restored to TN." 1991. *Indian Express*, 10 August, p. 7.

Peabody, Norbert. 1991. "In Whose Turban Does the Lord Reside?: The Objectification of Charisma and the Fetishism of Objects in the Hindu Kingdom of Kota." *Comparative Studies in Society and History* 33(4): 726–54.

Peterson, Indira Viswanathan. 1989. *Poems to Śiva: The Hymns of the Tamil Saints*. Princeton Library of Asian Translations. Princeton: Princeton University Press.

Peterson, Peter. 1895. "Stone-Inscription of the Temple of Bhadrakālī at Prabhās Pātana of the Time of King Kumārapāla." In *A Collection of Prakrit and Sanskrit Inscriptions*, pp. 186–93. Bhavnagar: Bhavnagar Archaeological Department.

Phukan, Shantanu. 1989. "From the Idol to the Icon: The Transformation in the Pratimā Pratiṣṭhāna Ceremony." Unpublished essay, University of Chicago.

Pichard, Pierre; Françoise l'Hernault; Françoise Boudignon; and L. Thyagarajan. 1994. *Vingt ans après Tanjavur, Gangaikondacholapuram*. Mémoires archéologiques 20. 2 vols. Paris: Ecole Française d'Extrême-Orient.

Platt, J. C. 1843. "The East India House." In *London*, edited by Charles Knight, 5: 49–64. London: Charles Knight & Company.

Pollock, Sheldon. 1993. "Rāmāyaṇa and Political Imagination in India." *Journal of Asian Studies* 52(2): 261–97.

Pope, G. U., trans. 1900. *The Tiruvācagam or "Sacred Utterances" of the Tamil Poet, Saint, and Sage Māṇikka-vācagar*. Oxford: Clarendon Press.

Postens, Lieutenant. 1838. "Notes of a Journey to Girnār in the Province of Kattywār, for the purpose of copying the ancient inscriptions upon the rock near that place." *Journal of the Asiatic Society of Bengal* 7: 865–82.

Prakash, Gyan. 1990. "Writing Post-Orientalist Histories of the Third World: Perspectives from Indian Historiography." *Comparative Studies of Society and History* 32: 383–408.

Price, Major David. 1839. *Memoirs of the Early Life and Service of a Field Officer*. London: J. Loder.

Price, Sally. 1989. *Primitive Art in Civilized Places*. Chicago: University of Chicago Press.

Prinsep, James. 1838a. "Note on Somnāth." *Journal of the Asiatic Society of Bengal* 7: 883–87.

———. 1838b. "Translation of Inscription in the Society's Museum." *Journal of the Asiatic Society of Bengal* 7: 557–62.

Quennell, Peter, trans. 1929. *The Book of the Marvels of India*. Golden Dragon Library. New York: Dial Press.

Rabe, Michael. 1995. "Royal Temple Dedications." In *Religions of India in Practice*, edited by Donald S. Lopez, pp. 235–43. Princeton Readings in Religion. Princeton: Princeton University Press.

Raghunathan, K., and R. Parthasarathy. 1991. "The Untold Story . . . the Men Who Got the Icon Back." *The Hindu*, 18 August.

Rajaguru, Satyanarayana. 1961. *Inscriptions of Orissa (c. 1045–1190 A.D.)*. Bhubaneswar: Sri Gauri Kumar Brahma.

Rajasekharan Nair, K. K. 1982. "Around the World in Search of Stolen Idols." *Indian Police Journal*, pp. 7–10.

Ramachandran, T. N. 1954. "The Nāgapaṭṭinam and Other Buddhist Bronzes in the Madras Museum." *Bulletin of the Madras Government Museum* n.s. 7: 1–150.

———. 1956–1957. "Bronze Images from Tiruvenkatu-Śvetāraṇya (Tanjore District)." *Lalit Kala* 3–4: 55–62.

Ramamurti, C. V. 1896–1897. "Nadagam Plates of Vajrahasta; Śaka-Saṃvat 979." *Epigraphia Indica* 4: 183–93.

Raman, K. V. 1975. *Śrī Varadarājaswāmi Temple—Kanchi: A Study of Its History, Art and Architecture*. New Delhi: Abhinav Publications.

Ramanujan, A. K., trans. 1973. *Speaking of Śiva*. London: Penguin Books.

———, trans. 1981. *Hymns for the Drowning: Poems for Viṣṇu by Nammāḻvār*. Princeton Library of Asian Translations. Princeton: Princeton University Press.

———. 1982. "On Woman Saints." In *The Divine Consort: Radha and the Goddesses of India*, edited by John Stratton Hawley and Donna Marie Wulff, pp. 316–24. Boston: Beacon Press.

Ranking, George S. A., trans. 1898. *Muntakhabu-t-Tawārīkh by ʿAbdu-l-Qādir Ibn-i-Mulūk Shāh known as al-Badāonī*. Bibliotheca Indica, vol. 97. Calcutta: Baptist Mission Press.

Rathnasabapathy, S. 1982. *The Thanjavur Art Gallery Bronze Sculptures*. Thanjavur: Thanjavur Art Gallery Administration.

Raverty, Major H. G., trans. 1881. *Tabakāt-i-Nāṣirī: A General History of the Muḥammadan Dynasties of Asia, Including Hindūstān*. Bibliotheca Indica, vol. 78. 2 vols. London: Gilbert & Rivington.

Rawlinson, George. 1898. *A Memoir of Major-General Sir Henry Creswicke Rawlinson*. New York: Longmans, Green.

Reynolds, James, trans. 1858. *The Kitab-i-Yamini: Historical Memoirs of the Amīr Sabaktagīn, and the Sultān Mahmūd of Ghazna*. London: Oriental Translation Fund of Great Britain and Ireland.

Reynolds, Juliet. 1989. "Captive Beauty." *The Spectator*, 2 September.

Richards, J. F. 1974. "The Islamic Frontier in the East: Expansion into South Asia." *South Asia* 4: 91–109.

Robbins, Kenneth X. 1985. "The Sculpture of India, 3000 B.C.–1300 A.D." *Arts of Asia* 15.5: 100–9.

Roebuck, Thomas. 1819. *The Annals of the College of Fort William*. Calcutta: Hindoostanee Press.

Rogers, J. M. 1973. "The 11th Century—A Turning Point in the Architecture of the *Mashriq*?" In *Islamic Civilization, 950–1150*, edited by D. S. Richards, pp. 211–49. Oxford: Bruno Cassirer Ltd.

Rosenthal, Franz, trans. 1958. *The Muqaddimah: An Introduction to History*. Bollingen Series 43. 3 vols. New York: Pantheon Books.

"Row Over Ownership of Nataraja Idol Ends." 1991. *The Hindu*. 25 May.

Roy, Sourindranath. 1953. "Indian Archaeology from Jones to Marshall (1784–1902)." *Ancient India* 9: 4–28.

Royal Society of Arts. 1910. "Proceedings of the Society: Indian Section, Thursday Afternoon, January 13th." *Journal of the Royal Society of Arts* 58 (4 February): 273–98.

Rubin, William. 1984. "Modernist Primitivism: An Introduction." In *"Primitivism" in 20th Century Art: Affinity of the Tribal and the Modern*, vol. 1, edited by William Rubin, pp. 1–81. New York: Museum of Modern Art.

Sachau, Edward C., trans. 1964. *Alberuni's India*. 2 vols. Delhi: S. Chand.

Salisbury, G. A. 1909. *Story of a Shrine, or the Legend of Srirangam*. Trichinopoly: Southern Star Press.

Sanders, E., C. Blood, J. Stoddart, and C. F. North. 1843. "Report of a Committee Assembled by Order of Major General Nott, to Report on the State of the Gates Brought from Ghuznee." *Journal of the Asiatic Society of Bengal* 12: 73–78.

Sanderson, G. J. S. 1986. "Report on the Evidence of Traditional Sanskrit Sources Concerning the Conditions under which a Hindu Idol Is or Is Not a Deity, With Reference to the Idols of the Viswanatha Swamy Temple in Tamilnadu." Unpublished report. London.

Sauvaget, Jean, trans. 1954. "Les merveilles de l'Inde." In *Memorial Jean Sauvaget*, edited by H. Laoust, pp. 187–309. Damascus: Institut Français de Damas.

Scerrato, Umberto. 1959. "Summary Report of the Italian Archaeological Mission in Afghanistan. 2. The Two First Excavation Campaigns at Ghazni, 1957–8." *East and West* 10: 23–55.

Schimmel, Annemarie. 1992. *A Two-Colored Brocade: The Imagery of Persian Poetry*. Chapel Hill: University of North Carolina Press.

Schwindler, Gary. 1976. "The Dating of South Indian Metal Sculptures." Ph.D. dissertation, University of California, Los Angeles, California.

Sharma, Dasharatha. 1969. "Some New Light on the Route of Mahmud Ghaznavī's Raid on Somanatha." In *Dr. Satkari Mookerji Felicitation Volume*, edited by B. P. Sinha et al., pp. 165–68. Chowkhamba Sanskrit Series, vol. 69. Varanasi: Chowkhamba Sanskrit Series Office.

———. 1975. *Early Chauhan Dynasties*. 2nd ed. Delhi: Motilal Banarsidass.

Shinohara, Koichi. 1994. "Changing Roles for Miraculous Images in Medieval Chinese Buddhism: A Study of the Miracle Image Section in Daoxuan's *Ji shenhou sanbao gantonglu*." Unpublished essay, McMaster University.

Shulman, David Dean. 1980. *Tamil Temple Myths: Sacrifice and Divine Marriage in the South Indian Śaiva Tradition*. Princeton: Princeton University Press.

———, trans. 1990. *Songs of the Harsh Devotee: The Tēvāram of Cuntaramūrttināyanār.* University of Pennsylvania Studies on South Asia. Philadelphia: Department of South Asia Regional Studies, University of Pennsylvania.

Singh, N. K. 1989. "Damage of Diplomacy." *India Today*, 31 March, pp. 94–96.

Sircar, D. C. 1961–1962. "Note on Nesarika Grant of Govinda III, Śaka 727." *Epigraphia Indica* 34: 135–40.

Sivaramamurti, C. 1964. *Royal Conquests and Cultural Migrations in South India and the Deccan.* Calcutta: Indian Museum.

Sivasankara Pandiyaji, S. N.d. *Celebration of the Navaratri Festival at Ramnad in 1892.* Miniature Hindi Excelsior Series, vol. 4. Madras: Adyar Theosophical Society Library.

Skelton, Robert. 1978. "The Indian Collections: 1798 to 1978." *Burlington Magazine* 120 (May): 297–304.

———. 1985a. "Collecting Indian Miniatures." In *Indian Miniatures: The Ehrenfeld Collection*, edited by Daniel J. Ehnbom, pp. 9–14. New York: Hudson Hills Press.

———. 1985b. "Indian Art and Artefacts in Early European Collecting." In *The Origins of Museums: The Cabinet of Curiosities in Sixteenth- and Seventeenth-Century Europe*, edited by Oliver Impey and Arthur MacGregor, pp. 274–80. Oxford: Clarendon Press.

Smith, H. Daniel. 1995. "Impact of 'God Posters' on Hindus and Their Devotional Traditions." In *Media and the Transformation of Religion in South Asia*, edited by Lawrence A. Babb and Susan S. Wadley, pp. 24–50. Philadelphia: University of Pennsylvania Press.

Snellgrove, David, and Hugh Richardson. 1980. *A Cultural History of Tibet.* Boulder, Colorado: Prajna Press.

Society for the Diffusion of Useful Knowledge. 1835. "Tippoo's Tiger." *The Penny Magazine* 4 (15 August): 319–20.

Somasundaram Pillai, J. M. 1965. *The Island Shrine of Sri Ranganātha.* Trichi: St. Joseph's Industrial School Press.

Sontheimer, Günther-Dietz. 1964. "Religious Endowments in India: The Juristic Personality of Hindu Deities." *Zeitschrift für Vergleichende Rechtswissenschaft* 67: 45–100.

Spencer, George. 1976. "The Politics of Plunder: The Cholas in Eleventh-Century Ceylon." *Journal of Asian Studies* 35: 405–19.

Spooner, D. B. 1919. "The Didarganj Image Now in Patna Museum." *Journal of the Bihar and Orissa Research Society* 5(1): 107–13.

Sreedhara Menon, A. 1962. *Kerala District Gazetteers: Vol. 1, Trivandrum.* Trivandrum: Superintendent of Government Presses.

Sreenivasachar, P., ed. 1940. *A Corpus of the Inscriptions in the Telingana Districts of H. E. H. the Nizam's Dominions, pt. II.* Hyderabad Archaeological Series, no. 13. Hyderabad: Hyderabad Archaeological Series.

Stein, Burton. 1980. *Peasant State and Society in Medieval South India.* Delhi: Oxford University Press.

Stein, Burton. 1983. "Mahānavami: Medieval and Modern Kingly Ritual in South India." In *Essays on Gupta Culture*, edited by Bardwell Smith, pp. 67–90. Delhi: Motilal Banarsidass.

———. 1989. *Vijayanagara*. In *The New Cambridge History of India*, vol. 1. Cambridge: Cambridge University Press.

Talbot, Cynthia. 1994. "From Mleccha to Asvapati: Representations of Muslims in Medieval Andhra." Paper presented at Association for Asian Studies Annual Conference. Boston, Mass., 24–27 March.

Tambiah, Stanley J. 1976. *World Conqueror and World Renouncer: A Study of Buddhism and Polity in Thailand against a Historical Background*. Cambridge Studies in Social Anthropology. Cambridge: Cambridge University Press.

Tanen, Ted M. G. 1991. "Festivals and Diplomacy." In *Exhibiting Culture: The Poetics and Politics of Museum Display*, edited by Ivan Karp and Steven D. Lavine, pp. 366–71. Washington, D.C.: Smithsonian Institution Press.

Tartakov, Gary, and Vidya Dehejia. 1984. "Sharing, Intrusion, and Influence: The Mahiṣāsuramardinī Imagery of the Calukyas and the Pallavas." *Artibus Asiae* 45: 287–345.

Taylor, William. 1835. *Oriental Historical Manuscripts*. Madras: C. J. Taylor.

Thakur, V. V. 1932. "A Short Note on the Charities of Devi Shri Ahilya Bai Holkar." *Proceedings of the Indian Historical Records Commission* 13: 139–44.

Thapar, B. K. 1951. "The Temple of Somanatha: History by Excavations." In K. M. Munshi, *Somanātha, the Shrine Eternal*, pp. 105–33. Bombay: Bharatiya Vidya Bhavan.

Thapar, Romila. 1966. *A History of India 1*. Harmondsworth: Penguin Books.

Thomas, Job. 1986. *Tiruvengadu Bronzes*. Madras: Cre-A.

Tod, James. 1839. *Travels in Western India*. London: W. H. Allen and Co.

"Too Stuffy for Gods to Live In." 1991. *The Hindu*, 10 August, p. 11.

Tripathi, Gaya Charan. 1986. "Navakalevara: The Unique Ceremony of the 'Birth' and the Death of the 'Lord of the World.'" In *The Cult of Jagannaṭha and the Regional Tradition of Orissa*, edited by Anncharlott Eschmann, Hermann Kulke, and Gaya Charan Tripathi, pp. 223–64. South Asian Studies. New Delhi: Manohar Publications

United Kingdom. High Court. 1988. *Union of India and Others v Bumper Development Corporation*. Blackwell & Partners. Transcript.

Van der Veer, Peter. 1994. *Religious Nationalism: Hindus and Muslims in India*. Berkeley and Los Angeles: University of California Press.

Venkatarama Iyer, M. K. 1964. *Advaita Vedanta According to Śaṁkara*. Bombay: Asia Publishing House.

Venkataramanayya, N., and M. Somasekhara Sarma. 1957–1958. "Vilasa Grant of Prolaya-Nayaka." *Epigraphia Indica* 32: 239–68.

Venkatramani, S. H. 1984. "Turning the Tables." *India Today*, 30 April, p. 136.

Vidyasagar, N. 1991. "Back Home—But Not Yet." *Aside*, 31 August.

Vigne, G. T. 1840. *A Personal Narrative of a Visit to Ghuzni, Kabul, and Afghanistan.* London: Whittaker.

Vogel, Jean Phillippe. 1911. *Antiquities of Chamba State, Part 1: Inscriptions of the Pre-Muhammadan Period.* Archaeological Survey of India New Imperial Series, vol. 36. Calcutta: Superintendent of Government Printing.

Von Stietencron, Heinrich. 1977. "Das Kunstwerk als politisches Manifest: Untersuchungen zur Frage nach der Existenz zeitgeschichtlich engagierter Kunst im fruhen indischen Mittelalter." *Saeculum* 27(4): 366–83.

Waghorne, Joanne Punzo. 1992. "Dressing the Body of God: South Indian Bronze Sculpture in Its Temple Setting." *Asian Art* 5(3): 9–33.

Wagoner, Phillip B. 1994. "Understanding Islam at Vijayanagara." Paper presented at Association for Asian Studies Annual Conference. Boston, Mass., 24–27 March.

Watson, J. W., trans. 1879. "The Fall of Pātan Somanāth." *Indian Antiquary* 8: 153–61.

Wellington, Duke of, ed. 1858. *Supplementary Despatches and Memoranda of Field Marshal Arthur Duke of Wellington, K.G.* London: John Murray.

Wensinck, Arent Jan. 1979. *The Muslim Creed: Its Genesis and Historical Development.* New Delhi: Oriental Books Reprint Corporation.

Wheeler, Monroe. 1956. *Textiles and Ornaments of India.* New York: Museum of Modern Art.

Wickremasinghe, Don Martino de Zilva. 1912. "Jetavanarama Slab-Inscription (no. 1) of Mahinda IV." *Epigraphia Zeylanica* 1: 213–29.

Wiginton, Robin. 1992. *The Firearms of Tipu Sultan, 1783–1799.* Hartfield, Herts: John Taylor Book Ventures.

Williams, Joanna Gottfried. 1982. *The Art of Gupta India: Empire and Province.* Princeton: Princeton University Press.

Wilson, Horace H. 1841. *The Oriental Portfolio: Picturesque Illustrations of the Scenery and Architecture of India.* London: Smith, Elder.

Wolpert, Stanley. 1993. *A New History of India.* 4th ed. New York: Oxford University Press.

Yates, William. 1824. *Memoirs of Mr. John Chamberlain, Late Missionary in India.* Calcutta: Baptist Mission Press.

Younghusband, George. 1921. *The Jewel House.* London: Herbert Jenkins Limited.

Yule, Henry, and A. C. Burnell. 1903. *Hobson-Jobson.* London: John Murray.

Zebrowski, Mark. 1983. *Deccani Painting.* London: Sotheby Publications.

Zvelebil, Kamil Veith. 1974. *Tamil Literature.* In *A History of Indian Literature,* edited by Jan Gonda, vol. 10. Wiesbaden: Otto Harrassowitz.

Bibliographic Appendix

List of Arabic and Persian Works, Chronologically (C.E.), with Translations

c. 800	Ibn al-Kalbī, *Kitāb al-Aṣnām*—Faris 1952
c. 950	Buzurg ibn Shahriyār, *Kitāb ʿAdjāʾ ib al-Hind*—Quennell 1929, Sauvaget 1954
1021	al-ʿUtbī, *Kitāb al-Yamīnī*—Reynolds 1858
1030	al-Bīrūnī, *Taʿrīkh al-Hind*—Sachau 1964
c. 1050	Gardīzī, *Zayn al-akhbār*
1091	Nizām al-Mulk, *Siyāsat-nāma*—Darke 1960
c. 1150	Nizām-i-ʿArudi, *Chahar Maqala*—Browne 1921
c. 1230	ʿAṭṭār, *Manṭik al-Tayr*—Bosworth 1966
1231	Ibn al-Athīr, *Kitāb al-Kāmil*—Elliot and Dowson 1867
1259–60	Minhaj-i Siraj, *Tabakat-i Nasiri*—Raverty 1881
1257	Saʿdī, *Būstān*—Edwards 1911
1274	Ibn Khallikan, *Wafayāt al-aʿyān*—De Slane 1868
1275	Zakariyya al-Kazwini, *Āthār al-Bilād*—Elliot and Dowson 1867
c. 1310	Amir Khusraw, *Khazāʾin al Futūḥ*—Habib 1931
1316	Amir Khusraw, *ʿAshīka*
1349–50	ʿIsāmī, *Futūḥ al-Salāṭīn*—Husain 1967
1357	Baranī, *Fatāwa-yi Jahāndārī*—P. Hardy 1960
1379	Ibn Khaldūn, *Mukaddima*—Rosenthal 1958
1444–46	Mīr Khāwand, *Rawdat al-Safā*—Elliot and Dowson 1867
c. 1580	Nizām al-Dīn Ahmad, *Tabakāt-i-Akbarshāhī*—De 1913
1596	Badāʾūnī, *Muntakhab-ut-Tawārīkh*—Ranking 1898
c. 1606	Firishta, *Gulshan-i Ibrāhīmī*—Dow 1770, Briggs 1966

Index

About the Author

Richard H. Davis is Associate Professor of Religious Studies at Yale University. Previous publications include *Ritual in an Oscillating Universe: Worshiping Śiva in Medieval India.*

9181694R0

Made in the USA
Lexington, KY
06 April 2011